The Young Lords

The Young Lords

A READER

Edited by **Darrel Enck-Wanzer**

FOREWORD BY IRIS MORALES
AND DENISE OLIVER-VELEZ

NEW YORK UNIVERSITY PRESS
New York and London

NEW YORK UNIVERSITY PRESS
New York and London
www.nyupress.org

Library of Congress Cataloging–in–Publication Data
The Young Lords : a reader / edited by Darrel Enck-Wanzer ;
foreword by Iris Morales and Denise Oliver-Velez.
p. cm.   Includes bibliographical references and index.
ISBN 978-0-8147-2241-1 (cloth : acid-free paper) —
ISBN 978-0-8147-2242-8 (pbk. : acid-free paper)
1. Young Lords (Organization)—History—Sources.   2. Puerto Ricans—
New York (State)—New York—Social conditions—20th century—Sources.
3. Puerto Ricans—New York (State)—New York—Politics and government—
20th century—Sources.   4. Puerto Ricans—New York (State)—New York—
Biography.   5. Political activists—New York (State)—New York—Biography.
6. New York (N.Y.)—Social conditions—20th century—Sources.   7. New York
(N.Y.)—Ethnic relations—Sources.   8. New York (N.Y.)—Biography.
9. Readers. I. Enck-Wanzer, Darrel.
F128.9.P85Y68   2010
305.868'72950747—DC22   2010020183

New York University Press books are printed on acid-free paper, and their
binding materials are chosen for strength and durability. We strive to use
environmentally responsible suppliers and materials to the greatest extent
possible in publishing our books.

Manufactured in the United States of America

C 10 9 8 7 6 5 4 3 2 1
P 10 9 8 7 6 5 4 3 2 1

Contents

An insert appears following page 160.

Foreword

Why Read the Young Lords Today?

IRIS MORALES AND DENISE OLIVER-VELEZ

"¡El Pueblo Unido, Jamas Sera Vencido! The People United, Shall Never be Defeated!" Ten thousand people chanted and marched through the streets of El Barrio heading downtown on Lexington Avenue in New York City. The Young Lords had called the march to the United Nations to demand the end of U.S. colonialism in Puerto Rico, freedom for Puerto Rican political prisoners, and an end to police brutality in our communities. Young people, artists, and community activists joined it, excited to be part of the momentous event. Looking from the hilltop on 100th Street, we saw the bright purple, black, and maroon berets of the Young Lords, the Black Panthers, and the Puerto Rican Student Union. Activists from the Puerto Rican Socialist Party, El Comite, Justicia Latina, and others were also present. Young people wearing jeans and t-shirts, military jackets, dashikis, combat boots, and big Afros carried Puerto Rican flags and huge, almost avenue-wide banners that read, "Serve the people" and "Fight U.S. imperialism." With confidence, we marched, believing deep in our hearts in the power of poor people to change the world. "¡Despierta Boricua, Defiende Lo Tuyo!" (Wake Up Boricua, Defend What Is Yours!) It was October 30, 1971.

Some of the issues we faced as political young people back in those early halcyon days of the movements of the 1960s and '70s have changed. We were "BC": "before crack." There was no AIDS pandemic. Youth gangs didn't have automatic weapons. No one had a computer, a cell phone, or email. There was no Homeland Security or PATRIOT Act. The World Trade Center hadn't been built, much less destroyed. There were no music videos or MTV. Our rap music was spoken word poetry set to the sound of conga drums or do-wops sung on street corners. Oprah Winfrey didn't have a TV show, and J-Lo hadn't been born.

The women and men whom we strove to emulate and live up to had names like Lolita Lebron, Don Pedro Albizu Campos, Sojourner Truth, Malcolm X, Blanca Canales, and Fannie Lou Hamer. The "Rainbow Coalition" was Fred Hampton's revolutionary vision of unity among poor people, not Jesse Jackson's poverty program.

When we entered the Young Lords in its early days, the leadership was all male. We helped to change that and to create an organization of young women and men struggling together to change the world and ourselves in the process. We connected to a larger movement in our opposition to the war in Vietnam. Inspired by the Cuban and Chinese revolutions and by the liberation struggles in Africa and Latin America, we believed that we could change the U.S. economic, political, and social system. Puerto Rican and African American youth joined the Young Lords, determined to change the status quo.

We awoke early each day to serve breakfast to school children, went door to door testing residents for lead poisoning and anemia, developed ground-breaking programs to deal with drug addiction, conducted community political education classes, and mobilized demonstrations. We advocated for community control of schools and educational curriculums that included Puerto Rican history and culture. We organized hospital and factory workers and worker-community alliances; and from the beginning, health care was a priority. We organized to change prison conditions and defined the prison system as another form of genocide. We raised awareness about the triple oppression of women of color by class, race, and gender. We wanted to change our communities, and perhaps while doing so, change our brothers. We organized high school and college students, and with the Puerto Rican Student Union formed "Free Puerto Rico Now" committees on college campuses. We published and distributed *Palante*, a bilingual newspaper, and produced a radio show on WBAI-FM, Pacifica, New York. We inspired, and were inspired by, our artists, poets, and musicians to play to the drumbeat of revolution. We were breaking new ground and lived each day as if there would be no tomorrow, and for some of our comrades and compañeras, the struggle ended in jails, institutions, and the Long Island cemeteries of Pedro Pietri's "Puerto Rican Obituary."

Latino youth and community activists have tried to keep the Young Lords' history alive, identifying with the group's spirit of resistance, its ideas about equality, and its bold and dramatic actions. When *Palante,* a book of essays and photographs about the Young Lords first published in 1971, went out of print, Latino students reproduced and circulated photocopies, and a bookstore sold a high-quality copy for years. *El Pueblo Se Levanta,* Newsreel's cinéma-vérité film produced in 1971, persists as a visual first-hand account. More than two decades later, Puerto Rican young people assisted in the production of *¡Palante, Siempre Palante! The Young Lords,* the Latino/a Education Network Service (LENS) documentary that continues to be screened in schools and community venues, connecting the Young Lords with another generation.

School curricula pay lip service to Black history, but Puerto Ricans didn't make the cut. Martin Luther King is an icon on a postage stamp, no longer part of an ongoing mass movement; but the struggle for human and civil rights did not end at his death. The Black Panthers, Young Lords, Brown Berets, I Wor Kuen, American Indian Movement, and the followers of Malcolm were too dangerous to even pay lip service to and have been relegated to the obscurity of a few documentary glimpses in art film showings. In 1996, public television broadcast two documentaries about Puerto Rico and the role of Puerto Ricans in America's history, both on the Island and in the United States, but since then it has not broadcast anything else.

We *were* there, and a body of our work remains, mostly unpublished until now, scattered about the country in old trunks, closets, and a few libraries, and on microfilm, waiting patiently to see the light of day, to give testimony to our struggle.

Why is it important for us to look back across the years and bring the Young Lords back into view, into the classrooms and the homes of those who may not have even been born when we first began to struggle? What is it that we hold in common with you, the reader, who may not have even heard of the Young Lords, or who may not be Puerto Rican or African American?

Though on the surface things appear different now, sadly, little has changed. The poor have gotten poorer, and the rich, richer. War is promoted as a fact of life. Big corporations move jobs globally to pay the lowest wages, forcing unprecedented numbers of human beings to migrate in search of a livelihood. Undocumented immigrants take on low-wage jobs in this country, without benefits or security, living in constant fear of deportation. Labor unions lose membership, and the national health care we called out for still eludes us.

New waves of brown and tan faces have replaced the ones in our old neighborhoods— where there were once African Americans and Puerto Ricans, there are now Mexicans, Dominicans, Nicaraguans, Salvadorians, Koreans, Africans, West Indians, South Asians, Vietnamese, Cambodians, Pakistanis, Arabs. . . . The demographics have shifted, but the objective conditions remain the same.

Where are you today? Are you sitting in the university deconstructing the latest paradigm shift, while your sisters in the street collect the next "baby daddy" and then die of AIDS? Are you watching your young brother trade in the newest Nikes for prison shoes with no laces?

Where are you? Are you worrying about how to make ends meet, pay off school loans, find a partner, or get out of a dead end job or relationship? Obsessing about being too fat or too thin, not pretty enough, smart enough, sexy enough? Trapped in isolation, assuring yourself that if you just study harder, compete better, you'll get that job, that raise, the success dangled in front of you to keep you chasing the American dream?

While you subdivide yourselves into yet another group or caucus, the world needs you to take action. (One campus has a Black students group, a West Indian/Caribbean Black group [no African Americans allowed], a Puerto Rican group, a Chicano group, a Dominican group—and the lone Brazilian on campus doesn't know which to join.)

You are our daughters, sons, nieces, nephews, goddaughters, and godsons, cousins, coworkers, students, lovers, and friends. We are saddened by much of what we see, but also encouraged by the young people who are resisting the relentless pressure to remain part of the problem and who are moving toward a solution.

If you don't know your history, you cannot assess where you are today, and where you are going in the future. The Young Lords' ideas about a just society opened up the imagination, offered hope, and inspired action. Its commitments connected the organization and the community to a national and international agenda. The Young Lords, situated in the relatively recent past, between the civil rights movement and the era of conservatism of the 1970s, offer insight into what was and was not effective in mobilizing communities.

Motivated by love for our people and outrage against an unjust system, we believed that the community's survival and well-being depended on collective action. We dedicated ourselves to organizing out of storefronts throughout New York City barrios and other urban centers, and later in Puerto Rico. Passionately guided by the idea of "serve the people," community organizing was our life, "twenty-five hours a day, eight days a week." We did it because it had to be done. We were young people from working-class families—primarily Puerto Ricans, first-generation born or raised in the United States, but also Cubans, Dominicans, Mexicans, Panamanians, Colombians, about 25 percent

African American and one-third women. We woke up each day to serve the people and went to sleep analyzing what we had accomplished, and at night we dreamed about the new society that we would create, convinced that the richest country on the globe had sufficient resources to make a better world. Granted, when we were young in the 1950s and '60s, there was a "movement" to join. By the time we were teens, some of us were veterans of demonstrations. We had joined the NAACP, CORE, SNCC, SANE, SDS, Black and Puerto Rican Student Unions, labor organizations, and a string of other movement groups prior to becoming Young Lords in our late teens and early twenties. We had role models.

Sojourner Truth asked simply, "and ain't I a woman?" Rosa Parks sat down and refused to move. Lolita Lebron said, "There is no victory without pain." Fannie Lou Hamer was "sick and tired of being sick and tired" and opted out of the two-party Democratic/Republican system to join the Mississippi Freedom Democratic Party. Malcolm X said, "The future belongs to those who prepare for it today." Don Pedro Albizu Campos said, "Los jóvenes tienen el deber de defender su Patria con las armas del Conocimiento" (Youth have the duty to defend the homeland with the weapons of knowledge). And Che Guevera reminded us that revolutionaries are guided "by great feelings of love." Those women and men were exemplars who inspired us to join hands with others to build a movement that rocked our generation and changed the world as we knew it.

Although we are no longer young, we still believe in the power of young people to change the world. As for us, some of us continue to engage in political struggle, albeit on different fronts and with different tactics. Others moved on, changed focus, and forgot about the movement, grabbing at opportunities that opened up for a slim few who could wiggle through the doors of the system. Still others, who were then uninvolved or on the sidelines, have emerged decades later to claim they were there as activists and not observers. But those of us who continue to fight and speak out have contributed to this book to make it a living will or testament in hopes that it will light a spark or strengthen your commitment to raise questions, confront issues, and take action.

The "movement," in disarray for a generation, was stifled and squashed by government and police repression, and internal divisions. The FBI counterintelligence program known as COINTELPRO targeted citizens, destroyed the sixties movements, and demoralized a generation of activists. Pressure to ensure that a new movement does not gain ground has intensified. Cooptation, media control, consumerism, and other diversions have all had a numbing effect, and we must rebuild.

"But what can we do?" we are frequently asked. "Change the society that creates these conditions," we say. As has been the case throughout history, each individual has a capacity to make change and to join hands and hearts with others to collectively make a difference. To quote singer/songwriter Buffy Sainte-Marie, "'Oh what can I do?' say a powerless few / With a lump in their throats and a tear in their eyes / Can't you see that their poverty is profiting you?"

"What can we do?" young men and women in community organizations, in high schools, and on campuses ask. "It was different for you . . . back then," they say. Our only response is that a movement begins with one person reaching out to join with one other. The Young Lords started with only a handful of us, some of us no older than fifteen, and the oldest, in the beginning, was an elderly twenty-two years of age. We had less access to technology than you do now, and probably fewer skills.

In the post-9/11 world, it has become clear that the United States perpetuates war, global exploitation, racism, and subordination of women, which has awakened interest in building resistance movements domestically and internationally. The world we lived in was not so different from the one we live in today, but the contradictions are becoming clearer as the gap widens between the haves and the have-nots. In some ways, the struggle is more difficult and more transnational. Attempting to grapple with this complexity, today's young people often tend to focus on single issues—gay rights, women's rights, the environment, antiwar activism, abortion, and racism—without an overarching vision, organization, or plan of action. The strength of the Young Lords was that we created a program and a platform, modeled on the Black Panther Party's, with international amendments, that outlined a clear vision of the interrelationships of oppression and of the need for systemic societal change.

In the following pages, we reach out to those of you we have never met—to share with you our past, to speak simply of who we are, where we have been and where we are now, and hopefully of where we are headed, together, in the struggle. What can we share with you? Our triumphs? There were many. Our defeats? There were plenty of those, too. Our dreams? They are vested in you. Remember—we were never alone in anything we did. There were always other women and men to support us, hug us, dry our tears, share our fears, and march out there united against a world that tried to stifle our every breath and dream. We hope the materials collected here illustrate the potential of people's power—that they show the infinite possibilities, the power of what people united can do, with very little or no money, but just the will to say, "*Basta Ya!*" "Enough!"

Pa'lante. The struggle continues.

Ever forward in solidarity.

Acknowledgments

I must begin by thanking all of the Young Lords across the country, without whom this book would have no purpose and without whom Boricuas would not have made the kinds of political and cultural advancements we have made. This book belongs to all of you. I especially want to thank Iris Morales and Denise Oliver-Velez for their insight, encouragement, and support on this book and on all of the research I have done and continue to do on the Young Lords.

This book was a challenging journey that could not have been possible without the assistance and encouragement of many individuals and institutions. Collecting materials over the course of multiple years would not have been financially possible without the generous support of Indiana University's Department of Communication and Culture, College of Arts and Sciences, and the Graduate and Professional Students Organization; the University of Georgia's Department of Speech Communication; the Latina/Latino Studies Program at the University of Illinois at Urbana-Champaign; and the Department of Communication Studies at the University of North Texas.

Several people deserve special thanks for helping me find materials and prepare them for this book. First, I want to thank the people of the Centro de Estudios Puertorriqueños at Hunter College of the City University of New York—which is the most important archive and library resource for Puerto Rican studies in the United States and, probably, the world—who have been invaluable for this project. In particular, Jorge Matos Valldejuli (formerly of the Centro) has been a tremendous resource and friend since I started researching the Young Lords in graduate school. John Louis Lucaites directed my dissertation on the Young Lords and to this day is a tremendous help as I embark on my career in higher education. I should acknowledge also that there is simply no way I could have transcribed all of these materials from their original formats (which were often poor copies of the originals) without the expert transcription skills of Carly Evans, a former student of mine from Illinois.

I am incredibly grateful to the editorial and production staff at New York University Press who have been so helpful in seeing this book through to publication. I particularly want to thank Eric Zinner, my editor, for taking on the project and being so supportive of it from our very first interactions over email. Thanks go also to assistant editor Ciara McLaughlin for her patience and guidance getting everything in order to make sure this book happened. Finally, thanks go to the magnificent copyeditor Emily Wright and managing editor Despina Papazoglou Gimbel, with whom it was a pleasure to work bringing the manuscript to a close.

Finally, I could not have done any of this without the loving support of my family and friends. In particular, I want to thank two people. My mother, Elba Iris Petersen (Arocho Rosa), has journeyed with me to discover and rediscover various aspects of our Puerto

Rican history, culture, and identity. Without her encouragement over the years, I probably would not have become so dedicated to my education and to educating others. I also want to thank Suzanne Enck-Wanzer, my partner, who always pushes me to find and follow my passions . . . and who tolerates me when I do. I probably could not have taken up a lengthy research program on the Young Lords without her help, her critical eye, and her loving support.

Introduction

Toward Understanding the Young Lords

DARREL ENCK-WANZER

In 1968, over half a century after U.S. citizenship was imposed on Puerto Ricans against the will of a democratically elected House of Delegates on the Island, Boricuas in the United States continued to face hard times. Economic conditions were lean: jobs were hard to come by (especially if you did not speak English), and those jobs you could find involved hard physical labor and little pay. More than one job was often needed to support a family. "Great Society" social programs should have helped boost economic conditions, but most of those benefits were lost in the messy bureaucratic web spun by the state in conjunction with local Puerto Rican–run professional organizations.[1] Politically, Puerto Ricans were still characterized as "docile," and the role of political activism in urban centers like New York had been monopolized by professionals, experts, and elites.[2] Furthermore, Puerto Ricans faced extreme and complex forms of racism and xenophobia.[3] By most accounts, life for the working-class Puerto Rican left much to be desired.[4]

The troubling situation was not unique to Puerto Ricans in urban centers. In fact, nationwide, deleterious social conditions sparked various political responses from a wide range of so-called marginalized groups. In the U.S. South, the Student Nonviolent Coordinating Committee (SNCC) changed its strategy to one based on the principles of Black Power—a radical, sometimes militant Afrocentric response to racist classism and classist racism. Across the country, the Black Panther Party articulated a militant Black Nationalist political program designed to address anti-Black racism at its roots and resist white oppression "by any means necessary." In the Southwest and elsewhere, Chicanos articulated a conception of Brown Pride that eventually included a separatist political strategy rejecting completely an Anglo-American conception of politics. It is within this period of political radicalism that the Young Lords street gang in Chicago became politicized and radicalized under the leadership of Jose "Cha-Cha" Jimenez, adopted the name "Young Lords Organization," and spread first to New York.

As with any of these (or other) social movements, the situation within which the Young Lords arose and operated was anything but simple. They were a group of twenty-year-olds and teenagers, second-generation Puerto Ricans living in impoverished communities. Some of the Lords were fortunate enough to attend college. Most of the Lords were motivated both by the virulently racist, classist, and sexist oppression they faced daily and by a sense of love of their homeland and people.[5] All of the Lords, virtually on condition of membership, were committed to articulating a new radical Puerto Rican identity aimed at the betterment of the Puerto Rican people in social, economic, and political arenas.

If only the history of this heterogeneous organization had been written by now. Instead, there are only a handful of scholarly articles on the Young Lords. One memoir of activism written by a former Young Lord (Miguel "Mickey" Melendez) has been published to date. A few doctoral dissertations have been written in whole or substantial part on the Young Lords, but none of them has yet seen publication. Worse still, the primary documents produced by the Young Lords—speeches, articles, posters, photographs, illustrations, poetry, etc.—have literally been disintegrating in boxes, basements, and landfills. While the record of the Chicago Lords' activities exists only in oral histories and archival news footage, many of the New York Young Lords' materials have been preserved by private collectors (all former Young Lords) and archives. Sadly, however, only fragmented pieces of that material are easily available for the general public and those without immediate access to the archives and collectors.

It is unjust that when the name "Young Lords" is uttered, most people have little or no understanding of what Marta Moreno calls "this group of young men and women of color who made significant impact on history." This book represents an attempt to right that wrong and to set the historical record straight about the Young Lords in their own words. Rather than rely on oral histories taken years after the fact or news reports propagated by a biased media, this book brings together material written, spoken, and otherwise produced by the Young Lords in their era. Organized around issues rather than personalities, this book offers a comprehensive collection of primary texts so that the Young Lords' memory can be preserved and that you, the reader, can decide for yourself what the Young Lords might mean to us today. Before embarking on such a historical journey, however, a brief introduction to the New York Young Lords history and activism is necessary.

Origins of the Young Lords

Palante: Young Lords Party, the group's historical and theoretical introductory book (a collection of narratives, explanations of their policy positions, and documentary photographs published in 1971), begins by addressing this issue of origins. A message from the Central Committee, the Young Lords' governing body, recollects, "Many people ask us, 'How did you begin?' A few people have the idea that 'some foreign power' organized us, or that we are a gang. This is our story."[6] For the most part, the story begins in January 1969, when a group of Puerto Rican college students gathered as a kind of consciousness-raising measure to understand better the situation of their brothers and sisters in El Barrio (East Harlem). By one former Young Lords' own admission, "the intentions of these people were good, but vague."[7]

As months passed, different people entered and left the group, which became known as the Sociedad de Albizu Campos (SAC).[8] In May 1969, the collective, partially organized by Miguel "Mickey" Melendez and including Juan Gonzalez, began to clarify its mission with the help of several key members. First, Pablo "Yoruba" Guzmán, who would become minister of information and one of the most visible and vocal members of the group, came to New York and joined the discussions. Next, David Perez, a political radical from Puerto Rico who came to New York via Chicago, met up with Guzmán and SAC. On their first night spent talking together, they came to an agreement that SAC needed to stop meeting and start acting.

Two weeks later, on June 7, 1969, they found their model for activism: the Young Lords Organization, a street gang "turned political" in Chicago. At this point, the members of SAC developed coalitions with other progressive Latino groups: a group of street photographers/activists from El Barrio and, from the Lower East Side, a group of former gang members and street activists who had taken the name "Young Lords."[9] After a series of mergers, a unified group, the New York Young Lords, received an official charter from the Chicago organization on July 26, 1969.[10] According to Guzmán, "we split from Chicago in April 1970 because we felt they hadn't overcome being a gang";[11] but, as described below, the reasons were even more complicated. At this point, the group became the "Young Lords Party," a name and mission they retained until changing, in 1972, into a different, decidedly Maoist, organization called the "Puerto Rican Revolutionary Worker's Organization."[12]

Phase One: Young Lords Organization (YLO)

In the beginning, the Young Lords Organization in New York was primarily a community service organization. Borrowing from the models offered by the Young Lords Organization in Chicago and the Black Panthers, in addition to their own experiences in community organizing, this new group of New York Lords sought first to address change at the local level in their immediate community through "serve the people" programs.[13] Three aspects of this early stage are particularly important. First, they were motivated by multiple traditions of thought and action. Second, they were focused on practical public tasks (cleaning up garbage, testing for disease, providing social services, etc.). Finally, they sought transformations in the community that cannot be measured sufficiently through lenses of "influence" or policy "success."

Unlike many Chicanos in the Southwest, the Young Lords were not exclusively oppositional. Rather than reject outright the Anglo political system (although they did reject voting as the means of political action) or accept entirely the Marxist critique of capitalism, the YLO occupied a liminal space among multiple political traditions. Through required political education courses, the YLO members and "friends of the Lords" broadened their critical vocabulary and became comfortable operating within and outside of dominant and subversive traditions at once. Everything was fair game, regardless of whether there was clear ideological consistency between their different traditions or vocabularies. Such theoretical liminality and paradox further worked its way into their practical endeavors in the local community; but it was also because of their community that they were so liminal and paradox ridden. One Young Lord explains the embrace of paradox by saying, "We find in our community—the Puerto Rican community—that things are compatible. For instance, people have Catholic saints and at the same time they'll have a Voodoo doll, you know, or a piece of bread above the door so that the evil spirits can eat that and leave in peace."[14] The YLO, then, embraced such "compatibility" in their theoretical articulations.

In practice, the YLO was most concerned with the immediate problems facing their community. Opening their first office on Madison Avenue in East Harlem (there is now a low-income housing project where their office used to be) and branch offices in the South Bronx, Brooklyn, the Lower East Side, and elsewhere, the YLO focused on health, sanitation, and other social issues with which the establishment did not adequately cope.

Beginning with the "garbage offensive," one day after they received their official charter to become the "Young Lords," the YLO directed their attention to making life better in the various Puerto Rican slums. They founded a lead paint testing program in response to countless children being poisoned by the paint in their homes. They ran a blood and x-ray testing program for tuberculosis. They established community education initiatives, a breakfast program for poor children, free clothing exchanges, and day care for working families. They also led the drive to renovate a hospital (Lincoln Hospital in the Bronx) that had long been condemned for being unsanitary and unsafe, and they established the first in-patient drug rehabilitation program for the working class. Some of these programs worked in opposition to the system by pointing out institutional racisms, while others were reformist in impulse.

While many of the programs and offensives the YLO implemented were successful in the conventional sense of meeting their stated practical goals, the success of the YLO should not be measured by such an instrumentalist standard. Such analysis overlooks the constitutive effects of the YLO's activism, namely, that the YLO constituted and cultivated a fundamentally political consciousness in El Barrio that offered residents a social imaginary through which an active political life could be led.[15] In part through such transformations in the people's consciousness, the YLO thrived in their communities and garnered the active support of both a broad membership (numbering in the thousands) and a loyal nonmember community base.

Phase Two: Young Lords Party (YLP)

As mentioned above, in May 1970, the New York Young Lords Organization made the decision to split from the national organization in Chicago. There were various reasons for the split, some having to do with differences of opinion and vision, others having to do with the New York group not feeling as though they were respected enough given the amount of work they were accomplishing (running the newspaper, leading a larger membership, etc.), still others related to the New York Lords believing Chicago had a hard time leaving their gang past behind, and yet others related to what the New York chapter felt was a need to have a truly national party.[16] With the split came a renewed sense of vision and direction for the New York Young Lords Party. Continuing various community programs (and, by this time, having branches throughout the Northeast), the YLP adopted a more explicitly political structure that was better aligned with their stated goals. Specifically, the YLP developed "mass people's organization[s, which] involve[d] the Puerto Rican people wherever they [were] at any level of struggle."[17]

There were five different organizations within the YLP during this stage. First, the Puerto Rican Worker's Federation took the struggle into places of employment in an attempt to challenge and, eventually, overthrow capitalist economics. Second, the Lumpen Organization enlisted the class below the workers, including those in jail, drug users, and the unemployed, in the struggle. This wing of the YLP was largely responsible for the (in)famous Attica prison uprising.[18] Third, the Women's Union sought to organize women in the struggle and challenged misconceptions about gender, sex, and sexuality. Fourth, the Puerto Rican Student Union mobilized students in high schools and colleges. Finally, the Committee for the Defense of the Community dealt most directly with different community issues such as health, land use, and breakfast programs. In all, according to Juan Gonzalez in a speech to Hawaiian students in November 1971, the YLP believed they were "trying to build a structure to involve our people in whatever level they wanted to involve themselves. . . . So, we see those people's organizations as the beginning, the seed of the people's self-government where the people train themselves to be involved in the revolutionary process and exercise their political power."[19]

During this phase of development (from May 1970 to July 1972), the YLP expanded operations, membership, and scope. In September 1970, the YLP successfully integrated its cadre and leadership along gendered lines, revising their Program and Platform to explicitly reject sexism and machismo and placing women in leadership roles on the Central Committee. They also began recognizing and tackling heterosexism in the organization. In March 1971, they expanded their operations to Puerto Rico, launching "*Ofensiva Rompecadenas*" (Chains Off Offensive) by opening branch offices in El Caño and Aguadilla and coming under the strict scrutiny of the FBI's COINTELPRO (Counter-intelligence Program).[20] The expansion, however, was short-lived when all the members of the Aguadilla branch resigned in April 1972.[21] The YLP left the island completely, concurrent with their decision to shift focus and change mission, which emerged from the First (and last) Party Congress held June 30 to July 3, 1972.

Phase Three: Puerto Rican Revolutionary Worker's Organization (PRRWO)

As a result of the Congress, the Young Lords entered their third and final phase, becoming the Puerto Rican Revolutionary Worker's Organization. Lasting until 1976, the PRRWO represented a radical shift from the YLO and the YLP. One of the most telling examples of the differences between the earlier iterations of the Lords and this final stage is found in their respective icons. Where for the YLO and YLP, iconic figures such as Ernesto "Che" Guevara, Pedro Albizu Campos, and Malcolm X were featured prominently, the PRRWO (on the cover of their publication that emerged out of the Congress) featured Karl Marx, Friedrich Engels, Vladimir Lenin, Joseph Stalin, and Mao Zedong. The PRRWO closed its community offices and organizations and directed full attention to the workers' struggle from an international Marxist perspective. Gone were the featured concerns for immediate community problems and the need to educate the people. The membership declined sharply, and those who remained were sent to work in factories to aid in developing a workers' consciousness through unionization. Furthermore, the PRRWO left behind its concerns for democracy in the organization and eventually devolved into a proto-authoritarian regime under the leadership of Gloria Fontañez. Loyal members were accused of being "spies" for COINTELPRO, some were placed on house arrest, and others were threatened and beaten. Only a handful of members remained when the PRRWO went defunct in 1976.

About This Book

This book developed out of my research in the Department of Communication and Culture at Indiana University. Writing about the Young Lords from Bloomington, Indiana, was quite an undertaking—especially considering that, at the time, only two microfilm reels that (a) included materials from the Young Lords and (b) were permitted to circulate through interlibrary loan existed in the United States. *Palante: Young Lords Party*, the group's book, was long out of print, and many libraries had reported their copies lost or stolen. *¡Palante, Siempre Palante!*—Iris Morales's 1996 documentary on the Lords—had been in circulation for some time, but its archival materials were primarily visual and fragmented. Over the course of a couple of years, then, I went to New York as often as I could to meet with former Lords and collect materials from individuals and institutions. Since then, I have posted some materials online; but the longer websites and Wikipedia entries were up, the more requests I started getting from students and scholars for information about the Lords. This book will help ensure that students, scholars, and community activists in the future will have a smoother start in their journey toward understanding the Young Lords.

Choosing materials for this volume was a challenge. Other books like this (most notably Phillip S. Foner's *The Black Panthers Speak*) organize their material around key figures in the organization. While this book could have been organized in such a manner, I felt that doing so would be contrary to the spirit of collective politics the Young Lords fought so hard to advance. Therefore, this book is organized around thematic and political offensives: organization, ideology, history, education, garbage, gender, the church, prisons, etc. In the editing process, I have introduced "silent corrections" of minor, meaningless, and distracting errors. As a rule, however, every effort has been made to preserve the texts as the Young Lords originally published them. In making the specific selections for each chapter, I sought first to choose pieces that seemed representative; that is, I looked for *content*, not *characters* that represented well the issue/theme at hand. It is important to note, though, that as careful as I was to pick pieces that I thought were representative (asking some Lords, too, if they were comfortable with my choices), what ultimately made it into this book is the result of decisions I have made. It is, no doubt, a cliché to say that this book only scratches the surface of a vast body of discourse by the Young Lords, but it is nonetheless true. This book is an attempt at a fair introduction that offers breadth and some depth; but it is far from a comprehensive collection.

NOTES

1. Antonia Pantoja, "Puerto Ricans in New York: A Historical and Community Development Perspective," *Centro Journal* 2, no. 5 (1989): 21-31; Carlos Rodríguez-Fraticelli and Amílcar Tirado, "Notes towards a History of Puerto Rican Community Organizations in New York City," *Centro Journal* 2, no. 6 (1989): 35-47.

2. Juan Flores, *Divided Borders: Essays on Puerto Rican Identity* (Houston, TX: Arte Publico Press, 1992), 13-60.

3. For a broad examination of the forms of racism Puerto Ricans face, see Flores, *Divided Borders*. For a comparison of Puerto Ricans to other ethnic and racial groups, see Ramón Grosfoguel and Chloé S. Georas, "Latino Caribbean Diasporas in New York," in *Mambo Montage: The Latinization of New York*, ed. Agustín Laó-Montes and Arlene M. Dávila (New York: Columbia University Press, 2001).

4. The History Taskforce of the Center for Puerto Rican Studies offers an explanation of the economic conditions of Puerto Ricans on the Island and in New York (and the relationship between the two) in History Task Force Centro de Estudios Puertorriqueños, *Labor Migration under Capitalism: The Puerto Rican Experience* (New York: Monthly Review Press, 1979).

5. See Young Lords Party and Michael Abramson, *Palante: Young Lords Party*, 1st ed. (New York: McGraw-Hill, 1971).

6. Young Lords Party and Abramson, *Palante*, n.pag.

7. Young Lords Party and Abramson, *Palante*, n.pag.

8. "Sociedad de Albizu Campos" translates as the "Albizu Campos Society." Pedro Albizu Campos was the Harvard-educated cofounder and leader of the Puerto Rican Nationalist Party in the 1930s.

9. Pablo "Yorúba" Guzmán, "Ain't No Party Like the One We Got: The Young Lords Party and *Palante*," in *Voices from the Underground: Insider Histories from the Vietnam-Era Underground Press*, ed. Ken Wachsberger (Ann Arbor, MI: Azenphony, 1991), 296-97.

10. Young Lords Party and Abramson, *Palante*, n.pag. and 73-74.

11. Pablo Guzmán, "La Vida Pura: A Lord of the Barrio," in *The Puerto Rican Movement: Voices from the Diaspora*, ed. Andrés Torres and José E. Velázquez (Philadelphia: Temple University Press, 1998), 157.

12. Guzmán, "La Vida Pura," 167-68.

13. Iris Morales, "*¡Palante, Siempre Palante!* The Young Lords," in *The Puerto Rican Movement: Voices from the Diaspora*, ed. Andrés Torres and José E. Velázquez (Philadelphia: Temple University Press, 1998), 213-14.

14. Felipe Luciano qtd. in Young Lords Party and Abramson, *Palante*, 31.

15. I draw this distinction from Ronald Walter Greene. See, Ronald Walter Greene, "The Aesthetic Turn and the Rhetorical Perspective on Argumentation," *Argumentation and Advocacy* 35 (1998): 19-29. An earlier and similar construction was made by Bruce E. Gronbeck, who distinguishes between the "instrumental" and "consummatory" functions of rhetoric in presidential campaigning. See, Bruce E. Gronbeck, "The Functions of Presidential Campaigning," *Communication Monographs* 45 (1978): 268-80.

16. For a good description of the rationale behind the split see Young Lords Party and Abramson, *Palante*, 10-11.

17. Juan Gonzalez, "Untitled Speech Given in Hawaii on November 16, 1971," in *Juan Gonzalez Papers* (New York: 1971), 6.

18. The uprising at Attica was rooted in prisoners' demands for humane treatment. After negotiations led by a panel of community activists and government officials were cut short, the standoff was ended by military-style assault on the prison in which numerous prisoners and guards were slaughtered.

19. Gonzalez, "Untitled Speech," 8.

20. Morales, "*¡Palante, Siempre Palante!*" 221-23.

21. Morales, "*¡Palante, Siempre Palante!*" 222.

1

Young Lords Platform and Rules

Modeling themselves in large part after the Black Panther Party, the Young Lords articulated a set of core principles that helped secure a direction for the organization and offered a resource for what today would be called "talking points." The "13 Point Program and Platform" was used to guide policy and grassroots activities and identified a core set of slogans for public recitation. The Program and Platform was revised substantially in 1970 to reflect and direct changes in the organization's cultural and political commitments. The "Rules of Discipline" laid out a set of principles under which the members would function on a daily basis. The "Program and Platform" and "Rules of Discipline" were printed in every issue of *Palante* published in New York.

....

13 Point Program and Platform of the Young Lords Organization (October 1969)

(From the newspaper *Palante*, 8 May 1970, volume 2, number 2)

THE YOUNG LORDS PARTY IS A REVOLUTIONARY POLITICAL PARTY FIGHTING FOR THE LIBERATION OF ALL OPPRESSED PEOPLE.

1. WE WANT SELF-DETERMINATION FOR PUERTO RICANS—LIBERATION ON THE ISLAND AND INSIDE THE UNITED STATES.

For 500 years, first spain and then the united states have colonized our country. Billions of dollars in profits leave our country for the united states every year. In every way we are slaves of the gringo. We want liberation and the Power in the hands of the People, not Puerto Rican exploiters. QUE VIVA PUERTO RICO LIBRE!

2. WE WANT SELF-DETERMINATION FOR ALL LATINOS.

Our Latin Brothers and Sisters, inside and outside the united states, are oppressed by amerikkkan business. The Chicano people built the Southwest, and we support their right to control their fight against gringo domination and its (puppet) generals. The armed liberation struggles in Latino America are part of the war of Latinos against imperialism. QUE VIVA LA RAZA!

3. WE WANT LIBERATION OF ALL THIRD WORLD PEOPLE.

Just as Latins first slaved under spain and the yanquis, Black people, Indians, and Asians slaved to build the wealth of this coutry. For 400 years they have fought for freedom and dignity against racist Babylon (decadent empire). Third World people have led the fight for freedom. All the colored and oppressed peoples of the world are one nation under oppression. NO PUERTO RICAN IS FREE UNTIL ALL PEOPLE ARE FREE!

4. WE ARE REVOLUTIONARY NATIONALISTS AND OPPOSE RACISM.

The Latin, Black, Indian and Asian people inside the u.s. are colonies fighting for liberation. We know that washington, wall street, and city hall will try to make our nationalism into racism, but Puerto Ricans are of all colors and we resist racism. Millions of poor white people are rising up to demand freedom and we support them. These are the ones in the u.s. that are stepped on by the rulers and the government. We each organize our people, but our fights are the same against oppression and we will defeat it together. POWER TO ALL OPPRESSED PEOPLE!

5. WE WANT COMMUNITY CONTROL OF OUR INSTITUTIONS AND LAND.

We want control of our communities by people and programs to guarantee that all institutions serve the needs of our people. People's control of police, health services, churches, schools, housing, transportation and welfare are needed. We want an end to attacks on our land by urban removal, highway destruction, universities and corporations. LAND BELONGS TO ALL THE PEOPLE!

6. WE WANT A TRUE EDUCATION OF OUR CREOLE CULTURE AND SPANISH LANGUAGE.

We must learn our history of fighting against cultural, as well as economic genocide by the yanqui. Revolution culture, culture of our people, is the only true teaching. LONG LIVE BORICUA! LONG LIVE EL JIBARO!

7. WE OPPOSE CAPITALISTS AND ALLIANCES WITH TRAITORS.

Puerto Rican rulers, or puppets of the oppressor do not help our people. They are paid by the system to lead our people down blind alleys, just like the thousands of poverty pimps who keep our communities peaceful for business, or the street workers who keep gangs divided and blowing each other away. We want a society where the people socialistically control their labor. VENCEREMOS!

8. WE OPPOSE THE AMERIKKKAN MILITARY.

We demand immediate withdrawal of u.s. military forces and bases from Puerto Rico, Vietnam, and all oppressed communities inside and outside the u.s. No Puerto Rican should serve in the u.s. army against his Brothers and Sisters, for the only true army of oppressed people is the people's army to fight all rulers. U.S. OUT OF VIETNAM, FREE PUERTO RICO!

9. WE WANT FREEDOM FOR ALL POLITICAL PRISONERS.

We want all Puerto Ricans freed because they have been tried by the racist courts of the colonizers, and not by their own people and peers. We want all freedom fighters released from jail. FREE ALL POLITICAL PRISONERS!

10. WE WANT EQUALITY FOR WOMEN. MACHISMO MUST BE REVOLUTIONARY . . . NOT OPPRESSIVE.

Under capitalism, our people have been oppressed by both the society and our own men. The doctrine of machismo has been used by our men to take out their frustration against their wives, sisters, mothers, and children. Our men must support their women in their fight for economic and social equality, and must recognize that our women are equals in every way within the revolutionary ranks. FORWARD, SISTERS, IN THE STRUGGLE!

11. WE FIGHT ANTI-COMMUNISM WITH INTERNATIONAL UNITY.

Anyone who resists injustice is called a communist by "the man" and condemned. Our people are brainwashed by television, radio, newspapers, schools, and books to oppose people in other countries fighting for their freedom. No longer will our people believe attacks and slanders, because they have learned who the real enemy is and who their real friends are. We will defend our Brothers and Sisters around the world who fight for justice against the rich rulers of this country. VIVA CHE!

12. WE BELIEVE ARMED SELF-DEFENSE AND ARMED STRUGGLE ARE THE ONLY MEANS TO LIBERATION.

We are opposed to violence—the violence of hungry children, illiterate adults, diseased old people, and the violence of poverty and profit. We have asked, petitioned, gone to courts, demonstrated peacefully, and voted for politicians full of empty promises. But we still ain't free. The time has come to defend the lives of our people against repression and for revolutionary war against the businessman, politician, and police. When a government oppresses our people, we have the right to abolish it and create a new one. BORICUA IS AWAKE! ALL PIGS BEWARE!

13. WE WANT A SOCIALIST SOCIETY.

We want liberation, clothing, free food, education, health care, transportation, utilities, and employment for all. We want a society where the needs of our people come first, and where we give solidarity and aid to the peoples of the world, not oppression and racism. HASTA LA VICTORIA SIEMPRE!

Young Lords Party 13-Point Program and Platform (revised November 1970)

(From the newspaper *Palante*, 20 November 1970, volume 2, number 15)

THE YOUNG LORDS PARTY IS A REVOLUTIONARY POLITICAL PARTY FIGHTING FOR THE LIBERATION OF ALL OPPRESSED PEOPLE.

1. WE WANT SELF-DETERMINATION FOR PUERTO RICANS. LIBERATION ON THE ISLAND AND INSIDE THE UNITED STATES.

For 500 years, first spain and then the united states have colonized our country. Billions of dollars in profits leave our country for the united states every year. In every way we are slaves of the gringo. We want liberation and the Power in the hands of the people, not Puerto Rican exploiters. QUE VIVA PUERTO RICO LIBRE!

2. WE WANT SELF-DETERMINATION FOR ALL LATINOS.

Our Latin Brothers and Sisters, inside and outside the united states, are oppressed by amerikkkan business. The Chicano people built the Southwest, and we support their right to control their lives and their land. The people of Santo Domingo continue to fight against gringo domination and its puppet generals. The armed liberation struggles in Latino America are part of the war of Latinos against imperialism. QUE VIVA LA RAZA!

3. WE WANT LIBERATION OF ALL THIRD WORLD PEOPLE.

Just as Latins first slaved under spain and the yanquis, Black people, Indians, and Asian slaved to build the wealth of this country. For 400 years they have fought for freedom and dignity against racist Babylon. Third World people have led the fight for freedom. All the colored and oppressed peoples of the world are one nation under oppression. NO PUERTO RICAN IS FREE UNTIL ALL PEOPLE ARE FREE!

4. WE ARE REVOLUTIONARY NATIONALISTS AND OPPOSE RACISM.

The Latin, Black, Indian and Asian people inside the u.s. are colonies fighting for liberation. We know that washington, wall street, and city hall will try to make our nationalism into racism; but Puerto Ricans are of all colors and we resist racism. Millions of poor white people are rising up to demand freedom and we support them. They are the ones in the u.s. that are stepped on by the rulers and the government. We each organize our people, but our fights are the same against oppression and we will defeat it together. POWER TO ALL OPPRESSED PEOPLE!

5. WE WANT EQUALITY FOR WOMEN. DOWN WITH MACHISMO AND MALE CHAUVINISM.

Under capitalism, women have been oppressed by both society and our men. The doctrine of machismo has been used by men to take out their frustration on wives, sisters, mothers, and children. Men must fight along with sisters in the struggle for economic and social equality and must recognize that sisters make up over half of the revolutionary army; sisters and brothers are equal fighting for our people. FORWARD SISTERS IN THE STRUGGLE!

6. WE WANT COMMUNITY CONTROL OF OUR INSTITUTIONS AND LAND.

We want control of our communities by our people and programs to guarantee that all institutions serve the needs of our people. People's control of police, health services, churches, schools, housing, transportation and welfare are needed. We want an end to attacks on our land by urban renewal, highway destruction, universities and corporations. LAND BELONGS TO ALL THE PEOPLE!

7. WE WANT A TRUE EDUCATION OF OUR AFRO-INDIO CULTURE AND SPANISH LANGUAGE.

We must learn our long history of fighting against cultural, as well as economic genocide by the spaniards and now the yanquis. Revolutionary culture, culture of our people, is the only true teaching. JIBARO SI, YANQUI NO!

8. WE OPPOSE CAPITALISTS AND ALLIANCES WITH TRAITORS.

Puerto Rican rulers, or puppets of the oppressor, do not help our people. They are paid by the system to lead our people down blind alleys, just like the thousands of poverty pimps who keep our communities peaceful for business, or the street workers who keep gangs divided and blowing each other away. We want a society where the people socialistically control their labor. VENCEREMOS!

9. WE OPPOSE THE AMERIKKKAN MILITARY.

We demand immediate withdrawal of all u.s. military forces and bases from Puerto Rico, VietNam, and all oppressed communities inside and outside the u.s. No Puerto Rican should serve in the u.s. army against his Brothers and Sisters, for the only true army of oppressed people is the People's Liberation Army to fight all rulers. U.S. OUT OF VIETNAM, FREE PUERTO RICO NOW!

10. WE WANT FREEDOM FOR ALL POLITICAL PRISONERS AND PRISONERS OF WAR.

No Puerto Rican should be in jail or prison, first because we are a nation, and amerikkka has no claims on us; second, because we have not been tried by our own people (peers). We also want all freedom fighters out of jail, since they are prisoners of the war for liberation. FREE ALL POLITICAL PRISONERS AND PRISONERS OF WAR!

11. WE ARE INTERNATIONALISTS.

Our people are brainwashed by television, radio, newspapers, schools, and books, to oppose people in other countries fighting for their freedom. No longer will we believe these lies, because we have learned who the real enemy is and who our real friends are. We will defend our sisters and brothers around the world who fight for justice and are against the rulers of this country. QUE VIVA CHE GUEVARA!

12. WE BELIEVE ARMED SELF-DEFENSE AND ARMED STRUGGLE ARE THE ONLY MEANS TO LIBERATION.

We are opposed to violence—the violence of hungry children, illiterate adults, diseased old people, and the violence of poverty and profit. We have asked, petitioned, gone to courts, demonstrated peacefully, and voted for politicians full of empty promises. But we still ain't free. The time has come to defend the lives of our people against repression and for revolutionary war against the businessmen, politicians, and police. When a government oppresses the people, we have the right to abolish it and create a new one. ARM OURSELVES TO DEFEND OURSELVES!

13. WE WANT A SOCIALIST SOCIETY.

We want liberation, clothing, free food, education, health care, transportation, full employment and peace. We want a society where the needs of the people come first, and where we give solidarity and aid to the people of the world, not oppression and racism. HASTA LA VICTORIA SIEMPRE!

Rules of Discipline of the Young Lords Organization

(From the newspaper *Palante*, 8 May 1970, volume 2, number 2)

Every member of the YOUNG LORDS ORGANIZATION must follow these rules. CENTRAL COMMITTEE members, CENTRAL and BRANCH STAFFS, including all captains, will enforce these rules.

Every member of the party must memorize these rules, and apply them daily. Any member found violating these rules is subject to suspension by the ORGANIZATION.

THE RULES ARE:

1. You are a YOUNG LORD 25 hours a day.
2. Any ORGANIZATION member busted on a jive tip which that member brought down on himself or others, can swim alone.
3. Any member found shooting drugs will be expelled.
4. No member may leave any illegal drug in his or her possession or in their system while on duty. No one may get drunk on duty.
5. No member will violate rules relating to office work or general meetings of ORGANIZATION ANYWHERE!
6. No one will point or fire a weapon of any kind unnecessarily or accidentally at anyone.
7. No member can join any army force other than the People's Army of Liberation.
8. No ORGANIZATION member will commit crimes against the people.
9. When arrested, YOUNG LORDS will give only name, address, and will sign nothing. Legal first aid must be understood by all members.
10. No member may speak in public unless authorized by the Central Committee or Central Staff.
11. The 13 Point Program must be memorized and the Platform must be understood by each member.
12. ORGANIZATION communications must be national and local.
13. No member may speak about another member unless he or she is present.
14. All ORGANIZATION business is to be kept within the ORGANIZATION.
15. All contradictions between members must be resolved at once.
16. Once a week all Chapters and Branches will conduct a criticism and self-criticism session.
17. All members will relate to Chain of Command. Officers will discipline officers, cadre, and so on. The O.D. is the final authority in the office.
18. Each person will submit a daily report of work to the O.D.
19. Each YOUNG LORD must learn to operate and service weapons correctly.
20. All Leadership personnel who expel a member, must submit this information, with photo, to the Editor of the newspaper, so that it will be published in the paper, and known by all Chapters and Branches.
21. Political Education classes are mandatory for general membership.
22. All members must read at least one political book a month, and at least two hours a day on contemporary matters.
23. Only assigned ORGANIZATION personnel should be in office each day. All others are to sell papers and do political work out in the community, including captains, section leaders, etc.
24. All Chapters must submit a weekly report in writing to National Headquarters.
25. All Branches must implement First Aid/Medical Cadres.
26. All Chapters and Branches must submit a weekly financial report to the Ministry of Finance.
27. No Chapter or Branch shall accept grants, poverty funds, money, or any aid from any government agency.
28. All Traitors, Provocateurs, and Agents will be subject to Revolutionary Justice.

29. At all times we keep a united front before all forms of the man. This is true not only among LORDS, but all Revolutionary Compañeros.
30. All Chapters must adhere to the policy and ideology put forth by the Central Committee of the Y.L.O. Likewise, all members will know all information published by the ORGANIZATION.

2

The Ideology of the Young Lords Party

This chapter reproduces part of a booklet, by the same title, that the Young Lords circulated among themselves, "friends of the Lords," and community members. The essays contained in this chapter lay out key theoretical and practical commitments of the Young Lords. While they are not reproduced in this volume, it is important to note that the booklet contained eight different images across forty-one pages of text. The booklet was first written in February 1971 and first printed in February 1972. The reader will find many (though not all) of the essays in the original booklet reproduced here.

....

Introduction

(From the pamphlet *Ideology of the Young Lords Party*, written February 1971, first printing February 1972)

This is the beginning of the ideology of the Young Lords Party. What is ideology? It is a system of ideas, of principles, that a person or group uses to explain to them[selves] how things operate in the world. Our ideology was developed out of the experiences of almost two years of struggling everyday with our people against their oppression.

The systematic ideas and principles in this pamphlet are guiding us as to the best way to lead the liberation struggle of the Puerto Rican nation. These are not fixed, rigid ideas, but constantly developed as we constantly work to serve and protect the people.

There are certain principles that are fixed and unchangeable to us, though. First, is collective leadership, not individual leadership. One individual can never see the whole of a problem. Only collectives of people, working together, can solve problems correctly. Second, we can understand nothing unless we understand history. One of the problems of the Puerto Rican and amerikkkan revolutionary movements is that they have not done systematic, scientific study of their history and so do not yet understand the countries that they wish to liberate. Third, a revolutionary must be one with the people, serving, protecting, and respecting the people at all times.

> "Wherever a Puerto Rican is, the duty of a
> Puerto Rican is to make the revolution."
> GLORIA GONZALEZ
> FIELD MARSHAL

....

Definition of Terms

(From the pamphlet *Ideology of the Young Lords Party,* written February 1971, first printing February 1972)

When we begin to read and study things on revolution, on how other people's [sic] have liberated themselves and how we can develop our revolution, we come across a lot of new words we have never heard or seen before. We should learn what the words mean and then learn how to explain those ideas to our brothers and sisters in ways they can understand.

NATION: A people who have had the same history, culture, language, and usually have lived in the same territory for a long period of time.

COLONY: A nation which is controlled economically, culturally, militarily by another country and whose government is run by that other country.

CAPITALISM: A way of running the economy of a nation, where a few of the people in the nation own the factories, trains, business, commerce, and the majority of the people work for those owners. The few capitalists make large amounts of money by selling what the rest of the people make—the products, like dresses, cars, copper, oil. This is called profit.

VENDEPATRIA: A sell-out. One who has sold out his or her people for money or power.

CONTRADICTION: When two things are opposed to each other, for instance, right and wrong, up and down, good and bad. When you have a contradiction you have a problem that has to be solved. If someone says that the way to get to a place is by turning right, and someone else says it's by turning left you can't get to that place until the contradiction is solved—it's either right or left.

JIBARO: The mixture of mostly spanish and Taino, but also some Blacks, who developed in the mountains and campos of Puerto Rico mostly as small farmers and as peasants. The language is spanish, the culture Spanish and Indian.

AFRO-BORICUA: The mixture of mostly Spanish and African who developed in the sugar cane plantations and coasts of Puerto Rico doing fishing, and whose ancestors were slaves. Most Black Puerto Ricans try to call themselves mulattos when the language is Spanish, but the culture and customs are still mostly African, and when the racist societies of Spain and Amerikkka still treat them as though they are inferior.

CLASS: The group of persons that an individual belongs to all of whom make their living the same way. For instance, lumpen make their living by surviving—stealing, prostitution, dope, etc. The workers make their living by working for someone. The petty-bourgeois make their living by working for themselves, the peasants make their living working on the land for themselves or someone else. The bourgeois make their money off the labor of everyone else. They don't work at all.

SELF-DETERMINATION: It means every individual, every nationality has the right to determine their own lives, their future, as long as they don't mess over other people. A nation should be free from control by another nation.

INDEPENDENCE: When a nation has a government made up of people from that country, but it is still controlled economically and culturally by another country.

NATIONAL LIBERATION: When a country is completely free from control by another nation. When the people are in control of the government, economy and army.

LOMBRIZ: A parasitic worm that produces intestinal disease, found in tropical countries. We use this word for all the Puerto Rican traitors, for the parasites they are.

> "The price of imperialism is lives."
> JUAN GONZALEZ

....

Protracted War in Puerto Rico

(From the pamphlet *Ideology of the Young Lords Party*, written February 1971, first printing February 1972)

The concept of Protracted War best describes the history of the Puerto Rican people. For many centuries our people have been invaded by one nation or another. Two oppressors were successful, the spaniards in 1493, and the yankees in 1898.

When a country is invaded by another, it becomes a colony, slave, of the occupier, and that control stops the normal development of the people.

In Boriquen, the Taino nation had its own economic, social and political structure, and was developing in its own way. When these people came they used the riches of the island to aid Spain's development and destroy the Tainos.

The Taino people rose up against the enemy. The war did not last long, because the Spaniards, with their plunder of the rest of Latin America, had more power and arms. Many Tainos died, some because of diseases the Spaniards had brought, others through the war, and the rest fled to the mountains to avoid slavery.

Then the Spaniards had the problem of who would be their slaves. Beginning in the 1500s, they showed how barbaric and criminal they were. They began to ravage the African lands, kidnapping our Yoruba brothers and sisters to serve as slaves. By the 1600s there had been four slave revolts. We were once again defeated, but they did not destroy us, as is shown through the influences of African culture in Puerto Rico.

Out of these temporary defeats, our people became stronger, and by the 1800s, the Puerto Rican nation, as we know it today, was formed, of the mixture of Taino, Yoruban, and Spanish, of the most exploited by those in power of men and women more determined than ever to be free. Among the many freedom fighters were Ramon Emeterio Betances, Maria Bracetti, and Segundo Ruiz Belvis. These were the ones who toward 1868 raised the cry for liberation on September 23, in Lares. Eventhough [sic] we were defeated again, Betances knew what a protracted war was and he said, "Men and women pass, but principles continue on and eventually triumph." And so our struggle for liberation continued.

In 1898, the Spaniards had war declared on them by the united states and were quickly defeated. As a result, Puerto Rico passed from one slavery into another. Now the invaders were Yankees, and on July 25, 1898, 18,000 amerikkkan troops landed at Guanica.

This new invader would be the most criminal and vicious that has touched our land, and with the new invasion began the new war of liberation.

The principles established by the Taino nation, by the African people, and then by the revolution of Lares were advanced by the Nationalist Party, which in the 1930s proved to the Yankees that our people suffered from unbelievable hunger and misery—that was the "democracy" the Yankees brought to us.

The Nationalist Party, under the leadership of Don Pedro Albizo Campos, became the defenders of the people. In 1936, the amerikkkans arrested Don Pedro and the rest of the leadership of the party, because they were considered a threat to their plans. It was during this period that occurred what we have to come to know as the Ponce Massacre. On March 21, 1937, the Nationalist Party organized a demonstration in Ponce. The day was the anniversary of the abolition of slavery in the era of the Spaniards. The demonstration was to let the Yankees know that our people would not tolerate either political prisoners or continued occupation.

Throughout this period the amerikkkans had one of their own as governor. At the time the criminal was called Blanton Winship, and he, along with the lombrice, Corsado, gave the order to assassinate the nationalists; 200 persons were wounded and 22 killed. With this act the united states declared war on the Puerto Rican nation. The enemies of our people continued their brutal attacks, arrested 2,000 persons, and sentenced many to 400 years of prison after the revolt of Jayuya in 1950. All if this had one sole aim—to end the operation of all the just struggle for liberty because we were receiving international support.

In addition to all of this, the yankees began operation "co-option." That is, they looked for sellout traitors, and during this period they began to heavily support the electoral parties, especially the Popular Party led by traitor Munoz Marin.

The combination of the repression of the Nationalist Party and the lies of the Popular Party created a lot of confusion among the people. Another important factor was

> **"If our people fight one tribe at a time, all will be killed.**
> **They can cut off our fingers one by one, but if we join together**
> **we'll make a powerful fist."**
> LITTLE TURTLE, MASTER GENERAL OF THE MIAMI INDIAN, 1791

that the Yankees tried to weaken us by dividing the people through "Operation Bootstrap," and they moved 1/3 of the Puerto Ricans to the united states, but our struggle continued.

It's true that they weakened us when they took away our revolutionary leadership, but what they did not understand was that it is impossible to stop a liberation struggle.

Once again, in the united states, we rose up in the belly of the monster. In 1965, we rebelled, together with Black people in Chicago, New York, Philadelphia, and in New Jersey; wherever there were boricuas, the cry of liberty was heard.

Out of those rebellions, developed the Young Lords Organization in Chicago, in 1969. With the example of the Afro-american people, who throughout their prolonged war inside the united states, raised consciousness among Puerto Ricans, and the principles

and examples of Don Pedro, Lolita Lebron, Dona Blanca Canales, the YLO began to organize the Puerto Ricans in Chicago. Meanwhile, in New York arose a group, Society of
Albizu Campos, young students and lumpen (lumpen are the class in our nation which
for years and years have not been able to find jobs, and are forced to be drug addicts,
prostitutes, etc.), all of whom had the same sole objective, the liberation of Puerto Rico
on the island and inside the united sates.

The Young Lords of Chicago united with the Society of Albizu Campos to create the
national organization. With a 13 point Program the organization began to serve and protect the people, with free breakfast programs, free health and clothing programs, and
with the taking of the People's Church, where the organization was recognized as a group
with support from the community.

Each day the organization won more support, but it found itself with many problems.
Because of its oppression, the Chicago group did not understand the necessity for discipline
and political education, which is needed to achieve our liberation, and was not able to further the struggle. In New York was the Eastern region with a much more disciplined and
developed leadership, which was anxious to advance the struggle. We split with Chicago
and formed the Young Lords Party. With three bases in El Barrio, another in New Jersey,
and another in the South Bronx, the Party began to analyze Puerto Rican society, and we
soon realized that 2/3 of our people, almost wholly unknown to us, lived on the island.

The analysis of Puerto Rican society made it clear that our nation is composed of distinct
classes and social groups and with this understanding we began to formalize ideas to bring
the Party to all sectors of our people. Always remembering that we are a revolutionary party
whose goal is complete national liberation, and about the job of uniting the nation.

In August, 1970, two leaders of the Party, Juan Gonzalez and Juan Fi Ortiz, made the
first official Party visit to the island. From that trip, we analyzed a number of things.

For example, we saw that the struggle in the united states was much more advanced
since the conditions in the u.s.—the racism, the oppression was much clearer; hunger
and oppression expose quickly the lies of the amerikkkan dream.

Although it's true that there were other established independence groups, the Movement for Puerto Rican Independence, founded in 1959, and the Puerto Rican Independence Party, founded in 1947, the origin of these groups was either from the petty or
upper bourgeoisie (the middle and upper classes). Also, they were either social movements or electoral parties. As the years have passed, these organizations have raised the
consciousness of the people, especially MPI, but for our revolution to succeed it's clear
that we need more revolutionary leadership. With this in mind, we began the prepara-
tions for the move to the island, this being the best way to unite the 1/3 of our people on
the island and the 2/3 in the u.s.

The Yankees have divided and weakened us in many ways—the analysis of Puerto
Rican society helps us to understand the divisions. First, we have to unite the two most
oppressed classes, the lumpens and the workers, and also the two social groups in which
our people are divided, the most oppressed Afro-Puerto Ricans and the jibaros. This is
not to say that we won't also unite the petty-bourgeoisie and the students. As we have
seen, with a little education, they will come in large numbers to follow the lead of the
people and will take part in the revolution.

Taking into account our region in the u.s., we began to analyze the 2/3 in Puerto Rico.

In the northeast of the island, are the towns of Loiza Aldea, Fajardo, Rio Grande, Canovanas: it was to these towns that the Spaniards brought the African slaves, and to this day these towns, with one third of the island's population, are Afro-Puerto Ricans, victims not only of exploitation, but of racism.

Carolina is one of the most industrialized towns where the Yankees have built many factories, and the people are all workers.

In this area are the big arrabales (slums), like El Caño, in Santurce, Barrio Obrero, Matrin Peña, Cataño, and the housing projects like Lloren Torres where 26,000 people live, and communities with large lumpen populations, like La Perla, in San Juan.

With this, we have briefly described the north of the island. The second area of major importance is the center—Lares, Adjuntas, Jayuya, and the south, Ponce, Cabo Rojo, Salinas, and Guanica. The social group of the center is what by the 18th century received the name Jibaro. The jibaro of that period was humble and illiterate because of their exploitation, very superstitious, and always ready to defend their honor.

It was rare when the jibaro or jibara visited the town. Their calendar was the many hurricanes that passed over the land. The jibaro of today continues to be illiterate, not so superstitious, and now not only visists [sic] but lives in the big towns, now that Yankees have forced them to leave their lands, turning them into tomato pickers in New Jersey or dishwashers in New York. The jibara, who once had her herd of pigs, her house in the mountains, now is a worker in a factory making a miserable amount, while producing brassieres. It's obvious why this group, a large part of our population, will give strength to the revolutionary movement. Our job is immense. We have called it the Chains Off Offensive (Ofensiva Rompecadenas). To reunite our nation, we began with a demonstration on the 21st of March, the 34th anniversary of the Ponce Massacre. Together with our revolutionary example, the Nationalist Party, we raised once again the cry of liberty in Puerto Rico.

There are many reasons why we chose Ponce. Ponce is the second largest city on the island, next to San Juan. The place where Don Pedro was born, it is also where the Yankees have established chemical plants, although the unemployment is immense. We have all sectors of our society living there—the lumpens and workers and also the different social groups Afro-Puerto Ricans and jibaros. Only unified can we break the chains of slavery.[1]

For the Puerto Rican nation this is another stage in our protracted war for liberation. To achieve our liberation we need a revolutionary Party, representative of all the people with one sole objective, national liberation.

In that way we will give our largest contribution to the other oppressed people's [sic] of the world, as the people of Vietnam have done for us.

> Liberate Puerto Rico now!
> Venceremos!

NOTES

1. This paragraph is crossed out with a hand-drawn "X" in all known copies of the booklet.

Colonized Mentality and Non-Conscious Ideology

(From the pamphlet *Ideology of the Young Lords Party*, written February 1971, first printing February 1972)

We are all fighting against an enemy, the Yankee and the Puerto Rican lombrices. The one major thing that holds us back in our fight to liberate Puerto Ricans and all oppressed people is a lack of unity. If we are not united, like a fist, we are weaker in our battle. In unity there is strength, and a nation divided is a weak nation. We have been divided geographically, with one third of the nation on the mainland and two thirds on the island. To be stronger we must unite. But even this unification will not be enough if we still fight against each other. One of the problems that we face is the fact that we have been taught to fight against each other. Capitalism is a system that forces us to climb over our brothers and sisters' backs to get to the top. It is like a race, in which the prize is survival, with 500 people in it, and only one person is the winner—the one who gets to the finish line first, the losers all starve to death. The prize money which is equal to life: We fight against each other to live, and we are divided into groups that fight against each other. These groups are formed out of artificial divisions of race and sex, and social groupings. The struggle between men and women, the struggle between lumpens and workers are all contradictions among the people. Contradictions among the people must be erased in order to form a solid fist, a fighting force to destroy the enemy.

Many of these divisions that exist are a result of colonization. Puerto Ricans are a colonized people. As a result of the oppression suffered for generations and generations, first under Spain and then under the amerikkkans we all develop a "colonized mentality." The colonizers divide us up, teach us to think we are inferior, and teach us to fight against each other, because as long as we fight against each other we won't deal with our real problems—slavery, hunger, and misery. We are [so] brainwashed by the newspapers we read, the books they write for us, the television, the radio, the schools, and the church, that we don't know what our real thoughts are anymore. We are afraid to be leaders, because we are taught to be followers. We have been told that we are docile [for] so long, that we have forgotten that we have always been fighters. We are afraid to speak in public because we have been taught not to speak out. We are told that we cannot exist without amerikkkans in Puerto Rico, and we believe it, even though we know that our nation existed for hundreds of years without them. All of this brainwashing, this "colonized mentality" holds us back from our liberation. If you take 10 rats and lock them up in a cage which is only big enough for 5 rats, some of them will kill each other and some of them will go insane, just as we kill each other in the streets for five dollars, or in a stupid argument, and just as we go insane and turn to drugs to cover up the ugly reality of our lives.

We can only unchain our minds from this colonized mentality if we learn our true history, understand our culture, and work towards unity.

This colonization is responsible for the racism that exists in our nation. We do not see it all the time, and most Puerto Ricans believe that we don't have any racism. Most people will tell you "we are all Puerto Ricans, we are all different colors, none of us are black or white, we are just Puerto Ricans." But that doesn't mean that racism doesn't exist. It is so deep that we just don't see it anymore. The darker members of every Puerto Rican family have felt it all their lives. We have been so brainwashed that it has become unconscious. The Young Lords Party calls this "non-conscious ideology." We believe that Black is bad and ugly and dirty, that kinky hair is "pelo malo," [bad hair] we call Black Puerto Ricans names like prieto, moulleto, and cocolo [dark-skinned, mulatto, and Black, respectively]. We are not proud that our ancestors were slaves, so many of us say we are "spanish" or "castillians." Our birth certificate says white even if the reality when we look in the mirror is very dark. The Spanish treated the slaves as if they were animals, and none of us want to believe that our ancestors were animals, so we "non-consciously" reject the Blackness we are all a part of. All Puerto Ricans have a Black heritage, in our culture, in the way Spanish is spoken, in the blood which flows through our veins. Having slaves for ancestors is not something to be ashamed of; one should be proud to know that one's ancestors were strong enough to live through the horrors of slavery, strong because of the rich and beautiful history of Africa. We are taught that Africans were savages, and this makes us non-consciously ashamed of our past. We must study true African history, of the civilization of Mali and Songhay, for this history is part of our history. The Young Lords Party is a Party of Afro-Americans and Puerto Ricans. Both have the same roots in the past, similar culture and the same types of "colonized mentality." Because of the Black Power and Black Pride movement inside of the united states, American Blacks are now able to hold their heads up high

"The Chains that have been taken off slaves' bodies are put back on their minds."
DAVID PEREZ

and be proud of their past. It is necessary that we understand and study Puerto Rican history, much of which is African history so that we can move on ridding ourselves of the barriers that exist between Afro-boricua and jibaro.

We should not be afraid to criticize ourselves about racism. We are all racists, not because we want to be, but because we are taught to be that way, to keep us divided, because it benefits the capitalist system. And this applies to racism towards Asians, other Brown people, and towards white people. White people are not the oppressor—capitalists are. We will never have socialism until we are free of these chains on our mind.

The other way in which "non-conscious ideology" divides our people is through machismo, or male chauvinism. We have said for a long time that sisters and brothers should be equal in the struggle, that men and women should work together and that Puerto Rican men should not oppress their wives, mothers, and daughters anymore. When we said that machismo is fascism, we were saying something that was true, but we couldn't understand the reasons why men became uptight when they were accused of machismo. Brothers could not understand why some of the ways that they treat sisters are wrong. Brothers did not know how to act differently than their fathers and grandfathers have always acted toward women. Is it all right to rap to a sister? Should I give a woman a compliment? Is it machismo if I want to protect a woman? Because we did not understand why there is this division we could not explain well enough, all we could say was machismo was bad, male chauvinism is wrong, you are oppressing your sisters.

On the other hand, we criticize sisters for being passive and docile. We want women to become leaders, to speak out in public, to stop being shy and timid, to learn to be strong. We tell sisters to change, the way our mothers have taught us to be, the way our mothers' mothers have always been. And again, we did not completely understand why our sisters had difficulty in understanding what passivity is, and how to change. Sisters still volunteered to cook and sew, to take care of children. Sisters still felt more comfortable letting the men be the leaders. Sisters don't like other women to be leaders either. We did not understand why women constantly get into arguments with each other. When a woman is strong and a leader she is considered to be a "bitch." When a man is strong he is a "good leader." But why?

We have realized that the division of the sexes between male and female have existed for such a long time, that all societies have accepted the "fact" that there is a difference between men and women. We know that the only differences are biological—women have a womb and ovaries and they make eggs, and men manufacture sperm.

All societies developed around the first oppression; man used woman as a worker, to reproduce, to make babies, while men were free to do other things. This ideology of a division of the sexes is called "sexism," just like the ideology of the division of the races is called "racism." Both are "non-conscious ideologies." From the simple fact that women produce babies and men didn't, developed all sorts of ideas that women were a certain type of human and men another type of human.

What is a man? What is a woman? "Non-consciously" we believe a man is strong, aggressive, hairy, bad, decisive, hard, cold, firm, intelligent. "Non-consciously" a woman is weak, timid, smooth, soft-spoken, scatter-brained, soft, warm, dumb, and loving. Both of these sets of descriptions are a result of the way we have been trained "non-consciously." From the time a baby is born it is taught by its parents and by society to be a "man" or a "woman." If it grew up alone, with no outside influences what would its personality be like? Just because it has a womb, would it be weak? If it had a penis, would it be aggressive and strong? No. These traits of personality are part of the way we are taught to be.

A little boy wears blue. A little girl wears pink. A little boy is given trains, trucks, toy soldiers and baseball bats to play with. Little girls get dolls and suzie homemaker sets. Little boys wear dungarees and can play rough and get dirty. Little girls wear dresses and stay at home near their mothers to play and watch them cook. When a little boy talks about what he wants to be when he grows up he dreams of being a fireman, a doctor, a lawyer, a cabdriver, a revolutionary. A little girl can dream, but everyone knows what she will be—a mother, a housewife. Anything else is strange and temporary. Any other job she has must be something for her to do part-time until she can quit and stay home. If she has to work she then has two jobs—the main one is the home. Women cannot exist in this society without a "man to protect them." Women who have no men are forced to make it in a world that doesn't accept them. Welfare mothers are women with no men. Women compete against each other to "get a man." So we don't just have division between men and women, sexism divides women against each other.

By the time a baby is six months old it has already been treated differently if it is a boy than if it is a girl, and acts and responds differently. Baby boys are more active. Baby girls cry more.

Because Puerto Rican society is structured in a sexist way, it is very difficult to fight against things that we are not aware of. If we want to change this society and develop a new one that no longer oppresses anyone we must try to eliminate the sexism that we "non-consciously" retain in our minds. We must become instead of men and women— new humans, revolutionary people.

Men should learn to cook, to care for children, to be open to cry and show emotions because these are all good things—needed to build a new society. Women must learn to be leaders, to speak out, to use tools and weapons, because our army must be made up of brothers and sisters. One of the ways that brothers can figure out if they are oppressing sisters is to ask themselves if they would treat another brother the same way. If you lived with another brother, would he always cook the meals and do the housework. If you lived with another brother and friends came over would you do all the talking? Sisters can judge their passivity the same way. How would you repair machines if there were no men around? Who would protect you if you were attacked? We must think about all the ways we have been brainwashed un-consciously and fight against it. It is a hard struggle, because everything around us is sexist—the books we read, the t.v. shows we watch, the institutions of our society. We will never be free until we have broken all the chains of our "non-conscious ideology" and our colonized mentalities.

....

The Party and the Individual

(From the pamphlet *Ideology of the Young Lords Party*, written February 1971, first printing February 1972)

The ideology of the Party is the framework from which we move. Everything we do relates to the principles on this paper. Ideology doesn't only talk about what the Party believes but also where the Party sees itself going. On the basis of those principles and ideas we do our work among the people. We call this practice.

As the Party grows and develops, we are going to be developing a bigger, more defined ideology and we will be faced with a continuous problem; how do we keep building that Party of our people that will put the ideas into practice? It is no good to have an ideology if all you can do is talk and not practice. In order to be involved in good practice, two things must be dealt with; first on the level of organization, and then on the level of the individual.

On the level of the Party, we ask ourselves, how do we develop the type of organization that can lead our people in a liberation movement? How do we structure it? How do we run the Party? We must remember that the structure is not for any one part of our people, it must suit the needs of all our people—lumpen, worker, student. Also, it must help develop people into good revolutionaries.

The Party is divided into levels of leadership and ministries. The levels of leadership are the branch, the leadership of the branch, and the leaders and coordinators of the Party in general. The ministries, Defense, Staff, Field, Information, Economics, and Education are specific fields of responsibility assigned to party members. The level of leadership is the army that does the organizing of the people, and the ministry is the function that aides [sic] the Party.

We have learned the hard way, through trial and error some of the problems involved. It is very important for parts of the Party to communicate with the whole. If this is not done, there will be no unified Party. Communication is done in many ways, regular reports, telephone, mail, personal visits. One of the most important things besides communicating is education. Without a structured educational system in the Party it is very hard for the Party to organize all sectors of the people. It is also hard for any individual to develop without political education.

Two of the cores of the Party are the general membership meeting, where democratic discussion and decision-making are done, and criticism—self-criticism, the key to Party democracy. The structure is still changing, but we should never be afraid of changing to progress.

On the level of the individual the question comes up, how do we train cadre? What is cadre? How do we develop individuals from different sectors of the society at the same time? In this field the Party went through many changes. We were organizing high school students, lumpens, college students, workers, and other sectors at the same time and we had to fight the bad traits that each group brings with it, like the impatience of high school students, the individualism of lumpen, the conservatism of workers, and the intellectualism of college students.

What is cadre? A cadre is a person in the Party who has gone through a change in himself or herself from just another Puerto Rican to leader of the people, a revolutionary. This change does not take place right away. First, a person becomes political, then they join the Party, then, after a period of time, they become a leader of the people. But it isn't as simple as that. There is a big change in the whole life of the individual. This change can be broken into two parts. First, losing the bad traits from the class they originated from, like individualism, machismo, sexism, racism, intellectualism, superiorities and inferiorities. This is called "de-classing." Once you become a cadre of the Young Lords Party, you are no longer a student, or a lumpen street-person, or a worker. You have that background, but what you are is able to organize best that class that you came from because you understand it best, have dealt with a lot of the negative parts of it, and have recognized the good parts.

Second, is the big change that the individual has in getting rid of the scars that capitalism has left in the person's mind, like liberalism (not doing something you know is right), pessimism, and the biggest of all, colonized mentality. Colonized mentality is the effects of oppression. Because we are taught that a spic is a lower form of human, we end up believing it and acting as if it were true. We shy away from responsibility, we think negative, we don't think we can learn and then we take [it out] on ourselves, persecuting ourselves and fighting with others. We call this change, "de-colonizing." This doesn't mean that before you become a Lord, you have completely succeeded in getting rid of bad traits—that takes years—but that you have made an effort and are succeeding. The change in the individual of de-classing and de-colonizing goes on at the same time and both complement each other. The developing of the Party should be seen as preparing internally for the prolonged war demands constant development and change.

3

The Origins and History of the Young Lords

This chapter contains a selection of resources that helps to chart the evolution of the Young Lords from their beginnings in Chicago to their various phases in New York and beyond. This chapter begins with an interview of the Chicago Young Lords Organization founder Cha Cha Jimenez (published in the *Black Panther*), which the nascent New York activists used as a model of their activism. What follows this interview are other articles published by the New York Young Lords that document organizational changes (e.g., the break with the Chicago Young Lords Organization) and political and community milestones related to their service and activism.

....

Interview with Cha-Cha Jimenez

(From the newspaper *The Black Panther*, 7 June 1969)

BM: Cha-Cha, how did the Young Lords come into existence, become an organization?

CHA-CHA: In 1959 the Young Lords was a gang, a street gang on the near North Side of Chicago in the area of Oldtown. It got together as probably being more or less for protection because it was primarily a white area and the Young Lords were Puerto Rican. Later on more and more Puerto Ricans came into the area as more and more of the racist whites moved out into another community which was closer to Oldtown. After a while they became a social club, they had parties for the benefit of raising money for sweaters and T-shirts. They had picnics, they had dinners for the families and slowly but surely they were changing organizationally into helping the people in the community. After a period of time of giving money to the people in the community, and giving donations of food and clothing, the Young Lords tried to sit down to cope with the needs of their environment. So they got together to find out what was the real problem, how could they help their people best. This was the main reason why the Young Lords Organization turned politically, because they found out that just giving gifts wasn't going to deal with the system that was messing over them.

BM: Cha-Cha I see that more and more in different medias [. . .] you are associated with different political groups such as the Black Panthers, which is a very political organization and they have a political line and a political platform and program which they follow. What inspired you to align yourselves with the Black Panther Party?

CHA-CHA: Well you see, we're still looking for that way in which we can help our people. Now we're starting to realize who our people really are, who our friends are and who our enemies are. And as we read and studied other organizations that are appearing now in the United States, we see and we recognize the Black Panther Party as a vanguard party, a vanguard revolutionary party. And we feel that as revolutionaries we should follow the vanguard party, this is why we follow them.

BM: Cha-Cha, I've seen in the news and it's been in different medias where you lost a member of your organization, he was shot down by some of the Chicago police. And in working in a political way as the Black Panthers do and knowing Mayor Daley and the officials or the power structure of Chicago to be, as they've demonstrated in the past, are you prepared and willing to deal with that situation or whatever for existence as a political organization?

CHA-CHA: As a political organization, I think we're well prepared to deal with it. I think we've dealt with it already, I think we've showed Chicago our following by coming out in 24 hours bringing 3,000 people to the streets which is something that isn't done very often. Manual Ramos was a regular guy from the Ghettoes of Chicago. He was just like most of us are right now. Like we said before earlier, we're still searching for a way to help our people, we're still helping search for a way towards protection. Manual Ramos was a regular member in the organization since the beginning. We feel that he was a true revolutionary for changing along with it, because most of us don't really understand all the basic issues. Most of us are new in the movement but we can see everyday, this is a common experience for us, you know, this is a common experience for people in the ghetto. Daley just this past week had a press conference four days out of five days, showing the people of Chicago that he is planning this repression against gangs. Fred Hampton, the Deputy Chairman of the Illinois Chapter of the Black Panther Party is in jail right now serving a two to five year sentence, the head of the CobraStones is in jail doing three to twenty. I have myself been arrested on a fake charge of aggravated kidnapping, the kidnapping of my own child they claimed, but I was released right away when they found out. The reason I say gangs, Fred Hampton, Deputy Chairman of the Illinois Chapter of the Black Panther Party and myself is because this is what he means when he talks about getting rid of the gangs, at least most gangs, are changing and are turning politically.

BM: Have you ever been confronted with or had to deal with any situation dealing with agent provocateurs trying to get into the organization or coming into the organization or creating situations that might have charges brought against you by the F.B.I, the C.I.A. etc?

CHA-CHA: Just the other day we had a march on the pig station because of the brother Manual, we demanded the arrest of pig James Lam and a group calling themselves the CornerStones came and threw stones at the demonstrators and we passed through Cabriddy housing project which is mostly a black populated area and we felt that the blacks were our brothers and we wanted them to come in.

We thought that they would join us, and they did. They joined us, except for these provocateurs. I wouldn't say that they were CIA or F.B.I, but I do say what they told me after the demonstration. They told me that the pigs were saying that we wanted to provoke a fight with them, that we were trying to take over their turf, you know, treating us more like a gang style and we talked to them. A couple of days later we took over McCormick Theological Seminary and there we had a meeting and we found out that the pigs were trying to pay them to attack us.

BM: Cha-Cha since you've been moving in a political fashion as a political organization how many people have been arrested?

CHA-CHA: How many people, I say it's hard to count. About five a week (an average) get arrested. This is including all the Lords. Some of the charges that come on us are like mob action, assault and battery on the pigs whether we touch them or not. Just the other day a brother was searched down, because they have this stop and frisk law in Illinois where they just search you anytime they want to, he was searched down and all of a sudden he came out with a bag of marijuana which he never knew he had in his pocket, he couldn't believe it. This is some of the charges that we get charged with. We got stopped for leafleting and and they say something about littering the streets, you know, like kidnapping or anything, or just basically disorderly conduct or resisting arrest. Basically disorderly conduct is usually a $25 bail, resisting arrest is $25 bail. Most of the bails are $25 or there are some up to $50. This is the basic bond for most people who do get arrested. Now when a Young Lord gets arrested it's a special case, sometimes the bails come up to $1,000, $10,000 and $25,000 and even higher than that, [. . .] $100,000. Excessive bails are given to the Black Panthers and the Young Lords and the Young Patriots, the coalition that we have formed.

BM: Since the Young Lords have become a political organization rather than a street gang how is it acceptable in the community? Do the people relate to and support you; how do they feel about the Young Lords; about this transition; Do you get more support?

CHA-CHA: In the beginning when we were just a regular organization, a gifting organization, giving gifts out to the people we didn't get too much support, but we did feel happier when we gave gifts. But now that we've started organizing people, getting them together and starting them to work politically, we've gotten much support in the community. We have given much aid to the Latin community especially in the school committee or any committee where no Latins or even Blacks could be found, but now these places are filled with Latins and blacks and poor whites. So the people in the community are for us and everyday we get new members.

BM: So then would you say that the people are beginning to recognize or they do recognize that the movement is one of a class struggle rather than a race struggle?

CHA-CHA: I think our organization just by the people, just by the content, just by being Puerto Rican, you just have to understand it's a class struggle, because we have light skinned people like myself, I'm very light, we have dark skinned people, we have red, we have yellow, we have all kinds of people, a rainbow of people. And this is why we can easily understand it is common sense to us that this is a class struggle. I can't relate to black people hating white people and Puerto Ricans getting hated by anybody, you know, and people can't relate to that, you know, we look to see which is our enemy, which is our commonest enemy and we just see that the pigs are the body guards of the capitalists pigs that are oppressing and exploiting our people. We look to see that this octopus, the United States, has been sucking all the resources from Puerto Rico and we see who our enemy is. We see that the United States is our enemy. And we look out for allies, you know, we look at Cuba, we look at Mao, we look at all these other countries that have liberated themselves from the monsters.

....

Origins of the Young Lords

(From the book *Palante, Young Lords Party*, 1971)

Many people ask us, "How did you begin?" A few people have the idea that "some foreign power" organized us, or that we are a gang. This is our story:

In New York City, in January of 1969, some Puerto Rican college students got together because they felt something had to be done to connect them with the people they had left behind in the ghetto. The intentions these people had were good, but vague. They didn't quite understand which was the best way to proceed. As the months wore on, the group met many times in El Barrio. People came and went, the group kept changing, and those who stuck around felt things were going nowhere.

Yoruba came into the group in late May (by this time it was called the Sociedad de Albizu Campos [SAC]). He was a student at the State University of New York at Old Westbury, and had just returned to the States from a stay in Mexico, which was part of his schooling. He was eighteen at the time. Most of his life before going to Mexico was related more closely to the struggle of Black People in Amerikkka than to that of Puerto Ricans. This was because his dark skin and Afro hair made it difficult for Puerto Ricans to relate to him, especially light-skinned ones.

However, Yoruba's stay in Mexico had made him aware of his Latin roots, so when he returned to Amerikkka he was looking for something to get into. A friend of the brother's who also went to Old Westbury was one of the people who stuck it through with the SAC from the beginning. He introduced Yoruba into the group.

Two weeks after the first meeting he attended sometime in May, Yoruba met David Perez. Old Westbury needed more ghetto spics to maintain its image of a "with it" institution, and it sent people out all over the country looking for these strange animals. They had found David in Chicago, where he was hustling an anti-poverty group. Whereas Yoruba was born in Lares, Puerto Rico. At ten, he came to Chicago, because his family, like hundreds of thousands of other Puerto Rican families, nearly starved due to the effects of "Operation Bootstrap."

When David arrived in New York, he was nineteen years old. He and Yoruba quickly got along, and they went to stay at night in the city. They stayed up all night rapping about the SAC in particular, and politics in general. Their points of view on a lot of things were similar, and one thing was especially agreed on: the SAC had to stop meeting and get into the street.

On June 7th, the Black Panther newspaper had a story about an alliance in Chicago called the Rainbow Coalition which the Panthers had formed with two other organizations and a story about one of the groups in the Coalition—The Young Lords Organization (YLO). The Young Lords were Puerto Rican revolutionaries!

The Lords had entered into an alliance with the Young Lords Patriots Organization, a street gang of white youths that had also turned political, and the Black Panther Party. This was called the Rainbow Coalition.

The Rainbow Coalition sent representatives to the annual Students for a Democratic Society (SDS) convention in Chicago, held in May of 1969. An SDSer from Florida, Jose Martinez, who was looking to get back to his Latin people, met Cha Cha, one of the founders of the YLO at the convention. Martinez told Cha Cha he was going to New York, and wanted permission to start a Lords chapter there.

When Martinez got to New York's Lower East Side, he soon managed to start a group that met regularly. This group heard that there was another group doing what they were doing—except in East Harlem. These young street bloods would clean up the streets of El Barrio at night and leave the garbage in the middle of the street the next morning. In this way, the Garbage (Sanitation) Department was forced to clean it up so traffic could get by. Jose met with this group's leader, Pickle, and the two groups became one, with the intention of getting recognition from Chicago. It was decided that the new group would work out of El Barrio.

At its June 7 meeting, the one where we discussed the Lords, the SAC talked about both New York groups. We felt that it was important for all the little groups that kept popping up to form one national party, and we felt the Young Lords Organization was that party. The SAC met with the group that had just merged, and a new merger was made. This merger represented the uniting of the street people with the students of working-class background.

Together, this new group, already calling itself the Young Lords, cleaned up the streets of El Barrio, rapping to people as they went. On July 26, the group was recognized by Chicago as the New York State Chapter of the Young Lords Organization.

On Sunday, July 27, the Lords of New York blocked the avenue of El Barrio. This action grew in size through the summer, as the frustrated, forgotten mass of Puerto Ricans joined in barricading the avenues and streets. Soon the garbage action turned into a confrontation with police, and the YLO became experienced in street fighting, in basic urban guerilla tactics, the hit and run. For the first time in years, the pigs came into the ghetto with respect and fear in their eyes. This period of the summer of 1969 is referred to as the Garbage Offensive.

By September, we felt that our people had accepted us, and that we were now a part of people's lives. We opened an office in a storefront at 1678 Madison Avenue, between 111th and 112th Streets. The leadership of the organization at that time consisted of David Perez, Deputy Chairman; Pablo "Yoruba" Guzman, Deputy Minister of Information; Juan Gonzalez, Deputy Minister of Finance. This was the Central Staff.

Juan Gonzalez joined the Sociedad de Albizu Campos just before we merged with Pickle's and Jose's group. He had just come out of jail, having done thirty days for contempt of court arising from the 1968 student uprisings at Columbia University. Born in Ponce in 1947, Juan came to the States at an early age. His parents felt that they should always "do better," and Juan's family kept moving from place to place, one step before the Puerto Ricans, two steps before the Blacks, and three steps after the whites.

Juan entered Columbia on a scholarship. To support himself, he took a poverty program job on the West Side of Manhattan. Here, as a community organizer, Juan would go from house to house, getting to know people, and seeing all that his parents kept moving away from. This led him to junk the books his professors would give him for books on how to change the people's conditions, books on revolution. He joined SDS and became a leader of the 1968 uprising.

Fi was a member of Pickle's group, stayed with the merger of Jose's group, and wound up a Young Lord. He was fifteen at the time of the merger. His father is a preacher who managed to save enough to buy a house in Queens. Most of Fi's time was still spent in El Barrio, and he rarely visited the house in Queens.

The brother refused to accept the nonsense taught in school, and he had been tossed out of practically ever high school in Queens, until in 1969, he wound up at Benjamin Franklin in El Barrio. Fi is a brilliant photographer whose work of the street scenes has been exhibited in museums. Many of the people in the photo workshops in 117th Street that he belonged to were also with him in Pickle's group. Although he was not a part of the central leadership in the beginning, the Central Staff soon saw the level he was on, and in September he was promoted to Deputy Minister of Finance.

The Central Staff decided that we would shift the Organization's tactics from street fighting to programs which served our people and which would also build the Organization's theoretical level. We began Free Breakfast and Lead Poisoning Detection programs, supported the struggle of the welfare mothers, and studied revolutions in other countries.

In October of 1969, we wrote the Thirteen Point Program and Platform (revised May 1970) and Thirty Rules of Discipline (revised December 1970).

That same month, we went to a Methodist church on the corner of 111th Street and Lexington Avenue and asked if we could use some space to run a Breakfast Program. We couldn't even get in the front door. We wrote letters, began attending services, and talked with the congregation, but the church's Board voted no. December 7 was the church's testimonial Sunday, when people from the congregation spoke. Felipe rose to speak, and twenty-five uniformed pigs that had been going to church with us for six weeks, ran in, attacking the Lords and our supporters. The ambush netted thirteen Lords and supporters. They and others who got away were treated for broken arms and heads.

For two following Sundays, we went back to the church and interrupted services again. The fact that blood was spilled in the church showed us the level the pigs wanted to go to. On December 28, we took the church, renamed it People's Church, and for the next eleven days, we ran free clothing drives, breakfast programs, a liberation school, political education classes, a day care center, free health programs, and nightly entertainment (movies, bands, or poetry). Three thousand people came to the church. This was our Second Offensive, the People's Church Offensive, and the action spread our name around the world.

Two things happened: our membership increased rapidly, and we were now seen as a legitimate threat to the enemy's balance of power.

It was obvious that we were no street gang; as Socialists and revolutionary nationalists, we had become a political force to be dealt with. Those in power knew, perhaps better than we, what could happen if Socialist, revolutionary nationalist Puerto Ricans in Amerikkka hooked up with the other two-thirds of our people living on the island. The explosion would be tremendous.

Our intention after People's Church was to build our organization to get back in regular touch with our people through our daily organizing programs, which had been suspended for the eleven days of the church. From January through March we did this; during this period there was a series of street battles with the police for allowing the drug traffic to come into the neighborhood, and then busting junkies instead of the big pushers. The YLO became involved in getting junkies to kick and in having them serve our people.

In October of 1969 we opened our second office, in Newark, New Jersey; the fact that we managed to run an office there, plus the success of People's Church, prompted National in Chicago to recognize us as the leadership for the East Coast Region, with the responsibility for organizing that area. The Central Staff moved up in rank and became the Regional Central Committee with the titles of Regional Ministers.

The Bronx Branch was opened in April of 1970. This was also the location of our Information Center. The leadership for the East Coast now noticed that Chicago was not providing guidance or example; a few things that bothered us were the newspaper, YLO, was not coming out regularly; that there was no political line to follow (which meant that we developed on our own—the Thirteen Point Program and Platform is an example), and that the only branches of the Organization were in Chicago, El Barrio, the Bronx, and Newark, while our people were calling for us everywhere. There was also a branch in Heywood, California, but they were in less contact with Chicago than we were. They are now disbanded.

To offset the problem of not having a newspaper which regularly gave our position to the people, in October, 1969, we had begun publishing a mimeographed packet called Palante, the voice of the YLO–East Coast. On May 8th it came out for the first time as a full-size newspaper. The paper has grown in content and circulation. We also have a weekly New York radio program called "Palante" that went on the air on WBAI-FM in March.

In May of 1970, the East Coast Regional Central Committee went into a retreat. We discussed where we had been, and where we hoped to go. We knew that we could not continue to run an effective organization on our own personal dynamism, that definite political principles would have to be laid down for others to follow. As a group, we started studying more, and formulated methods of work that would develop other leaders. One of the main areas that we attacked was machismo and male chauvinism. If we wanted to have power in the hands of the people, it would be necessary to have all the people fighting now. The attitudes of superiority that brothers had towards sisters would have to change, as would the passivity of sisters towards brothers (allowing brothers to come out of a macho or chauvinist, superior bag).

It was felt that the vague relationship with Chicago would have to be cleared up. We went deeply into what we felt were the responsibilities that Chicago was not fulfilling. After the retreat, we went out to Chicago. After a series of meetings, we felt that we had to split from the YLO and move ahead with the work that was urgently needed. We had now become the Young Lords Party.

Since October of 1969 we had been active in the field of health, both from the patient's point of view and the hospital worker's. Our work in lead poisoning detection led to deep investigations in New York City that uncovered epidemics; we did the same for tuberculosis.

Ninety per cent of the hospital workers in New York City are Black and Puerto Rican. To meet their demands for better conditions, and to serve the needs of patients, the Health Revolutionary Unity Movement (HRUM) was created, made up of these hospital workers, in the early fall of '69. HRUM has the ideology of the Young Lords Party. It became involved in several health struggles, like Gouverneur Hospital on the Lower East Side.

The Young Lords Party and HRUM, along with the Think Lincoln Committee, a patient-worker group, took Lincoln Hospital in the South Bronx in July of 1970. This was our Third Offensive; we ran programs, like TB and lead poisoning detection services, and a day care center, in a building the hospital was not even using. This highlighted the oppressive conditions in Lincoln (the building was condemned by the city), which could have been found in any ghetto hospital. Just before Lincoln was taken, a city-run TB x-ray truck was liberated in El Barrio. This was a good education for our people as they saw the difference between what the government did and what we did; whereas the city was lucky if it tested 300 people in a week, we examined 300 people in one day .

On July 26, 1970, the Party celebrated its first anniversary. Soon afterward, in August, a branch was opened on the Lower East Side.

In August of 1970, Felipe Luciano was demoted from the Central Committee to the position of cadre in the Party. He left the Party in October. This was one dramatic example of a series of internal problems, and the Central Committee met early September to get the Party moving again. One of the results of this was the establishment of a definite system of work and responsibility within the Party. This is called democratic centralism; briefly, it means that there is a top-down, centralist chain of command in the Party, and that at each level (central committee, branch staff, etc.) democracy is practiced.

For this series of meetings there was a new minister, Denise Oliver; afterward, there were some changes on Central Committee, and also, another minister was added, Gloria Gonzalez. Juan was now the Minister of Defense; Fi was Chief of Staff; Denise was Minister of Finance (now Economic Development); and David and Gloria were Field Marshals.

Denise had joined the Party in October of 1969, when she was twenty-three. Before, she had attended the State University at Old Westbury, the last of several universities she had attended, all filled with empty promises. Denise had been raised in a "Black Bourgeois" (really middle-class) family, but she knew that reality was in the ghetto, with the people of the streets, and the workers who came home late for little pay. This is where Denise made her home.

Once, Denise worked in an El Barrio anti-poverty program. In the Lords, she rose to her natural level, and went through the ranks to become a minister. Besides contributing to the struggle against male chauvinism and female passivity, she has helped in eliminating the racism that exists both within the Party and among our People.

(In March of 1971, Denise Oliver left the Young Lords Party to join the Eldridge Cleaver faction of the Black Panther Party. This was not part of a collective decision by the Central Committee, but rather was an individual decision on Denise's part. We in the Lords still relate to Denise as a sister, in the same manner as we would relate to any other Panther. As a result, the position of Minister of Economic Development is now vacant.)

Gloria became a Lord in February of 1970. Born in Puerto Rico, she was a strong supporter of the Nationalist Party. To make a living in New York, she became a health worker in Gouverneur Hospital. There she saw conditions which led her to join community struggles for better health care. For this, the sister was fired, but not until she had helped found HRUM and its newspaper, For the People's Health, two people's tools that still fight on. That ain't bad for a junior high-school dropout.

Through HRUM, she came in contact with the Party; Gloria went through the People's Church Offensive, and joined the Party afterward. She rose through the ranks aided by her organizing of our Health Offensive that reached a peak in Lincoln Hospital in July. In August she and Juan celebrated a revolutionary wedding. She joined the Central Committee in September, at age twenty-six.

On September 22 and 23, the Young Lords Party and the Puerto Rican Students Union sponsored a conference for Puerto Rican students at Columbia University. The theme was the liberation of Puerto Rico. Over 1,000 high school and college students attended. September 23, El Grito de Lares, the conference marched for a celebration to Plaza Borinquena in the South Bronx.

In August, our branch in Philadelphia was recognized. This has been one of our most effective branches, having dealt with the drug problem (pushers) in the colony, taking over a church to support the demands of rebelling prisoners, and now organizing a conference for church people on the problems of brothers and sisters in the prisons. For this, they have undergone practically the heaviest attacks of any branch; there have been numerous beatings, false arrests, and several firebombs which have wrecked their offices.

We first got involved in the prisons struggle when the prisons in New York City first got taken by the inmates. Many of the sisters and brothers in jail had come from the streets we had worked in, and had read Palante, or were reading smuggled copies. In October of 1970, an organization that arose from the prison rebellion came from the concentration camps to become a section of the Young Lords Party. This was the Inmates Liberation Front (ILF).

Our attention had turned from the prisons toward organizing a national demonstration when we were brought sharply back to the brutal oppression of the inmates. For years, there had been reports, many published in the press, of Puerto Ricans and Blacks committing suicide by hanging in precincts and jails. Such a large number of these deaths were reported that the circumstances were highly suspicious. On October 15, 1970, a Young Lord joined the statistics. Julio Roldan, arrested on the whim of a pig in El Barrio, was said to be found hung in his cell in the Tombs, the Manhattan Men's Prison. We were told it was a "suicide."

We knew we were being taken for a ride. Julio was a Young Lord, and we are not about useless, wasteful suicide. There had to be some action taken to provide an example for our people; a demonstration just wasn't going to make it.

On October 18, at the end of a funeral procession of 2,000 people for Julio Roldan through the streets of El Barrio, we took the People's Church once again. Only this time we took it armed, with guns. Our message was clear: When attacked, defend yourselves. This was the Party's Fourth Offensive.

Where does the Young Lords Party go from here? At this point, we are going ahead with plans to step up the forward progress of the Puerto Rican national liberation struggle. On October 30, 1970, the anniversary of the day in 1950 that the Nationalist Party started a rebellion in Puerto Rico, we organized a march to the U.N. of 10,000 people. On March 21, 1971, we held a demonstration in Ponce, Puerto Rico, in remembrance of the massacre of innocent people in 1937 by Amerikkkan orders. We announced that day that a YLP branch had opened in Ponce. This has been done to unite our people on the island and the mainland with a common goal: liberation. Wherever a Puerto Rican is, the duty of a Puerto Rican is to make the revolution.

Our new branch in Bridgeport is carrying the Party line to Connecticut. This line carries our belief that national liberation will be won by uniting the most exploited parts of our society, the street people and the workers, in a common effort. We also believe that our fight here on the mainland is fought at the side of many peoples, particularly the people of the Third World, people of color. We are eliminating the racism that divides us.

Our past examples, our past work, and our future successes make victory certain, because we are backed by our people. The enemy, the United States Government, respects us because of our people; we are always humble before our people, and will always be vicious before the enemy.

> LIBERATE PUERTO RICO NOW!
> VENCEREMOS!
> Central Committee

....

Before People Called Me a Spic, They Called Me a Nigger

(From the book *Palante, Young Lords Party*, 1971, narrative by Pablo "Yoruba" Guzman)

People always look for beginnings of the Party. We started Young Lords because we just knew something had to be done. If we didn't find or create an organization that was gonna do something then everybody was gonna get shot, see because it would have gotten to the point that people got so frustrated, they would just jump on the first cop they saw, or just snap, do something crazy.

At first the only model we had to go on in this country was the Black Panther Party. Besides that, we were all a bunch of readers, when we first came in we read Che, Fidel, Fanon, Marx, Lenin, Jefferson, The Bill of Rights, Declaration, Constitution—we read everything. Now there ain't too much time for reading.

We also felt that the potential for revolution had always been there for Puerto Rican people. If we had gone into the thing from a negative point of view, we wouldn't have made it, right. 'Cause a lot of times when things were really rough, it's been that blind faith in the people that keeps us going. The problem has been to tap that potential and to organize it into a disciplined force that's gonna really move on this government. Puerto Ricans had been psyched into believing this myth about being docile. A lot of Puerto Ricans were afraid to move, a lot of Puerto Ricans really thought that the man in blue was the baddest thing going.

Things were different in the gang days. Gang days, we owned the block, and nobody could tell us what to do with the street. Then dope came in and messed everything up, messed our minds up and just broke our backs—dope and anti-poverty. Anti-poverty wiped out a whole generation of what could have been Puerto Rican leaders in New York City.

For example, in '65, the time of the East Harlem riots, we held East Harlem for two days. We had the roof-tops, the streets and the community—no pigs could go through. It was like back in the old days. A lot of people really tripped off that, a lot of junkies who had been in gangs remembered that shit. To end it they shipped in anti-poverty. They brought it in full-force, and they bought out a lot of the young cats who were leading the rebellions. A lot of dudes who were throwing bricks one day found themselves directors of anti-poverty programs the next, or workers on Mayor Lindsay's Urban Action Core.

So we had no leadership, and we had no people—our people were dying from dope. But we knew that it was *there*, man, 'cause we knew that the fire was there. Those of us who got together to start the thing, we knew we weren't freaks—we didn't feel that we were all that much different from the people. There's a tendency to say "the people" and put the people at arm's length. When we say "people," man, we're talking about ourselves. We're from these blocks, and we're from these schools, products of this whole thing. Some of us came back from college—it was like rediscovering where your parents had come from, rediscovering your childhood.

Our original viewpoint in founding the Party was a New York point of view—that's where the world started and ended. As we later found out, New York is different from most other cities that Puerto Ricans live in. But even in New York, we found that on a grass-roots level a high degree of racism existed between Puerto Ricans and Blacks, and between light-skinned and dark-skinned Puerto Ricans. We had to deal with this racism because it blocked any kind of growth for our people, any understanding of the things Black people had gone through. So rather than watching Rap Brown on TV, rather than learning from that and saying, "Well, that should affect me too," Puerto Ricans said, "Well, yeah, those Blacks got a hard time, you know, but we ain't going through the same thing." This was especially true for the light-skinned Puerto Ricans, Puerto Ricans like myself, who are dark-skinned, who look like Afro-Americans, couldn't do that, 'cause to do that would be to escape into a kind of fantasy. Because before people called me a spic, they called me a nigger. So that was, like, one reason as to why we felt the Young Lords Party should exist.

At first many of us felt why have a Young Lords Party when there existed a Black Panther Party, and wouldn't it be to our advantage to try to consolidate our efforts into getting Third World people into something that already existed? It became apparent to us that that would be impractical, because we wouldn't be recognizing the national question. We felt we each had to organize where we were at—so the Chicanos were gonna have to organize Chicanos, Blacks were gonna have to organize Blacks, Puerto Ricans Puerto Ricans, etc., until we came to that level where we could deal with one umbrella organization that could speak for everybody. But until we eliminate the racism that separates everybody, that will not be possible.

What happened was, in 1969 in the June 7 issue of the Black Panther newspaper there was an article about the Young Lords Organization in Chicago with Cha Cha Jimenez as their chairman. Cha Cha was talking about revolution and socialism and the liberation of Puerto Rico and the right to self-determination and all this stuff that I ain't *never* heard a spic say. I mean, I hadn't never heard no Puerto Rican talk like this—just Black people were talking this way, you know. And I said, "Damn! Check this out." That's what really got us started. That's all it was, man.

We started by trying to pick something that would introduce us to the community. It had to be an action. See—it was summer, it was hot, the people were just, like sweltering in the heat, nobody was doing nothing. For four year there had been no action. Puerto Ricans hadn't had a good riot since 1965, not even a good fight, a good brawl. Something had to happen that would stun the community. It had to be something with a sense of drama, and a flair, right—but it also had to be something that was real, so the people would know that this wasn't just a bunch of young punks messin' around.

The best thing to hook into was garbage, 'cause garbage is visible and everybody sees it. It's there, you know. So we started out with this thing, "Well, we're gonna clean up the street." This brought the college people and the street people together, 'cause when street people saw college people pushing brooms and getting dirty, that blew their minds. It also got us out of our shyness. When we began, people said, "Well, what are you doing, with those berets?" and "What are you doing with those buttons?" and "What does 'All Power to the People' mean?" and things like that. The bolder ones in our group would get out there and yell to people, and everybody else would jump with shock. It was frightening, man, to go on the street and to walk up to some strangers and just start rapping and give 'em a leaflet—that's frightening shit. And we just forced ourselves to do it, and it got to a thing where nobody wanted to be the one who didn't talk that day, because everybody else would criticize you.

At first some people thought we were part of Lindsay's Urban Action Task Force, and some thought we were just a gang that was trying to be a social club. People couldn't figure us out, man. If we said, "All Power to the People," some of them who read the *Daily News* right away said, "Well, those are the Panthers, and they're Communists." A lot of people thought we were the Panthers, and to that we got a bad reaction, 'cause they were afraid of us. But some people just came out and looked.

This is all we did for the first two Sundays—clean up the street, make it look nice, and put the stuff in garbage cans. We picked Sunday 'cause that was one of the few days when everybody could get together. Some of the members of the Party got pissed. We'd have general meetings and they'd say, "I didn't do this for this shit, to clean up no garbage. I came here to off the pigs"; they were comin' from that, right. So, it was hard, man, 'cause we had a bunch of crazy people who just loved fighting, loved getting into shit. And cleaning garbage was not where it was at, so it was a kind of discipline for us, to go through that and learn patience. We didn't realize that what we were doing at that time was building the proper conditions for struggle. I mean, we could have gone underground and started blowing shit up—the thing is, nobody would have understood where it was coming from. Those people who didn't think it was the pig, would think it was some lunatics, and they'd probably be right. So we were just getting ourselves known.

By the second time around, everybody said, "Hey, here they come again! Here come these nuts!" They were calling their friends out—"Look at these fools cleaning off the street!" It was a big thing. They were coming from blocks around. We cleaned 110th Street from Second to Third to Lexington.

By the third Sunday we did something we had learned from what we had read about the Chicago group, and that was to get the people involved through "observation and participation." This time we got the people to clean the shit up with us. We knew somehow we would take them through some kind of struggle, we didn't know where the hell we were going, but we had to get them involved.

And then came the Sunday of July 27, when we had a lot of people and not enough brooms, and we went to the Sanitation Department. . . . Now understand this—for the Young Lords Party, this July 27 is probably a historical date. It was a Sunday, right? When four of us went to pick up some brooms, they told us, "Well, you can't have any brooms." And we said, "Why?" and they said, "Because it's Sunday." Now the sanitation cats are just second cousins to the cats in blue, 'cept that they wear green. This fool at 106th Street which was the nearest branch of the department asks us, "What area are you cleaning up?" So we tell him 110th between Second and Third. He says, "That area is serviced by 73rd Street and York." So we had to go about a mile and a half outside where we were, when there was this place four blocks down. And the dude at 73rd and York says, "Well, you can't have any brooms." So, we were pissed, you know. We had gone through all the legal machinations, and now were pissed. We were looking for a rationale for what was going to come next.

In the car on the way up, the four of us said, "Look, we're going to take the garbage and throw it in the street and that's all there is to it—we're just going to dump it." And that's what we did. We blocked Third Avenue to traffic, right. The people, they went and blocked 111th Street and Third Avenue, blocked 112th, and what was developing was a riot situation. When we saw that happening, we set up a line of garbage cans at the end of 112th Street and we set up a line of Lords and said, "We ain't lettin' nobody through." There was this one cat who said, "Let's go! Let's take it all the way up to the Bronx." This cat was freaking out, and we were saying, "No, you ain't going noplace—we're stoppin' right here because if we keep going, this is what the pigs want, they just going to pick us off. You ain't got no guns, you know." And this guy kept saying, "No, no, let's go! We got all these people here!" 'Cause people had come out, they came from all over East Harlem for this, they moved a truck into the street, they turned cars over, they were ready to go crazy. The pigs showed up and didn't do nothing, 'cause the pigs believe that Puerto Ricans are docile, you know. We didn't know what kind of reaction we'd get. I mean, all we were doing was throwing some garbage in the street, but we saw that it turned the people loose, it was what they needed, it just set them going. So, we had a quick rally and signed up some recruits, and we said, "Well, we're gonna do this again next Sunday."

When we went back the next Sunday, more people came—but it was a different thing. This time it wasn't "Here come those nuts . . ." but "Here come those people who started the shit last Sunday—let's get together." And people were just, like, waiting, waiting like this on the corner, waiting for us to throw the garbage so they could get involved in the shit.

The next day, Lindsay's office called a meeting. Gottehrer and all those dudes came down to East Harlem to this poverty place. That's when we found out what poverty pimps were really about—they're like outposts in Indian territory, like Fort Apache and Fort Savage, they are the eyes and ears of the mayor of any city. And they're supposed to keep the savages down, right. In this case, we weren't working with the poverty pimps. This was coming from the people, and the poverty pimps are far removed from the people. When they couldn't explain to their masters what was going down in East Harlem, they said, "Well, we have this under control . . . there are these leaflets that are going around. . . ."

We found that a lot of people thought we were there just to throw garbage in the street. They couldn't understand that we were really there for a Socialist revolution, we were really there to off the government of the United States. They just couldn't deal with that, you know. So we tried setting up political education classes.

I remember a lot of those being really funny. Juan had become Deputy Minister of Education, because he knew the most, he had the clearest mind. Juan was dealing with books right, but like, ain't nobody could read the books, and then those who could read, let's say something like Che on *Man and Socialism*, threw the book away and said, "This is boring." Juan could not understand how Che Guevara could be boring. You know, it blew his mind. We had to try to find some way of reaching brothers and sisters who did not dig school, the concept of school or the classroom. And how the hell were we gonna do this? This is a problem we're still dealing with. We tried everything, man, from jokes to getting high together, everything to try to bring the point across.

Then there were other problems like people's commitment. Like, "Well, how come you wasn't here last Sunday?" "Ah, man, you know, my mother told me not to come," or, like, "I was out late Saturday night, and I just wanted to sleep. . . ." I mean, how do you build up discipline? If you were going to divide fifteen people into three groups that could block an avenue at a given time you needed discipline. How could you cool out cats who knew nothing about fighting and say to them, "Listen, this is not when you hit this pig—you do not hit this pig now."

It was very difficult, it was very hard to do. . . .

Well, after the First Offensive, the Garbage Offensive, all Puerto Ricans in New York knew about us. Then it was the People's Church Offensive that put us on a national level in terms of the United States and Puerto Rico. This was through the correct use of the media. We said, "Look, you know, the media is gonna have to be used. Until we can put out the *Daily News* regularly, until we have a TV station and a radio station, chalk it up. Everybody on welfare got a TV set, everybody got a radio, everybody buys the *Daily News* and *El Dario*, so as long as the people already got access to these things, we might as well use them to the best of our advantage.

It was December 28 that we took the church and during the eleven days we were in there we learned a lot of things about the media. The first day there was this quick press conference on the steps of the church. That night I saw myself on TV, and I didn't like myself, you know. I came across as this stereotyped image of what a militant was supposed to be—the Afro and the shades and all this. I was up there talkin' all kinds of shit about this, that, and the other. And it was so routine and blasé, I said, "Damn," you know. I didn't dig myself. So the next day we had the press conference indoors behind a table. It was a relaxed atmosphere, I had my clear glasses on, so people could see my eyes, and as the press was settling down, I said, "How you doing?" introduced myself and got into raps. All the time we were in that church we had something to give the media people every day, that's how we had 'em going, 'cause they had no other news going on at the time. I got to know 'em, I know everybody in New York City in the media, you know, and we developed a kind of rapport, 'cause they understood they could talk to me, and that meant they could talk to the Party. I learned a lot of things out of that. I learned that a reporter could be your best friend, you shouldn't classify a reporter immediately as being a pig, especially now that they are letting a lot of Black and Puerto Rican reporters in. The real enemy is up on top—management levels. I had some good things for us—the editors came and hacked the shit up, and it was nothing like what they put in, and they proved it to me, 'cause, like at first I distrusted them also. There's a whole Movement orientation toward distrusting and watching out for the media—a lot of times, man, the Movement people come up there and treat the media people like shit, you know. Then they say, "Well, they put me on the air bad." *Of course* they put you on the air bad, you came across like an idiot.

And TV gets into somebody's house, man. You know, when you're on the screen in somebody's crib, you better not be saying things that come out with a lot of blips on the screen, 'cause you're gonna turn off whole families like that. You should understand what you're doing. The whole thing is to forget the person behind the mike that's asking the questions and imagine that you are talking to 300 of the most assorted kind of Puerto Ricans in the world in one room, in one little room—just do it like that, and as long as you keep the people in your eyes, you've got it.

Too many people tend to get into arguments with reporters. There are some reporters that come in there red-baiting—what you gotta do is use that, and that's where a little humor doesn't hurt. You can turn things around to make them look like jackasses and expose their game to the people right there on TV or radio. The people dig an underdog, that was the great appeal of the Mets at one time, and you have to understand that that's exactly what we are, underdogs. Once the people can start digging us for that, we can tell them, "Dig yourself for that."

When we're standing up there tellin' the pigs off—they dig that, man, whether or not they're of the same political persuasion. When the chips are falling down for us, a lot of times there have been Puerto Rican reactionaries that have defended us—sometimes *before* the Puerto Rican liberals, because at least they realized that one thing they can never say about us is that we are against the nation. We know for a fact that because of the way we've used the media, people dig our audacity, they love us, they feel like we're their grandchildren.

There was a period in our Party from July of '69 when we first started, to about August of 1970 or July of 1970 when we ran really on the personal magnetism of the leadership. But as we started to grow we said, "Look man, there ain't no way you can get a party going on that—you can't build a national liberation movement on the charisma of five or six people." 'Cause that would mean they would always have to be traveling everyplace to keep the whole machinery together. And if you want to keep a thing together, you've got to lay down certain principles that people can pick up on and go to town with—like the Thirteen Point Program and Platform. We have also developed our own political analysis. Right now we are going through a whole big thing of teaching ourselves to think in scientific terms, to study the theories of other revolutionary philosophers—people like Marx, Lenin and Mao.

Actually, we have made *two* analyses because we have to think of two struggles which are interrelated and at the same time not related—like the law of opposites. In other words, we have to make one analysis for the Puerto Rican nation that includes Puerto Rico, the island and the mainland; then another one for the Puerto Ricans who are struggling in the United States.

Within the Puerto Rican nation, there have been many groups who have been struggling for a long time, and our analysis has shown that the correct method of bringing about revolution is to isolate the enemy to as small a number as possible and unite the greatest number of people. Our major goal at this point is defeating the U.S. enemy. Right now we work with anybody who has the same goal. We're trying to work with the greatest number of people. In doing this, one of our most important concepts is that we are humble before our people, and vicious before the enemy. If you read *History Will Absolve Me,* you will see Fidel is *very* good at isolating the enemy into this little clique. See, when people think the enemy is this big mass, it wears away at the will to fight, but when people see that the enemy is just this bunch, right—this *Tame* Bunch—people begin to move.

The first segment of our people that will join, work with, and support the revolution is the *lumpen*, the street people: prostitutes, junkies, two-bit pushers, hustlers, welfare mothers. That's the group that got the Party through its first two years. Marx and Lenin said the working class would be first, right. But we have to examine the Puerto Rican reality. The street people come into the revolution because they've got nothing to lose. And it's a law of revolution that the most oppressed group takes the leadership position.

After the *lumpen* come the lowest classes of workers. For a long time in America, for a lot of reasons, the importance of the worker has been understated, and when people have said "Power to the people," they have talked about only one segment, and have sort of isolated everybody else. In the phase we are entering now, we are pushing very strongly for a *lumpen*-worker alliance as being the basis for the revolution within the Puerto Rican nation—an alliance of working people and street people, which will build and see this revolution through to the end.

We're going very heavily into worker organizing while we continue the organizing of street people, and we will continue to create situations where the two can come together because this system has created an antagonism between the working people and the street people of the same nation. In the ghettos of the city you have poor working-class people living in projects, and poor street people living in the tenements, and the people in the tenements can't stand the people in the projects. I mean, there are junkies ripping off the working people when they come home from the subways with their paychecks, and then the workers want to get together to form vigilante groups. . . . So we have gone out into the community to end this antagonism. This is one of the things that came out of the Second People's Church, this alliance. We know this will bring on a lot of repression from the enemy, because that's been one of their greatest games—like racism, like sexism—to keep the lower classes fighting each other, because they have the greatest revolutionary potential.

The group that comes in between the *lumpen* and the worker is the student. A student is this weird thing—a student actually could be classified as *petit bourgeois,* because the student, see, doesn't have much to do, the student is not working, has nothing to support except himself or herself. The student just has to worry about term papers and grades and scholarships. Once the student gets over that hangup, the student then begins to join the struggle. But the student doesn't have the same kind of gut commitment that the *lumpen* has, or the same kind of overall response coming from prolonged pressure that the worker has.

Many of us in the Party were students. But after checking it out, we saw that we were the children of workers or *lumpen,* so this prevented us from tripping out into a real *petit-bourgeois* vacuum.

Among *petit-bourgeois* people—lower *petit-bourgeois* people like teachers, certain poverty pimps that ain't gettin' too much bread, middle-class professionals—there's almost a fifty-fifty split in the time of revolutionary struggle. Some will join, and some go against, there's a left-wing *petit bourgeoisie* and right-wing *petit bourgeoisie*.

When you get to the ruling class, you'll find very few of our people there. And very few of the people who are actually a part of the elite in Puerto Rican society are going to join and support our struggle. Anybody who comes along is considered a bonus.

When we talk about our role in terms of creating the American Revolution, we are not saying we are going to take Puerto Rican people and ship them back to Puerto Rico. We are saying that we have been here in this country for two generations—in some cases, maybe three generations—we've been here for so long, right, that it would be too convenient for us to move back now, and just create a revolution there. We're saying that we want pay back for the years that we have suffered, the years that we have put up with the cockroaches and rats. We had to put up with snow, we had to put up with English, we had to put up with racism, with the general abuse of America. And we are gonna hook up with everybody else in this country who's fighting for their liberation—and that's a whole lot of people. We know that the number-one group that's leading that struggle are Black people, 'cause Black people—if we remember the rule says the most oppressed will take the vanguard role in the struggle—Black people, man, have gone through the most shit. Black people, along with Chicanos and native Americans, are the greatest ally we can have. So we must build the Puerto Rican-Black alliance. That is the basis of the American Revolution for us. Actually, the first group in America that we had a formal coalition with was the Black Panther Party. Also we must further the Latino ties, especially as we move west, and here in New York City, we must work with Dominicans—to further eliminate the racism that has deeply divided Black people and Spanish people.

We are also coming very close together with the struggle of Asians in this country, Asians who have been disinherited from the land that was theirs. Hawaii, for example, was made a state. One of our immediate struggles is to prevent that from happening in Puerto Rico. The Asian struggle is, like, twice as hard, because now they have to free a state, which is different from freeing a colony, right. That's actually going in and busting up part of a union.

Now the time has come for the Young Lords Party to begin organizing on the island. I mean, that's inevitable—we're not fighting just for Puerto Ricans in the States, we are fighting for all Puerto Ricans, you know and in turn, we're fighting for all oppressed people. In the fourth point of our Thirteen Point Program and Platform, we say we are revolutionary nationalists, not racists. That also means that we recognize the struggle of white people.

One thing we always say in the Young Lords, "Don't ever let any particular hatred you have prevent you from working. Always take it into you and let it move you forward. And if it's strong, change it, because it stops your work." We tell all Puerto Rican youth to listen to this. High school–age Puerto Ricans are into a *big* thing about whitey, and we tell them, "Man, it's not white *folk*. What we are trying to destroy is not white people, but a system created by white people, a capitalistic system that has run away from them to the point that it is now killing white people, too." And in fact, in that struggle, we're gonna hook up and we're gonna be allies with white people, like the Weatherpeople. The fact that the Weatherpeople rose is important to us because for a long time it was very theoretical talking about white allies. Every time we talked about it with somebody, the brother or sister would say, "Well, where are they?" And it was a good point. You know, where was everybody when Fred Hampton was killed? So that the emergence of the Weatherpeople—their beginning was very shaky, but it's a good, solid, steady group now—has given us a lot more trust and has helped us a lot in relating to other white people.

You know, when we meet somebody from the Third World, we immediately call them brother or sister, right. And then they have to prove to us through their practice that they are not our brothers or sisters—like Gene Roberts, who infiltrated the Panther Party. We view white people, when we first see them, with mistrust, suspicion, and then they have to show us by their practice that they are really our brothers and sisters—and that is the difference in the two.

It would be totally naïve for us to openly embrace white people, even if they are in the Movement, simply because they're supposed to be revolutionary. We've gone through too many frustrations with white people in the Movement to have that happen. 'Cause you really want to hope that once you get into the Movement there ain't no more racism. But that's a joke. In many cases racism becomes sicker than what you see in the so-called "straight" world, because it's kind of like a psychopathic hero worship. You know everything the Panthers do is right simply because they're Black, the Young Lords are fantastic because they're Puerto Rican. That's ridiculous. The Young Lords make mistakes, and if we make mistakes we want our white *companeros* and *companeras* to criticize us. If they really love us, that's what they'll do. That's one of the weaknesses of the Movement, you know, that people do not want to criticize the Panthers because the Panthers are Black. But in doing that they do more harm to the Panthers than they do good.

We try to encourage honesty in our relationships with white people. I think that we've gone a long way toward eliminating a lot of the shit in the Movement. And I think a lot of people get good vibes when they're around us. I think a lot of people in the Movement dig us because of that.

The Young Lords Party today is the fastest-moving group of people inside the Puerto Rican nation. We're moving faster than anybody else, and this means that all contradictions that exist among our people are much more highlighted among us, that things come out much more quickly. That's why you have the Young Lords arguing about male chauvinism, female passivity, racism, Viet Nam. People on the street ain't talkin' about all those things yet, you know. We try to take that word "vanguard" and give it a new definition, because the definition that it has now is that the vanguard is some elitist group, that they're better than everybody else, and they tell all the other groups, "Go fuck yourself." Like, to us, the vanguard means that we have a great responsibility. It means that we are in front of the people and show the people the way, but at the same time we are among the people, because we are the people. We are also in back of the people, you know, because sometimes you got to lay back to check the people out. And that's where we get our strength from.

We're here because we are trying as best we can to take the power of the State and put that back in the hands of the people who for so long have been denied everything. It's a very deep, emotional thing, you know, for people who have been told for so long that they're fucked up, that they're niggers, spics, that they ain't worth shit, to be doing this.

We are showing people an alternative to living under a capitalistic society—an alternative to the tenement, to the street, to the workplace, to the *fanguito* [mudhole/slum]. Each generation that comes up is taught that this is the only way things can be done, this is life, right. It's a fact of life that you're poor, that there are some people on top, and that most people are on the bottom. It's a fact of life that this is a dog-eat-dog world, and if you want to make it you got to make it by yourself. But we're gonna take them facts of life and turn them around. We're saying that it is gonna be a new fact of life that what counts first is not so much the individual but the group, and in order for the individual to survive, the group, the nation, has to survive.

There's a whole new way to live, you know, if people together are planning where their nation's gonna go, how their government is running, how much they're going to produce, who's going to produce what, and what they're gonna do with it once they get it. In cold, scientific terms this means that production and distribution get put in the hands of the people. That's a phrase that everybody can sing by rote, but if we think about it and if we understand it, it's a whole mindblowing concept to oppressed people, because we've never been shown that we can succeed in anything.

You know, there was a way that the people used to walk in the street before 1969, before the Young Lords Party began—people used to walk with their heads down like this, and the pigs would walk through the colonies, man, like they owned the block. They'd come in here with no kind of respect in their eyes. They'd *walk* through, they wouldn't ride through. See, when a pig *walks* through the street that means they got less respect than if they gotta ride. But after the Garbage Offensive and the People's Church it was a whole new game.

As these things started to happen, as each one came, it was like boom, boom, boom. You and the enemy are standing there like this, right, and the enemy's been kicking your ass. But suddenly you throw up a couple of blocks, right, and you land a couple a solid ones, and people start digging this, and they see you're landing more solid ones. You're fighting toe to toe and, like, you're takin' some shit, but you know you can take his best. For 400 years, you've taken the best that this motherfucker could throw at you, and now you're gonna deal. So now, what's he gonna do? He wants to land his haymaker, he wants to round everybody up—you know that's coming. But we are a tempered people, we have been tempered like the blade of a knife by years, man, of living under this shit. When fascism comes, people gonna be ready for it. It's gonna blow the pigs' minds, right, but we ain't gonna give up. Because the people have seen that there's a way.

At the Second People's Church, we brought guns out into the open, and these guns were definitely illegal, they were unregistered, right. But because we had our people with us, Mayor Lindsay had to say the guns were legal. He had to hold his police back, because the white racists in the department wanted to kill us, you know, and they couldn't. And when people saw this, they said, "Wow!" We took the guns out of the church and we showed them—like we say in the street "we showed our shit" and got away clean. We still ain't been popped for that one.

Now, when they catch us, when they start rounding up the first bunch of Lords, they're gonna throw everything on us. But the point is the people now have hope. They can round me up, they can round up the Central Committee, but they're gonna have a hard time. First of all, the explosion that's gonna come if they touch any body in the

Central Committee will be tremendous. We already know what happened when they tried to take out Chief of Staff, Fi, and that was months ago. The main thing is that they can take any Young Lord now, because now they've got to kill an idea. Like, we have a second, third, fourth level leadership. This is one of the greatest things we've done. Ain't nobody done this in the Puerto Rican nation—build something that's gonna live on. The Nationalists tried and failed because they were centered around this one cat—Albizu Campos.

Our people have been taught to believe that when they rounded up Albizu Campos and two thousand members of the Nationalist Party they broke the back of the Nationalist Party. But now the people can think about Albizu and all of a sudden it seems like the Nationalist Party has just been going through different kinds of changes for twenty years. "Well man, we thought you all lost—it looks like we're gonna start winning." And, like, the concept of winning, right, that is the number one contribution of the Young Lords Party—that is what we are, man, the concept of winning.

One thing about us I really dig is that we don't get so hung up in theory that we don't move. We can still jump out into the street, we still do battle with the pigs, we still haven't lost our heart. That may sound like a whole big *macho* thing, but it's not, see, because it's important that we understand that the thing that kept the Puerto Rican nation intact, the thing that made us was the soul and strength of our men and women. That's what did it. When people would get up against the wall, it wasn't because they had read Marx or Mao, it was because deep down inside there was this basic nationalist feeling that said, "Get off my back, you don't belong here—you ain't got no business bugging me. Get the hell out! And if you don't, I'm gonna punch you in the mouth!" This is the thing that is in our core, this is our nationalism.

Now, there are some people who would say that there's a contradiction in being a revolutionary nationalist—in fact, they say you can't be a Nationalist and a Socialist at the same time. Well, that's wrong. See, for these people I would quote Mao, where he says that loving your people and your country and fighting to liberate your people is the best way to aid the struggle of all peoples around the world. It's ridiculous to say you're an internationalist and you're going to struggle for all oppressed people, without picking a particular segment of people you're gonna work in. Because the people, you know, are divided along nation and class lines, and we have to recognize both. In this country, for example, racism is like a stick that the pigs are clubbing you on the head with. Now you got to grab the other end and hit them back with it—and the other end of the stick is nationalism. And if you do it righteously, if you do it with the interest of the people and with the backing of the people, then it becomes revolutionary. Now that's revolutionary nationalism—that is the kind of nationalism that says, "Yes, we are proud to be Puerto Rican, we are proud to be number one—but we want everybody else to be number one too, and we're gonna help everyone else be number one." See, 'cause the other kind of nationalism is reactionary nationalism—where you say, "Well, I'm number one. Fuck everybody else."

We've seen how the Black colony in America has been divided in terms of culture versus politics. We don't want to see the Puerto Rican colony divided that way. We don't want to create divisions where there need not be any. So that we do promote interest in the culture of the nation, right—but we only want to take from the culture what has been good. We're not gonna go into a trip glorifying the *pava* which is a straw hat, or a *guayabera*, which is a kind of shirt, 'cause there ain't no hat or shirt gonna free anybody. But the fact that our people, when put up against the wall, have managed to kick ass for centuries—that is good, that is part of our culture, right. That's why we say that the most cultural thing we can do is pick up the gun to defend ourselves.

Culture, see, is the gun—as long as we understand that it is not the gun that should control us, but the Party that should control the gun. That is a rule that our Minister of Defense has made very clear. And that was the whole lesson of the People's Church. It can be said that the Second People's Church, when we took the church with guns, when we armed ourselves in our own defense, was probably one of the most cultural events in the history of the Puerto Rican nation—on the same level with the uprising at Jayuya in 1950, and *El Grito de Lares* in 1868. The only cultural form that's gonna go beyond that is armed struggle.

We are not nihilists, you know, we're not just destroy, destroy, destroy. We're saying to our people, yes we've got to destroy, but we have a new system that we're already starting to build, right. Taking the whole Puerto Rican nation into account, we're a small group, we're dealing socialistically with one another in a very human manner, and as we move, that influence is gonna spread out in many ways.

....

YLP Editorial: Separation from the YLO

(From the newspaper *Palante*, 5 June 1970, volume 2, number 4)

The Young Lords Organization began in January of 1969, when Cha Cha Jimenez reorganized what was then a Puerto Rican street gang into a revolutionary political party. The aim of the Organization was to fight for the independence of Puerto Rico and liberate Borinquenos here in the united states from the oppression we suffer. The news of the Organization spread to New York where a group of us heard about it and decided to form a chapter here in the Barrio to work for the liberation of our people. We wrote to Chicago and in July became the New York State Chapter of the Young Lords Organization.

We have found it necessary to leave the Young Lords Organization in Chicago and form a new political party with the same goals—freedom for our people.

We are now the YOUNG LORDS PARTY.

We are the same YOUNG LORDS who threw garbage in the streets with the people of El Barrio. We are the same YOUNG LORDS who took over the People's Church on 111th Street and Lexington. And we will continue to wear the purple beret.

There are many reasons for the split between us and Chicago, our old National Headquarters. In order for us to make a revolution in this country, there is a need for a national political party to educate people about what has been happening on the island and why Puerto Rico must be free.

The only way you can build that kind of revolutionary political party is to have strong leadership and a strong national headquarters.

The National Headquarters has a responsibility to:

1) Publish a national newspaper regularly that will educate and inform our people all across the country.

2) Create a political platform and program to educate our people to the reasons why we want liberation and what we stand for.

3) Build a strong Central Committee to lead our people.

4) Educate and train members of the Party into responsible revolutionaries, who can love, serve, and protect our people.

5) Establish rules of discipline, because a revolutionary must be disciplined enough to endure hardship in times of struggle and must be able to follow orders.

6) Develop ministries to do specific tasks, like a Health Ministry to start health programs in the community; an Education Ministry to teach political education to the members as well as people in the community; a Defense Ministry to protect all of us from the police and armies that attack us; an Information Ministry to put out a newspaper and leaflets to our people.

7) Initiate programs that serve the needs of our people, like the Free Breakfast Program, Free Clothing Drive, Community Political Education, Lead Poisoning and T.B. Detection.

Because Chicago had and still has many organizational problems, they were unable to fulfill these responsibilities. The Central Committee in Chicago was constantly changing; the only person who remained constant was Cha Cha Jimenez. Consistent leadership is necessary to set a revolutionary example for the members and the people. The members were not disciplined and many did not report regularly, so that important political work could not be done in this community all the time. This is one of the main reasons that National Monthly newspaper (YLO) came out only 6 times in 18 months. Political education was not given to the members, so that many of them still functioned the way they had when the Young Lords was a gang and not a revolutionary Puerto Rican organization. No political platform or program was developed to give our people what we stand for and what we believed. When there is no political education and no program, the members flounder, become discouraged, and so do the people. Very few programs were developed in Chicago, and those that were started could not function because there was no consistent manpower.

We in New York made many attempts to go to Chicago to work things out, and to help supply manpower and leadership; but these only gave temporary relief and did not solve the problems. Finally, we went on a retreat in May to figure out the political direction of the New York Chapter. That discussion included our relationship with National. We decided that a solution was to have leadership from Chicago come here, to join with us to build a real National Political Party. The only other solution was to abandon our people and programs in El Barrio and the South Bronx and all go to Chicago. We could not, because we are serving them and have many ongoing programs and a newspaper to put out.

As revolutionaries, our first duty is to make the revolution. When we went to Chicago to ask them to come here, they refused. They felt that they could eventually solve their problems. They did not think the problems were as basic and unchangeable as we did. They were just beginning a health program that they didn't want to abandon.

We criticized their decision and gave them our decision to form the YOUNG LORDS PARTY. We left them as revolutionary compañeros with no name calling. We hope that some time in the future we will be able to struggle together for the liberation of Borinquenos and Latinos all across the nation and on the island.

The National Headquarters of the YOUNG LORDS PARTY will be at 1678 Madison Avenue, and the YOUNG LORDS will be everywhere.

LIBERATE PUERTO RICO NOW!
POWER TO ALL OPPRESSED PEOPLE!
Falipe Luciano, Chairman
Pablo "Yoruba" Guzman, Minister of Information
Juan Gonzalez, Minister of Education
Juan "Fi" Ortiz, Minister of Finance
David Perez, Field Marshall

CENTRAL COMMITTEE
YOUNG LORDS PARTY

....

Central Committee

(From the newspaper *Palante*, 19 April–1 May 1971, volume 3, number 7)

We are presenting these short biographies, or histories, of our Central Committee. As you read this, you will see that the Central Committee (our National Leadership) is made up of different types of Puerto Ricans, and that they are much the same as other Puerto Ricans.

Juan Gonzalez, Minister of Defense, 23: Juan was born in Ponce, P.R. When he was young, his parents came to New York. They were concerned with trying to give a "better life" to their children, and constantly moved from one neighborhood to the next, leaving one slum for another. This is a common feeling among working-class Puerto Ricans, as Juan's parents were—trying to maintain some kind of dignity and respect, and seeing that their children get "the best."

Juan went to Franklin K. Land High School while he lived in Brooklyn, then took advantage of being a Puerto Rican to get a scholarship to Columbia University. He got an anti-poverty job in New York's Westside, where many Latins live. Here he came into close contact with his people once again, going into apartments and seeing dwellings some people call "homes." He asked himself, "What am I doing? Here I am, at Columbia, and for what? For who? Me? What about these people, my people?"

Juan quickly went through a lot of changes, working with the most radical group on campus at that time, Students for a Democratic Society (SDS), and was a leader of the 1968 uprising at Columbia. For this, he was expelled four days before graduation, and did 30 days in jail. After jail, Juan met a group of Puerto Ricans who were trying to do something, and through this became a founder of the Young Lords Party.

Juan "Fi" Ortiz, Chief of Staff, 17: Fi's father is a pentecostal minister, and his parents also wanted to give their children "something better," and they moved out to Queens. Fi couldn't relate to this, and stayed in El Barrio, visiting the house in Queens occasionally. At school, Fi heard so many out and out lies, distortions and omissions, that he constantly made fools of his teachers, asking embarrassing questions. Fi's parents were told their son was "a born delinquent" because of this. The brother was kicked out of practically every high school in Queens until he finally landed in Benjamin Franklin High School in El Barrio.

While going to Franklin, he studied photography at a community center with other brothers and sisters. He was good enough to have the pictures of his people and El Barrio shown in museums and on television. Eventually, Fi got angry at the conditions he was photographing, and the people responsible for them. He and his friends formed a group that wanted a better life for Puerto Ricans, and through this Fi became a founder of the Young Lords Party.

Gloria Gonzalez, Field Marshal, 27: Gloria was born in El Fanguito, near San Juan. When she was ten, she was brought to New York. Here, she took to the street gangs and soon became a junior high school dropout. Gloria seemed to be on the course thousands of other Puerto Rican women are forced into: early marriage, housework, a quick old age and no laughter in life.

She worked in garment centers, small orchard street stores, and finally as a nurses' aid for six years. But an opportunity to do something different came up while she lived in New York's Lower East Side. Gloria went once a year to Puerto Rico, and in both places, she saw what the gringos' racist neglect and total lack of concern did to the health of our people. She worked with other people in the community to try and get better treatment from Gouvernier Hospital. Anti-poverty and the hope that "these people" could be bought off created a Community Health Advisory Board, and Gloria sat on the board while working in the hospital as a Mental Health Assistant. She refused to be bought off, and intensified her efforts, convinced that preventive medicine means giving people health check-ups and treatment before they get sick to prevent future illness. In this amerikkkan society, doctors' greed makes this unreal. In her fight, Gloria helped found the Health Revolutionary Unity Movement (HRUM), and joined the Young Lords Party in January of 1970. In September, she was made Field Marshal and a member of our Central Committee.

David Perez, Field Marshal, 21: David was born in Lares, and came to Chicago when he was 10. Like so many other Puerto Ricans, his parents were told things were "better" in the states. And like so many other Puerto Ricans, the Perez family learned they had been told a lie, and settled into the rut of slum living. David's people are from campesino and campesina background, and the ways of the city were foreign to his nature. But he knew enough when somebody was lying to him, or trying to take him for a fool, and this was what teachers were doing in school. With a friend, he organized a strike at his high school; and for this he was promptly expelled.

David hustled around in the streets for a while and then saw what seemed to be an easy hustle, a job at an anti-poverty agency. It is fitting in a way that the anti-poverty organizations created by president johnson provided the means for many Blacks, Puerto Ricans and Chicanos to live until they could grab johnson and his friends by their throats. At this job, David met a representative from the State University of New York at Old Westbury, which was looking for ghetto people to maintain its image of a "with-it" institution. With no high school diploma, David got into college, simply by being a spic. In New York, he met up with the Puerto Ricans who were tired with the way things were, and said, "This is for me." David went on to become a founder of the YLP.

Pablo "Yoruba" Guzman, Minister of Information, 20: Yoruba was born in El Barrio, and raised in the South Bronx. His parents represented a mixture of working-class Puerto Ricans and a growing class among our people, the lumpen. The lumpen are the lowest in the social order, including welfare mothers, hustlers, pimps, prostitutes and junkies.

Yoruba went to the Bronx High School of Science. After a year there, he saw how empty his thinking was, and only did well enough just to get by, while he concentrated on hanging out in the streets. But after two years, he left that once his crowd started using hard drugs.

Trying to figure out what it was that turned so many people you know into junkies, he saw that this happened all over, in greater numbers, and Yoruba began studying new books now, about the politics of change. He passed on to Old Westbury, and during his year there, rediscovered his Puerto Rican roots after taking a trip to Mexico. Yoruba is an Afro-Boricua, a brother with dark skin and an afro, and up until that time the racism he found from lighter skinned Puerto Ricans put him into a heavy Black thing. He even refused to listen to Latin music. Soon he saw that it was an outside enemy that turned brothers and sisters against each other. With David, he left Old Westbury and helped found the Young Lords Party.

....

2 Years of Struggle

(From the newspaper *Palante*, 24 July–7 August 1971, volume 3, number 13)

July 26 is the second anniversary of the Young Lords Party. Last year at this time we had a special anniversary issue describing all the things we had done in our first year. We'd like to use part of this issue to do something similar to that—but this time we'd like to explain more clearly the reasons behind many of our actions and the changes that the Party has gone through in the last year.

We've done a lot of things this year and we've made mistakes too. We didn't make these mistakes on purpose, because we want to serve our people not hurt them. They happened because we are trying to do something—make revolutionary changes—and there are no specific guidelines for our situation. So we make mistakes, because we are human too. We have come to recognize these weaknesses and move to correct them as soon as we are aware of what is wrong. We also understand that the only people who don't make mistakes are the people who don't do anything.

We want to serve our people as best as we can. We try to analyze our own strengths and weaknesses so that we can more totally be the People's Party. This article will talk about some of the things we have done and also some of the weaknesses and strengths we have. This has been made possible by the people, both in the Party and outside the Party, who cared enough to take the time to give us constructive criticism (criticism to help us develop).

LINCOLN HOSPITAL

Since we began, we recognized the basic need for community control of the institutions in our communities. One such struggle was the takeover of the Lincoln Hospital Nurses' Residence on July 14. We were working with community groups and the Health Revolutionary Unity Movement (HRUM) to win community-worker control of the hospital. Together we demanded a $140 minimum weekly salary for all workers, a 24 hour a day child care center, and a community-worker board to run the hospital. In September, members of the community fired j.j. smythe, the man who ran the inadequate abortion program at Lincoln. The community held smythe responsible for the death of Carmen Rodriguez, the first legal abortion death in New York. On November 11, the 6th floor of Lincoln was seized by

ex-addicts, workers, and community people who were demanding a detoxification program for the South Bronx. 15 people were arrested. As a result of their work, there is now a
community-worker controlled drug program in Lincoln Hospital. The fight for control of
Lincoln Hospital—between the city, and the workers and community—is still going on.

STUDENT CONFERENCE

On September 22 and 23, we called a Student Conference along with the Puerto Rican
Student Union. Over 1,000 students attended this conference and we laid the ground-
work for increased activity on the campuses and the forming of a Third World high
school group.

At the conference we also set up Liberate Puerto Rico Now Committees in different
cities. But because we failed to follow up on these groups and didn't give them enough
guidance and political education, they fell apart.

JULIO'S MURDER

On October 14, Julio Roldan and Bobby Lemus were arrested after the people of El
Barrio burned garbage in the streets to protest a lack of garbage pickups by the sanitation
department. Julio was killed in the Tombs, New York's Manhattan House of Detention
for Men, on October 15. On October 18, the Young Lords Party held a funeral march
for Julio. We were joined by about 2,000 concerned people. At the end of the march
we seized, for the second time, the People's Church on 111th Street and Lexington Avenue. We were armed because one of our members had been killed and because we didn't
intend for any more of our people to die without protecting ourselves. In this action we
received the support of Puerto Ricans in New York. The police knew we had support and
stayed away from the church. However, once we had the church we failed to do a thorough follow-up on the programs that we had started inside. So the programs didn't really
get off the ground like we wanted them to. And the people lost interest, and we lost their
support. After awhile, the church got a court order on us, and we left the church. The
People's Church is still sitting in the middle of our community, unused 6 days a week.

Bobby Lemus' case is going to court in September. The pigs are trying to convict him
and sentence him to 30 years. By saying Bobby is guilty, they can justify the death of Julio
Roldan. See you in court in September.

PHILLY'S PEOPLE'S CHURCH

On November 5, the Philadelphia Branch of the Young Lords Party took over the
Kingsway Lutheran Church and turned it into a People's Church with programs to serve
the community. Again, after the takeover, the Party did not put enough emphasis on
follow-up and the programs slowly fell apart. The day after the takeover, the office of the
Philly Branch was bombed. Another bombing took place at the end of December. This
showed how uptight the city administration was about the church takeover. (Philadelphia is the fourth largest city in the u.s.)

INMATES LIBERATION FRONT

After Julio's death in the Tombs, the Party became very involved in work around the
prisons. The Inmates Liberation Front, a group of brothers in jail, became a part of the

Party, and we became involved in cases where brothers had been killed in jail (Lavon Moore, Anibal Davila). Eventually, however, the ILF became a reformist group—that is, trying to bail brothers and sisters out of prison one by one, rather than work to change the whole prison system.

OFENSIVA ROMPECADENAS

In January, Central Committee returned from a long retreat (a meeting where our work is evaluated and our future work is planned). Plans were announced for the opening of a branch in Ponce, Puerto Rico in March. We were all very excited about uniting the 1/3 and the 2/3's. (1/3 of all Puerto Ricans live in the u.s. and 2/3's live in Puerto Rico.) We all knew that this was a big step and that we would have to tighten up the organization. We went into a period, where we concentrated on raising money, studying a lot more about Puerto Rico, and training the group that was to go to the island first. So, many people began to ask "Where are the Young Lords? Have they disappeared?" We were not as involved in community programs as before, so our people did not understand what we were doing. In order for us to move forward in one area—preparing for the move to Puerto Rico—we had to sacrifice in the area of community work.

As part of tightening up, we exposed four agents that had infiltrated the Party. We knew federal and local police had sent agents into our organization. We felt now was the time to throw them out—before they could sabotage the important move to Puerto Rico. We found out about the agents through tips from friends inside the police department (not all police are pigs), by checking on the information they had given us, and by investigating their backgrounds.

Ofensiva Rompecadenas was for the most part successful. We did tighten up enough to send a group to open branches in Puerto Rico. Originally we were going to open a branch in Ponce, but instead we opened two branches, one in El Cano and the other in Aguadilla. Ponce turned out to be a bad place to start off in, because the government and the right wing is very strong there (it is ferré's hometown).

During Ofensiva Rompecadenas, the district attorney in New York began building a conspiracy case against the Party. The homes of Party leaders were broken into and papers and notebooks were stolen. We felt that the best defense against a conspiracy bust was to let people know what was going on, so we began to publicize the district attorney's plans to jail our leadership. This publicity bought us some time, but the case is still sitting in the files at the district attorney's office. We can probably expect some kind of conspiracy charges in the near future.

MARCH 21

On March 21, the anniversary of the Ponce Massacre, Boricuas everywhere took to the streets. 700 people marched in Ponce in the biggest demonstration ever held there on March 21. 7000 Boricuas marched in New York, 30 in Bridgeport and 300 in Philadelphia.

HRUM

In January, the Health Revolutionary Unity Movement officially became a people's organization of the Party. A people's organization is an organization that follows the political ideology of the Party and works very closely with the Party. Some of its members are members of the YLP but the majority are not.

HRUM organizes Third World health workers, and on May 15 and 16, HRUM held a conference at City College in NYC. Out of this conference, new HRUM chapters were formed.

PUERTO RICAN DAY PARADE

The last three issues have talked a lot about the Parade so not much more needs to be said. We'd just like to stress, one more time, that our demand was that POOR PEOPLE march at the front of the Puerto Rican Day Parade, because most Puerto Ricans are poor and the Parade should represent what is happening to the majority of our people.

The police attack upon Puerto Ricans there was unjustified and very brutal. There was no excuse for it no matter what the police say.

RESTRUCTURING OF THE PARTY

We constantly evaluate our work. In January we came out of such an evaluation, and we saw the need for the Party to get to more areas where our people are and especially to organize workers. We set this as our major goal after Ofensiva Rompecadenas. We tried and we tried, but we still were not organizing our people in the best way. So we had to check and see what was wrong. What we found was that the way the Party was structured according to functions—with an education ministry, economics ministry, etc.—had become an obstacle in our way. So we decided to reorganize the Party according to sections. We did this in NYC and later plan to restructure in Puerto Rico, Philadelphia, and Bridgeport according to sections.

Each section organizes a certain class or social grouping of our people wherever our people are at. The different sections are workers, lumpen, community, students, women and GI's.

So the Party is now in the process of change. The offices (branches) are being turned over to the community with the name of Committee to Defend the Community. Only a few Lords are left in the offices to help community people organize their areas. The community sections have suffered a lot because we took people out of this area to do other organizing. That is why some of the offices have been closed a lot lately; we are recruiting community people to do community work. There are now Committees to Defend the Community in El Barrio, the Lower East Side and Brooklyn.

We have also set up an organization for workers called the Federation of Workers. All of the members of the Federation, including the Lords, are workers, so the organization doesn't demand that members spend too many hours in meetings. Right now, the Federation has begun showing films about workers in the community, and studying workers' struggles in the past. This organization will be putting out a newspaper dealing with the interest of workers. This is very important because our working class people are not being organized for liberation.

The Bronx office has been turned over to the lumpen organization, Lumpen Unidos Rompecadenas. This group too has only a few Lords working with it, and it is concentrating now on fighting for community control of drug programs.

The Third World Student League, an organization of high school students, has begun working and will call for a high school strike on September 23, the anniversary of El Grito de Lares. The theme of the strike will be that high school students should not salute the amerikkkan flag while amerikkka continues to occupy Puerto Rico, IndoChina, and the Black and Latin communities in the u.s. Third World Student League groups will be set up in many high schools in September.

We also have a Women's Union, which puts out a paper called La Luchadora. Again, most of the members are not in the Party. But there are Party members there. The Union is concentrating on setting up a child care center for women in the Union and on doing political education.

There is also an organization dedicated to organizing GI's and ex-GI's. This organization is called the New 65th Infantry.

INTERNAL DEVELOPMENT

While all of the things we have discussed were going on, the Party was also going through a lot of internal (inside) changes. In September, the Party began to move towards collective leadership where decisions are made by a group of people rather than by individuals. This was very important, because more people had to take responsibility. In addition to Central Committee, we now have a National Staff, which is the second level of national leadership in the Party.

Last summer was also the time when we stepped up the struggle against machismo in the Party. We began to criticize brothers for not treating sisters as equals, for not respecting the abilities of sisters, seeing them in an inferior role. The more the brothers acted this way, the more sisters were afraid to speak up, to take leadership, and they just accepted men making all the decisions. This keeps sisters from developing as human beings. It keeps them from developing as leaders of our nation. Over half our nation is sisters, and we must struggle real hard to eliminate anything that holds back half of our people. This is part of what we call "the Revolution within the Revolution." National Liberation and self-determination are our major goals. The fight against machismo is part of the struggle.

NEW BRANCHES

In November, the Bridgeport Branch was opened. The opening of this branch was very important because it was the first time the Party opened in a small working class city. The Bridgeport Lords became involved in organizing tenants, and after a rent strike in Bridgeport, police and slumlords destroyed our office. The tenants that were on strike won their demands.

In April, two branches were opened in Puerto Rico. We now have 7 branches altogether.

PARTY SCHOOL

In February, the Party started a Party School. After over a year, we were finally able to set up a system for training officers and leaders. We are now in the second session of Party School, with a new group of officers being trained.

OVERALL EVALUATION

One of the main weaknesses we see is that we have been moving too fast. In one year we have done much more than one year's work. Because we were trying to do so many things at once, we sometimes didn't follow up on things we started.

Another weakness was that we didn't explain everything clearly to the people so that many people are still confused about what we have been doing. Now that we have restructured the Party and offices are Committees to Defend the Community [sic], many people think the Lords have abandoned the struggle. This has to be explained so that people understand that there are still Lords in each community working with community people. And in addition, there are Lords organizing in factories and schools. If we had explained everything clearly, people would know that most of the people who work in the community offices are not Party members.

Another weakness was that the Party moved a lot according to the conditions in New York City. The conditions in New York are not the same as in Bridgeport, Philly, Boston, El Cano, or Aguadilla. Not taking the whole Party into account led us to take actions that hindered (held back) the Party organizing in other areas.

The Party has grown a whole lot this year, as has the entire Puerto Rican movement. We have succeeded in opening branches in Puerto Rico and are working with Boricuas in communities around the country. We are moving to correct the weaknesses that we are aware of.

Our people must be strong to struggle for liberation. We want to continue to grow and to serve our people. We can do this best if you tell us what you think and what you need. We must criticize each other so that we can find out our weaknesses and strengths.

¡QUE VIVA PUERTO RICO LIBRE!

National Staff
YOUNG LORDS PARTY

....

The Young Lords Party (speech by Juan Gonzalez, 16 Nov. 1971)

(From the Juan Gonzalez Collection, Center for Puerto Rican Studies, CUNY Hunter College)

Juan Gonzalez
Minister of Defense
Young Lords Party
16 November 1971

I'm gonna rap for awhile, so if you get tired . . . because we don't get a chance to come out to Hawaii very often so when we come, we like to tell you all that we have learned to share with you and learn all that you have learned in your struggles to share with us so we can take it back. So if you get tired, leave or complain.

Well, what I'm gonna try to talk about today is first of all, let you know how we got here. We're going across the United States now and to Hawaii in a tour trying to bring two things to the American people and the other colonized people living inside the

United States. One is a film that was made of the Party—the Young Lords Party—which covers our history for a one-year span from October of 1969 to October of 1970. And we have that film and we can't show it here, unfortunately, but we will be showing it tomorrow night, here at the University in one of the lounges—you remember the name of the lounge? Hemenway Lounge tomorrow night. So that if any of you haven't seen the film, you can come tomorrow night.

And what we've been doing is taking the film around to different cities throughout the United States over the last four weeks. We've been in Connecticut, been in Ohio, in Dayton, Cincinnati, and Yellow Springs, and Cleveland, been in Detroit and Auburn and Chicago, San Francisco. Now we're here and we've still got to go on to L.A., to Boston, back to Connecticut and finally, back to New York.

And what we're trying to do with this trip is to educate as many people as possible about the situation of the Puerto Rican people, both on the island and inside the United States, and try to express our values with other colonial peoples of the American government and with the American people and the struggle against what we consider the common enemy. And maybe some of the people don't even know that we got an enemy in common yet. Try to let them know about that, too. So, we've been essentially showing the film and then explaining what's been happening in the Party since then.

Now, somebody was telling me before when I asked them what should I rap about to the students here and they told me that a lot of people were talking about how the political movement, the revolutionary movement was quiet or dormant or dead. And we've been across the United States now and we have a sense of what's going on. And it's true that one part of what was known as a political movement in the past is dead. For the most part, the college campuses are dead . . . ain't nothing happening on the college campuses, which is good and bad. The good part of that is that the people who were involved in political struggle over the last few years who used to be on those college campuses are no longer there. They're out now organizing different aspects as part of the American society, whether it's working people, professional people, students, so forth, but they're outside in the real world organizing, mobilizing people, setting their roots for a long and protracted revolutionary struggle. That's the good aspect of the fact that there's nothing happening on the campuses. The bad aspect is that the campuses should continue to be a source of consciousness raising [for] the rest of the society and that's not happening. That's mostly the fault of the people who are here and not of the people who have left.

And so, what we have just in the various collectives and organizations that we've met across the country, organizations like the Black Workers' Congress in Detroit and Chicago. They're rising up angry in Chicago like the revolutionary unions in Southern Ohio, like Los Siete de la Raza, and I Wor Kuen, and Venceremos, and various other organizations in San Francisco. There are numerous revolutionary organizations all around the United States trying to organize and mobilize people to deal with the government that's rapidly becoming impossible for most of the people of the world to sustain or deal with. So that, that's a hopeful thing I want to bring to you in case you didn't know because you're not gonna read about it in the newspapers. There are thousands of people organizing the masses of American people. It's gonna take awhile for the effects of that to be felt because it's going through a new level of struggle now. It's no longer a small group of young people that are involved in rebellion against the United States government. It's broadening now into a deeper movement. It's gonna take time for people to see that, maybe two years, three, four years. But that's okay because it's a young movement and we got a lot of time and we shouldn't be in a hurry.

Now, we were out here in January of last time and in the ethnic studies thing we have a long rap about the history of Puerto Rico to acquaint people with the situation of the Puerto Rican people. And I'm gonna rap through that . . . no, I'm not gonna go through that because that would take too long. I'm just gonna backtrack a little bit, at least to the period of American entry into Puerto Rican history.

Alright, we were captured in 1898. In 1898, there was a war—they called it the Spanish-American war. But it wasn't fought in either Spain or America. It was fought in the Philippines; it was fought in Cuba; it was fought in Puerto Rico. And the prize of that war was the Philippines, Puerto Rico, Cuba, and Guam. The United States defeated Spain and took over those four countries, four separate nationalities, four separate peoples. It became the war booty of the United States. And the American troops invaded Manila and invaded Guanica and Puerto Rico, invaded Havana, invaded Guam. They said they had come to liberate the people from Spanish yoke, Spanish oppression. And they stayed in the Philippines until 1946 liberating the Philippine people. They stayed in Cuba until 1904 until they got the Platt Amendment, which gave them the right to come in anytime they wanted to. They're still in Guam and they're still in Puerto Rico. And it took two wars by the Philippine people even to make a dent in the U.S. getting out. And they only got out politically because they're still there economically to control the Philippine nation. So that, that's the colonial situation, we call that colonialism.

What the Americans did is they came at Puerto Rico and they changed our economy overnight with sugar cane plantations—one large sugar cane plantation. Right, very similar, we'll check it out here. And pineapples, too, pineapples and sugar cane. After awhile, around 1930, they decided they didn't need Puerto Rico for sugar anymore because they were getting 6 million tons from Cuba and they were getting 2-1/2 million tons from Santo Domingo. And we were so small anyway, 100 miles by 35 miles, we were producing only 500,000 tons of sugar. It wasn't worth it to the American capitalists.

So they got themselves a commission. They called it the Brookys Institute. And they said to Brookys, go down there and find out what we can do with that island. So the Brookys Institute went down there and did a study. And they studied the economy of the island and they came with their report. And their report said it's not worth it to keep it an agricultural economy. Industrialize the island because you have lots of cheap labor. It's a small island, build lots of factories, put all those Puerto Ricans to work in the factories, get them off their land and you'll make a lot of money that way.

So the U.S. government dug the proposal. The problem was that at the time the capitalists were a little uptight. It was 1930, the depression had just occurred or was occurring. There wasn't that much money for them to invest. So they had to shelve the report for awhile, putting it in their records, and wait for better days. And after World War 2, when they had rebuilt their economy off of the World War, they were ready. They got the report out of the files, they began to implement. And in 1945, they began Operation Bootstrap to industrialize Puerto Rico.

They got themselves some puppet traitors to come in. They gave them some money to form a party—a political party called the Popular Democratic Party. And that Popular Democratic Party, under leadership of a traitor named Munoz Marin, put forth the slogan of Bread, Land and Liberty—"Pan, Tierra y Libertad." And after he got elected, because all the people dug that slogan, things were bad. So after he got elected, he then said, liberty can wait—let's deal with the economic situation. And the socioeconomic situation meant bringing in all the American companies.

And over the next few years, from 1945-65, the peasant class of Puerto Rico was destroyed. People were herded into the cities, San Juan, Mayaue, and Ponce to work in the factories. And over one million Puerto Ricans were forced to leave their homelands to come to the United States to work in the steel mills of Gary Indiana; the migrant labor camps of eastern Massachusetts, Long Island, Wisconsin, and New Jersey; the garment factories of Philadelphia and New York; the ship building industry of Connecticut. A whole bunch of Puerto Ricans were even brought out here to Hawaii to help along and combine their knowledge about sugar cane cutting and some of them left eventually and ended up in San Francisco and Haywood, California.

So that one-third of the Puerto Rican people were forced to leave their homeland because the Americans had so messed up the Puerto Rican economy. And the people came here, my parents came here in 1950 looking for decent jobs, for better opportunity, looking to implement all the advertisements that they were getting over there from the American companies about the type of life that there was in the United States. And now, thirty years later, they are still working in the same factories they started working in in 1945, the same restaurants, the same hotels, the same bus boy jobs, same waiter jobs. And nothing has changed. They just spent thirty years in a foreign country suffering under racism, bad education, overcrowded housing and the rest of a situation that is the reality of Puerto Rican and Black people and other poor people in the country and the United States.

So, out of that condition came up the Young Lords Party—started viewing the situation. And we arose in the summer of 1969, in Chicago and New York. Began to build what we call a National Political Party for the Puerto Rican people. Now it is not a political party like other political parties; not like the Democratic party or the Republican party because we don't participate in elections. That's not why we're building a political party. We are building a political party to involve our people in political activities. Elections don't involve you in political activity. Like the government treats you like fool. They herd you into voting booths once every four years to elect one or another oppressor. And they tell you that is democracy. And every four years you elect one slate of lying politicians who came back the next four years to try to explain to you why they couldn't succeed the last four years and promise you they are going to succeed in the next four years if you'll vote for them. So the people play their game every four years.

We say that the way people should be involved, the oppressed people should be involved in the political problem is on a constant basis—running the society, not voting for oppressors to run it for them. So that, we are building a political party that is going to mobilize and organize the masses of the people to become involved in the transformation of the Puerto Rican society and to participate in the transformation of American society. Our position in terms of elections in Puerto Rico is somewhat different. They have elections in Puerto Rico. They have about three or four political parties that they got together. And those political parties are just carbon copies of the American political parties. And they each have a factor lying to the different American political parties. Our position is that it is impossible to have [free] elections in Puerto Rico. You have 50,000 American troops who have never left since 1898. You have all the radio, t.v., and press controlled by American companies. So how is it possible to have a free election inside Puerto Rico? We maintain that we are for free election. We're for free election once the Americans are out of Puerto Rico. It's the same position that the Vietnamese people have, get out and then we will have our election to decide what our future is going to be. But as long as you are in our country, it's not possible for us to have free elections because you are going to be in control. That's your situation that we put forth in the American Government.

Now, what we've tried to do is to begin to deal with some of the major ways that our people are divided and oppressed. The first one, the most obvious one, is the division of the Puerto Rican nation. 700,000 Puerto Ricans inside the United States; 2,700,00 on the island. We are divided like North Vietnam and South Vietnam, North Korea and South Korea, East Germany or West Germany. And we want reunification of our people. We believe that the way we're going to get reunification of our people is through national liberation of Puerto Rico. And we believe that if we can build an independent and socialist Republic of Puerto Rico, a majority of our people who now live in the United States will leave the U.S. because they never wanted to come here in the first place. They'll leave the U.S. and return to Puerto Rico. Now, there will be large numbers of Puerto Ricans, especially youths, who have grown up in this country and become accustomed to the United States and will want to remain in the U.S. And in that case, the Party will continue to fight for self-determination of the Puerto Rican people inside the United States on an equal basis with all other National minorities and all other peoples of the United States.

By self-determination, we mean complete equality in society. We don't mean abstract idealistic equality, which the government tries to put across to us now. You see, the government of the United States is very slick. They have a Bill of Rights, an abstract Bill of Rights which says to you, you have freedom of speech, the freedom to vote, the freedom to so and so and so and so, well that is true. I do have freedom of speech. Nelson Rockefeller has freedom of speech. A whole bunch of other people have freedom of speech. But Nelson Rockefeller's able to implement his freedom of speech in the material real world when he can buy as many television stations as he wants. And our material ability to implement that freedom of speech on some street corner or before a few hundred students is very different. Because of his wealth and his power, he can get his freedom of speech across to a whole country, to millions and millions of people. And we can't get our freedom of speech across to hardly anybody. It's very rare that we get invited to places like this. So that, that is the difference between an abstract right and a material reality. That is an abstract right. The same thing with votes. Votes are an abstract right, everyone has one vote. But once again, Nelson Rockefeller's vote is worth a whole lot more than your or my vote. Because, I mean, his voting doesn't even matter because he chooses the people we're going to vote for. So that, that abstract right of one vote, one person, is different from the material reality of what actually happens. So we feel that we don't want abstract equality rights, we want material equality. That means the redistribution of the wealth in this society. And that means that people like Nelson Rockefeller and Henry Ford or the Bishop Estate or Dillingham or whatever, they have to redistribute the wealth that they have robbed from the poor working people of the world. I mean, they made if off our backs. Henry Ford, he made the first Model T. After that, who made all the other cars. So it wasn't him, it was the people who work in the automobile factories, who sweat in 100 degree temperatures; who risk industrial accidents for a lousy $150 a week. And he makes millions every year. And he ain't produced shit. I mean, he just sits behind his desk and writes papers, either that or signs checks. That's the reality of the way society functions. And what we say, we do want a redistribution of that wealth—spread it among the people it's been robbed from. Return it to the people it belongs to.

Now, we feel that one of the solutions to one of our problems of the division of the Puerto Rican nation has been that we have expanded our Party of Puerto Rico. In the last year, we began operating in our homeland. We now have two branches. One in Aguadilla, Puerto Rico, and the other in San Juan, Puerto Rico. Aguadilla is a small town about 50,000 people in the west coast of the island. Aguadilla is on the side of a plateau running down to the ocean. All right, this is like a plateau here—on the top of the plateau in the best land in all the [country] is the United States Randy Air Force Base, Strategic Air Command. And so, we chose that city to organize in because we feel that the people have a very high consciousness of American oppression because they live in that base and they're forced to meet the needs of that base everyday. Then we have a branch in a swampland, shanty town in San Juan called "El Cano." And when you come tomorrow night to see the film, you'll be able to see the place where one of the worst conditions that our people live in, in Puerto Rico.

So, we have opened the Party on the branches in Puerto Rico to begin reunifying the Puerto Rican people in one common struggle. You see, there is no difference in Puerto Ricans on the island and the Puerto Ricans inside the United States. We're the same nation except that we're divided. We've been divided by a forced plan of the American government from the 1930's. So that, that was the first thing we did.

Now, the next thing we did is that we felt that somehow or other, we had to begin to develop forms and methods to build the mass revolutionary movement of the people. Because we don't believe that revolutions are made by a small group of people or a minority or an elite. Because that's just a coup, a seizure of power that happens all the time. It happens in Greece, Brazil, Argentina, happens all the time. We don't want coup, we want revolution. So is the transformation of society. And in order to do that, all the people, the masses of people, have to be involved in the revolutionary movements as if it was a fad—it's not. It's a very serious thing.

Revolutions have been part of the historical process of the development of human beings. From the French revolution to the American revolution to the Algerian revolution to the Vietnamese revolution—that's part of the process by which society moves forward, it changes and transforms. We're building part of that historical process. And it's not a fad; it's not a joke; it's not a do-your-own-thing. It's a real way by which society functions and progresses and moves forward when no other alternatives are available to the mass of the people.

So, we're trying to build what we call mass people's organizations. They're organizations that involve the Puerto Rican people wherever they are at any level of struggle. We have the first and most important which we call the Puerto Rican Workers' Federation which is taking our struggle into the factories, the hotels, the restaurants, the places where our people work and sweat away for American capitalists everyday. And we're organizing a federation of all Puerto Rican workers to begin attacking those businessmen, demanding more decent conditions. It's under one simple slogan that we're building the Workers' Federation. The factories belong to those who work them; the work places belong to those who work them. That's our slogan, that's how we're going to build a revolutionary workers' movement.

Then we have another organization called Lumpen Organization which organizes that part of our people who are either in jail, on dope, on welfare, or prostitutes. That part of our society that wasn't even allowed a chance to get a slave job in some factory. But who were forced by some conditions in our society to have to go on drugs, rob or kill to stay alive, who had to fight for survival. And society considers them as criminals. We consider them as results of the conditions of this society. So we're trying to organize what we call a Lumpen Organization to organize inmates inside the jails, to organize our welfare mothers and the people on drugs. And one of the results of that type of organization, or the little parts that we played in it, was played by the Attica section of the Young Lords Party, which was organized in Attica about six or seven months ago. And the Attica section of the Party represents the Puerto Rican inmates inside the prison, joined with black inmates inside the prison and poor white inmates inside the prison. [. . .] And I want to read to you a letter we received from the Attica section of the party after they seized control of D-yard.

This is a letter from an inmate, the Party section in Attica, before Rockefeller ordered the massacre:

To Central Committee and our People. All of us have got to go out of here. We are automatically dead men if we remain here. The representatives of the people whom we are, will be the ones who will die first at the hands of the fascist pig. Please get us out of this concentration camp. I repeat we will die if we remain here. You know what happened to comrade George Jackson in San Quentin, and what will happen to sister Angela Davis. Not only we the representatives of the Young Lords Party will die, our black comrade will also die. Brothers, we are not jiving—this is for real. The pig is already talking about sacrificing our hostages to get at us. They have already ambushed some cons and have criminally and with malice, have fought or beaten them senselessly. Brothers, we want out, now, as soon as possible. We have a dying necessity for a transfer to a safer place, any place else, just out of here. If possible, we are willing to leave this country if we are granted safe passage out. We are not Americans, we are Puerto Ricans and Blacks and as such, we do not belong in fascist America. Please consider we are leading and representing the people, that is why we are going to die no doubt. We are acting for the people. We are the voice of the people. We the people are merely reacting to the criminal acts perpetrated against us by the society of America. Please, you must get a Federal Judge to help us. Also, we want full amnesty of all the racist surprises which the pig is definitely contemplating of doing to the people. Please contact our loved ones, advise them of all there is occurring, tell them the full truth. Do not withhold anything from them. We need the full unmitigated support of the world out there. Please, you must above all, get the public support. If we must die, we will proudly die fighting for the cause. Finally, we will back up to the wall, but we will fight for liberation. We saw it necessary to carry this out. We will continue to do our job and we expect of you, your support as much as they need ours. These are times, brothers and sisters, the population in general are determined to die fighting provided that you give them your support. We have stopped begging for crumbs. We are human beings and we will die to prove that fact. We only want to be treated as respectable, decent and civilized people. This is the time to realize that racism, oppression, and retaliation must cease. In our conclusion, we raise our banner high with words and actions that can never be taken away—"QUE VIVA PUERTO RICO LIBRE, QUE VIVA LA LUCHA, PALANTE A VICTORIA!"

Some of these inmates were killed soon afterwards when Rockefeller ordered an outright massacre of the inmates. [. . .] National Guards and State Troopers came in shooting with M-1's and M-16's, tear gas at Attica prison and not only killed thirty-two inmates and ten guards. They didn't care, they were just shooting anybody. At [. . .] first, they tried to spread all kinds of rumors how guards had been castrated and killed and mutilated because they wanted to stir up opposition by the American people to the Attica rebellion. But little by little, over the next few weeks as the facts became clear that there were no guards that were mutilated, there were no guards who were killed, but the fact that some of the inmates tried to protect some of the guards when the shooting started. Then it became clear that it was just an outright massacre that had been ordered by Nelson Rockefeller. So that, that is some of the example of the work we've been trying to do in the building of the People's organizations, the Lumpen Organizations.

Then, we have other organizations that we've been building. One is called The Women's Union, whose job it is to organize and mobilize Puerto Rican women to become involved in liberation struggles and to wage a relentless struggle against an incorrect idea that's been around for a long time, especially in the heads of men, that men are superior to women. It's an incorrect idea that's been around since the breaking up of primitive communities and has resulted in oppression for years on end of one-half of the human race, especially the poor and oppressed one-half of the human race. And [. . .] the Women's Union's job is to organize and mobilize Puerto Rican women and defend their rights in their society against oppressive men and against capitalism.

Then we have the Puerto Rican Student Union whose job it is to organize and mobilize students both in the colleges and in the high schools to fight for the liberation of Puerto Ricans to fight against their own administrations in the way in which they oppress them.

And finally, we have a committee for the defense of the community, whose job it is at a community level to organize against people who try to take away our land, either for highway construction, urban renewal or university expansion or whatever trick they try to pull to take our land away, organizing housing strikes against landlords who don't even give decent services, health programs, breakfast programs and so on and so forth. And so we have built five People's organizations: the Workers' Federation, the Lumpen Organization, the Women's Union, the Puerto Rican Student Union and the Committee for the Defense of the Community. We believe we're trying to build a structure to involve our people in whatever level they wanted to involve themselves into. That means it involves giving a little bit of money to organization, or three hours a week, ten hours a week or whatever it is. We are involving the whole nation in the liberation struggle. And the People's organizations, we feel, is the nucleus of our new society, or our new state government because we plan to seize power away from the present state government of the United States that's oppressing us. And [. . .] we have to replace that with a new state power, a new government. And we don't want a situation where our people are involved in a revolutionary struggle or a people's war and end up not being able to run the society after they've kicked the Americans out. That has happened, too, in the past. It happened in Algeria, it happened in a few other countries. The people became involved in long wars of independence only to find out afterwards that they couldn't run the society and have to go back either to the same capitalists who they kicked out to help them run their society or they had to go over to some of the supposed socialist countries, we don't consider them socialist countries, like the Soviet Union, to look for aid. So that, we don't want that type of situation to develop among our people. And we're training and preparing ourselves to be able to govern our new society because we're completely confident of victory. So, we may as well plan for after the victory and how we're going to build a new independent and socialist Puerto Rico. So that, we're training ourselves now. We are training all Puerto Rican college students to get skills that are necessary to bring back to the people economic, architecture, or whatever skills we're going to need in the new society.

So, we see those people's organizations as the beginning, the seed of the people's self-government where the people train themselves to be involved in the revolutionary process and exercise their political power. We've been confronted now with the problem of how do you wage a revolutionary struggle. We know that we need a disciplined, scientific organization which we call a party. This is as centralized and as disciplined as the enemy is. We know that we need a mass organization of the people where the people are involved democratically in the running of the society. We know also that we need a people's army to protect that people's movement. No we don't think we need a people's army because we like violence, we don't like violence. We're peaceful people. But we have come to study history; we study history because we want to change history. Because we want to build a new society. So we have to study how this one was made; what forces made it, so that you can deal with whatever forces created it and changed it.

So we study history and we check out that very rarely have people been ever able to achieve anything in social changes unless they were capable of defending themselves and backing it up. Because if we were able to go into Nelson Rockefeller's office and I was able to go in and say, "Nelson, you and your father and your grandfather have been seized, have been robbing from working people for years. How about redistributing your wealth?" And if Rockefeller said "Juan you are right. I have been a thief and a crook and Standard Oil has been oppressing the people to work for years. Take it back, redistribute it among the people." There will be no need for war; there will be no need for violence. But the capitalists won't do that; they will defend themselves; they will defend their right to maintain that oppression and that exploitation.

So what are we going to do in the place of that? We are going to just sit by and say, "Kill us, go ahead and keep oppressing us." We will turn the other cheek and say, "Hit us some more," or we are going to begin to organize and defend ourselves. Or we are going to organize to build the people's movement because if we had 10,000 people or a hundred thousand people, we march into Washington—well Washington is kinda rough; you need more than one hundred thousand people for Washington—let's say any local city government. 255,000 people are going to march down to city hall and take over the government. They just walk in; they'll be the majority. There is only the mayor and a few other people standing around. But they couldn't do that. Why can't they do that? Because the mayor has the police force, the mayor has the national guard, and finally he's got the army to back him up. They have force, they have military force. Because they have that force they can do whatever they want in the long run. When it comes down to a question of numbers they can do whatever they want as long as they have that military capability over people. So we have to equalize the stakes and then let the number of people decide. The only way we can equalize that is if they have an army, we have to have an army. That is the only way we are going to survive. Not because we want to but because that's the only way that's possible to achieve our liberation. So, we're realists, we're not utopian, we're not idealists, we're not saying because we want peace, therefore, we will act peaceful because if acting peaceful is going to get us killed, then we can't be peaceful. That's not being realistic. So we're materialistic. We deal with the material real world so we're being forced to build a people's army eventually. But first, right now, our concern is to build a party and building a mass movement. We don't think we need a people's army right now. We think that will come, though in the future.

So that is how we see, essentially, the three ingredients necessary for the liberation of Puerto Rico. We see the necessity for a strong, disciplined, scientific party. We see the need for mass revolutionary movement of the people, and we see the need for a people's army to defend that party and that mass movement. Those are the three ingredients for Puerto Rican liberation and that's what we're trying to build.

Now the question then is, once you know what you want to do and once you know what some of the forms of the organization that you're going to use, how do you go about accomplishing such a big thing like saying you're going to build a revolution to liberate your people? Because the United States is a powerful country. Puerto Rico is a very small country. There are 5 million Puerto Ricans on this earth; there are 200 million people in the United States. The United States is very big; Puerto Rico is very small. The United States is very wealthy; Puerto Rico is very poor. So how are we going to achieve our liberation?

Well see, basically, we're very hopeful because once again we're studying. We're dialectical in our viewpoint and the point of view of the world is our way of looking at the world and we check out like the forces that play. Now, let's check out the supposed unity in the sense of the United States of America.

First thing that we have discovered, that maybe a lot of other people haven't really thought about or in practice, it happens everyday, that there is no United States of America. The United States of America isn't a nation, it's a conglomerate; it's a combination; it's an empire. Every one of the fifty states was named after a native American people that was wiped out in that particular area—Illinois, California, Nebraska, conquered lands. Every bit of that territory is conquered land. And what you have inside the United States is a whole bunch of different national minorities, not one nation. A nation is a people with a common history, culture, language, and national territory. That's not true of the United State. What you have inside the U.S., we feel, is a lot of allies. I mean, we have 30 million black people as our allies; we have 10 million Chicago people; 500 thousand Chinese people; 250 thousand Japanese people; we have about 500 or 600 thousand Hawaiian people that we consider our allies—maybe the rest of the 700 thousand might not be our allies. But at least 400 or 500 thousand of the Hawaiian people, we consider our allies. We have 700 thousand native American people that are our allies and millions of poor white people and white youths as our allies. So when you add up all those figures, the power of the U.S. becomes a little less. When you add the fact that the U.S. is dis-united states, with local state governments fighting national government, fighting local city governments. I mean, they can get very little done in the United States on a regular, consistent basis because the country is disunited. When you add to that, the fact that we deal with the situation in international viewpoint, the United States is not isolated from the rest of the world. In fact, it controls one-half of the world. So that, we're dealing with this thing on international viewpoint.

So then, we count among our allies, 800 million Chinese people, 40 million Koreans, 40 million Vietnamese people, 7 million Cuban people. So then the numbers you even get the outnumbered United States when you deal with our international viewpoint. And so, we're very confident of victory. We have no doubt, we have no doubt of our ability to achieve liberation from the United States government. And by the way, when I say the United States, I do not mean the American people. For the majority of the American people don't even know what the United States government and the businessmen do. The majority of the American people are miseducated, have been filled with a lot of incorrect ideas in their heads. Some of the incorrect ideas, it's obvious to me they're incorrect. It's obvious to the Young Lords Party that it's incorrect. It's been filled into the minds of the American people by the government. So what we're going to do is to eradicate these incorrect ideas from the minds of most white Americans and Europeans. We will do that through practice. We will demonstrate our equality through practice over the next few years. And little by little, people will have to learn to deal with us on an equal basis because they'll see our practice. And in that way, we'll eradicate that incorrect idea from the minds of the American people and help them to be able to move forward under the leadership of the Third World people for a better society.

So, what we're trying then to do is to build that revolutionary movement with those three ingredients—the party, the mass movement, and the people's army. And we feel not only that the United States is weak in terms of internal situation, but right now, the United States is dealing with two main contradictions—two main unsolvable contradictions that are going to determine its downfall as an empire in the world.

The first contradiction is the Indochina war. For ten years, they've been trying to resolve that problem. But the only thing, the only way they can think of resolving that problem is by winning. And there ain't no way that they can win in Indochina. No way except by destroying all the Indochinese people. So it's gotten so bad that Nixon only can rely on about 2,000 pilots because he can't rely on his army anymore because it won't fight. His army won't fight anymore so all he can depend on [is] an elite of about 2,000 or 3,000 pilots that drop bombs on Indochina. That's the only sure fighting force that they have. Why do you think they want those prisoners of war released from North Vietnam? Not because they have any great love for those prisoners of war. All those prisoners of war are pilots. They were all shot down over North Vietnam. Every one of them is a Major and up. They're experts in bombing. That's why they want those pilots released because they're running out of good trained pilots and they want them back to bomb more of North Vietnam and South Vietnam. It's not that Nixon has any love for prisoners of war all of a sudden. He just wants his pilots back. So that the reality of the first contradiction, the external contradiction that the United States faces, is that when the Indochina war started, the United States was undoubtedly the leading power in the world. Now that the Indochinese war is ended, the United States has been dismantled as a world power. It has been unmasked. It has been shown how weak it is as a world power. It has been overextended.

It was so overextended that when it was fighting in Indochina and Palestine, it had to give up on Latin America. The United States has given up on Latin America because it's too overextended. It can't deal with Indochina, Palestine, and Latin America too. They're letting Chile go by, they're letting the nationalizations in Ecuador go by, the nationalizations in Peru and Bolivia. Now they haven't given up completely on Latin America. Their foreign policy has now decided they're gonna hold onto Brazil. They're willing to give up Ecuador and Peru and Uruguay but they are gonna hold onto Brazil. Why? Because Brazil has one-half of Latin America's population, all of Latin America's wealth and mineral resources. So they figure if they can hold onto Brazil, establish a fascist dictatorship in Brazil, they at least have a chance to maintain most of their wealth and their power. But they're giving up on Chile, Ecuador, Peru. They don't really care what happens to them anymore because they realize there's a limit now to their power. They can't control things the way they used to. So there's that external contradiction of the international scene and international scene sells revolution from Palestine to Uruguay, Santo Domingo to Indochina.

They also have the second aspect of the external international scene which is that they are now involved in a new competition among the advanced capitalist countries of the world. After World War 2, the United States had established homogeny [hegemony] over the world, they controlled everything. They rebuilt Europe, they rebuilt Japan because they were in complete control. But now what happens? Their cousins are getting powerful. Japan is moving up, West Germany is moving up, France is moving up. The capitalists are in competition again. Last time the capitalists were in competition, they created the depression of 1930. Guess what's happening again? There's another depression heading our way. It's the depression of the 1970's. If you haven't [illegible] then you haven't been reading the newspapers or checking out the unemployment line. Because there's a new depression hitting the United States and when a depression hits the United States, it hits the world like the last depression hit the world. And at a time like that, millions and millions of people who before were well off, who before had a house and car, now find that they're losing their job and they can't make the payments on the car, they can't make the payments on the house. And all of a sudden they realize that capitalism is not a very secure system. That capitalism can collapse at a given moment when the poor capitalists are so busy competing with each other that they don't care about the needs of the people.

So that, the United States is now facing an economic depression. On a worldwide scene, what they're trying to do now is protect themselves. So Nixon comes out with a wage-price freeze and he comes out with import tariffs. Now check this out, import tariffs. What do they do? They figure that since the American economy is in bad shape, we're gonna raise tariffs so that way Volkswagens will cost more and people will buy more Fords. So they raise import tariffs. So now, they can't just raise them just to the European countries because that would become an outright excuse for economic war. They can't do that so blatantly. So what they do is that they raise their import tariffs against the whole world. So who suffers when they raise the import tariffs? The advanced capitalist countries? No, they can get by, I mean they're wealthy. The ones who suffer are the oppressed and underdeveloped countries. So the U.S.A. raises import tariffs, then the Australian wood industry is collapsing. The U.S.A. raises import tariffs and the Argentinean beef industry is collapsing. So what's happening is that they're creating unemployment throughout the world and to all those countries who are dependent on the U.S. trade for their sustenance. That's what imperialism is all about when one country controls the economic life of another country. So what they're doing is, they're postponing the unemployment and depression in the U.S. but they're causing it in the rest of the Third World. And all the parts of the Third World are still under the capitalist system.

So what they're just doing is buying time, like cities buy time by selling bonds when they don't have the money to do something, so they float bonds. That's just buying time, postponing the debt to the future. The United States is trying to buy time with its import tariff. So what's going to happen? Germany is going to raise their import tariff; Japan is going to raise their import tariff. And you're going to start economic war. And economic war is predecessor to turning into a military war. So who knows if we're not heading for our third world war? The oppositions, we're not afraid of a third world war, while the capitalists were fighting, 200 million people turned to socialism of the Soviet Union. After the second World War, when the fascists fought a capitalist society, 600 million people turned to socialism in China. So we think maybe after the third world war, the whole world might turn into socialism. So we're not worried at all about a third world war.

So that, our situation, we look hopefully towards the future because we see that over the last century, even though in your schools and in your textbooks, people make preludes that Marxism and ideals of socialism have been bankrupt, the reality is that all around the world, the masses of people have turned to socialism over the last century. And now, one third of the world is making more living under socialism. And now, it's come to the point where they have to recognize that one fourth of the humanity is developing and advancing at such a fast rate that they got admission into the United Nations. They recognize that they exist. They finally recognize that one fourth of humanity is existing and building a socialist society. And now, they got to deal with them and bow down to them. Nixon is now going to China to lick the feet of Mao Tse-tung and Chou En-lai and see what he can do. He still thinks that he can deal with deals. That's the only way they think—deals. What deals can we make? Now they've become as powerful as we have, how can we get together? That's the way they think. I mean, Nixon's a fool and he comes out with this stuff so heavily. What happens? China was admitted to the United Nations. And what happens? Just because some delegates clapped and cheered in the United Nations, Nixon comes out with a statement and he says that every one of those countries who clapped and cheered, we're gonna cut off your economic aid. That's what he said, I read that, check it out. I mean, he's so blatant with this stuff. That's what makes the United States such a hated country in the world. Wherever you go among the people of the world, the United States government is hated. It's that kind of behavior that's caused so much misery and oppression in the world.

So that, we have a lot of faith in the possibilities of building a revolutionary movement over the next few years. And we see that we're young—I'm twenty-four. The Party's two and a half years old. We got all our lives to destroy the U.S. imperialism. But they've been here for so long and so many people have suffered under this, so it takes a little while, be a little patient. And we have to take our time so we can organize the masses. But we got time, we got time. There's no other alternative so we may as well take our time and build it well. Because people have tried to rise up their liberation in the past. French peasants rose up for their liberation against the kings and queens and they were replaced with capitalists. They failed. The slave class rose up numerous revolts. The Haitian revolution, the masses of people rose and petty bourgeois people took over. The Algerian people rose up in revolutionary struggle and they found out that other petty bourgeois people took over. So what we're trying to do, we wanna build a scientific revolution. One that involves the masses of the people and doesn't permit the possibility of other oppressors rising up again as they did in the Soviet Union; as they have in all the Eastern supposedly socialist countries to oppress the people once again.

And that's our goal, national liberation of Puerto Rico and self-determination for Puerto Ricans inside the United States. Inside the U.S., we see ourselves allied with all Third World people, poor white and working class people. See, because right now, what's happening is the economic collapse is occurring. Working people before were closed to politics, they didn't want to hear about politics. And now they're saying what's going on? Why are the cities falling apart? What's the chances of it falling apart? What's with the war? Why aren't the soldiers fighting? All these questions are going through people's minds. And at this time, the people now, in this time of crisis, the forces will try to educate and mobilize the people now, in this time of crisis, the forces of the counter-revolution and the forces of revolution, the forces of fascism, and the forces of liberation and socialism. Check out Hitler, what did Hitler say to the German people in the middle of depression? What did he say were the causes of the problem in German? He said it was the Jews, he said it was the communists, and he said it was the people who sold out in the World War 1. Those were the three forces responsible for the downfall of Germany.

What are Nixon and the other neo-fascists saying nowadays? What is the cause of the crisis that we have in our country and the United States and Puerto Rico and Hawaii? What are the causes? Well, it's the communists, it's the Third World people instead of the Jews this time, and it's the peace people. Same lines. Fascism always has the same lines. Fascism is a dictatorship, a capitalistic dictatorship. When things fall apart they started a dictatorship. Because Hitler didn't get rid of the capitalists, because they kept manufacturing, he just controlled them a little bit. So that, fascism would try to tell the people that this is the reason things are happening. And then the forces of socialism would tell the people, what's the surprise? This happens under capitalism all the time, every thirty years they have a depression, or every twenty years. The system falls apart. The system's not made for working people, it's made for the rich. And so, what we have to do is transform the system, change it and take society to a higher level. Develop it as it's been developing from primitive communities to feudalism, or from slavery to feudalism to capitalism to socialism to move society forward, move the productive forces forward, to eliminate the obstacles to the progress of human beings, the present obstacle being capitalism. So that two forces will try to organize the masses of people. And if we don't hurry and we don't get ourselves disciplined enough and we don't talk and we get out there among the masses of people, the forces of fascism will organize more. And then we'll have to go through, like the Germans, in the United States. And what we're trying to do is get out with as many people as possible and explain to them why the economic system is failing once more. And you've got to be convinced it's failing, wait two or three more years. They ain't getting out of this one. There's no more countries to conquer, they have conquered all the countries in the world at one point or another. They have drawn all the wealth they can. So what they have now is limited returns. They have diminishing returns on their ventures. More and more countries are being liberated. Markets are becoming fewer and fewer. That's why they're going to China now. They're so uptight at the markets, they have an idea they can open up China as a market and begin selling their goods to China. That's their idea.

Anyway, that's about all I got to say except to make a few comparisons about the situation in Hawaii and the situation in Puerto Rico. You were invaded about 1895 when the Queen started to resist the traders that came in and invaded the country, the merchants, not the traders. And you were annexed in 1898 by the United States government the same year we were annexed. And you were colonized for a number of years, you're still a colony. I mean, some people may consider you a state but we check it out. We see you not as a part of the United States, you are in no way connected with the United States. Even the United States is not really the United States. So how could you be a part of that, I don't know. I mean, they have a hard time proving to the rest of the world that Alaska and Hawaii are states of the United States. And so they're trying to make us a state, too. They're going to have a plebiscite in 1947 and they're going to try to make us a state. But they're not going to succeed. And so we think that the situation is the same. You are, essentially, a bunch of people sitting on America's main military base in the Caribbean. We play the same role. You're the first line of defense against the Asian people and we're the first line of defense against our own people, the Latin American people. So it's so heavy. So what we have to do is check our situation out. Check out that we're still colonies. The colonial situation of Hawaiian people is different because the national composition is varied, it has a number of different nationalities. But all those nationalities, especially the poor and oppressed people are in those nationalities, have helped to construct this country, the country called Hawaii. They've helped to construct it with sweat and their labor. They were forced to migrate here by American companies in one way or another who went over to Hong Kong or wherever it was and got people to sign contracts they couldn't even read and go to a country they didn't even know about.

So that, we feel that there's great hope for the possibility of the Hawaiian people, all the welfare people and even poor white people in Hawaii, if there are any. I don't know, I haven't done enough investigation to know to be able to launch a struggle to secede or establish your own independent republic. And if you don't think you can live independently from the United States, that's what they tell us in textbooks in school that we couldn't possible live without the Americans; that we would die of hunger. We never believed that anyway. But just to assure ourselves, we checked it out and studied it and we got all the economics down. We're sure we can easily go on without the United States and we went without the United States before 1898. There wasn't no problem, no hassle. We're sure we can build an independent and strong Republic. And that we can continue to express our solidarity with the Hawaiian people and the Puerto Rican people to the Hawaiian people. So that, if they liberate Puerto Rico now, they liberate Hawaii now—

ALL POWER TO OPPRESSED PEOPLE!

4

On History

The Young Lords was a historically minded organization. Because Puerto Rico has such a complex and troubled colonial past, the Young Lords worked actively to construct a serviceable history of Puerto Rican and "Third World" activism in the United States and abroad. In so doing, the Young Lords produced a variety of essays exploring the actions of particular individuals (mostly Puerto Rican or African American) and broader historical surveys (e.g., the history of Puerto Rico). Not "mere" history, these essays articulate particular sociopolitical commitments of the organization in their attempt to bring about a "New American Revolution." In other words, in a U.S. culture marked by historical amnesia where Puerto Rico is concerned, these selections are representative of the Young Lords' efforts to articulate a collective memory that *did political work*.

Puerto Rican Obituary (by Pedro Pietri)

(From the book *Palante, Young Lords Party*, 1971)

They worked
They were always on time
They were never late
When they were insulted
They worked
They never went on strike
Without permission
They never took days off
They were on the calendar
They worked
Ten days a week
And were only paid for five
They worked
They worked
They worked
And they died
They died broke
They died owing
They died never knowing
What the front entrance
Of the first national bank looks like
Juan

Miguel
Milagros
Olga
Manuel
All died yesterday today
And will die again tomorrow
Passing their bill collectors
On to the next of kin
All died
Waiting for the Garden
    of Eden
To open up again
Under a new management
All died
Dreaming about america
Waking up in the middle
    of the night
Screaming Mira! Mira!
Your name is on the winning
    lottery ticket
For one hundred thousand
    dollars
All died
Hating the grocery stores
That sold them make-believe
    steak
And bullet proof rice and
    beans
All died waiting dreaming
    and hating
Dead Puerto Ricans
Who never knew they were
    Puerto Ricans
Who never took a coffee break
From the ten commandments
To **KILL KILL KILL**
The landlords of their cracked
    skulls
And communicate with their
    Latin Souls
Juan Miguel
Milagros
Olga
Manuel
From the nervous breakdown

streets
Where the mice live like
    millionaires
And the people do not live
    at all
Are dead and were never alive
Juan
Died waiting for his number
    to hit
Miguel
Died waiting for the welfare
    check
To come and go and come
    again
Milagros
Died waiting for her ten
    Children
To grow up and work
So she could quit working
Olga
Died waiting for a five
    dollar raise
Manuel
Died waiting for his
    supervisor to drop dead
So that he could get a
    promotion
Is a long ride
From Spanish Harlem
To the island cemetery
Where they were buried
First the train
And then the bus
And the cold cuts for lunch
And the flowers
That will be stolen
When visiting hours are over
Is very expensive
Is very expensive
But they understand
Their parents understood
Is a long non-profit ride
From Spanish Harlem
To long island cemetery
Juan

Miguel
Milagros
Olga
Manuel
All died yesterday today
And will die again tomorrow
Dreaming
Dreaming about Queens
Clean cut lily white
    neighborhood
Puerto Ricanless scene
Thirty thousand dollar home
The first spics on the block
Proud to belong to a
    community
Of gringos who want them
    lynched
Proud to be a long distance
    away
From the sacred phrase:
    Que pasa?
These dreams
These empty dreams
From the make believe
    bedrooms
Their parents left them
Are the after effects
Of television programs
About the ideal
white american family
With Black maids
And Latin janitors
Who are well trained
To make everyone
And their bill collectors
Laugh at them
And the people they represent
Juan
Died dreaming about a new
    car
Miguel
Died dreaming about new
    anti-poverty programs
Milagros
Died dreaming about a trip to

Puerto Rico
Olga
Died dreaming about real
    jewelry
Manuel
Died dreaming about the Irish
    sweepstakes
They all died
Like a hero sandwich dies
In the garment district
At twelve o'clock in the
    afternoon
Social security numbers to
    ashes
Union dues to dust
They knew
They were born to weep
And keep the morticians
    employed
As long as they pledge
    allegiance
To the flag that wants them
    destroyed
They saw their names listed
In the telephone directory of
    destruction
They were trained to turn
The other cheek by
    newspapers
That misspelled who
    mispronounced
And misunderstood their
    names
And celebrated when death
    came
And stole their final laundry
    ticket
They were born dead
They died dead
Is time
To visit Sister Lopez again
The number one healer
And fortune card dealer
In Spanish Harlem
She can communicate

With your late relatives
For a ressonable fee
Good news is guaranteed
Rise Table Rise Table
Death is not dumb and disable
Those who love you want to
    know
The correct number to play
Let them know this right
    away
Rise Table Rise Table
Death is not dumb and disable
Now that your problems are
    over
and the world is off your
    shoulders
Help those who you left
    behind
Find financial peace of mind
Rise Table Rise Table
Death is not dumb and disable
If the right number we hit
All our problems will split
And we will visit your graves
On every legal holiday
Those who love you want to
    know
The correct number to play
Let them know this right
    away
We know your spirit is able
Death is not dumb and disable
RISE TABLE RISE TABLE
Juan
Miguel
Milagros
Olga
Manuel
All died yesterday today
And will die again tomorrow
Hating fighting and stealing
Broken windows from each
    other
Practicing a religion without
    a roof

The old testament
The new testament
According to the gospel
Of the internal revenue
The judge and jury and
    executioner
Protector and eternal bill
    collector
Secondhand shit for sale
Learn how to say Como Esta
    Usted
And you will make a fortune
They are dead
They are dead
And will not return from the dead
Until they stop neglecting
The art of their dialogue
For broken english lessons
To impress the mister bosses
Who keep them employed
As dishwashers porters
    messenger boys
Factory workers maids stock
    clerks
Shipping clerks assistant,
    assistant
To the assistant, assistant
    dishwasher
And automatic smiling
    doorman
For the lowest wages of the
    ages
And rages when you demand
    a raise
Because it's against the
    company policy
To promote SPICS SPICS SPICS
Juan
 Died hating Miguel because
    Miguel's
Used car was in better
    condition
Than his used car
Miguel
Died hating Milagros because

Milagros
Had a color television set
And he could not afford one
    yet
Milagros
Died hating Olga because
    Olga
Made five dollars more on the
    same job
Olga
Died hating Manuel because
    Manuel
Had hit the numbers more
    times
Than she had hit the numbers
Manuel
Died hating all of them
Juan
Miguel
Milagros
Olga
Because they all spoke broken
    english
More fluently than he did
And now they are together
In the main lobby of the void
Addicted to silence
Under the grass of oblivion
Off limits to the wind
Confined to worm supremacy
In long island cemetery
This is the groovy hereafter
The protestant collection box
Was talking so loud and proud
    about
Here lies Juan
Here lies Miguel
Here lies Milagros
Here lies Olga
Here lies Manuel
Who died yesterday today
And will die again tomorrow
Always broke
Always owing
Never knowing

That they are beautiful
     people
Never knowing
The geography of their complexion
PUERTO RICO IS A BEAUTIFUL PLACE
PUERTORRIQUENOS ARE A
     BEAUTIFUL RACE
If only they
Had turned off the television
And tuned into their own imaginations
If only they
Had used the white
     supremacy bibles
For toilet paper purpose
And made their Latin Souls
The only religion of their race
If only they
Had returned to the
     definition of the sun
After the first mental
     snowstorm
On the summer of their senses
If only they
Had kept their eyes open
At the funeral of their fellow
     employees
Who came to this country to
     make a fortune
And were buried without
     underwears
Juan
Miguel
Milagros
Olga
Manuel
Will right now be doing their
     own thing
Where beautiful people sing
And dance and work together
Where the wind is a stranger
To miserable weather
     conditions
Where you do not need a
     dictionary
To communicate with your

hermanos y hermanas
Aqui se habla español all the
    time
Aqui you salute your flag
    first
Aqui there are no dial soap
    commercials
Aqui everybody smells good
Aqui TV dinners do not have
    a future
Aqui wigs are not necessary
Aqui we admire desire
And never get tired of each
    other
Aqui que pasa Power is
    what's happening
Aqui to be called negrito y
    negrita
Means to be called LOVE

Malcolm Spoke for Puerto Ricans

(From the newspaper *Palante*, February 1970, volume 2, number 1)

February 21st is the anniversary of the assassination of Brother Malcolm X. When Malcolm spoke (or does he still speak?) of being proud of our heritage, Black People were awakened to a new truth: "We are beautiful." And when Malcolm moved on, and told us to take it ("Nobody can make you free!"), well many of us are still wondering what The Man meant by that. His message is crystal clear: Political Power (That means freedom) comes from the barrel of a Gun. Simple. Yet hard. It took a Huey Newton to put Malcolm's words into practice.

Brothers and sisters, look at the awareness of our Afro-American companeros. Our own Albizu Campos also taught us that to be Boriqueno is a good thing, yet we are not aware of the oppression our island faces each day in the hands of the Yanqui.

We still have time to drive the capitalistas to their graves. It is not much time, but it is here, and we must SEIZE IT! While we can. In the name of Albizu and Malcolm X, join with the YOUNG LORDS ORGANIZATION and the BLACK PANTHER PARTY. May we have Power; then, Peace.

HONOR MALCOLM—STAY HOME FEB. 20

IN THE NAME OF THE PEOPLE, MALCOLM
YOU SHALL BE AVENGED

PABLO "YORUBA" GUZMAN

DEP. MINISTER OF INFORMATION
NEW YORK CHAPTER
YOUNG LORDS ORGANIZATION

....

The Vote or the Gun

(From the newspaper *Palante*, 22 May 1970, volume 2, number 3)

Juan Gonzalez
MINISTER of EDUCATION
EAST COAST REGION

The Young Lords Organization is a revolutionary political party fighting for the liberation of Puerto Ricans and all oppressed people. We are the answer to the 400 year need of Latinos for a political party to lead our struggle for liberation.

From the first invasion of Borinquen by christopher columbus in November 1493, our people have been resisting the foot on their back. The Tainos fought the Spanish adventurers and money-hungry pirates. The people of the Yoruba Nation, kidnapped from their African homeland, resisted the Spanish slave traders, and consistently rebelled for their freedom.

In 1868, the Puerto Rican people rose up for the first time as a nation. In El Grito de Lares, we were saying—we are not Spaniards. We are the mixture of African and Indian, born in Borinquen, speaking Spanish. We are Puerto Ricans, an island nation, oppressed by the Spanish empire.

Led by Ramon Emeterio Betances, Segundo Ruiz Belvis, and Manuel Rojas, our first patriots, we took up aim for independence. The revolution was defeated. But for the first time someone had tried to build a political organization to lead the people. In every city revolutionary juntas had been formed. They used names of secret societies to fool the Spanish police; names like La Torre del Viajo, Centro Bravo, Capa Prieto.

They had good leadership. They raised money, got arms, politicized the people. They understood that the enemy is well organized and that if the people wish to win their freedom, they too must be well organized and prepared to deal.

The revolution was defeated, though, because it was not organized enough. The patriots did not have military training. An arms supply from The Dominican Republic never reached them. They did not go into the countryside where the poorest and greatest number of Puerto Ricans—the jibaros, the campesinos, were.

Electoral System

After the revolution, our only political parties all tried to work within the Spanish and then American political structure. The Puerto Rican Republican party or Barbosa, the Federal Party of Munoz Rivera, the Independence Party of Matienzo Cintron, all worked within the structure set up for Borinquen by the amerikkkan occupiers. Some of the parties wanted independence, but all of them accepted the amerikkkan invasion, and hoped to convince amerikkka to someday free our people.

While they talked, the U.S. destroyed our economy, impoverished our people, imposed citizenship, destroyed our farmland, set up amerikkkan governors to rule us, and put military bases on the island to guard their businesses against all Latinos.

In 1932, the Nationalist Party, after ten years of trying to win independence through electoral means, decided that only through war against the U.S. would Borinquen be free. The newspapers, radio, the assembly, the businesses and latifundias [large estates, haciendas] all were controlled by the U.S. There could not be free elections. Only armed struggle would free our nation.

Don Pedro Albizu Campos, leader of the Party said, "The electoral fight is a regular farce to keep the Puerto Rican family divided." The Nationalist Party, like the secret parties of 1868, said "Basta Ya" to the vendepatrias (traitors) of our history. It said there are two alternatives—slavery or freedom/colony or independent nation/oppressed or liberated.

From 1932 to 1954 the second War of Independence was waged. The Ponce Massacre, the battles of 1948, the Revolution of 1950, the attack on Truman and Congress were all battles of that war.

Patriots Defeated

Again the patriots were defeated. Don Pedro was jailed for life, the Nationalist Party destroyed. There were three main reasons for the defeat:

the repression of the Gringo government which jailed or killed hundreds of Nationalist Party members, like Nixon-Mitchell are doing to freedom fighters of the Black Panther Party.

the sell-out of vendepatria Munoz Marin who organized the Popular Party and Puerto Ricans saying "Bread, land, liberty." He then made a deal with the Gringo: he would become the first Puerto Rican governor if he would agree not to push for independence and accept his puppet role. The biggest traitor in Puerto Rican history is this lackey, Luis Munoz Marin, who shipped our people by the hundreds of thousands to New York because he could not provide jobs for them; who taught our people to be white middle class americanos, when they were poor, oppressed boricuas; who destroyed the jibaro with operation bootstrap, moving thousands off the land into the slums of San Juan, and Ponce, and let all our money go to u.s. capitalists. He was the apostle of non-violence for profit.

Finally, the Nationalist Party was destroyed by its own internal problems, by its emphasis on immediate shootouts with police instead of organizing a guerrilla army to lead the nation in people's war in the countryside; by its failure to organize the Black Puerto Rican as well as lighter skinned boricuas, and by its failure to provide concrete programs to meet the immediate needs of the people.

Revolution is the most serious of jobs. It is not an ego-trip or a party. When the people join in revolutionary war, they do so because they have been convinced by both actual conditions and political education that there is no other way out, that their lives and those of their family, are threatened.

Revolution is a complete change, an overturning of dead soil, a new way of life, with new government, new laws.

Revolution is not something we want to do. It is bloody and cruel, but it is something we have to do to live decently and free.

The Young Lords Organization is a revolutionary political party. We are the political party for Puerto Ricans in amerikkka and on the island, for all Latinos oppressed directly by the U.S. We are not the Democratic Party, Republican Party, or Popular Party or any other electoral party.

Ours is a party of the people.

Our motto is serve and protect.

We serve the needs of our people and educate them that only through revolution will all our needs be met. Only through organized change will we end addiction, eliminate landlords, build new cooperative housing, provide jobs for all, assure decent health for everyone, end all wars, and achieve independence for Puerto Rico.

Our party defends our people from greedy businessmen, racist teaching systems, rats and roaches, disease, police brutality, robbery and murder.

No matter how many promises they make or what they do, the other political parties will never give you freedom. Freedom is taken, not given.

That is why we organize. Wherever there are Puerto Ricans there will be YOUNG LORDS. Wherever there is oppression there will be armed people fighting for their dignity.

We are in the period where revolutionary education is more important than revolutionary war. We are in a period of preparation.

We have lost twice before. We will not lose again. We cannot lose again. The Puerto Rican nation is being destroyed by the Yanqui and our vendepatrias.

Soon, that revolutionary war will start and the oppressed people of the United States, led by the Young Lords Organization, the Black Panther Party, the Comandos Armados para la Liberacion, will slay Goliath, burn Babylon, throw the moneylenders out of the temple, and then we, the last, shall be the First.

> Power to all oppressed people
> Liberate Puerto Rico Now!
> The party guides the gun.

> Juan Gonzales
> Minister of Education
> East Coast Region

....

Lolita Lebron: Puerto Rican Liberation Fighter

(From the newspaper *Palante*, 22 May 1970, volume 2, number 3)

On March 1, 1954, the members of the u.s. house of representatives were busily discussing their empire, making decisions that would affect people the world over. One of the topics to be discussed that day was the status of the Chamizal district between Texas and Mexico, that the Mexican government wanted back (and which the u.s. did not want to give up). The rulers of the united states empire were also going to discuss Puerto Rico that day since our nation was still reacting to the attempted revolution of 1950. It was twelve noon when a woman and three men stood up in the spectators gallery. The small, slender woman grabbed her .45 automatic with both hands, fired the first shots and kept on going until her clip was empty. Her three companions did the same and for the five minutes that they shot down into the house floor, the fat, old, self-proclaimed rulers, looked like chickens with their heads cut off running in every direction, and scared to death. As all four emptied their guns, and the house guards came at them, Lolita Lebron, unfurled the Puerto Rican flag, wrapped it around her arms and yelled for the world to hear, "QUE VIVA PUERTO RICO LIBRE."

Lolita Lebron, 31, Rafael Cancel Miranda, 25, Irving Flores Rodrigues, 23, and Andres Figueroa Cordero, 23, struck a blow against the united states colonial power that day that is only equaled in its daring, courage, and dedication to the cause of the liberation of the Puerto Rican nation by the attempted assassination of president Truman in 1950 by Oscar Collazo and Griselio Torresola. They managed to wound five congressmen that day (including one from New York very seriously). Their intent was to show the united states congress (whose house committee on Insular Affairs and senate committee on Territorial and Insular Affairs rule every aspect of Puerto Rican life) that the people of Puerto Rico would rather die fighting for our liberation than sit idly by and watch our destinies and lives decided and determined by northamerikkkan rulers.

BLOW FOR ALL THIRD WORLD

In many ways those four Borinquenos struck a blow not only for Puerto Rico but for all Third World people in the united states and around the planet. One of the four, Rafael Cancel Miranda, had long been an advocate of liberation for Afro-american people in the united states. He had been arrested in Puerto Rico in 1948 for refusing to be drafted into the u.s. army and had been sentenced to three years in jail. During his time in the Atlanta, Tallahassee, and other federal prisons, he actively tried to organize black brothers to fight against the racism and oppression that they faced more than other prisoners. Because of the effectiveness of his activities and his courage (he frequently kicked guards in their asses for abusing him or his brothers), he spent most of his time being transferred from one jail to another or being kept in solitary.

As always, the united states treated this act of liberation as an excuse to repress more Puerto Ricans, especially those who had been active in the campaigns to free the political prisoners of 1950. Along with Lolita, Rafael, Andres, and Irving, eleven other Boricuas from New York were charged with attempting to overthrow the government of the united states. In Puerto Rico, Don Pedro Albizu Campos was sent to jail for saying to a reporter that the four patriots had "realized an act of sublime heroism." Don Pedro had been pardoned after serving four years of a life sentence for his role in the revolution of 1950. But now, through a blatant violation of their own jive laws, colonial puppet governor Luis Munoz Marin retracted the pardon and sent Don Pedro back to jail just for making a public statement. He stayed in jail until he was killed through "treatments" in 1965.

This plus the fact that the Chamizal land between Mexico and the united states was being discussed that day caused people all over Latin America to label the four Puerto Rican warriors, "LOS CABALLEROS DE LA RAZA." This means that they struck a blow not only for Puerto Rico but for all people of the Third World (La Raza).

Lolita, Rafael, Andres, and Irving were all Puerto Ricans of humble working backgrounds who had been living in New York and building up the Nationalist Party Junta (mission) here. Lolita Lebron, the valiant leader of the group, worked in a factory in New York just like most of our sisters still do. She had two children and at the time of the attack was head secretary of the Junta in New York City. She was small in size (about 4 feet, 10 inches—95 pounds) but had the courage and energy of ten people. Since the attempted revolution in 1950, she had been active in the publicity and fund raising campaigns to free the political prisoners and keep Oscar Collazo from being murdered in the electric chair.

Rafael Cancel Miranda was a tall (6 feet, 2 inches) brother who was known throughout the Nationalist Party for his strength, intense political activity, and hatred of the northamerikkkan oppressor. He often smacked gringos or colonial police who showed disrespect or abused our people. He was fast with his hands and as the house of representatives action showed, fast with a gun. Rafael also had two children and at the time of the attack was, like Lolita, working in one of New York City's sweat shops.

Andres Figueroa Cordero was a short brother who walked with a limp. He had worked for years at Pedro and Julia's bodega on the corner of 103rd Street and Park Avenue as a butcher. He was a cadre of the Nationalist Party Junta in New York and like Irving Flores, also a cadre, was very active in doing the work of trying to free all of the political prisoners that had been jailed in 1950.

50 YEARS IN JAIL

Conrad Lynn and Mark Lane were among the many lawyers who defended "LOS CABALLEROS DE LA RAZA" and the eleven other brothers and sisters. After much propaganda about the "violent attempt to overthrow the government," the court sentenced Lolita Lebron to 25 to 50 years in jail; and Rafael Cancel Miranda, Irving Flores Rodriguez, and Andres Figueroa Cordero to 25 to 75 years in jail. All four are still in federal jails, with Lolita in Virginia and the three brothers in Leavenworth, Kansas. The other eleven brothers and sisters were given 6 to 10 years, and some of them are out on parole or done with their sentences now.

The lessons that we must learn from our valiant sister and brothers is that we Puerto Ricans in the united states are not New Yoricans or any such bullshit non-people. We are Borinquenos, whether or not we have been taught about our warriors, our history and our island. Most importantly, we should understand that everything that happens in our country affects us here, and likewise everything we do here, as our compatriots did in the house of reps, affects our people there. They showed us that it is up to us here to pick up the gun from Lolita, Rafael, and Oscar Collazo, and follow the path towards liberation and the brothers firmly believed and practiced the teachings of Albizu that "In order to take our nation, they must first take our lives," and "The Nation is Valor and Sacrifice." These are not empty words or mere slogans. They express the experiences of our colonized people who have struggled for 72 years to free us from united states imperialist control. Unless we heed the words of our fallen brothers and sisters, we will become the last generation of Puerto Ricans who bugalooed, shot-up, or poverty-pimped their time away while genocide was being brought down on us.

In accordance with point number 9 of the YLO Program (We want freedom for all political prisoners), we demand the release of "LOS CABALLEROS DE LA RAZA." Lolita

Lebron, Rafael Cancel Miranda, Irving Flores Rodriguez, and Andres Figueron Cordero must be set free for they have committed no crime, but have instead tried to liberate us from colonial domination.

IMMEDIATE FREEDOM FOR
"LOS CUATRO DE LA RAZA"
FREE ALL POLITICAL
PRISONERS!
QUE VIVA PUERTO RICO LIBRE!

Carlos Aponte
Ministry of Education
East Coast Region

Sojourner Truth: Revolutionary Black Woman

(From the newspaper *Palante*, 5 June 1970, volume 2, number 4)

Sojourner Truth was born a slave in Ulster County, New York in 1797. Her slave name was Isabella, and as soon as she was old enough to travel alone, she ran away from her slavemaster and went to the city, where she got jobs as a domestic worker. She earned her living scrubbing floors and cleaning white people's homes. In 1843, Isabella, an older woman now, with five children felt the urge to speak out against slavery. She had run away but her brothers and sisters were still living in the horrible conditions that she had left behind. Isabella was a deeply religious woman, and truly believed that all men and women were created equal under God. One day in the spring of 1843, she felt inspired by God and decided to walk around the country, to speak out against slavery, to set her brothers and sisters free. "I felt so tall within. I felt as if the powers of the Nation was with me," Isabella said. She decided to change her name to Sojourner Truth, which would represent her travels preaching the truth, to Blacks and whites all around the country. She not only spoke for the rights of Blacks but for the rights of women as well. When Sojourner would speak to large crowds she was always the main figure, the center of attention, because she had a deep powerful voice and she spoke from the heart for she knew what slavery was all about. Sojourner Truth became very famous, and everyone knew her name. For this reason the people who believed in slavery tried time and time again to stop her and silence her. She was stoned and beaten, but Sister Truth continued her battle against the slave owners.

At that time women never spoke in public and were supposed to stay at home, cooking and sewing and having babies, which is what capitalist society does to sisters today. Sojourner Truth was accused of being a man in women's clothing. At one rally, when she was accused again the sister ripped open her dress, bared her breasts, and declared that the men should come up and look. She said "These old breasts fed five children of mine, and other people's children too, and you say I'm not a woman. These strong arms have pushed a plow, and scrubbed your floors but I've had many children and could bear twelve more and you say I'm not a woman. I don't need your help to cross no puddles and to get in and out of carriages, and I don't faint at the sight of blood, but I'm more of a woman than you are a man. If you don't believe me come on up here and see these tired old breasts." With these words, Sojourner shamed the men in the audience who had doubted her womanhood.

Once, when riding on a streetcar, that had recently been integrated, two white "ladies" got on and sat down across from her. When they saw Sister Truth they started whispering and giving her dirty looks. They finally called the conductor and asked him if "niggers were allowed to ride." The conductor was embarrassed and answered "yes," and the "ladies" started talking about how terrible it was for clean, decent white people to have to ride in a car with niggers. Sojourner said aloud enough for them and everyone else on the car to hear "Of course black people ride on these cars 'cause they are meant for us and poor whites too. Carriages are for ladies and gentlemen!" The ladies took the hint and got up to leave. "Oh," said Sojourner, "now they are going to to take a carriage. Good-bye ladies!"

It is important for us to know the history of Puerto Rican and Black women who fought for freedom of our peoples. We are not taught about them because even today people believe that women had no role in history. People still believe that women are only supposed to stay at home, cooking and sewing and raising children. These are the same things that were said to Sojourner Truth over a hundred years ago and they are still being said now. Women who speak out against injustice and fight for revolution are accused of acting like men, and we must understand that revolution is the job of men and women, brothers and sisters. We must learn from great women like Lolita Lebron, Carmen Perez, Antonia Martinez, Kathleen Cleaver and Ericka Huggins. This is what Point 10 of the YOUNG LORDS PARTY 13-Point Program and Platform means when it says "We want equality for women; machismo must be revolutionary and not oppressive."

REMEMBER SISTER TRUTH!
FORWARD SISTERS AND
BROTHERS IN THE STRUGGLE!!!
LIBERATE PUERTO RICO NOW!!!

Denise Oliver
Communications Secretary
YOUNG LORDS PARTY
New York State Chapter

History of Cuba Part Three

(From the newspaper *Palante*, 28 August 1970, volume 2, number 10)

[EDITOR'S NOTE: "History of Cuba" was originally a five-part series.
Parts 3 and 4 are reproduced here.]

In 1898, after the spanish-amerikkkan war, the united states occupied both Puerto Rico and Cuba; and the second age of misery for Latin America began. Spain had ruled

Latin America with an iron grip for 400 years. The whole continent and the Antilles were a colony—under political, military and economic control. The u.s. was slicker than spain. McKinley and the other presidents had seen that when you are too openly oppressive, the people rise up, like Jose Marti and Maximo Gomez, like Betances, like Simon Bolivar, like the American Revolutionaries. So the u.s. developed a new form of control—neo-colonialism. Neo-colonialism was a new type of colony, a colony where the government is elected by the people of that country, but where the real power (political power, economic power, military power) is controlled from the outside. They kept Puerto Rico as an outright old-fashioned colony, but made Cuba and the rest of Latin America neo-colonies.

What does it mean to be economically controlled by another country? Well, imagine that you went shopping on 34th Street, or downtown Brooklyn, or Broad Street in Newark, or Boston Commons, or Michigan Avenue in Chicago and all the stores you shopped in were owned by germans. Imagine that all the factories in your country were owned by germans, that all the food you ate was imported from germany, that the telephone company and power company were german. In other words, all the money you had would be going to german companies and the profits would be going back to germany. That is neo-colonialism. Germans would have more to say about your country than you. They would finance politicians running for office. They would lobby for or against taxes or wage increases. Wealth controls absolutely. The u.s. controlled Cuba absolutely.

The Platt Amendment to the Cuban Constitution gave the u.s. the right to intervene in Cuban affairs whenever the u.s. felt that the "democracy" of Cuba or the lives and property of amerikkkan businessmen in Cuba was threatened. When the people heard that the Platt Amendment would mean u.s. control of spanish control, they understood that the revolution of Marti had been sold out, and they reacted. On March 2, 1901, the day the Platt Amendment became law, 15,000 Cubans demonstrated against it in Havana, just as Puerto Ricans fought against the imposition of u.s. citizenship 16 years later in 1917. The u.s. took steps to teach the Cuban ruling class how best to keep the people in line. The New York chief of police went to Cuba to train and equip the Havana police. The guardia, rural police, were trained in the u.s. military forts.

When the u.s. arrived in Cuba, campesinos and small landowners were the majority and most of the businesses and sugar plantations were owned by Cubans. By 1943, 40% of the compesinos had lost their land as amerikkkan carpetbaggers came in droves. 13,000 money-hungry, scheming, sly wolves descended on Cuba, all of them parasites looking for a way to live off the people.

The history of Cuba after 1902 is the story of one vendepatria after another selling himself to the u.s. government in order to become president. Estrada Patra was the first. When he tried to reelect himself for a second term, the people rebelled and he had to call on u.s. forces who occupied the country from 1906 to 1909. The next piti-yanqui, Jose Miguel Gomez, brought with him to office the amerikkkan brand of racism and discrimination. But the Cuban liberation army of national independence had been about 70% Black, and the Black Cubans were not about to stand for this kind of racial discrimination. So in 1908 another leader of the people, Evaristo Estenoz, organized Black Cubans into the Partido Independiente de Color. The party was declared illegal, and its leaders were hunted down. On May 20, 1912, the Black people of Cuba rose up against Gomez. The movement was defeated, Estenoz was killed, and the u.s. demanded a wave of killings of Black revolutionaries—over 3,000 Blacks were killed.

As the u.s. businessmen, united fruit company, american sugar company, j.p. morgan & sons began to buy up Cuban land and business, reshape Cuban eceonomy, turn the country into a strictly one-crop sugar supplier of the world, they needed more labor, so they got the Cuban immigration laws changed and began importing large numbers of Jamaican and Haitian day-laborers who worked for subsistence wages.

Over the years, one million persons emigrated to Cuba from the Caribbean, europe and Asia. In 1917, the u.s. got Cuba to declare war against germany, then used that as an excuse to land 2,000 troops on the island. The troops stayed until 1922 when the next lackey Cuban president, zayas, reminded the gringos that the war was over. During zayas' presidency complete control of the Cuban economy was accomplished. 1925 began the reign of machado, the most unpopular president in Cuban history. In the middle of the depression, conditions in Cuba got worse. Thousands were unemployed, many were landless; Cuban businessmen were being squeezed out by amerikkkans. machado repressed all protest against these conditions. The value of the sugar crop dropped from $200 million in 1929 to $42 million in 1933. Students were shot and killed in the streets for protesting. In 1933, after a student was killed in Havana, the people rose up in strikes, demonstrations, and battles across the country.

The revolutionary force of the people frightened the u.s. government and it urged machado to flee Cuba. He did, as Cuban peasants retook their lands, and armed students and workers battled police and troops in the streets. For months one government after another fell. Meanwhile, fulgencio batista, a sergeant in the army, gained in stature and power within the ranks of the army. Finally peace came, and in 1940 a new constitution was written. It was liberal, decent. batista was the first president. But as soon as peace returned, the greedy vendepatrias began again to sell their land and their country to the gringos.

Carlos Prio Socarras was the president in 1952 when batista pulled a coup, seized power, and established a dictatorship. He suspended the constitution of 1940. For the next few years under batista, terror and death reigned in Cuba. The campesinos lost their homes. The workers' rights were denied. Living conditions became worse. Havana became the whorehouse of the Caribbean where every gringo businessman could buy himself ten prostitutes. Dope traffic and the underground market flourished. And the people starved batista's secret police [illegible] hunted all leftists.

In 1948, Jose Mendez, the Black leader of the Cuban Communist Party, was shot by batista's police. Finally, in 1953, the people arose again in the Moncada Assault, led by a lawyer named Fidel Castro.

VIVA MONCADA!
VIVA PUERTO RICO LIBRE!

Juan Gonzalez
Minister of Education
YOUNG LORDS PARTY

....

History of Cuba Part Four

(From the newspaper *Palante*, 11 December 1970, volume 2, number 16)

Amerikkka tries to teach all of us, Puerto Ricans, Blacks, the poor, that revolutionaries are caused by outside agents from Moscow, China, and Cuba; that communism is brought from other countries.

If you asked who brought in their revolution in 1776, the yankees will tell you, "no one, we are fighting for independence." But they refuse to believe anyone else, any other country, should also be fighting to free itself from oppression.

The Cuban revolution that overthrew Fulgencio Batista was one of those fighting for freedom—like the Algerian, Vietnamese, Mexican, and Chinese revolutions. In March, 1952, Batista overthrew the free-elected government of Cuba when he saw he was going to lose the election for President.

Fidel Castro, a young Cuban lawyer, went to the courts of Cuba and demanded that Batista be arrested as a criminal. The judges, frightened by Batista's army, refused. Fidel realized that the only way to end the dictatorship was through revolution.

He organized about 200 young men and women, mostly students from the University of Havana, trained them for a year and then attacked Fort Meneada, the second largest fort in Cuba. His plan was to take the 1,000 soldiers by surprise, broadcast over the radio the liberation of the island and call on the people to overthrow Batista. The attack on July 26, 1954 was defeated and Batista ordered the cold-blooded murder of over 70 of the young revolutionaries.

Fidel and six leaders were put on trial. Batista was so frightened of the people's support for the revolutionaries, that he did not allow Fidel to attend his own trial: 100 soldiers were in the court and only six reporters who had their stories censored. Before being sentenced to 15 years in jail, Fidel was given a chance to speak. His speech, called "HISTORY WILL ABSOLVE ME," lasted five hours. He admitted trying to overthrow Batista. But, he insisted that Batista was the criminal and that he was trying to bring freedom to Cuba. He showed how throughout history, in the american and french declarations of independence, in all writings of great government leaders, it has always been seen as the right of the people to destroy a government that oppresses them instead of serves them.

His speech did not only talk about the injustice, the oppression, the racism of the government and the amerikkkans who controlled Cuba with their money, but it also gave concrete examples of how the country could be liberated. The YOUNG LORDS PARTY has always said that revolutionaries must deal with concrete problems of the people, land, health, housing, education, jobs, and industry. Fidel had definite plans as all true revolutionaries should have. Fidel also knew his nation inside and out. He had analyzed the different classes in Cuban society. He knew that most Cubans, like most Puerto Ricans, were either workers, campesinos, or unemployed, and he knew who was making money. He said:

"The future of the country and the solutions of its problems cannot continue to depend on the selfish interests of a dozen financiers, nor the cold calculations of profits that ten or twelve magnates draw up in their air-conditioned office." He had trust in the people and their power, when united and organized, to change Cuba.

At the end of his speech, he said, "It is understandable that honest men should be dead or in prison in this Republic where the president is a criminal and a thief" (in History Will Absolve Me).

Sentenced to 15 years, he was released on May 15, 1955, when the pressure of the Cuban people made Batista give him amnesty.

He went to Mexico to prepare an army and return to Cuba. As the army was being built and trained by an old expert in guerilla warfare, General Alberto Bayo, Fidel traveled especially to the united states, raising funds. In cities like Bridgeport, Tampa, Union City, and New York, he found small colonies of Cubans who contributed money, guns, and supplies to the revolutionaries. Finally, after months of training, in December 12, 1956 the yacht Granma, loaded with 82 men, arms and supplies, landed in Oriente Province. From the beginning they were lost and trailed by Batista's army.

In the end, only twelve men escaped to the Sierra Maestra, Fidel Castro, Raul Castro, Che Guevara, Camilo Cienfuegos, Calixto Garcia, Faustino Perez, Calixto Morales, Universo Sanchez, Efigenio Almejerias, Ciro Redondo, Juan Almeido, and Rene Rodriguez. From there they began organizing guerrilla war.

Guerrilla war is the type of war the people use when they are outnumbered, have poor arms, and are fighting on land they know. The armed struggle in Puerto Rico and in Amerikkka will use guerrilla war. In the cities and countryside.

As the months passed, the small band grew larger. They would hit and run, only attacking the enemy when sure of victory, just as Antonio Maceo had done years before in fighting the spanish. At the same time, the revolutionaries protected and served the campesinos in the mountains.

They paid for everything they borrowed, not like Batista's thieves and killers. They started country hospitals for their soldiers and the people. Within two years, Che Guevara, the Argentine doctor, and Fidel's right-hand man, had set up over 30 schools for the campesinos. A land reform program that took the land from the rich and latifundistas [large estates, haciendas] and gave it to the campesinos was started.

A newspaper, CUBA LIBRE, was printed and distributed in the cities by student and worker leaders, like Frank Pais, who supported the movement. In 1958, a radio station— Radio Rebelde was also set up and all the people were victorious, and Fidel Castro, Raul Castro, Che Guevara, and Camilo Cienfuegos were the leaders of the new society.

The Daily News and other amerikkkan trash sheets carried stories about Fidel the monster, who executed hundreds of innocent people. In fact, Fidel prevented thousands of deaths. The Cuban people wanted to begin attacking all their local oppressors. During the dictatorship, Batista's army had killed over 20,000 people, and all those families wanted revenge. Fidel said no. He insisted that all the criminals would be tried in revolutionary courts, just as the allies in the World War 2 had tried the Nazis, or the Israelis tried Adolf Eichmann. In the end 700 murderers and criminals from Batista's army were executed and put in jail. But the amerikkkans, who had supported Batista's army with money and military trainers, and military weapons, wanted right away to isolate the Cuban Revolution for freedom from the rest of the world it controlled and oppressed.

CUBA, PUERTO RICO!
UNIDOS VENCEREMOS!

QUE VIVE CHE!

QUE VIVA CAMILO!

Juan Gonzales

Minister of Defense

YOUNG LORDS PARTY

....

Editorial (Betances)

(From the newspaper *Palante*, 25 September 1970, volume 2, number 12)

This issue of PALANTE is dedicated to EL GRITO DE LARES and the revolutionaries who, on September 23, 1868, began the fight for liberation. This year, the YOUNG LORDS PARTY has called for a conference of all Puerto Rican students in the colleges and high schools in order that we may continue the work begun by our own ancestors.

The YOUNG LORDS PARTY stands for the intensification of the struggle that began on September 23, 1868. We aim to be around to its conclusion—and beyond.

All of us, whether or not we are Puerto Ricans, can learn from EL GRITO DE LARES. These women and men fought against amazing odds to liberate a town from the spanish rapist. Inspired by Betances and his followers, the first generation of what we know today to be the Puerto Rican—African, Indian and Spanish combined—a new Nationalist Party arose in the 1930's to overcome the amerikkkan plunderers. In 1950, this group, led by Albizu Campos, started a rebellion on October 30 in the town of Jayuya, a rebellion that quickly spread to surrounding towns. While this was happening two Puerto Ricans showed us what a correct support position is for revolutionaries here. They went to Washington D.C. to off the president of the united states. For that attempted action, Oscar Collazo is still in Leavenworth.

In 1953 Lolita Lebron led three brothers in what has become one of the most audacious acts carried out by a colonized people against the yanqui, shooting at the lawmakers who keep us enslaved while they were in session.

Mad, you say? You say these spics are mad? We're damned insane! The YOUNG LORDS PARTY and a whole new generation of crazy Puerto Ricans have been born, tempered by the ghettos of amerikkka, and are moving quickly on the enemy. We fight now not only for the socialist liberation of Puerto Rico, but for the right to self-determination for all Puerto Ricans. We fight for the million in New York City, the hundreds of thousands in Chicago, Cleveland, Hartford, Philadelphia, Hoboken, Newark, and Wilmington.

We fight for the 1,000 spics in Alabama.

We fight for the 75,000 spics in Hawaii.

This generation is learning from history. One reason why Betances and Albizu failed is because they led movements based mainly on charisma and petty bourgeoisie liberals. To correct this, the revolution is now based among the people, the most oppressed people, on principles of socialism.

One thing we have in common with our ancestors: the gun. Petty bourgeois liberals they might have been, but they weren't using bottles at Lares or bricks at Jayuya. Some of us who have been listening to the enemy's propaganda for too long as to how peaceful we are better dig the fact that Betances, Albizu, Blanca, and Lolita were packin'. The bottle ain't been made that can stand up to a .38.

So this year we intend to celebrate EL GRITO DE LARES, not only on September 23, but every day. Through the Liberate Puerto Rico Now Committees we will build a movement strong enough to crush the enemy. We intend to unite with other Latin and Third World struggles because we can't do it alone.

Every day from now on must be another day lost to the enemy, another day won for the people. We cannot spend any more time jivin'. Really, this may well be the last generation of spics. Each day brings a new chance to strike, to build, to organize.

We must not fail. To do so would be to condemn our ancestors to failure. Anything less than victory from now on would deny the future of our nation and of humanity in general. We must wage war in order to have peace.

> STRIKE TO WIN!
> USE WHAT YOU GOT TO GET WHAT YOU NEED!
> Editor

....

El Grito de Lares

(From the newspaper *Palante*, 25 September 1970, volume 2, number 12)

For centuries, we have been taught that we are a small, quiet, insignificant, shuffling people who cannot even govern ourselves and who are very happy having outside governments control our lives. We have been taught that Puerto Rico is a beautiful island for tourists on summer vacations. We are taught that revolution is the work of maniacs and fanatics and has nothing to do with nice, docile spics. Yet we have not been quiet; the people of Borinquen have struggled for liberation from the time of the Taino Indians to the present.

The first revolutionary action of the Puerto Rican nation took place on September 23, 1868—EL GRITO DE LARES—when a group of short, quiet, shuffling, machete-carrying spics tired of taking shit picked up arms against spain. These Puerto Ricans became revolutionaries after a long struggle to improve conditions which resulted in nothing, a struggle similar to the civil rights movement in the u.s.

For being revolutionaries, Ramon Emeterio Betances, Segundo Ruiz Belvis and others were exiled and ordered to go to spain. The two brothers refused and fled to New York where they continued to make plans for the revolution. (The u.s. government allowed them to operate freely because it was interested in Puerto Rico and Cuba for itself but wasn't ready to hassle spain at that time.) In New York they hooked up with different groups that were planning the liberation of all the islands in the Caribbean.

To get money and guns for this, Belvis went to Chile to speak to President Vicuna Mackena, an old friend of his. A week after his arrival, Belvis was found dead unexpectedly and mysteriously in his hotel room.

In the meantime, Betances continued working with the Cuban revolutionaries in New York and kept contact with the secret organizations in Puerto Rico. He went to St. Thomas and issued a proclamation calling for armed revolution in Puerto Rico and a 10-point program that included the abolition of slavery and the right to carry guns. From there he went to Santo Domingo—the headquarters for the revolution—to lead the Revolutionary Committee for Puerto Rico whose purpose was to organize a revolution to make Puerto Rico an independent democratic republic. These committees were established in certain cities: Lares, Mayaguez, San Sebastian, Camuy, and Ponce. The job of the committees was to educate and organize Puerto Ricans for revolution. Puerto Ricans then lived in their own country as second-class citizens to spain just like Puerto Ricans today live as second-class citizens to the u.s. The committees also educated Puerto Ricans that they have the right to rebel against the government when it is working against their interest which is what we tell our people today.

Out of the Lares committee came the flag of EL GRITO DE LARES and the national anthem, la Borinquena, written by Loia Rodriguez del Tio whose revolutionary lyrics were later changed to fit the image of a docile Puerto Rican.

In the middle of July, 1868, a revolutionary brother, Pedro Garcia, who had been collecting money for the revolution, got caught with a list of names of people who were donating money for guns. The leaders were caught by surprise and arrested; all the revolutionary records were confiscated. They were betrayed by juan castenon, a captain of the militia of the spanish army, who had infiltrated the movement.

The leaders in different towns were alerted. Some responded and others held back. However, they decided to mobilize their forces in Lares on September 23, in advance of the predetermined date of September 29.

Betances sailed for Curacao to pick up a shipment of rifles. He got them, but still needed more. He returned to St. Thomas where he organized an expedition to sail from there to reinforce the revolutionary forces in Puerto Rico. He could count on 10,000 warriors with 4 mortars and an adequate [amount] of rifles and machetes. He was to leave with his expeditionary force aboard the streamer Telegrafo, but a message stopped him, telling him that the revolution had been discovered and that the entire coast of Puerto Rico had been alerted and a landing was impossible.

On the afternoon of September 23, 1868, nearly 100 men from Mayaguez met with 400 men from Lares. Most of these men had no military experience. Some were armed, with rifles, hand guns, and carbines; others, recruited from among the jibaro, didn't have anything but knives and machetes. They marched into Lares in formation with shouts of "Liberty or Death" and "Long Live Puerto Rico!" and seized Lares. The revolutionaries held Lares for one day.

The following day the Spanish military came in and systematically crushed the rebellion from town to town. Everyone that was not killed was jailed. The jails of Arecibo and Aguadilla were packed. Even before coming to trial, 36 of these political prisoners died of a flu caused by the filthy, overcrowded, unsanitary conditions of the prisons. During the trials, seven revolutionaries were condemned to death and five others were sentenced to long terms in the prison of Ceuta in North Africa. For the time being, the movement was crushed, but the revolutionary spirit continues among the people.

September 23, 1868 proclaimed us to the world as a colonized nation fighting for independence. One hundred and two years later we are still a colonized nation continuing to struggle against the oppression of our people, this time by the u.s. We are the continuation of the struggle of EL GRITO DE LARES. It is the duty of every Puerto Rican woman,

man, and child to follow the example of the revolutionaries of the present, like CAL, MIRA, and the YOUNG LORDS PARTY.

> THE DUTY OF EVERY PUERTO
> RICAN IS TO MAKE THE
> REVOLUTION!
> QUE VIVA PUERTO RICO LIBRE!
>
> Iris Morales
> Education Captain
> YOUNG LORDS PARTY
>
> SEPT. 23 A NAT'L HOLIDAY FOR ALL BORICUAS

....

Albizu Campos

(From the newspaper *Palante,* 30 October 1970, volume 2, number 14)

When we ask our parents who Albizu Campos was, many of them answer that he was a violent man, crazy and full of hate for the yanqui. Others say that he was an intelligent man, even the most intelligent Puerto Rico has produced, but that he used very bad methods, that he tried to do it the hard way, and that is why he failed in his purpose. We may still find others who say that don Pedro Albizu Campos was the greatest patriot of this century; the most valiant Puerto Rican of our history, equal only to Betances; the father of our country. If today we ask one of the many yanquis who from their universities and government offices write their own interpretation of Puerto Rican history, they will say that Albizu Campos was a violent man, a racist, alone, without any contact with the daily life of the Puerto Rican. And what will we believe, we Puerto Ricans who never heard his voice, never saw him in action, nor participated in the fight for liberation of our country which he led?

Of his actual life we know a lot. He was born at the beginning of this century in Ponce, the pearl of the south. When he was a small boy, as he himself reported years later, he was able to hear the great patriot Jose de Diego recite his nationalist poems and from those days in high school he felt the great love for his country that later on served as an example to every Puerto Rican. With the help of a priest he won a scholarship to a college in New Hampshire. From there he won another scholarship to Harvard University. When the first world war broke out, he enlisted in the American army as a lieutenant. He graduated from Harvard with various honors and diplomas and returned to Puerto Rico after the war was over.

In those 1920's, Puerto Rico was just beginning to know and organize against the north american invaders, who had 20 years of military occupation, economic control and cultural aggression against Borinquen. The Union Party was a coalition of different social classes in Puerto Rico who were trying to fight against those Puerto Ricans who were selling out our country; the pitiyanquis, as they were called for being very friendly with the invaders. Albizu joined the Union Party. But in 1922 the Union Party withdrew independence for Puerto Rico as one of the demands in their platform, and the young radicals left the party and started a new party with independence as their major demand and not as one among others. Among the young militants was the young lawyer from Ponce, Pedro Albizu Campos. They formed the Nationalist Party of Puerto Rico.

Albizu joined in the launching of the new party, but pretty soon he started on a trip through Latin America that lasted almost five years. During this time he met Latin American revolutionaries, learned about their conditions and at the same time spread the word about the colonial conditions of Puerto Rico. He returned to Puerto Rico in 1930 when the Nationalist Party was in the midst of a great debate about its course of action. As the colonial elections got closer, a faction of the party wanted to discard the elections because they considered them a waste of time. After 30 years of elections, the yanquis controlled more than ever the daily life of the Puerto Ricans and their lands.

This faction proposed that the party should take up arms and launch armed struggle as the only road to freedom. The other faction proposed that the party should participate in the elections once more; that as they believed, there was the possibility of winning and in that way they could secure independence from the yanquis. Albizu entered in this debate and in the process was elected president of the party.

The party lost the elections that year and again in 1932. Finally in 1932, the nationalists launched armed struggle. Albizu spent the next six years educating the people to the reality of the north american occupation. There were many shoot-outs; and in one of them, two nationalists killed Colonel Riggs, yanqui chief of security forces. For this action the two were killed in jail without a trail, and Albizu and the party leadership were arrested and accused of conspiracy to overthrow the government of the united states. At the trial the Puerto Ricans found them innocent and the north American guilty. The north American governor got a jury from the united states composed mainly of yanquis and sentenced him to 10 years in the federal prison in Atlanta, Georgia. He came out of jail in 1947, sick and weak from the electrical tortures that did not let him sleep. Even so, he started to reorganize the party.

In 1950, munoz marin was planning the slaughter of the Nationalist Party so he could go ahead with his plans to set himself up in the new "commonwealth." Even though the revolution had been planned for 1952 and they weren't prepared yet, the Nationalists threw themselves into battle rather than wait and be murdered in jails or shot in the back on dark streets. In Jayuya, Arecibo, San Juan and other towns in the Island, the Nationalists fought against the yanqui armed forces and their hirelings. Don Pedro was captured after three days of gunfire in his house in Old San Juan. His body limp from tear gas, but with his gun still in his hand. He was thrown into jail again, with the majority of the other Nationalists, many of whom were killed. In 1953, munoz marin, trying to gain the sympathy of the voters for the elections, freed him. But in 1954, when Lolita Lebron and the three other Nationalists shot-up the congress of the united states, Albizu was rearrested and was kept in jail until 1965. He was tortured again in jail and besides was given cobalt-ray treatments that killed him little by little. Not wanting him to die in jail, the colonial government released him. He died three months later in 1965.

Given this long history of struggle against the yanqui occupier, why is there so much confusion about the real importance of Albizu? Why so many different opinions?

First, since the beginning of his struggle in the Nationalist Party, Albizu was attacked by the yanqui government as all those who rebelled were attacked. The yanquis said that the reason why Albizu fought back was because he loved his country. They also said, as they say today against anyone who talks about armed struggle as a means to freedom, that taking up arms was an inexcusable madness. They tried to deny that there were no other open ways for us to get our freedom—when actually they maintained themselves in Puerto Rico because of their own arms. Because the united states controlled the press, the schools and the government, all public information gave a negative impression of Albizu. So a great number of Puerto Ricans who never knew Albizu had only that impression.

Second, Don Pedro was a man who spoke beautifully, and for the Puerto Ricans with a long history of colonization, education and a nice way of expressing yourself was something that every poor, oppressed person longed to have. This created an image of Albizu as a man of great intelligence, whom everybody respected and admired, even though they didn't always understand completely his political message. This increased the tendency of his being looked at as a great genius and not like a very simple man, representing the daily life of every oppressed Puerto Rican. Then what is the importance of Don Pedro?

Albizu was the first man to take up arms against the yanqui invader. He did this at a time when the majority of the Puerto Ricans were accommodating themselves to the growing military occupation, the elimination of our language, the theft of our land. This uprising with arms was with courage unequaled in our history since the time of Betances. It serves as an example to us today. Albizu was very much aware of the necessity for courage to obtain liberation when he said, "The motherland is courage and sacrifice," and the many times he showed his own valor.

He also brought out the importance of studying and knowing Puerto Rican history and culture at a time when the yanquis were doing everything possible to make us forget both. We consider Albizu a great man and a great fighter in the long and hard struggle for our liberation that has been carried out by the people of Puerto Rico. But at the same time that we praise him, we cannot make him a saint.

Today the struggle of Puerto Ricans in the island and here in the bowels of the yanqui beast has advanced since Albizu's times. We see that when the leadership of the Nationalist Party was arrested, there was no trained cadre to continue and intensify the struggle. That is why today we concentrate on the development of all PARTY members. We see that Albizu never dealt with the reality that we are mainly an African country and that the intermixing of spanish, Indians, and Africans did not leave us being more spanish as he said. We also know today that to launch armed struggle you have to organize and create a popular movement first that can sustain and carry on a people's war of all Puerto Ricans and not just a group or party.

Finally, with Puerto Rico today at the point of extinction at the hands of the north american companies that make us provide riches which they keep for themselves, that rob us of our copper, land, forests, and islands—we know that it will be necessary to go beyond independence in our objectives. We must find other means to manage our society and economy different from the existing capitalist one that the yanquis have used to

rob us of our wealth. We understand the necessity of an authentic Puerto Rican socialism that will develop from our daily struggle.

But all these improvements in our struggle do not take away from Pedro Albizu Campos his greatness as a Puerto Rican who dedicated and gave his life for the liberation of
the Puerto Rican people.

> Carlos Aponte
> Education Lieutenant
> YOUNG LORDS PARTY

....

History of Boriken 1

(From the newspaper *Palante*, 29 January 1971, volume 3, number 2)

It is important that we study our history, our true history. We have to know where we
came from to know who we are; and we have to analyze the past and the present to find
out what laws will apply for the future. Part of being oppressed is constantly being told
by the slaveowner that we have no roots, no history, no past, nothing from which we can
build. We are told that anything that might have come before us didn't amount to two
cents anyhow, and that the reality of things is that we have to start from scratch. Every
new generation is made to believe that in order to move against the enemy, we have to
start from the beginning, rather than take a look into our collective history, and see what
mistakes and successes were made before. This is how capitalists remain on top; through
lies and gaps of their educational system they are able to maintain their false superiority.

This is the generation that has broken the cycle of always beginning again. Black people
in amerikkka began by making it important to know Black history, and to be proud of
being Black. Of course, when people get into a bag of just studying their history, without
putting their new knowledge into meaningful practice, or if people are proud of what they
are to the point of thinking and acting as if they're better than someone else, this is wrong.
This was taken up by the Chicanos of the West and Southwest of amerikkka, and then by
the Puerto Ricans. Asian people who live in amerikkka are also studying their past.

We now know why we must study history:

- To analyze the mistakes and successes of our past.
- To see if a pattern develops in the enemy's tactics.
- After analyzing both our people's development and the enemy's tactics, to see if we can
  make guidelines for the future and
- To be proud of having a rich history, of having roots.

Let's get into these roots:

Puerto Rico is an island lying in the Caribbean Sea, part of a cluster of islands, called
the Greater Antilles. Two other islands in the Greater Antilles which have been closely
linked to Puerto Rico's history are Santo Domingo and Cuba. The island is over 100 miles
long and 35 miles wide, about the size of Connecticut. Strategically, Puerto Rico lies 1,050

miles southwest of Miami, between North and South America, at the entrance to the Caribbean. This accounts for much of Puerto Rico's value to imperialists.

Three-fourths of the island is mountainous or hilly. Although there is much rain on most of Puerto Rico, there are only 50 rivers, none of which are suitable for large ships. Temperature is usually about 80 degrees in the summer and low 70's in winter.

The earliest known people to live on the island were the Arcaico Indians. They probably came from southern Florida, by of way of Cuba. The Arcaicos lived mostly as a fishing people. They were conquered by the Igneri, who rowed canoes from Venezuela. The Igneris in turn were dominated by the Taino Indians, who also occupied the Dominican Republic.

The Tainos called the island Boriken, which means Land of the Noble Lord. They lived in small tribes, bound together by a larger federation. This was an early form of socialism. Tainos were short, and copper-colored, with straight black hair and high cheekbones. All went naked except the married women, who wore a small cotton wrap called the nagua (where we got our word for enagua, for slip, from). The fact that the Tainos made the kind of distinction between man and woman that put the woman in lesser positions, shows that they were a male chauvinist society as well. This also means that oppression of women began before capitalism, that it can exist under socialism, and that to make sure this does not happen, we must work extra hard to eliminate all false divisions based on sex.

The Indians placed their yucayeques (villages) near salt or fresh water and lived in small bohios. They relaxed in hamacas (hammocks) which were made from woven cotton fibers. The women tended the crops, while the men hunted. The men also smoked tabaco or inhaled it during religious rites. Nets, hooks, and traps were used to catch fish in the sea and rivers; certain plants in the river waters were used to drug the fish (most of this specific information for this part comes from a new book, "Puerto Rico: A Profile," by Kal Wagenheim. How you drug fish, I don't know). They raised some animals, including a now extinct type of mule, multi-colored dog, which they fattened and ate. The Tainos also caught wild birds and rodents.

The Taino chieftain was called a cacique, who wore a golden disc around his neck called the guanine. When he died, his successor would be chosen by going along his mother's line to his first sister's son, or his first sister who had a son. The Taino Indians believed in a supreme creator called Yukiyu, who lived in what is now El Yunque (the anvil). Their evil spirit was called Jurakan, who unleashed violent storms. There were also lesser spirits which each village and family had called a cemi. The dead were buried with water, food, arms, and adornments, since there was a belief in life after death. A cacique was buried with his favorite woman, who was buried alive with him.

The villages had plazas called bateyes, where religious ceremonies called areytos were held. History was passed along at these ceremonies by telling tales. Music was made from hollow tree trunks and sticks, maracas or guiros. Human bones were used for flutes. The only weapons the Tainos had were bows, arrows, hardwood swords called the macana (which is what we call the pig's billy club today), and stone axes with wooden handles. The Indians had corn, tobacco, and rubber, and some of the many Indian contributions to our language are canoa, maiz, guiro, maraca, sabana, and cayo.

By 1493, there were 30,000 Tainos living in Borinquen. On November 19 of that year, the peaceful life of the Indians was disturbed by an intrusion from a fool named christopher columbus, while on his second voyage to the americas. Columbus stayed awhile but sailed on to what is now the Dominican Republic, and in 1496 the city of Santo Domingo was founded. This was to be spain's headquarters for its imperialist operations in the so-called "new land."

After 1493, Borinquen was ignored. (columbus renamed it San Juan Bautista, after the son of the king and queen of spain). As though it were some prince's play thing, the rights to colonize San Juan were tossed back and forth in spain. While the oppressors were playing with it there, one of their kind had already received permission from the governor general of the Indies. His name was Juan Ponce de Leon, and he sailed from Hispaniola (Dominican Republic, which the Indians called Quisquella), landing in San Juan (Borinquen) on August 12, 1508. He conned the Indian chief there, and returned with him to Hispaniola (Quisquella).

He went back to San Juan in March of 1509. Sailing with him was a Black freeman named Juan Garribo. Garribo had been born in Angola, lived for some years in Seville, spain, won his freedom and became a Christian. He went with De Leon to Florida. Later, he went to Mexico with Cortes.

By August of 1509, Ponce de Leon had done such a good job of enslaving the people that had welcomed him, that king Ferdinand made him governor. He was ordered to give land and Indians to the colonizers and thirty more oppressors who were on their way from spain.

Oppression, racism, disease and the beginnings of People's War had come to Borinquen.

> THE DUTY OF A PUERTO RICAN IS TO MAKE THE REVOLUTION
> LIBERATE PUERTO RICO NOW!
> PONCE—MARCH 21
> Pablo "Yoruba" Guzman
> Minister of Information
> YOUNG LORDS PARTY

....

History of Boriken 2

(From the newspaper *Palante*, 19 February 1971, volume 3, number 3)

When ponce de leon first landed in Puerto Rico on August 12, 1508, he tricked a Taino cacique, Agueybana the Elder, into thinking he was a friend. By 1510, Agueybana's newphew was in rebellion against anything spanish. What had happened?

What happened was that ponce de leon was the spearhead for the spanish colonization, enslavement, of Puerto Rico. When he returned to the island in May, 1509, after going to the Dominican Republic (spain's headquarters in the "new world") for more orders, he brought African slaves for his household. governor de leon brought Franciscan friars in to "teach religion" to the Tainos. This follows the classical pattern used by western conquerors—first, the "discoverer," then the colonizer, then the priest. The plan is to get the "natives" so hung up on religion that they're too busy singing to realize they live in chains. Drugs were used in a similar way to bust up the gangs in the u.s.

Despite the fact that the Indians had been able to survive for thousands of years without spanish help, it was "obvious" to the racist conquerors that the Tainos needed help. A type of welfare system called the encomienda was started. Under this plot, anywhere from 30 to 300 Indians headed by a cacique were given to each spanish colonizer. The colonizer put them to work in the mines or elsewhere. The cacique was used as luis a. ferre, governor of Puerto Rico, is used today—a middleman for the boss. The generous Spaniards taught the Indians Catholicism and spanish culture, as payment for their services. Part of the spanish culture meant that the Indians had to cover their bodies, as though it were something to be ashamed of. Throughout history, western culture has always done this, and shown itself to Third World (people of color) People for what it really is—sick. The good ol' encomienda was slavery of the Indians.

The Indians, because of their armor, guns, horses, cattle and pigs of the Spaniards, believed them to be white Gods. (A myth helped along by the spanish who taught religion: "We are the children of God. You . . ."). After Agueybana the Elder's death, his nephew, Agueybana II, had more influence on the Tainos. ponce de leon had given Ageuybana II and his people to a rapist named sotomayor, a cruel sub-human being. Only the lie of the spaniards' immorality prevented a revolt.

Urayoan was an old cacique who had seen many things pass, and as far as he could tell, these spanish trespassers were not Gods. In November 1510, a Spaniard, diego saliado, asked Urayoan for some brothers to carry him and his bags across the Guarrabo River (check that out). The Taino brothers, like good boys, carried him and when they got to midstream, dropped him. They held poor diego under for several hours, then carried him ashore. Next they sat and watched. According to the stories the Spaniards had told, their God was dead three days, and then came back to life. Since they were children of God, made in God's image and likeness, the spanish reasoned, why they could do it too. After three days, diego refused to come back to life, and his stinking, decaying body was dragged back to Urayoan for inspection.

The spaniards sure as hell were not Gods. Sometimes it seems as though we will have to carry a politician like the mayor or the president across the river to show people what we mean, that the enemy also sleeps.

Agueybana and other caciques went to war. Spaniards caught on isolated plantations were killed. On a major assault against ponce de leon, Agueybana was killed, and the Indians were in disorder (that is why today we can't have only one strong leader. We must all become leaders). de leon offered amnesty to the Indians. Two traitors accepted, one of them was named gaquax, who was given the region now called Caguas. The other Tainos either went to the mountains or rowed to neighboring islands. Those who had been captured, killed their children and committed suicide, rather than serve a spanish beast. De leon asked king ferdinand for help to run the mines. He could not understand what was wrong with these Indians, as he sent his troops out to deal with the Indians who were still fighting in the hills. He left to find the fountain of youth. The facts we have today about how many Indians survived the brutality of the spanish varies so widely that we cannot say exactly how many there were. Most Indians did refuse to work for

Spaniards. Plantation owners protested because they had no Indians, not even one for housecleaning.

In 1511, a Dominican friar told governor diego columbus (son of chris) of the Dominican Republic, that he had sinned for persecuting the Indians. In 1512, the Dominican friars pressured the king for reforms, until a principle of freedom for the Indians was established—colonizers had to reduce the working hours, care for sick Indians, and baptize them. At least one Indian had to be taught to read and write. Married Indian women did not have to work in the mines, and children under 14 did not have to do hard labor.

Because the order came all the way from spain, a great distance away, it was hardly followed.

Once the gold mines stopped turning profits, the colonizers turned to agriculture to support the economy. As a boost to the economy, African slaves were brought in. This was around 1519. As payback for being made slaves the Africans carried smallpox they picked up from the whites on the ship to the spanish, who died like flies in a massive epidemic.

The next few years saw Carib Indians attack San German, killing five friars, and row into San Juan Bay under cannon to attack a nearby town (guerrilla warriors). The french also attacked San German, sacking and burning it. In 1530, the gold mines were practically dry. A series of storms hit the island and colonizers who had mortgaged their crops to buy African slaves went broke. So many people wanted to leave Puerto Rico, the governor made it a serious crime. Severe punishment, like cutting off a leg, was given to anyone trying to leave.

Desperate for an economy, the colonizers turned to sugar. With the good weather and African slaves as cheap labor, the sugar business turned a profit. Puerto Rican society changed. What was once a class of colonizers and miners became a new class of landholders. Shopkeepers and artisans prospered in San Juan. charles v ended slavery for Indians. A Nation had been destroyed in 50 years.

In 1521, emperor charles v ordered the freedom of all Indians except those owned by people who lived on the island who were not members of the crown. This could be done easily now that Africans were working. All 600 Indians, who were still living as slaves, were rounded up and sent to Toa, a royal farm. This is what the u.s. does in Vietnam. It rounds up Vietnamese people from different towns where it believes the NFL has support (which is just about every town) and places them in a specially created "town," really a concentration camp. It is called the "strategic hamlet," or "pacified village." Also that year, the island's name changed from San Juan to Puerto Rico, and the city that had been called Puerto Rico was changed to San Juan.[. . .]

In 1521, ponce de leon, looking for the fountain of youth, was killed by the Tainos' Indians comrades in Florida. 1521 was a good year.

Prosperity was short-lived. Other islands in the Antilles, properties of powers besides spain, developed better ways of sugar production, taking away Puerto Rico's markets. Slave trade diminished and pirate attacks cut down on shipping.

England was becoming the power of the seas, and spain turned Puerto Rico into a military fortress (as the u.s. uses it today). El Morro was completed, and annual aid came from the Mexican treasury (another spanish property). Although sir francis drake of england was defeated at El Morro, george clifford took San Juan in 1598. However, the "invisible weapons of the tropics" (disease) drove them away. The dutch sacked and burned San Juan in 1625, but it remained a spanish possession.

NEXT ISSUE: THE BIRTH OF THE PUERTO RICAN

PONCE—MARCH 21
ROMPE CADENAS
LIBERATE PUERTO RICO NOW!

Pablo "Yoruba" Guzman
Minister of Information
YOUNG LORDS PARTY

....

History of Boriken 3

(From the newspaper *Palante*, 5-19 March 1971, volume 3, number 4)

In the last issue, we saw that Puerto Rico developed a one-crop economy based on sugar. When other islands in the Antilles that were owned by powers besides spain developed cheaper ways to produce sugar, our island's economy sunk. Cattle, ginger and tobacco became the chief products, but they were all second rate compared to the number one Puerto Rican industry in the 17th and 18th centuries: smuggling.

Puerto Rico, as a colony of spain, was allowed to trade with only one other spanish port. (As a measure of our "progress," check out how Boriken as a colony of amerikkka is now allowed to trade with only a few u.s. ports.) Because of this poor economic situation, smuggling and piracy thrived as the main means of income. The main smuggling centers were Aguadia, Cabo Rojo, Arceibo, and Fajardo. Government officials, as they do today, looked the other way while their palms were greased with some pesos.

Boriken, from the late 1600's to the early 1800's, was practically ignored by europe, which was then the center of the world. In a one year period, not one ship from europe came to San Juan harbor. The spanish soldiers stationed on the island had nothing better to do than rape our Taina and African sisters and put down slave uprisings. From five towns in 1690, Puerto Rico had 14 in 1750.

The amerikkkan revolution in 1776, which served only the upper class (they got power), meant that the new united states could not trade with england or its ports. spain was eager for the amerikkkan trade, and soon ships from Philadelphia traveled to San Juan, carrying slaves and foodstuffs, in exchange for molasses, which was turned into rum and then traded for more slaves. The economic system that existed among the europeans then was mercantilism, which is a stage of development between feudalism (when there were castles owned by a baron and peasants who tended his land whose lives he ruled over) and capitalism. Mercantilist thinking believed that colonies were to be exploited, sucked dry of all they had, for the benefit of some powerful country, the top three of which were france, engand, and spain.

It's interesting to note that in school european history is all that we are taught. Yet what about China, with ¼ of the world's people? What about India, one of the largest countries in the world?

When the 13 amerikkkan colonies rebelled against England, they touched off a wave of democratic thinking in europe that bounced back to Latin America. Many of the sons of wealthy families in Latin America (never the daughters—women weren't supposed to learn anything) studied in european schools, the most liberal of which were in france. After the french revolution in 1789, france made up a constitution in 1791 that was a model for other democratic revolutions. Revolutions were taking place all over, and different types of people fled to Puerto Rico.

In 1765, spain sent a no-nonsense Irishman, Field Marhsall Alejandro O'Reilly, to look things over on the island. O'Reilly looked at the sad state of administrative affairs and went to work. He conducted a census, listing 39,846 spaniards and 5,037 slaves. O'Reilly reported that in the country people were living in small huts with hammocks, eating fruits and vegetables and planting small crops of coffee, sugar cane and tobacco.

The person he found in the country was the jibaro. Every country has a folk hero whom the people talk about and admire for having certain qualities. In amerikkka, it is the cowboy and the successfully crooked businessman; in Cuba, it is the guajiro; and in Puerto Rico, it is the jibaro. Jibaros first appeared in the 1700's, the result of the Tainos who fled to the hills, joined with Spaniards and later Africans. Somehow, the jibaros and jibaras, were catholic, although they were supersititious too. This combination is the basis for espiritismo. Today, the jibaro is our campesino or peasant, a landless worker slaving for one of the giant farm-factories or coming into town every so often to sell some cheap products. The term jibaro is used by some of us to put down other Puerto Ricans, meaning a "hick." This is a stupid, needless division we make among ourselves. [. . .]

The African slaves revolted in 1527. The slave revolts, which were taking place on all the islands and in the u.s. (more on that in the next issue), continued in intensity. In Puerto Rico, we are taught that the slaves never did this, that they "accepted their fate with bowed head." Jive. The Africans struggled so hard at tearing off the chains that in 1796 fascist measures had to be taken by the spanish forbidding meetings, etc. In 1821, 1822, and 1825 conspiracies were broken up in Guayama and Ponce. With 30,000 Africans recorded in 1834, the rebellions continued. A massive uprising gripped the island in 1843. This was followed by a revolt in Ponce in 1848.

In 1808, Napoleon invaded spain, and King Ferdinand VII cut out. To gain support against the french, several spanish leaders got together to rule in the king's name. This became the spanish cortes. The cortes made a slick political move: they declared the colonies "an integral part of spain," and then told the colonies to have elections and send a representative to sit on the cortes. Not only was this supposed to tighten the spanish empire against the french empire, but it was also supposed to help unify the colonies against the spanish possessions that were fighting for freedom, like Simon Bolivar in Venezuela. However, when Puerto Rico's militia was sought to fight rebels in Venezuela, the spanish official in charge of this business found out by means of a note nailed to his door one night that no Puerto Rican would fight fellow oppressed people who wanted freedom from spain.

The cortes gave Puerto Rico a few civil rights in 1809. Ramon Power y Giralt, one of those liberal, reform intellectuals whose imagination had been turned on in europe, represented the island. He helped draft the spanish constitution of 1812 (which was modeled after the french version of 1791), which guaranteed the rights of the individual, with the cortes as their protector.

Notice what had been done. The empire was threatened at its base, and gave its properties some vague rights, which amounted to sending a representative to spain. What could Ramon Power really do in spain? Taking a page from spanish history, the u.s. empire was to do this much later.

So far in this series, we have mentioned that Spaniards, Tainos, and Africans lived in Puerto Rico. We said that in the 1700's, the jibaro first appeared. The merger of the various blood lines continued until, in the early 1800's, a unique nation of people was born, arising from the soil. These people came into the world oppressed, and their African or Taino mother also knew nothing but the chains of slavery and cruelty at the hands of the spanish rapist. As soon as this new nation breathed the air of Boriken (this was the original spelling), a determination to be free set in, and a change was demanded.

This was the Puerto Rican.

As the 1800's began, Puerto Rico had been a colony for 300 years. Three hundred years. Since we are still a colony, we are the oldest, uninterrupted colonized people in history.

Although the new Puerto Rican had no political parties, there were three definite political tendencies: conservatives, who were loyal to spain, liberals who wanted a kind of union with spain, but self-rule and reform; and separatists, who wanted spain to go to hell.

This political storm that was brewing still goes on today. As Puerto Ricans came into the world and checked out history, an important question was asked: What were the spanish doing here?

LIBERATE PUERTO RICO NOW!

Pablo "Yoruba" Guzman
Minister of Information
YOUNG LORDS PARTY

....

History of Boriken 4

(From the newspaper *Palante*, 19 March–2 April 1971, volume 3, number 5)

No history of Puerto Rico would be correct if we didn't mention the activities of people elsewhere in the world. As we said last issue, Africans in the Antillean islands and in the u.s. revolted against slavery. One of the most significant uprisings occurred in Haiti. The success of the struggle on this island encouraged other slaves to do the same. Haiti was a french colony. When the revolution broke out in france in 1791, the colonies seized this moment to break for freedom.

Toussaint L'Ouverture was born a slave in Haiti. When the wave of uprisings hit Haiti in 1791, Toussaint quickly became its leader. In 1793, the National Convention in france outlawed slavery. At 50, L'Ouverture (meaning "the opening," for his ability to smash through enemy lines) was no longer a slave. Haiti prospered under L'Ouverture, who put Black people in power. Some people called him "The Black Napoleon" because he defeated the best of that emperor's generals. Actually, it would be more correct to call napoleon, "the white Toussaint L'Ouverture."

Ramon Power, elected to the vice-presidency of the spanish cortes in 1812, continued talking to deaf ears about Puerto Rico's needs for better schools; the right to form labor guilds (like a union); and preference for Puerto Ricans for public posts. He could have used the same arguments in the u.s. congress today.

The new spanish constitution, representative of a hurried liberal breeze in Madrid over to the threat of napoleon, was effective for Puerto Rico in March, 1812. Now Puerto Ricans were not colonial subjects; they were citizens of spain. Goodness, the u.s. certainly knows spanish history (one old dog passing tricks on [to] the new one). Ramon Power died in spain in 1813, still talking to deaf ears.

Too bad. The brother missed out on 1814. If he had been around, he might have started picking up the gun. That year, the french pulled out of spain, ferdinand VII went back on the throne as spain's king, and Puerto Ricans, Spanish citizens for almost two years, were now colonial subjects—again.

Simon Bolivar was leading a successful campaign against french rule in Venezuela. The Dominicans began fighting spain. They encouraged the separatists of Puerto Rico to do the same. Correctly, it was felt that spain, with problems at home, could not deal with rebellions in all of its colonies at once. Che Guevara knew the same thing about the u.s. when he said "two, three, many Vietnams" had to occur. The people of the world are using this strategy today in Brazil, Vietnam, Angola, Hawaii, the Philippines, and inside amerikkka itself. General Antonio Valero was a Puerto Rican who was in the spanish army, but saw spain for what it was, the enemy of his people. He joined the revolution in Mexico in 1821, then left to fight spaniards in Columbia [sic]. On the way over, pirates forced his boat to dock in Havana for safety. There the spanish picked him up and had him jailed. Cuban patriots helped him escape, and he fought in Columbia [sic]. Bolivar was going to have Valero lead a force to Puerto Rico in 1827, but it was called off. Antonio Valero should be a model to Puerto Rican g.i.'s of a brother to help his people defeat that enemy.

As you can see, revolutionary activity, against spain and other empires was on the rise everywhere. Practically all of South America was up in arms, including Columbia [sic], Venezuela. and Peru. In the rest of Latin America, there were wars being fought in Mexico, Cuba, Santo Domingo, and Martinique. In Puerto Rico, a conspiracy was discovered and crushed.

ferdinand VII, still not fully in charge of his empire, restored the 1812 constitution in 1820 as a smokescreen of reform. But in 1823, when he was in complete control, he threw the constitution out again. This time, he was looking to bring in fascism, complete, all-out repression in the colonies.

What stopped his plans short was that the united states, flexing its newfound muscles, instituted a thing called the monroe doctrine, saying european powers were to keep out of the Americas. This flim-flam stated that the u.s. would not tolerate outside interference. Fine, but why were the Americas supposed to tolerate the u.s.? Rather than come in with total crushing power, ferdinand set up military governors to rule over the island. For the next 42 years, a parade of 14 of these clowns ruled as little caesars. The first of these, Miguel de la Torre, at first used police state tactics, then changed his regime to the three B's: baile, butella, y baraja. By keeping the people partying all the time, he hoped to make them forget reality. Watch for other rulers later in our history who used variations of the three B's (drugs).

Finally in 1833 the king died. The liberals in spain and the colonies now put together a revolt that restored the 1812 constitution.

[EDITOR'S NOTE: The text ends abruptly and does not continue elsewhere in the issue or subsequent issues.]

....

History of Boriken 5

(From the newspaper *Palante*, 5-19 April 1971, volume 3, number 6)

On January 2, 1868, Betances drafted a Provisional Constitution for the Puerto Rican Republic while he was in Santo Domingo. Talk went around that spain was thinking of selling Puerto Rico and Cuba to the u.s. All of the Antillean revolutionary leaders quickly met on February 24, 1868, to plan uprisings.

lieutenant general juan prim, who set up the bando negro, was succeeded in 1848 by lieutenant general san juan de pezuelas, as governor of Puerto Rico. pezuelas felt that too much education made people subversive. He passed a law that required all persons "without means" (the average Puerto Rican) to carry a passbook, called the libreta. The libreta had all sorts of identifying information about a person, and when stopped by police, it had to be produced upon request, or else you went to jail. When this kind of condition exists, that is when fascism (police state) is most obvious. A day will come when in El Caño, in La Perla, and in the South Bronx, Puerto Ricans will have to carry a libreta for the gringo. The libreta lasted 19 years.

pezuelas was a true fascist. He passed laws that said people couldn't move to another house, travel between cities, or have parties without permission. When fascism is the order of the day, any kind of activity which could in the least possible way raise the people's spirits is banned.

A cholera epidemic plagued the island from 1855-1856, killing 30,000. A doctor in Mayaguez did such selfless work among the people that everyone soon knew and loved him. His name was Ramon Emeterio Betances. Betances was born April 8, 1827. In 1856, when he was 29, Betances went into the first of what was to become a series of exiles from Puerto Rico. Betances' work in Mayaguez during the epidemic brought him in touch with the African slave. His first exile resulted from his campaign to end slavery, and his desire to make Puerto Rico free.

By this time, there were definite political parties in Puerto Rico: the loyalists, who favored spanish domination, the liberals, who wanted spanish protection but also wanted Puerto Ricans to rule the island; and the Separatists, who wanted nothing of the spanish, and wanted to set up an independent republic. The Separatists, led by Betances, believed that they were not alone in their struggle against spain. They felt a unity with other peoples in Latin America whom spain controlled. Betances believed in an Antillean Federation that included Puerto Rico, Cuba, Dominican Republic, and Haiti. For all the years that Betances struggled, until his death in 1898, the patriots in all these countries worked together, trying to coordinate the pace of the different revolutionary movements in their countries.

In 1864, an armed revolt swept though the Dominican Republic. Separatists in Puerto Rico circulated a document throughout the island declaring solidarity with the Dominican, Cuban, and Haitian peoples' struggles for freedom. The document called the Puerto Rican people to arms. The new governor, messina, ordered Betances, who had returned from exile two years before, to meet him at the governor's palace, La Forteleza. He threatened Betances with hanging if he continued organizing the people against spain. Betances told him that on the night after his hanging, he would sleep better that day than messina.

Needless to say, Betances went into exile again, to St. Thomas in the Virgin Islands. From St. Thomas, he issued his "Ten Commandments" to Puerto Rico, a basic ten point program around which to unite Puerto Ricans. The ten points included:

1. Abolition of slavery.
2. Right to vote on budgets.
3. Religious freedom.
4. Freedom of speech.
5. Freedom of trade.
6. Freedom of press.
7. Right of assembly.
8. Right to bear arms.
9. Rights of citizenship.
10. Right to elect own rulers.

A new governor, marchessi, came into power. Meanwhile in spain, the decline of that empire was setting in. An attempt was made to maintain some kind of grip on power by inviting representatives from the colonies to spain (readers of this series will know that spain used this trick many times in the past). The Cuban and Puerto Rican representatives raised hell and mounted pressure on the spanish.

In Puerto Rico, a revolt of local artillery men occurred, and Betances, who was back again from exile, was given the blame. It is doubtful as to whether or not Betances had anything to do with this. At any rate, marchessi was trying to send Betances and another Separatist leader, Segundo Ruiz Belvis, to Madrid. Belvis and Betances fled, first to Santo Domingo, and then to New York. At that time, a revolutionary junta of Cubans was operating in New York, and they were supporters of Betances' Antillean Federation.

The revolutionaries in Latin America knew that spain was getting weaker, and liberation would be gotten much easier than if the u.s. was to control the islands. However, agents that had infiltrated the revolutionary ranks and the big mouths of idealistic patriots combined to tip the spanish off, and the conspiracy was busted.

In danger of being arrested again, Betances went to St. Thomas. Working with Separatists on the island, Betances built up a force of 10,000 at St. Thomas. The revolutionaries, who had set September 29 as their target date, had fighters led by generals in many key cities. All through the Antilles, revolutions were set to take place in the fall of 1868 also.

The revolution was betrayed. All along the coast of Puerto Rico, facing St. Thomas, spanish soldiers were stationed, waiting to repel an invasion. The main leaders were rounded up and arrested throughout Puerto Rico. Word that the plans had leaked out reached Manuel Rojas in Lares, who in turn contacted an American, Mathias Bruckman, who was heading the revolutionaries in Mayaguez. Bruckman took his troops to Lares, in time to meet the advanced September 23 date for the uprising.

The revolutionaries took Lares on September 23, the day we call "El Grito de Lares." The following day, spanish troops crushed the patriots at Lares. The wave of repression that followed Lares was so overpowering that the jails of Arecibo and Aguadilla could not hold any more people. New jails were built all over the island.

general prim, who had set up the bando negro, led a movement in spain that ended monarchies (kings and queens as rulers), and rulers were created and elected to office.

On October 10, the Cuban war for Independence began against spain with the Grito de Yara, similar to the Grito de Lares. The Cuban Revolution was more successful, and fighting lasted over a period of years.

Betances, meanwhile, continued the struggle from abroad. When it seemed that his companeros y companeras at Lares were going to get the death sentence, he urged activity among the people. The people responded so well that the death sentences weren't given out. Betances' Antillean Federation supporters won in the elections. Betances was offered the Presidency, but he declined.

Ramon Emetrio Betances was among the first to warn of the growing danger the u.s. posed to Latins. spain, unable to maintain the grip it once had abroad, gave Puerto Rico the right to elect their own officials, on November 28, 1897. The elections were held February of 1898; the government began functioning July, 1898. The u.s. battleship maine blew up (suspiciously convenient for amerikkka) in a Cuban harbor, and the states declared war against spain. So, in July 25, 1898, a general nelson miles landed in Puerto Rico at Guanica with 16,000 troops. The reason why amerikkka ran through Puerto Rico and not Cuba was that an armed revolt was taking place in Cuba. One of the great Puerto Rican patriots and revolutionaries died in France on September 16, 1898. Betances died saddened: the Spaniards were out, but what was to become of Puerto Rico under the gringo?

> APRIL 8—BETANCES' BIRTHDAY!
> THE DUTY OF EVERY PUERTO RICAN IS TO MAKE THE REVOLUTION!
> LIBERATE PUERTO RICO NOW!
> Pablo "Yoruba" Guzman
> Minister of Information
> YOUNG LORDS PARTY

....

History of Boriken 6

(From the newspaper *Palante*, 19 April to 1 May 1971, volume 3, number 7)

Now we are about the see some truly horrible things happen to our people since the amerikkkans landed. In the u.s., capitalism was changing over from free enterprises to monopoly capitalism. At one time it was possible for almost any white male in the u.s. to work hard, compete in business, and with skill, make some money; this was free enterprise. What happened was that the true greed of certain people surfaced (which is inevitable under capitalism), and a clique of capitalists began to take shape. These thieves eliminated their opposition, often by murder, and took absolute control in certain areas, such as railroads, steel, shipping, etc. . . . In amerikkkan schoolbooks, these crooks are called "Captains of Industry"; "Robber Barons" would be more correct.

Some of these Robber Barons were john d. rockefeller, cornelius vanderbilt, andrew carnegie, and marcus a. harman. All of these were backers of then president mckinley. Big business, which is what these "gentlemen" represented, looked for new markets to carry their disease of capitalism. It was clear that the amerikkkans were looking for some weak country with property to defeat so they could take these lands for their own.

One country fit the bill well: spain. By this time a large amount of Puerto Ricans and Cubans were living in New York. Most of these were supporters of revolutions for independence in their countries. However, there were a few traitors in their midst. Right after the u.s. battleship maine blew up, suspiciously, in Havana Harbor, dr. julio j. henna, one of these Puerto Rican traitors, went to washington d.c. to meet with senator lodge from massachusetts. lodge was a part of an even more openly imperialist clique than mckinley, which was headed by theodore roosevelt, who was under secretary of the navy at the time. After meeting with henna, lodge took him to see Roosevelt. henna then told Roosevelt of the positions, strengths and weaknesses of spain's army in Puerto Rico, how the people would react, where support would come from—in short, this fool actually was trying to get the u.s. to invade Puerto Rico! His words flattered roosevelt tremendously, and Puerto Rico fell under amerikkka's expansion gaze.

The spanish-amerikkkan war lasted 115 days; of these, only 17 were fought in Puerto Rico. general nelson miles, who commanded the invasion force of 16,000 troops, lost only four soldiers, with 40 more wounded. When miles landed on July 25, 1898, he declared: "We have come not to make war upon the people of a country that for centuries have been oppressed, but on the contrary to bring you protection . . . to promote your prosperity, and to bestow upon you the immunities and blessings of the liberal institutions of our government."

Needless to say, these were words of honey miles used to throw the people off. Also, one of the main problems that was to occur for a long period of time was that miles spoke english. A common saying at the time was "at least you could understand the spanish." The plan miles actually was going to proceed with on the island was in his pocket sent to him by the secretary of war:

DEFENSE DEPARTMENT SUBSECRETARY'S OFFICE WASHINGTON D.C.

"This department, in agreement with the State and Navy Department, judge it is necessary to complete the instructions given for the future campaign in the Antilles, with some observations relating to the political mission that falls on you as Commander in Chief of the Armed Forces.

"The problem of the Antilles has two aspects: one relating to the Island of Cuba, and the other to that of Puerto Rico, and thus our aspirations and our politics must be observed in a different manner for each case.

"In regards to Puerto Rico, this is an acquisition we must make and preserve, which will be easy because the change in rule will bring more benefits than losses to the interests created there, because they are more cosmopolitan than Spaniards.

"For this conquest the necessary methods are relatively easy, proclaiming carefully the observance of all the precepts of the laws between civilized and Christian nations and only in extreme cases must fortified cities be bombed. To avoid conflict our troops will land in unpopulated areas on the South of the Island. The lives and properties of the civil population will be respected.

"I recommend you forcefully and specifically that by all the means necessary you try to obtain the good will of the colored races for two purposes: the first to have their help in case of a plebiscite for the annexation, and, in second place, taking into account the main motive and object of the expansion of the U.S. in the Antilles is to resolve quickly and efficiently our racial problems that will continue to increase each day due to the propagation of the blacks, who will follow to the West Indies once they are convinced of the advantages."

That was the real message.

amerikkka was now in possession of Guam, the Phillipines, Cuba and Puerto Rico. On all these islands, the people didn't know what the amerikkkans were talking about when they spoke about "liberating you people from oppression." In Cuba at the time of the amerikkkan invasion, an armed revolt for independence was already under way. This prevented the u.s. from getting a firm grip on the island, as they were able to do in Puerto Rico. However, people in Puerto Rico didn't feel particularly "oppressed" either; they had just won control of their government and with time could have built an independent economic base. But the gringo changes all.

A country is not really free unless the people have absolute control over their political, military, economic and cultural lives. The u.s. proceeded to impose its authority in all four areas.

Political: From 1898 to 1908, Puerto Rico was ruled by military governors; then in 1901, the u.s. congress passed the foraker act, which said a civil government was to be set up on the island. However, all top officials were gringos appointed by the president of the u.s.

Military: the u.s. army immediately set up shop on the island, as the spanish army withdrew. The initial military footing was given between 1898 and 1901, when the military governors placed Puerto Rico under u.s. rule, thus forbidding Boricuas from bearing arms, as this would be a traitorous act against the u.s.

Economic: Here the u.s. worked its most subtle and vicious crimes. Under the second governor, gen. guy v. henry, who began his rule in 1899, the currency of Puerto Rico was changed from the spanish peso to the amerikkkan dollar. Since there was more gold and silver in the spanish peso, the u.s. gained more than 60-cents per peso, or $200 million, with the passing of one law. Most of the island's economy at that time (2/3 of all exports) was coffee. Forty-one percent of the land was taken up by coffee; 91% of this belonged to peasants. The u.s. then imposed high tariffs, or taxes on all coffee being sent abroad. And for a final blow, in 1899, a great hurricane, San Ciriaco, wiped out the coffee crops, killing 3,000 people and leaving 1/4 of the population of one million homeless. These things (currency devaluation, tariffs, hurricane) drove people bankrupt overnight. The peasants (campesinos y campesinas) left the country and their land to go to the city looking for work. Arrabales (slums) began to rise in San Juan. amerikkkan business bought acres and acres of land from people who sold it for practically nothing. These Robber Barons, like Vanderbilt (who once said: "What do I care for the law when I have the power"), gloated while extreme poverty hit the island. An example of their racist attitude is that the u.s. congress gave the hurricane victims what amounted to 80 cents each. Eighty cents!

We will move on to the cultural exploitation of our people next issue.

QUE VIVA PUERTO RICO LIBRE!
DRIVE THE GRINGO INTO THE SEA!
ALL POWER TO OUR PEOPLE!
Pablo "Yoruba" Guzman
Minister of Information
YOUNG LORDS PARTY

....

History of Boriken 7

(From the newspaper *Palante*, May 1971, volume 3, number 8)

The cultural takeover of our People was made possible by the political domination of Puerto Rico by the gringos. amerikkkan teachers were brought into the elementary schools, and English was taught. spanish could now be studied, like Russian or french, as a "foreign language." These teachers taught amerikkkan history, or "george washington is the father of our country and abraham lincoln freed the slaves" (whose country? whose slaves?). In short, the u.s. managed, in one generation, to intensify the replacement of western standards of acceptance for third world people (people of color) standards. When a culture is destroyed, killed off, by another culture's aggression, this is called cultural suicide.

So now the foothold was firmly entrenched.

The Foraker Act of 1900 had established the u.s. as the "legitimate" government on the island. At this time, the u.s. congress was trying to decide what to do with its newly ripped off lands. Some people called for eventual statehood. But Whitelaw Reid, who helped frame the treaty that ended the spanish-amerikkkan war, wrote: "In no circumstances . . . should they (Puerto Rico, Cuba, etc.) be admitted as states of the union. Their people come from all regions, all races, all conditions, from pagan ignorance and the verge of cannibalism. . . ." Reid later said: ". . . the enemy (u.s.) is at the gates. . . ." Another racist, Neely, wrote that the Puerto Rican population ". . . varies much even in race and color, ranging from spanish white trash to full blooded Ethiopians." And these are the feelings of the people who came to "liberate" us. You can see how the enemy used racism to further divide us.

Meanwhile, some political tendencies formed into political parties. One started in 1902 and was called the Amerikkkan Federal Party. Another, formed in 1903, was the Republican Party. Both were opportunist, or cunning, because their basis of existence was not for the people's interest, but their own: they hoped to get close to the u.s. and pass themselves off as the leaders of the Nation so that they would be the Party in power.

The greatest opportunist of this time was Luis Munoz Rivera, a leader of the Federal Party. Rivera led a group that in 1904 founded the Union Party, claiming to be more patriotic than the republicans. The republicans were in power.

Against con artist reformists like Munoz were patriots like Jose de Diego, who spoke out eloquently for national liberation.

Munoz Rivera eventually boot-licked his way to the resident commissionership in washington d.c. From there, he ran for assembly from Mayaguez in 1912, leaning towards an "independence" ticket. The fighters for freedom, like Jose de Diego, pushed a bill calling for national rights to self-determination. Naturally, rivera could not back this.

The first world war began in 1914, except for the u.s. The states decided to wait until they could come in late and strong and take a bigger share of the loot. In 1917, the jones act made Puerto Ricans u.s. citizens; a few months later, the u.s. entered the war! This conveniently made us eligible for the draft, and we've died in wars ever since. We must organize and refuse, as a strange country, to make us fight for them against another country that is really friendly to us.

Then the u.s. pulled a flim-flam (trick) of the type that has earned it distinction as the most degenerate country in history. Since many Puerto Ricans were furious over becoming u.s. citizens, the gringos smilingly said, if you wished, you could sign a statement refusing to be a citizen. Of course, this was like walking into an fbi office and admitting you bombed the capitol. Those of us who didn't sign loyalty statements or signed as being opposed to citizenship were subject to constant police harassment, files were kept on them, they couldn't get jobs, etc.

During "the war to make the world safe for democracy," in 1917, a young harvard law graduate entered the draft, and being a dark-skinned Puerto Rican, transferred to Puerto Rico in the hope that he would not be segregated. But he was assigned to an all black regiment. He made lieutenant. After the war, the brother began a journalism career exposing the u.s. as an imperialist power. Meanwhile, the union party fell through many changes, developing within it opposing tendencies. One formed itself as the nationalist association around 1925, and the other became known as the liberal party.

This became clear at a birthday rally for Jose de Diego on April 16, 1925. The first speaker saluted the flag of the united states, which flew at the rally, and said how it stood for liberty and justice. He made an appeal to the conscience of the gringo (what conscience?) to let Puerto Ricans rule themselves.

The next speaker started off by saying, "Flag of the u.s., I do not salute you! Because while it is true that elsewhere you might have stood for liberty and justice, here you stand for piracy and plunder." The young speaker received tremendous ovation, and, needless to say, it was the journalist. His name was Pedro Albizu Campos.

That year he became vice-president of the Nationalist Association. Later, he was to travel throughout Latin America, building ties of solidarity with similarly oppressed nations who have been close to us in history, such as the Dominican Republic, Haiti and Cuba. The freedom lover returned in 1929, after three years, and saw the nationalists needed strong organizational help.

In 1930, Albizu Campos became president of what is now the Nationalist Party of Puerto Rico.

With sights aimed at their targets, the Nationalists gave the u.s. hell for the next twenty years.

LIBERATE PUERTO RICO NOW!
DRIVE THE GRINGOS AND ALL TRAITORS INTO THE SEA!
Pablo "Yoruba" Guzman
Minister of Information
YOUNG LORDS PARTY

....

History of Boriken 8

(From the newspaper *Palante,* May 1971, volume 3, number 9)

Before we pass on to the growing struggle between the u.s. and Puerto Ricans, spearheaded by the Nationalist Party, let us look for a moment at the history of the Puerto Rican in amerikkka.

Puerto Ricans were in New York as early as the 1860's. But by 1910, there were only 500 Puerto Ricans in the city. A great leap was made when the jones act was passed in 1917, which imposed u.s. citizenship on us. There were 2,000 of us in New York by 1920. Steamers arrived from Puerto Rico in Brooklyn at pier 35. Although the main target was New York and its jobs, some steamers went to New Orleans. The trip took five days. Passage cost from $20 to $30, but the way money is worth today, this is higher than the plane fare between Puerto Rico and the u.s.

The first Puerto Rican colony of size in amerikkka was Brooklyn, in an area occupying President Sackert, Union, Degran, Van Broat, and Callor Streets. During World War 1, Puerto Ricans were employed in industry and commerce, especially in the Brooklyn Navy Yard. But as the war ended, Puerto Ricans were the first to be laid off to make room for the returning soldiers. Other Spanish speaking people during this time could go to their consulates when they were harassed, and get immediate action. This was a privilege given to them because they were from independent countries. Puerto Ricans could not go anyplace to complain when the "authorities" didn't enforce the laws, as we were from a colony, a property of the states.

The need to unite in a foreign land was great, and so the social clubs formed. The oldest that still exists today is La Razon, founded in 1901. Puerto Rican political organizations, "legal" ones, were mostly all democratic. Puerto Ricans went this way to obtain help from democrats who saw a chance to have a large future voting bloc. The democrats actually did something in the beginning, like busting a white slave ring, bringing sisters to the u.s. on a promise of work. The racket of selling phony baptism certificates was also busted.

El Barrio began to contain Puerto Ricans in 1922. Cubans and other Latins had begun living there earlier, and the streets were filled with political exiles, artists, writers, and intellectuals. What is known as La Marqueta started ceatering to Puerto Rican tastes in 1935. Botanicas, or shops where herbs can be bought for our people who still believe in espiritismo, also opened up then. As soon as Boricuas in New York could do so, we began playing bolita, gambling on the horses. An outlaw operation, today bolita can take in one million dollars a day, ahead of general motors. One large bank in El Barrio does $20,000 a day in business. The Cubans brought bolita over in the 1920's, but were displaced by the Italians.

By 1930, 45,000 Puerto Ricans lived in New York City, and we were spreading throughout the Eastern cities and westward to Chicago and Cleveland.

In 1930, when Albizu was President of the Nationalist Party, theodore roosevelt was one of the greediest imperialists the u.s. ever had for a president. He had the nerve to call himself the "jibaro of La Fortaleza."

Albizu and the Nationalist Party ran in the 1932 elections to show up the foolishness of the vote for an oppressed people. Like the Young Lords Party, the Nationalist Party has never been to elections since. As Don Pedro says, elections are a divide and conquer trick, splitting the nation on the question of the vote. The answer, he said, was to "smash the machinery."

The gasoline strike of 1933 was led by the Nationalist Party, and Albizu went from town to town, boosting the strike and spreading a message of revolution against the u.s. In 1934, a general farm workers strike again followed the Nationalist Party lead. The waves of a growing, grass roots liberation movement reached governor gen. Blanton winship and the police chief, colonel riggs. When they saw the mood of our people, they began plotting to stop the Nationalist Party in general, and Albizu Campos in particular. The gasoline strike won, and Don Pedro became the idol of the working class.

In October, 1935, Albizu gave a speech condemning president franklin d. roosevelt, the so-called "legal" Puerto Rican Parties, and the passivity of our students.

He was invited to speak at the University of Puerto Rico at Rio Piedras. The Nationalist Party Intelligence Section discovered that winship and riggs had a plan to assassinate Don Pedro, through traitorous students. A Nationalist Party leader, Ramon S. Pagan, went instead. Enraged that Campos had escaped, police killed Pagan and three other Nationalists in their car, wounding another (later tried for terrorism and attempted murder). In retaliation, two patriots later assassinated col. riggs. They were Elias Beauchamp and Hiram Rosado.

A lesson was taught: an eye for an eye, a tooth for a tooth. One fault was that a People's Army, silent and effective, had not been formed. So repression hit the Party.

> DRIVE THE ENEMY INTO THE SEA!
> LIBERATE PUERTO RICO NOW!
> Pablo "Yoruba" Guzman
> Minister of Information
> YOUNG LORDS PARTY

....

History of Boriken 9

(From the newspaper *Palante*, June 1971, volume 3, number 11)

After the shooting of colonel riggs on February 21, 1936 by Hiram Rosado and Elias Beauchamp (the cops later beat them to death in the stationhouse), shootings continued in the streets. Don Pedro's speeches attracted more and more hundreds of thousands of poor Puerto Ricans to the Liberation cause. Clearly, this man and his movement had to be stopped.

In June of 1936, Don Pedro heard he was to be arrested and walked into a police station to confront his enemy. They said they knew nothing of his arrest; the next day, he and 7 members of the Nationalist Party leadership were arrested for "conspiracy to overthrow the u.s. government established in Puerto Rico." Some day the u.s. government will bring these or similar charges against the Young Lords Party.

The day of the arrests, Nationalist headquarters all over the island were raided. (One rifle was found.) Sedition (subversion) was added to Don Pedro's charges. Under Puerto Rican law, there is no such charge as sedition, but slaveowner's law overrules even a puppet governor's law. We must learn that we will not really be free until our people control the government, the army and the economy—entirely free of outside domination. It is foolish and suicidal for us to believe otherwise and vote. The minute you step into the voting booth, you're saying that the gringo has the right to keep a foot on your back, shoving you into the mud.

The first trial for the eight patriots had a jury of 7 Puerto Ricans and 5 amerikkkans. In 15 days they reached a hung jury, as in the recent case of the Black Panther Party Chairman Bobby Seale and Sister Ericka Huggins. Even though the judge dismissed it, the amerikkkan enemy ordered a second trial. General blanton winship, the governor at this time, picked a jury of ten amerikkkans and two Puerto Ricans, who were traitors anyways. Don Pedro's companeros got six years and he received ten to be served in Atlanta Federal Penitentiary.

A point is reached at different times in the struggle, which the Vietnamese call the "Thoi Co." This means "critical moment," and it is that time when conditions are most right for a great leap to be made by the people. But when the time comes, people must be ready to seize it, or the enemy will take advantage. Revolutionaries build the conditions for "Thoi Co," and must also be good at preparing the forces just before the critical moment and keeping the forces steady afterwards. The Nationalist Party did not rely primarily on analyzing conditions surrounding and within our people's freedom movement, so they did not make best use of the "critical moment" period. A people's army was not being built that could deliver strong blows and escape. Also the popular classes (the "people"—workers, lumpen, and some of the petty bourgeoisie. For a definition of lumpen see the article in this issue) were not being developed to assume positions of leadership in the Party. Nonetheless, a critical moment in the period of u.s. control over Puerto Ricans was approaching built by the Nationalist Party.

The enemy moved from their end to seize the time, too. Jaime Benitez, who is now head of the University of Puerto Rico and a traitor who orders beatings and murders of students who protest the presence of the amerikkka he works for, spoke out at that time condemning u.s. brutality and in favor of "independence." The u.s. enemy was cunningly pushing individuals out of nowhere as "leaders." In reality they would sell our people out once elected or listened to. The enemy will use this trick today as another "Thoi Co" or "critical moment" is approaching in the liberation struggle. In case the sentiment for freedom gets too "hot," they will use as a safety valve the trick of "giving" us "independence." Some of us will even be leaders in the new "independent" government. But we will not really be free as amerikkkan business will still control the capitalist economy, and therefore be a major influence on the "independent" government.

The most treacherous snake of all that the amerikkkans produced from the "instant Puerto Rican leader" grab bag was luis munoz marin. Marin campaigned with benitez to free Don Pedro. More will be said about this snake later in the series.

Most important our people were moving to free Don Pedro. One march of 100,000 people went through all the towns of the island. As it neared San Juan, winship ordered his troops to "shoot to kill." Under such conditions the Nationalist Party leadership did not take the march into San Juan. Laws were passed against demonstrations or showings of the freedom spirit of any kind; not even wreaths of flowers could be placed at the graves of fallen companeros y companeras. On March 21, 1937 thousands of people gathered in Ponce's town square to march anyway. This was the anniversary of the abolition of slavery, a victory made possible long before by the work of Ramon Emeterio Betances. On the orders of winship and riggs' successor, colonel orbeta, police opened fire. 22 people were killed and over 200 were wounded. This is known today as the "Ponce Massacre."

The succession of events, the assassination of riggs, the killing of Rosado and Beauchamp, the arrest of Don Pedro, and the Ponce Massacre combined to bring about the "critical moment"—u.s. rule was in its most contested stage.

> POWER TO THE POPULAR CLASSES!
> DRIVE THE ENEMY INTO THE SEA!
> LIBERATE PUERTO RICO NOW!
> Pablo "Yoruba" Guzman
> Minister of Information
> YOUNG LORDS PARTY

....

History of Boriken 10

(From the newspaper *Palante*, 4-18 July 1971, volume 3, number 12)

A "critical moment" approached over the future u.s. role in Puerto Rico. The u.s. enemy thought they could stop the growing liberation feeling by imprisoning Don Pedro as they did in June of 1936. Before his imprisonment, Don Pedro had been raising nationalist feelings through his speeches to Puerto Ricans all over the island. At that time, in the 1930's, the world, including the u.s., was going through the Great Economic Depression. Capitalism the world over suffered a breakdown that lasted 10 years. This is happening now—the u.s. is in economic trouble, what nixon calls a "recession."

Since the depression was on, thousands of Puerto Rican workers were out of work or working for practically nothing. Don Pedro spoke to and received much support from these workers. However, he spoke to them on the basis of their being Puerto Ricans and not on the basis of their being workers. He appealed mainly to their nationalism, because the Nationalist Party did not have an understanding of the different classes in our society. Therefore, they did not organize workers, but instead around their being Puerto Rican. It is important to recognize the class nature of capitalist society, because class divisions are the major cause of antagonisms (conflicts) and divisions among the people. (For more on class, see *Palante* Vol. 3, No. 10.)

Workers' power first had a formal voice in Puerto Rico with the rise of the Socialist Party in 1900, the first political party in Puerto Rico with a clear ideology (system of thinking). The Party grew out of a May 1st Workers' Congress held in 1900. (On September 25 of this year, the Young Lords Party will conduct a Workers' Conference in the u.s. similar to the one in 1900, out of which a workers' organization will be formed.) That year, 5500 workers were Socialist Party members or members of a Socialist Party workers organization (syndicates). By 1920, there was a membership of 28,000 workers. Seeing the growth in their numbers and their unity around common interests created a consciousness in workers' minds of their class status (proletarians, or working class) and increased their militancy.

In 1914, this workers' party won the city elections in Arecibo, the first time workers controlled an administration in the western hemisphere. The Socialist Party made the mistake of thinking it had won power. Power is won only when all the political machinery, the economic base and the military are in the hands of the popular classes (the most oppressed classes: workers, lumpen, and some segments of the petty bourgeoisie. For a definition of lumpen, see last issue of Palante), and this will never happen through the vote, but by armed struggle. The Socialist Party was formally constituted in Cayey in 1915. In the 1917 elections, the Party polled 24,000 votes. By 1920, this had increased to 83,000 votes, and by 1936 to 144,000 votes. The enemy, who is fully aware of class divisions and the strength of workers since they cause those divisions and employ workers to make their profits, became alarmed.

The success of the Russian Revolution in October of 1917 brought on a change in the Socialist Party strategy from one of reform (just wanted to change the system a little by seeking better conditions for workers, higher wages, greater voice in the government, etc.) to that of revolution (complete change), and the Party led great strikes during the Depression. It also educated workers in factories and sugar centrals as to the nature of the present order of things, and how workers have a right to change that order.

The Socialist Party was founded by a Spanish worker in Puerto Rico named Santiago Iglesias Pantin. Iglesias said that the leading class should not be made up of doctors or lawyers who trained and studied in europe or the u.s. and therefore separated themselves from the people. Nor should the leading class be made up of businessmen, but rather it should be made up of those directly exploited by business, the workers. However, Iglesias took the Party on an opportunist path (allying with liberal representatives of the exploiters, the republican party) in the "critical moment" period of 1936-1937, just when true workers' power could have brought a crippling blow to the u.s. rule. His opportunism (taking advantage of a situation to better one's own position) grew and he began to see the successes of the Socialist Party as the product of his efforts, instead of the combined efforts of all the workers. As a result, the Socialist Party began to speak again of social reforms. This was also brought on by the Party's internal splits which allowed the republican party, a party of wealthy (bourgeois) liberals, to take most of their base, while the Popular Party, made up of middle class (petty bourgeois) liberals, adopted a radical sounding program and matching rhetoric.

Also the Socialist Party became influenced to a large extent by Samuel Gompers and the Amerikkkan Federation of Labor (AFL). This man and this union sold out the workers' struggle in the united states by merely pushing for social reforms.

During this period of the "critical moment," liberals from the dominant classes, influenced by the high sounding ideals of amerikkkan "democracy" and Samuel Gompers, did not see the Puerto Rican reality and created a strong movement for reform instead of revolution. The republican party made an alliance with the now-reformist Socialist Party. The Popular Party sounded a little more radical talking about "independence" like the Nationalist Party, but still being basically reformist (not really recognizing the u.s. as a deadly enemy). Afro-Boricuas, suffering the racism of Puerto Ricans, and being extremely poor as a group, nevertheless supported the republican party, which had been headed by Jose Celso Barbosa, a Black Puerto Rican who had made it in politics, was friendly to the u.s. and tricked Afro-Boricuas into pressing for reform instead of revolution. These reformists therefore served the interests of the oppressed Puerto Ricans. In a time of the "critical moment," the enemy will, if forced to make a choice, give in to reforms so that they can gather strength and control the people with more power at a later time.

> POWER TO THE POPULAR CLASSES!
> DRIVE THE ENEMY INTO THE SEA!
> LIBERATE PUERTO RICO NOW!
> Pablo "Yoruba" Guzman
> YOUNG LORDS PARTY

....

History of Boriken 11

(From the newspaper *Palante*, 24 July–7 August 1971, volume 3, number 13)

The amerikkkan capitalists have control of Puerto Rico. How did they do this and how did this affect the Puerto Rican workers?

In the late 1800's, Puerto Rican business was beginning to form. One example of this was the creation of the Banco Popular in 1893, and of the Banco De Credito y Ahorra Ponceno in 1895. From 1898, the yanquis began to expand and set up Amerikkkan companies all over our nation. Bankers from Boston working with banks in Puerto Rico established a Ford company on the island in October of 1898. In February that year, Ford had already invested in the Hacienda Aguirre Sugar Plantation. The capitalists, by putting money in the most important areas of the Puerto Rican economy, got to control it. In this way, Puerto Rico's economy was in the hands of owners who lived miles away in the states and knew nothing and cared even less about our people or our country. This kind of ownership is known as absentee ownership.

The Hacienda Aguirre continued to buy land until in 1899 it became the Aguirre central syndicate with a capital of $525,000, a large amount of money for that time, made from the sweat of our people. In 1900, a group of New York capitalists formed a corporation in Puerto Rico called the South Porto Rico Sugar Company with a capital of $5 million. Many other amerikkkan companies did the same thing, like Fajardo sugar company, established with a capital of $2 million in 1905; in 1907 the Loiza sugar company was established. With such large amounts of money to use, Puerto Rican business from the beginning had no way of competing against the yanquis so that the yanquis quickly got control.

From the beginning, the tobacco industry was in the hands of absentee owners. The coffee industry, Puerto Rico's main industry under spain, was done away by foreign businessmen, who were buying up land and changing the production of sugar. This left Puerto Rican business, which was mainly in coffee, out to die. By this time, over half of the economy was financed by the national city bank of New York, the royal bank of Canada, and the bank of Nova Scotia. The rest was financed by Bancos Popular and Crédito y Ahorro Ponceño, and two new banks, Banco de Ponce and roig commercial bank.

As the number of independent Puerto Rican companies got smaller, more products had to be bought from the united states. By 1901, 78% of all products were bought from the u.s. Today, Puerto Rico is the fifth largest buyer in the world of u.s. goods. This is an important reason why the u.s. fears revolution in Puerto Rico: it would severely cripple amerikkkan economy, which is already in bad shape.

As was said last issue, the class that suffered the greatest direct exploitation from the rise of capitalism was the working class, as it always is. This is because workers provide the labor to make products. The capitalists sell these products for profits. But the workers only receive a ridiculously low amount in wages. Workers must take control of everything the capitalists now own. In this way the workers will receive the benefits. This way will also create more jobs, and will do away with the abandoned class of capitalist society, the lumpen, the unemployables, people for whom there will never be work.

The First World War caused splits in the world socialist movement which affected the internal unity of the Socialist Party, the Workers' Party in Puerto Rico. In 1934, the Nationalist Party was involved in the first great sugar workers' strike. The Communist Party of Puerto Rico (founded in 1934) was under the direction of the CP-USA which in turn was under the direction of the CP in Moscow. The political line of the CP-USA was one of reform, pushing for better conditions and higher wages, etc., for workers, and not that of revolution, which would push seizing control of the economy and the government. The Nationalist Party still believed Puerto Ricans should control the economy and the government. This put the Nationalist Party in conflict with the reformist demands of the Socialist and Communist Parties.

In 1937 there was a strike at a button factory in Villa Palmeras; the first congress of the Chauffers' Association was held in San Juan in 1937; in Toa Baja, Dorado and Bayamon, sugar workers organized and in 1938, a general dock strike ended in victory after 42 days.

The rise of workers' power was seen as a threat to the bosses. So the enemy established a reformist union, the General Confederation of Workers (CGT) in 1940. The CGT adopted a Nationalist like speech, and thus won the support of Puerto Rican workers who had been inspired by Don Pedro and turned off by the stand of the Communist Party towards nationalism. It was power in the hands of reformists and the Second World War that carried the u.s. safely through the "critical moment" and left 175 years of domination over Puerto Rico intact.

POWER TO THE POPULAR CLASSES!
LIBERATE PUERTO RICO NOW!

Pablo "Yoruba" Guzman
Minister of Information
YOUNG LORDS PARTY

....

History of Boriken 12

(From the newspaper *Palante*, 16-29 August 1971, volume 3, number 14)

By 1940, Puerto Rico was deep in an economic crisis. Living conditions were so bad, that it was clear to the popular classes ("the people"—lumpen, workers, and parts of the petty bourgeois) that great changes were needed. The united states, afraid that people would go all the way to revolution (taking control of the power of the state), wanted to stop things halfway with reforms (higher wages, more schools, etc.; things that only serve the immediate need but don't really take care of the problem, and years later you wonder how things got worse). The first thing the u.s. did was to stop the Nationalist Party—Don Pedro and the Party leadership had been imprisoned since 1936.

The next thing was to find the right kind of treacherous opportunist who would tell people what they wanted to hear and string them along so things would "cool out." From the Bohemian circles of Greenwich Village, the enemy found luis munoz marin, son of luis munoz rivera, another traitor. marin had come out against Albizu's imprisonment and was a well-known liberal. His gringa wife had given him contacts with the Socialist Party of the u.s. He dumped her to puck up ines maria mendoza, who loudly proclaimed her proinde-pendence views, to strengthen his image. In 1938, he founded the popular democratic party (pdp). For the 1940 elections, the populares came out with the line that "the question of the final political status of Puerto Rico is not an issue." This threw the independence move-ment into confusion, as great noise was made about "solving our economic problems first, then worrying about independence or statehood later." marin's party raised the slogan, "pan, tierra, libertad—bread, land and liberty" and he campaigned extensively throughout the countryside, passing himself off as a Jibaro who had been to school. The populares symbol was the pava, the straw hat the campesino wears. And on his travels, marin told people that if they voted for him, independence would be right around the corner.

And the people believed him. The faith of much of the Nation was placed in the hands of this dog, this agent of the u.s. government. populares came into power in 1940 (they still could not be governor, for governors were still gringo civilians appointed by the u.s. president). marin was senate majority leader. In 1941, roosevelt appointed rexford guy tugwell, part of his brain trust, and a liberal, to replace winship as governor. tugwell and marin got their heads together to plot the island's destiny. For the 1944 elections, marin again declared "the political status is not the issue," and many populares left in disgust in 1945 to set up the Puerto Rican Independence Party (PIP)

In 1946, tugwell resigned and truman appointed jesus t. pinero, a Puerto Rican, as governor. In 1947, PIP had gone to the UN to demand immediate action on Puerto Rico's colonial status. What alarmed the u.s. enemy even more was that in 1947, Don Pedro returned to Puerto Rico. They had hoped he would die from the tortures he received in prison. Afraid he would die in his cell, in 1943 he was sent to die in Columbia Presbyterian Hospital in New York, but in a 2 year period, he recovered. So he was sent back to Atlanta Federal Penitentiary. But in 1947, his ten year sentence was up. To combat the certain rise of the freedom spirit that would result from Don Pedro's work, the u.s. decided to hold "free" election in 1948 for governor. In the campaign, marin and the PPD were not bothered, while PIP and others were harassed by fbi and other agents. You can imagine what treatment the Nationalists received, who condemned the elections, all elections run by a foreign power, as a fraud, and that freedom must be won by fighting.

In 1948, students at the University of Puerto Rico invited Don Pedro to speak. jaime benitez rexach, then chancellor (now president), refused, and a four month strike began. The repression benitez ordered, and the fact that he was a leading ppd member, drove home to the students the nature of the enemy and their struggle. That year marked the beginning of today's Puerto Rican Student Movement.

marin, of course became governor in the "free" elections. Now he announced that Puerto Rico's political status could be decided—the island would be estado libre asociado (ela), free associated state, or commonwealth. marin followed the orders of his bosses in Washington D.C., and "decided" the question of either independence or statehood by coming up with a new animal, the commonwealth. Puerto Rico was now a u.s. colony, but had elections to elect u.s. puppets. That was the freedom!

> LIBERTY FOR PUERTO RICANS NOW!
> POWER TO THE POPULAR CLASSES!
> DRIVE THE ENEMY INTO THE SEA!

> Pablo "Yoruba" Guzman
> Minister of Information
> YOUNG LORDS PARTY

....

History of Boriken 13

(From the newspaper *Palante*, 11-23 September 1971, volume 3, number 15)

After marín became governor in 1948, the next step was to eliminate those forces which would oppose his scheme. Notice how amerikkkan "democracy" works. In 1947, 1300 Nationalists and independentistas were in jail; in 1950, the government—in San Juan and Washington—decided to wipe them out altogether. Early that year, u.s. secretary of war Jordan met in La Fortaleza with marín and other "officials." A plan for the total destruction of the Nationalist Party and the liberation movement in general was created, called the "Jordan Plan." The Nationalist Party had an intelligence system that penetrated even into La Fortaleza, and soon news of the "Jordan Plan" was brought out to our people in August of 1950. This delayed the execution of the plan to October 26. That day, a car containing 4 Nationalists was stopped and they were arrested. The Party knew this was the beginning of the plan.

Don Pedro decided to fight rather than go to jail peacefully so that an example would be set for us all. On October 30, 1950 Nationalists led by Blances Canales captured the town of Jayuya. A Nationalist group attacked La Fortaleza, while uprisings occurred in Arecibo, Utuado, Naranjito and Mayaguez. The 30th and 31st of October, troops laid siege to Don Pedro's home. He was finally arrested November 2nd, when the beginnings of "order" was restored throughout the island.

All communications and travel between the states and Puerto Rico were cut off. At the Nationalist Mission in New York, the unreliable radio broadcasts said Don Pedro had been killed. To avenge the murder, two patriots, Oscar Collazo and Griselio Torresola, set out for Washington D.C. On November 1, they attacked the home of the u.s. president truman. Torresola was killed, and Collazo is still in jail.

The October 30 uprising gave the u.s. and its regime in San Juan an excuse to break the back of the liberation movement. Although 300 Nationalists participated in the uprisings, 2000 Puerto Ricans, ranging from liberals to moderates to those formerly unconcerned about politics, were arrested.

fomento, Puerto Rico's Ministry of Economic Development, was the vehicle used to carry out the final step at securing u.s. hold of the economic base, and so in turn of the political machinery. Under the over all name operation bootstrap, formento representatives went to the u.s. to encourage industry to begin in Puerto Rico while employing Puerto Ricans in the u.s. This cheap labor force would serve amerikkkan business needs, since unskilled laborers were fighting in the Korean War, and the thousands of Puerto Rican poor could be shipped off the island to the u.s. The marín government propagandized all over the island about the jobs and riches awaiting in amerikkka. Between 1950 and 1954, 100,000 Puerto Ricans went to the u.s. By 1955, manufacturing passed agriculture as the major form of production on the island. So it was that in 55 years, a process that took at least 110 years in the u.s. and Europe was done in Puerto Rico. This quick change over is a major psychological and economic trick used by the capitalists to destroy a people.

Forty-three thousand Puerto Ricans fought in the Korean War, with 3,650 wounded, missing or dead. One out of every 42 u.s. soldiers killed in Korea was Puerto Rican. While gringo injuries came to one out of every 1,125 amerikkkans in the u.s. 1 out of every 660 Puerto Ricans on the island died in Korea. When you see this imbalance, we get a clearer picture of how we are exploited as a colony—as cannon fodder.

marín "pardoned" Don Pedro in 1953; in 1954, Lolita Lebrón led 3 brothers in a shooting of the u.s. congress, to show the world the enemy that really ran the island. Don Pedro went to jail again, this time for good. Lolita and the brothers are still in prison. The student movement organized itself officially with the start of FUPI, Federation de Universitatios Pro-Independencia (The Federation of University Students Pro Independence). In 1959, MPI was created. Rather than stop the liberation movement, a whole new generation stood ready to fight the oppressor.

DRIVE THE ENEMY INTO THE SEA!
Pablo "Yoruba" Guzman
YOUNG LORDS PARTY

From the newspaper *Palante*, 11-23 September 1971, volume 3, number 15.

5

On Education and Students

In New York, it was principally young people who had been attending various colleges in the state who founded the Young Lords; that said, the Young Lords was a community organization, not a student organization. Doing work in their immediate communities, the Young Lords partnered with students in high schools and colleges to bring their principles and politics to an even younger generation. The articles in this chapter document some of those relationships and the Young Lords' commitment to radical student politics. Furthermore, the Young Lords did not limit education to a formal institutional context; rather, they were leaders in community education and regularly taught classes out of their community offices. As other chapters and their Program and Platform illustrate, education was a core principle and goal of the Young Lords.

....

Community Education

(From the newspaper *Palante*, 5 June 1970, volume 2, number 4)

When the amerikkkan army landed in Guanica in 1898, they brought with them not only soldiers, but teachers, administrators, geologists, biologists, etc. When they got there, they threw away history books written by Puerto Ricans and had gringos rewrite our history. This new version ended in 1898, and in it the spaniards were the bad guys and the amerikkkans the good guys.

What they were doing behind all this was trying to wipe out the minds of Puerto Ricans, our culture, language (they also changed the official language to english in the schools), history and our collective understanding of what we are, a nation.

They had psychologists study us day in and day out, to prove that Puerto Ricans are a docile, passive people, who go around saying "ay bendito" and do nothing more than have babies, play the conga, la bilita, and get stoned.

Now, the YOUNG LORDS, in the tradition of Urayoan, Betances, Albizu Campos, and Alfonso Beal, have picked up from where our Brothers and Sisters have left off, and intensified the struggle for the liberation of our people, our nation. The YOUNG LORDS PARTY is now running many programs which serve our people and educate us as to the way that this capitalistic system oppresses us, like the lead poisoning, t.b. testing, and anemia testing programs.

In addition to these, we are bringing to our people community education programs. These are held in El Barrio and in the South Bronx at 7:30 every Tuesday evening. In El Barrio, St. Edwards Church, 109 St. between Madison & 5th Ave. In the South Bronx, St. Anthanasius old school, on Fox St. near Tiffany St. The sessions will educate and prepare our brothers and sisters to deal with the society in which we live. That society is racist and capitalistic and has as its desire a world empire (imperialism) built on the backs of Puerto Ricans and other Third World people. Our children must relearn spanish, our young brothers and sisters must learn of our history and culture, and our warriors, men and women, must learn of the greatness of the Puerto Rican nation. Puerto Ricans must also understand the necessity for armed struggle or be wiped out through genocide. Our brothers and sisters on the streets must learn that the pig takes many forms, from dope to genocide in the hospitals, to brutality and murder at the hands of the patrolling pigs, and imperialist robbery at the hands of the army and navy who are stealing our island of Culebra today and will try to steal the rest of Borinquen tomorrow.

We invite all Boricuas to attend our community education sessions and to bring your friends and relatives.

EACH ONE TEACH ONE!

THE DUTY OF A PUERTO RICAN IS TO MAKE THE REVOLUTION!

LIBERATE PUERTO RICO NOW!

Carlos Aponte
Education Lieutenant
YOUNG LORDS PARTY
Bronx Branch

....

Student Conference

(From the newspaper *Palante*, 16 October 1970, volume 2, number 13)

The first National Puerto Rican Student Conference was held on September 22 and 23 at Columbia University. The conference marks the first time since Puerto Ricans were brought to this country that we got together on a national scale to intensify the struggle for the education and liberation of our people.

Over 1000 Boricuas, mostly students, came from all over the united states and Puerto Rico to attend the meeting called for by the YOUNG LORDS PARTY and the Puerto Rican Student Union. The conference had two main purposes: to organize Liberate Puerto Rico Now Committees all over the u.s. and Puerto Rico; and to plan for a massive demonstration at the UN on October 30, 1970.

The conference was both an opportunity to organize and an opportunity to learn. Workshops were held dealing with: revolutionary Puerto Rican history and culture; the role of women in the revolution; high school students, college students; Latin American and Latin unity; the military and the draft; political prisoners; Third World unity; education and the media; and socialism. The people in some workshops came out with specific recommendations for organizing in their areas. The high school workshop, for example, decided that all high school groups would support any high school struggle in the city. They also recommended that our people stop pledging allegiance to the amerikkkan flag and only salute the Puerto Rican or Black Liberation flags.

Representative from various revolutionary groups spoke at the conference: MPI, the Chicano movement, FERD (Frente de Estudiantes Revolucionarios Dominicanos), FUPI, PRSU, I Wor Kuen, and the YOUNG LORDS PARTY.

Liberate Puerto Rico Now Committees were set up around the country to publicize the fact that Puerto Rico is a colony of the united states and is controlled economically, politically, and culturally by amerikkka. The Committees will be organizing for the October 30th action at the UN to demand independence for our homeland.

We feel that the Student Conference was a first step in bringing together our people to begin our fight for the right to determine our own destinies. But it was only the first step. We still have much work and a long struggle before us. Unidos Venceremos.

Ministry of Information
YOUNG LORDS PARTY

. . . .

H.S. Revolt!

(From the newspaper *Palante*, 16 October 1970, volume 2, number 13)

Bullets and bombs aren't the only ways to kill people. Bad hospitals kill our people. Rotten, forgotten buildings kill our people. Garbage and disease kill our people. And the schools kill our people.

Inefficient administrators + racist uncaring teachers + overcrowded classrooms + irrelevant curriculums + old, lying textbooks + an attitude of "don't ask too many questions" + a prison atmosphere = genocide (the mass killing of people). But students and parents everywhere are rising up against these conditions. We understand that by herding us into these brainwashing centers, our enemy is trying to kill our desire to learn, to destroy our ability to get the skills and knowledges we need to fight a society that needs us only for cheap labor and manpower for its racist wars against other Third World people.

Benjamin Franklin HS is on 116th Street and Pleasant Avenue. It can seat 2400 students but 4400 are enrolled. Three classes are held in the cafeteria during the second period. Classes are also held in the auditorium balcony and the infirmary. One office, Room 138, is being used as a "classroom" for 24 students. Room 138 is only 21 feet long and 15 feet wide. How can people learn under these conditions?

Benjamin Franklin is 99% Puerto Rican and Black. Three years ago it had the second highest dropout rate in the city—60% (Morris HS in the Bronx had the highest—64%). In January, 1969, 47% of the graduating class were refused diplomas (the highest percentage in the city). At the same time, only 4% of the graduating class applied for college (the next to lowest percentage in the city). In predominantly white schools the number of students applying to college is always over 50%.

Concerned parents, students, and community groups at Franklin feel that a first step in dealing with these conditions and problems is appointing a principal that will serve and be accountable to the community. They have chosen Melvin Taylor, a brother who grew up in the area who worked as a teacher, advisor and dean at Franklin; who has demonstrated his ability to relate to Black and Puerto Rican students; who has had extensive experience in high school and college administration; and who possesses a State Certificate for Principalship of Secondary Schools. Although the brother has all the credentials necessary for the job, the Board of Miseducation has said "no good" and has given the people a "choice" of 7 lames (all white) that they can consider for principal.

We know that the Board has no right to tell us who we can pick to run our schools. These are our brothers and sisters, our children, who are being turned off to learning and are being pushed out into the streets and out of frustration into dope and crime. The Board of Miseducation has no right at all. They are public servants, not rulers. Our taxes pay their salaries, and they're supposed to do whatever the people want them to do.

The issue at Franklin is not just a matter of a principal—it's a matter of whether or not we have the right to control our own lives. The existing structure has shown through their practice that they are not going to move against the high dropout rates and over-crowding of schools in our communities; while at the same time, they would not let these conditions exist in their own communities. If they are not going to do their job, we'll have to take it into our hands.

Already we've seen the reaction of the people who control the school system. They're scared. Principals who say they're for freedom of speech will not allow YOUNG LORDS or Black Panthers to talk with our people. Why is it that they are so afraid of words? What are they trying to hide? Sisters and brothers are being hassled and threatened with suspension for organizing, postering, leafletting, and selling literature (Jane Addams H.S. and Alfred K. Smith HS, both in the Bronx, are two places where this is happening). In other words, "Sure, you have freedom of speech—as long as I approve of what you say."

We know what the problems are. But what are we willing to do about them? Are we going to let our sisters and brothers at Franklin, Jane Addams, Smith, and Morris struggle alone? Or are we going to come together from all parts of the city to present a united front and take care of business? At the Puerto Rican Student Conference, students in the high school workshop decided that they would no longer allow our enemy to isolate each school struggle. When one school goes they all go! The time is coming for us to put these words into practice. We are being oppressed as a people, as a nation, as Puerto Ricans and Blacks; and we have to fight as a nation, not as individuals.

The YOUNG LORDS PARTY is fighting to return the educational system to the people. Point 5 of our program says, "We want community control of our institutions and land." We will publicize and support as best as we can all battles for community control of the schools. Write to us at 949 Longwood Avenue, Bronx 10454, or call 887-1225.

To all our brothers and sisters in school—if your school is messed up, if the administration and the teachers don't care and don't teach—don't let them force you to drop out. Throw them out. The schools belong to us, not to them. Take all that anger and put it to work for our people. Make revolution inside the schools. If the schools don't function for us, they shouldn't function at all!

ALL POWER TO OUR PEOPLE!
UNIDOS VENCEREMOS!

Richie Perez
Information Captain
YOUNG LORDS PARTY

From the newspaper *Palante*, 16 October 1970, volume 2, number 13.

....

Seize the Schools!

(From the newspaper *Palante*, 15 January 1971, volume 3, number 1)

On December 31, a fire bomb was thrown into the Information Center of the YOUNG LORDS PARTY in Philadelphia. We believe this attack grew out of our work in the Philly area schools. Every time any revolutionary political party moves to awaken the minds of the people, some kind of repression comes down.

The schools in Philadelphia, like all the schools in amerikkka, are used to brainwash our children, to teach them to hate our sisters and brothers around the world, to hate other countries that are fighting for their freedom. We are taught that the imperialist amerikkkan empire is really the "land of the free" just trying to help its "backward neighbors" fight off the "communist conspiracy." We are taught an incomplete and incorrect history of the united states and are given a totally distorted view of our sisters and brothers who are struggling to be free of greedy amerikkka.

Understanding that the schools are an institution to indoctrinate our people, Lords began to organize and expose the true nature and purpose of the school system. In Dobbins, for example, almost an entire class was flunked, and the students revolted. They said that the atmosphere was not made for learning. "It's just a type of classroom atmosphere where you can't ask too many questions." The students clearly saw that their teacher Mrs. Caldwell, did not understand that education means the free exchange of ideas, the examining of all possibilities, the asking and answering of questions. They asked for her removal. Other students in the school supported the demand. They too understood that the schools are supposed to function for the people, and if they don't, they shouldn't function at all. When the demand for Mrs. Caldwell was not met, the students walked out.

In Edison, another school in the area, the students had a slightly different problem. In this school it was the administration that wanted a teacher taken out. They wanted

Mohammed Togani removed because he was teaching the true history of racist amer-ikkka. The school system wants to play down the fact that every time amerikkka has dealt with Third World people it has reacted the same way. The Indians were killed for their land. The Chinese were used as slave labor to build the west coast. Chicanos were exploited to build the southwest. The Japanese were killed by an atomic bomb and were put into concentration camps here in amerikkka during world war 2. Black people were brought to this country in chains and have systematically been killed and abused for 400 years. Puerto Ricans have been used as a source of cheap labor and now that new technology is eliminating the need for unskilled labor we are being killed off. These are the things that this country doesn't want students to know. Because when we find out the truth, we're going to kick their lying asses. After the students at Edison showed that they wanted to hear the truth, the frightened school system got an injunction to prevent any Lord or Mohammed Togani from speaking in or around any Philadelphia school. But they're fools—you can never stop an idea whose time has come, or a people who have been awakened.

The struggle in the schools will continue. Meanwhile we are rebuilding our office, part of which was destroyed by the fire bomb. We ask our People to donate food, money, ply wood, or any other materials we can use for repairs. Please send them to: Young Lords Party, 1540 Franklin Street, Philadelphia, Pennsylvania 19122.

SEIZE THE SCHOOLS!
QUE VIVA PUERTO RICO LIBRE!

Casper
Ministry of Information
YOUNG LORDS PARTY
Philly Branch

....

Puerto Rican Student Union

(From the newspaper *Palante*, 19 February 1971, volume 3, number 3)

In September 1969, many students at the University of Puerto Rico were beaten and jailed after the rotc (reserve officers training corps) building on the Rio Piedras campus was burned down.

On the mainland, a group of Puerto Rican students began to look for a way to help our brothers and sisters on the island. Meeting at Lehman College in the Bronx, they collected money and sent telegrams to the colonial government and the administration of the University of Puerto Rico, protesting the persecution of students there. Eventually, the people at Lehman realized that many schools were doing the same thing, but the work was not being coordinated—each school was isolated and no one knew what was going on in other schools.

After a series of meetings, the idea of a united Puerto Rican student movement developed. The movement would: organize high school and college students to fight in the schools and in our communities against the problems all Puertorriquenos face; support the struggle of all Third World (Latino, Black, Asian, Native American) people; and struggle for the liberation of Puerto Rico. In the past, high school and college groups had been isolated from their people. This time would be different. Students had learned that they can't separate student problems from community problems. "We're students for 4 years, but we're Puerto Ricans all our lives," they said. In December of 1969, a two-day conference was held in El Barrio. The group became the Puerto Rican Student Union. In their first action, members of PRSU joined in the Young Lords Party's liberation of the People's Church on 111th street. (This was the first takeover of the church in December 1969). Ten members of PRSU were among the 106 people arrested after a huge police force occupied El Barrio and arrested everyone inside the church.

PRSU soon became involved in a struggle at Bronx Community College over the Bilingual Program. This was supposed to be a program where spanish-speaking students took their courses in spanish and got credit for them. At the same time they would take classes to learn english. But the prejudiced school administration decided that they weren't going to give credit for classes taken in spanish. They said that students had to repeat the classes in english. One teacher in the program was so bad that she made students pay 5 cents every time they spoke a word in spanish. To protest this racism and to demand student control of the program, PRSU, the Bilingual students, and the Young Lords Party seized both Bronx Community College and the Board of Higher Education. The Bilingual Program has since been switched to Lehman College and the fight continues.

In April, Oswego College had a conference called "Puerto Rico: A Story of Success." PRSU, MPI, and the Puerto Rican Alliance seized the microphone and the stage. They tore down pictures of ferre and munoz marin and replaced them with a picture of Don Pedro Albizu Campos. When they talked to the audience, they explained, "We are a colony—not a success story."

In March, PRSU opened a storefront office on 138th Street and began working in the areas of welfare and housing. People from the community began coming to the office regularly for help. In one building, a successful rent strike was organized and now tenants pay only $1 a month rent and have heat all the time. Because the people have been able to unite and stop city marshalls from throwing people out of their apartments.

PRSU found itself working not only in the schools, but also in the community. Along with the YLP and HRUM (Health Revolutionary Unity Movement), they fought against bad conditions at Lincoln Hospital. At a health rally in the Bronx, 7 members and sympathizers of PRSU were arrested and brutally beaten.

An empty lot was turned into Plaza Borinquena. People came and worked with PRSU to paint and fix up the lot. Now it is used as a playground as well as a place for community education classes and rallies.

In September, PRSU and the YLP held a Puerto Rican Student Conference at Columbia University. Over 1000 students attended and we were able to decide together on the direction of the student movement.

On October 30th, we marched together with thousands of our sisters and brothers to the UN where we demanded "Liberate Puerto Rico Now."

The Puerto Rican Student Union has gone through a lot of changes and like all organizations that are dedicated to serving and protecting, they are continuing to change and develop—to grow stronger. They see a need for working closer with other organizations and for tightening up their school chapters. They know that only by being disciplined and strong can we free our Nation. All of us together,

UNIDOS VENCEREMOS!
PONCE—March 21!
LIBERATE PUERTO RICO NOW!

Richie Perez
Deputy Minister of Information
YOUNG LORDS PARTY

6

On Revolution, Nationalism, and Revolutionary Nationalism

The Young Lords considered themselves "revolutionary nationalists," which is a complex term. Eschewing reactionary or exclusionary nationalist politics, the Young Lords' brand of nationalism seemed to translate into two theoretical commitments. First, they favored Puerto Rican independence on the Island and the Mainland. In this way, they were aligned with various *"independentista"* movements. Second, their general nationalism reached beyond a strict focus on Puerto Ricans to encompass all "Third World" and "oppressed" peoples. Essays and illustrations in this chapter help demonstrate how the Young Lords articulated "revolution" and "nationalism" as a racially and ethnically heterogeneous ("mixed") organization.

....

On Revolutionary Nationalism

(From the newspaper *Palante*, 8 May 1970, volume 2, number 2)

PUERTO RICANS, WHEREVER THEY ARE, WHETHER IN THE united states OR IN BORINQUEN (PUERTO RICO), CONSTITUTE A COLONY AND THEIR OPPRESSION IS THAT OF A COLONIAL PEOPLE SUFFERING FROM THE HANDS OF "EL PATRON."

DECISIONS AFFECTING THEIR LIVES ARE NOT MADE BY THEM BUT FOR THEM BY THE u.s. INSTITUTIONS. SCHOOLS, JOBS, CHURCHES, AND POLICE STATIONS ARE THE INSTITUTIONS THAT GOVERN THE LIVES AND DEATHS OF PUERTO RICANS, AND WHERE CRIMINAL POLICIES ARE MADE, TAILORED SPECIFICALLY FOR THE "SPIC."

EL PATRON HAS NO INTENTIONS OF ALLEVIATING THE PLIGHT OF THE 20TH CENTURY SLAVES BECAUSE THEY SERVE HIS ECONOMIC POLITICAL AND CULTURAL INTERESTS. NOR SHOULD WE EXPECT THE PUNK TO DO SO. IT WOULD BE LIKE EXPECTING A MAN TO COMMIT SUICIDE TO KEEP YOU FROM DROWNING WHEN HE WAS THE DUDE WHO PUSHED YOU IN.

PUERTO RICO IS OPPRESSED AS A NATION. IT IS A COLONY OF THE united states AND THE COLONIAL STATUS OF PUERTO RICANS FOLLOWS THEM FROM THE COUNTRYSIDE TO NEW YORK CITY. FORM CHANGES, SUBSTANCE DOESN'T. IN PUERTO RICO THE WHOLE DAMNED ISLAND, COMPOSED OF RICANS, IS OPPRESSED. IN THE u.s. BORINQUENOS ARE ONE OF THE MANY COLONIZED PEOPLES LIVING IN A COLONY WITHIN THE INTESTINES OF THE SNAKE.

WE MUST LOOK AT ONE OF THE MANY FORMS IMPERIALISM TAKES IN ORDER TO CLEARLY SEE HOW THE u.s. OPPRESSES PUERTO RICO AND HOW WE SHARE THE SAME FATE.

ECONOMICALLY, amerikkka MONOPOLIZES ALL OF THE INDUSTRY IN PUERTO
RICO. NORTH AMERIKKKAN COMPANIES ARE ALLOWED TO OPERATE 10 TO 17
YEARS WITHOUT BEING TAXED AFTER WHICH THEY OPEN UNDER ANOTHER
NAME AND STILL GET EXEMPTED. YEARLY PROFITS FOR CAPITALISTS TOTAL 28%
SO THAT AFTER A 3 YEAR PERIOD THEY ARE GUARANTEED TO SAY, 85% OF CAPI-
TAL INVESTED IN PUERTO RICO IS amerikkkan, WHICH SIMPLY MEANS RICANS ON
THE ISLAND DON'T EVEN GET TO SMELL THE MONEY.

AT THE SAME TIME, PUERTO RICANS SERVE AS A CHEAP SOURCE OF LABOR,
EARNING 1/3 THE WAGES OF A north amerikkkan WORKER, YET, THEY HAVE TO
PAY 25% MORE FOR CONSUMER GOODS THAN north amerikkkans HAVE TO PAY.

COLONIALISM'S EFFECT

IN THE U.S. PUERTO RICANS ARE STILL IN THE FACTORIES WHERE THEY
LANDED IN THE FIRST PLACE, TEACHERS AIN'T TEACHING; JOBS AIN'T JOBBING,
BUT THE COP IS COPPING, SO MUCH SO THAT IN THE CITY JAILS 44 OUT OF
EVERY 100 PRISONERS ARE PUERTO RICANS, AT THE BRONX COUNTY JAIL, 85%
OF THE PRISONERS ARE BORINQUENOS.

COLONIALISM HAS MESSED OUR MINDS SO BADLY THAT PSYCHOLOGICALLY
WE DON'T EVEN KNOW WHO WE ARE NOR WHERE WE COME FROM. WE REJECT
OUR CULTURAL VALUES AND BASIC HUMAN VALUES BY IMITATING THAT WHICH
IS NOT NATURAL TO US AND BY STOMPING ON OUR OWN REFLECTIONS. WE'VE
BEEN SYSTEMATICALLY TAUGHT TO HATE OURSELVES WHILE BEING REMINDED
CONSTANTLY BY RACIST AMERICA THAT WE AIN'T HER KIND OF PEOPLE
EITHER.

PUERTO RICANS HAVE SUFFERED AS A GROUP, RACIALLY AND CULTURALLY,
NOT AS INDIVIDUALS. THEREFORE, THE FIGHT AGAINST amerikkkanism MUST
BE A GROUP STRUGGLE, A NATION STRUGGLE. THE ASSIMILATIONISTS WOULD
HAVE US BELIEVE THAT BECAUSE THEY "MADE IT" AS INDIVIDUALS (NOT REAL-
IZING THAT CAPITALISM ALWAYS ALLOWS A SELECT FEW TO BECOME COLLEGE
STUDENTS AND HEADS OF CITY INSTITUTIONS IN ORDER TO ENFORCE GENO-
CIDE AGAINST THEIR OWN) PUERTO RICANS AS A WHOLE CAN MAKE IT. IT MUST
ALWAYS BE REMEMBERED THAT RACIST amerikkka WOULD DO NOTHING TO HARM
HERSELF. THE INDIVIDUAL SHE PICKS TO BE SPIC OF THE MONTH IS ALWAYS
GOING TO BE AN ASS KISSER.

BASICALLY, WE ARE TALKING ABOUT NATIONALISM. TO COMBAT PSYCHOLOGI-
CAL IMPERIALISM WE COULD BEGIN BY TEACHING OUR PEOPLE PRIDE IN BEING
BORINQUENOS, THAT PUERTO RICAN SPANISH IS NOT A BASTARD TONGUE, AND
THAT WE SHOULD ALL ATTEMPT TO LEARN IT, THAT OUR WOMEN AND MEN ARE
WARRIORS AND ARE TO BE RESPECTED AND THAT WE ARE PROUD OF OUR INDO-
AFRO HERITAGE (THE SPANIARDS CONTRIBUTED NOTHING BUT RACISM, RAPE,
VENEREAL DISEASE AND GENOCIDE). BUT WOULD THIS NATIONALISM BY ITSELF
RESOLVE THE QUESTION OF LIBERATION FOR OUR PEOPLE ON THE ISLAND AND
SELF-DETERMINATION FOR PUERTO RICANS IN amerikkka? CULTURE WITH-
OUT REVOLUTIONARY POLITICS IS LIKE A SWORD WRAPPED IN FOAM RUBBER.
WE MUST MAKE A DISTINCTION BETWEEN CULTURAL NATIONALISM AND REV-

OLUTIONARY NATIONALISM. CULTURAL NATIONALISTS WOULD VIEW CALLING
PUERTO RICANS "BORINQUENOS," THEN CLAIM THE REVOLUTION HAD COME.
WE COULD WEAR GUAYABERAS AND PABAS FOR DAYS AND THAT WON'T CHANGE
THE POLITICAL SITUATION IN THIS COUNTRY. BACARDI WOULD HAVE A SERIES
IN LIQUOR STORES ON "FAMOUS" SPICS (YOU KNOW DAMN WELL ALBIZU, OSCAR
COLLAZO, AND DISC JOCKEYS WILL BE CALLING CORTIJO THEIR GODDAMNED
BROTHER).

amerikkka THRIVES ON COOPTATION OF OPPRESSED PEOPLE'S LIFE STYLES AS
LONG AS YOU DON'T SNATCH HER POCKETBOOK. WE CAN'T WIN THE REVOLU-
TION WITH RICE AND BEANS UNLESS YOU POISON IT AND GIVE IT TO THE NEXT
PIG WHO COMES TO ONE OF OUR RESTAURANTS. WITH CULTURAL NATIONALISM
PUERTO RICANS WILL BE PLAYING CONGAS IN THE JOINT.

SPIC CAPITALISM?

AS FOR SELF-HELP OR SPIC CAPITALISM, DON'T EVER THINK YOU'LL COM-
PETE WITH GENERAL MOTORS, CAUSE THEY'LL KILL YOU BEFORE GOD GETS
THE MESSAGE. THIS IS NOT TO SAY THAT THE YOUNG LORDS ORGANIZATION IS
AGAINST INSTILLING PRIDE IN OUR PEOPLE, AS LONG AS THAT PRIDE LEADS US
TO A POLITICAL OBJECTIVE. YES, WE MUST TEACH OUR PEOPLE WHO THEY ARE
AND WHERE THEY COME FROM. BUT IT IS ONLY RELEVANT TO THE EXTENT THAT
IT EDUCATES THEM AND US TO WHERE WE SHOULD AND MUST BE LEADING—
ARMED STRUGGLE.

REVOLUTIONARY NATIONALISM IS THE COMING TOGETHER OF PUERTO RICANS
BECAUSE OF A SIMILAR CULTURE, LIFE STYLE, AND A SIMILAR POLITICAL REAL-
ITY, OPPRESSION, FOR THE PURPOSES OF FORMING A MASSES-ORIENTED ORGA-
NIZATION TO IMPLEMENT A COMMON IDEOLOGY WHICH WILL STRUGGLE FOR
LIBERATION OF OUR PEOPLE THROUGH ARMED STRUGGLE.

THIS DOES NOT MEAN THAT REVOLUTIONARY NATIONALISM IS RACIST. CON-
TRARY TO CULTURAL NATIONALISM, REVOLUTIONARY NATIONALISM WORKS
WITH EITHER GROUPS AND/OR INDIVIDUALS FROM DIFFERENT NATIONALITIES
AND RACES PROVIDED THESE GROUPS ARE REVOLUTIONARY IN THEORY AND
PRACTICE. THESE GROUPS ARE USUALLY WORKING IN THEIR OWN RESPECTIVE
COMMUNITIES TO EDUCATE THEIR PEOPLE TOWARDS REVOLUTION AND AWAY
FROM RACISM. WE MUST ALL LEARN TO RESPECT AND LOVE CULTURAL DIFFER-
ENCES. BUT THESE CULTURAL DIFFERENCES MUST NEVER BECOME IMPENETRA-
BLE BARRIERS.

STATE POWER WILL BE WON WHEN ALL OF THE REVOLUTIONARY ORGANIZA-
TIONS IN DIFFERENT COLONIES IN THE U.S. BECOME (THROUGH REPRESSION AND
POLITICAL UNDERSTANDING) REVOLUTIONARY INTERNATIONALISTS. FORMING A
VIABLE LIBERATION FRONT IS THE STEP BEFORE RIPPING OFF COMPLETE STATE
POWER.

THE U.S. KEEPS PUERTO RICO ECONOMICALLY DEPENDENT ON HER BY DEVEL-
OPING INDUSTRY THAT IS NOT INDIGENOUS TO THE ISLAND. EVEN THOUGH
SUGAR AND COFFEE AND TOBACCO ARE THE TRADITIONAL ECONOMIC MAIN
STAYS OF THE ISLAND THESE ARE NOT DEVELOPED.

INSTEAD, MOST OF THE FACTORIES PROCESS RAW MATERIALS TO BE USED BY OTHER COMPANIES AS RAW GOODS. THE BASIC MATERIALS FOR THIS PROCESSING COMES FROM FOREIGN COUNTRIES AND ARE SOLD TO FOREIGN COUNTRIES BY THE U.S. BECAUSE WITH ANY OTHER COUNTRIES THAN THE U.S. IN EFFECT WHAT YOU HAVE IS MORE INSTANT COFFEE COMING INTO PUERTO RICO THAN NATURAL COFFEE GOING OUT. ALSO, THE WORK FORCE OF 700,000 PEOPLE HAS 98,000 UNEMPLOYED AND 100,000 UNDEREMPLOYED, ADD THAT TO THE FACT THAT 13% OF ALL THE ARABLE LAND IS OCCUPIED BY MILITARY BASES, 80,000 BROTHERS [. . .] AND SISTERS ARE DROP-OUTS BECAUSE OF RACIST TEACHING PRACTICES, AND 100,000 AGENTS [ARE] IN THE ARMED FORCES, CIA, FBI, ETC. AND YOU GET A GRAND TOTAL OF ZERO FOR SPICS.

REVOLUTIONARY NATIONALISM IS NOT CHAUVINISTIC. IT SHOULD NOT MAKE DISTINCTIONS BETWEEN CULTURES, BUT FUNCTION SO THAT PUERTO RICANS FEEL PRIDE IN THEIR UNIQUENESS AND UNDERSTAND AND LOVE THE COMMON CULTURAL-POLITICAL TIES WITH BLACKS, INDIANS, ASIANS, AND OTHER LATIN PEOPLE.

THE YOUNG LORDS ORGANIZATION IS A REVOLUTIONARY NATIONALIST PARTY BECAUSE WE SEE THAT THE POLITICS OF THE PUERTO RICAN COLONY EVOLVES FROM A COMMON CULTURAL AND COMMON POLITICAL OPPRESSION AND THEREFORE, MUST BE DEFINED BY THOSE WITHIN IT. AS PUERTO RICANS, WE MUST, THEN, FIND AND DEVELOP WAYS OF EDUCATING OUR PEOPLE TO WAGE RIGHTEOUS STRUGGLE AGAINST IMPERIALISM HERE AND ABROAD.

THE TACTICS WILL BE DIFFERENT FROM THE BLACK, INDIAN, ASIAN, AND WHITE POOR COMMUNITIES, THE POLITICAL OBJECTIVE, HOWEVER, FOR THE ENTIRE PUERTO RICAN NATION MUST BE THE SAME AS ALL OPPRESSED PEOPLE'S IN THE united states—SELF-DETERMINATION IN amerikkka, AND LIBERATION OF OUR ISLAND AT ANY COST.

ALL POWER TO OPPRESSED PEOPLE!
LIBERATE PUERTO RICO NOW!

FELIPE LUCIANO
CHAIRMAN
YOUNG LORDS ORGANIZATION
EAST COAST REGION

....

Puerto Rican Racism

(From the newspaper *Palante*, 17 July 1970, volume 2, number 7)

The Taino Indians were the first people of Borinquen, the Indian name for the island that is still used today. The spaniards came to Borinquen in 1493, changed the name to San Juan Bautista, and forced the Tainos into slavery, exploiting their labor in the gold mines and on plantations. The enslavers divided the land and people among themselves getting all the benefit and profit from the work of the Indian. In return the Taino was given barely enough to keep him alive. The Taino women were also exploited, not only their labor, but their bodies as well. In the early days the Spanish did not bring any of their women, so they took, abused, or raped our Indian sisters. They justified this inhumanity and murder, saying the Indians were savage, unchristian, and of another race.

Quickly, the colonizer killed, enslaved, or chased into the mountains our first ancestors. The spaniards then had to look to Africa for a new source of slave labor. In 1598, the first contract to bring in large numbers of Africans was signed. The oppressor accepted slavery as normal: the church never condemned it; and the government never enforced the laws against it. Our African sisters were also raped and used as breeders of more slaves. The number of African slaves was important to the sugar plantation owners who made a lot of money off the sugar cane fields where they put the African to slave. Again, the spanish justified slavery and rape, saying that the African was inferior, uncivilized, and of an alien race.

From the 16th to the middle of the 19th century the Africans and Tainos rebelled against spanish colonialism, many times united to fight the common oppressor. By 1868, when the Puerto Rican nation emerged and fought the Spanish in "El Grito de Lares" as Puerto Ricans, Blacks were still slaves. Black slavery was not abolished in Puerto Rico until 1873.

Puerto Ricans don't like to talk about racism or admit that it exists among Puerto Ricans. Boricuas talk of an island that is free from racism, or they say that the amerikkkans brought it in. Although the amerikkkan did make it worse, racism in Puerto Rico began with the spanish. According to them, one drop of white blood meant you were white and better than your Black compatriot. Acceptance was given according to the "degree of whiteness." The upper classes were white, descendents of the spanish or creoles. The spanish colonizer had certain economic interests in Puerto Rico and Latin America: that's why they used racism as a justification for exploiting labor to get economic profit.

When the u.s. invaded Puerto Rico in 1898, racism was reinforced and intensified by them. The white upper class, empowered by the spanish before, now made deals and got money from u.s. industries to stay in power in return for supporting u.s. policies. The u.s. took advantage of the racial and class divisions within our country to better control by playing one group against the other. Puerto Ricans have developed a phrase that is constantly referred to and taught to all Puerto Ricans from generation to generation as a basic axiom of life; "Hay que mejorar la raza," which means "One must better the race." Every Puerto Rican grows up with this concept and learns to view as ugly—dark skin, thick lips, a broad nose, and kinky hair. When referring to a person's profile, "perfile and perfilado" are used to indicate whiteness. Puerto Ricans believe that to better the race you must marry a light skinned Puerto Rican. As a result every Puerto Rican family has light and dark Puerto Ricans. That's why we say "EL QUE NO TIENE DINGA. TIENE MANDINGA" [basically meaning "everybody's black"]. That's why we ask: "Y TU ABUELA, DONDE ESTA?" [And your grandma, where is she from?]

During the 1940's Puerto Ricans were forced to emigrate to the u.s. Here the formula for racism says "one drop of Black blood makes you Black." As a result, Puerto Ricans as a mixed people are considered Blacks, and all Puerto Ricans become victims of u.s. racism. Amerikkkans cannot accept us because they believe that the racial mixture has caused a decline in our mental and physical capabilities. That's why, at best, the amerikkkans are paternalistic or just out and out racist pigs. Only recently have even the most radical whites been changing this deeply imbedded racism and paternalism.

Amerikkkan racist influence has really succeeded in dividing Puerto Rico along color lines especially within the last ten years. According to one study, 96% of the upper class is white, 94% of the middle class is white, and 60% of the lower class is Black on our island of Puerto Rico. On top of all of this is u.s. capitalism controlling the economy of the island and making bundles of money in alliance with the Puerto Rican capitalist class (people like pig governor ferre).

Back in the u.s., Puerto Ricans and Blacks are put in the same communities. Both are victims of racism, drugs, unemployment, the draft, bad health care, bad housing, and miseducated. Yet each is taught that the other is inferior and to be avoided or hated. For Puerto Ricans this means that the light skinned Puerto Ricans start viewing themselves as white and their compatriots as Black, reflecting amerikkkan society. Many Black Puerto Ricans cling to being Puerto Rican in order to negate their blackness. Many light skinned Puerto Ricans say "I'm American, I'm spanish," or "I'm White" in order to avoid identification as Puerto Ricans. Both Black and light skinned Puerto Ricans adopt racist attitudes towards Afro-American brothers and sisters.

We the YLP are revolutionary nationalists and oppose racism. We realize that capitalism has used racism to keep oppressed people fighting each other while the faggot pig makes the money. We must rid ourselves of the racist attitudes that exist among our Puerto Rican people. We must end the racist attitudes towards our Afro-American brothers and sisters. We grow up together, are victims of capitalism together, so we must pick up the gun and fight the racist, capitalistic pig together!

UNITY AMONG PUERTO RICANS AND ALL OPPRESSED PEOPLE!
REVOLUTIONARY NATIONALISM
NOT RACISM!
LIBERATE PUERTO RICO NOW!

Iris Morales Luciano
Ministry of Education
YOUNG LORDS PARTY
El Barrio

....

Felipe on Political and Armed Struggle

(From the newspaper *Palante*, 31 July 1970, volume 2, number 8)

The YOUNG LORDS PARTY has 2 basic goals: to liberate Puerto Rico from the yanqui oppressor and his Puerto Rican puppets and self-determination for Puerto Ricans and all oppressed people inside the united states.

It has been the experience of our parents, our people that you cannot get freedom by the vote or by prayers, only by fighting for it. Those who own the hospitals, the banks, the stores and the railroads are not going to give us anything. We, the people must make them bleed in order for them to understand that we are so serious about our freedom that we are willing to kill and even die ourselves in order to taste the fruits of victory. We Puerto Ricans must wage a people's war here and in Puerto Rico.

There are many odds we must overcome. First, this country has embedded its teachings and its laws into our people's heads. They have taken the chains off our hands and put them on our minds. What better way to pacify people but to make them believe that Puerto Rico cannot survive without the help of the united states. Or to make them think that they are poor because they're lazy and good for nothing but drinking and making babies and killing each other. Amerikkka has taught Puerto Ricans that the law is for everybody, and we believe it even though the majority of the people in the jails are Puerto Ricans and Blacks. I've even heard Puerto Ricans say they're living fine while rats are sleeping with their babies, and the bathroom roof is caving in. Amerikkka makes sure that though we have eyes, we don't see; and though we have ears, we don't hear; and though we have tongues and minds, we don't think or speak about the cruelties and injustices we go through every day on the job, in school, in the army, or on the streets.

Amerikkka also tries to teach us to forget who we are and where we come from. She tries to tell us we're amerikkkans. But, if we are amerikkkans, then why is it that we don't have the rights that white amerikkkans have. They have the fancy cars and the nice houses and the private schools and the best food. We don't have those things so how can we call ourselves amerikkkans? So what if we were born here. That's like a cat being born in a stable and calling himself a horse.

We are Puerto Ricans, a proud people, born of the mixture of Taino Indians, Spaniards, and African. We have never been a passive people and our history proves it. We fought against the Spanish, and now we're fighting against the amerikkkan government.

Second, the other odd we have to overcome is the fact that the u.s. has more guns, more money, and more soldiers and police. Those people this country cannot "teach" to be afraid, she tries to physically force into accepting her brutalities. For example, the administration of this city knows that it cannot buy the YOUNG LORDS PARTY off so it tries to beat us up and put us in jails. When they realize that doesn't work, they'll try to kill us to let other Borinquenos know that they will not tolerate any spic jumping up saying, "I'm Puerto Rican, love my people, and I want my island back, and I want my people to be able to rule over their own lives in the united states." They want us to fear them. But guns will only scare people as long as they allow them to. Once the people find out that the oppressor bleeds too and heavily, they'll rise against him.

However, because these odds are major ones they cannot be ignored. We must learn then to fight the money hungry monster on 2 levels.

First, we must fight a battle for our people's minds. Second, we must wage struggle against the pocketbook of this country and those who protect it.

Political Struggle and Armed Struggle

The first phase of any revolution is political struggle. It is this phase that the YOUNG LORDS PARTY is presently involved in. We must first educate our people to struggle before we begin to take up arms by the thousands. The worst thing to have in a people's war is a politically ignorant person with a gun. He will either shoot the wrong person or use it for personal gain. Many Puerto Ricans have guns today and know how to use them; the problem is that they kill each other with them instead of killing their oppressors because they haven't learned to think politically.

The first question that must be answered is why political struggle. Don't Puerto Ricans know what's happening to them? The answer is NO!

A. We must teach our people to struggle.

Not only Puerto Ricans, but all oppressed people, have been taught in racist schools to be non-violent to the oppressor—the landlord, the doctor, the big supermarket, the generals and the government—and violent towards themselves and their neighbors. It's okay to fire a gun and murder Asians in Vietnam and Cambodia, but not at the government when you come home and find yourself without a job or a decent place to live.

The aggression in our people is directed inward, not outward, causing a severe sickness called self-hatred. This brings us to our second point.

B. We must teach our people who the real enemy is.

Puerto Ricans hate other Ricans or Black people rather than hate the amerikkkan government that makes us live like pigs. Who has the money and influence to tear down all these slums and give us decent housing? Is it Black people, who are poor themselves, or the government? Who is sending our sons, our husbands, our lovers to Vietnam? Puerto Ricans or the amerikkkan government? Many Puerto Ricans blame their own people for prostitution and dope and murder. But they never ask themselves why does it happen only among poor people. Were Puerto Ricans born to shoot dope or to sell their bodies?

Or is it that when a government does not allow them to develop to their fullest potential in schools or jobs because they're spics, those same young people turn to dope and robbery and murder because they see no hope and want to escape? Who is to blame, the young people or the amerikkkan government?

C. We must teach our people the value of Socialism.

In amerikkka we have been taught "what is mine is mine and what is thine is mine too!" I have heard many Puerto Ricans say "Look, I have my raggety [sic] car and my sloppy apartment and my beer every Saturday night. I don't give a damn about anything or anybody else," or "The only friend I have is this dollar in my pocket."

Socialism means sharing. Sharing like our parents and grand parents had to do their farms in the countryside of Puerto Rico. They couldn't have survived without helping each other out with tools, food, and labor. Socialism means we take care of each other because we care about each other. There is a song taken from a poem that goes, "No man is an island, no man stands alone." We are being oppressed as a group so we must fight as a group not as individuals.

Socialism is the most mis-understood concept among Puerto Ricans. We have been taught to hate it, but we don't even know what it means. Socialism means that after armed struggle instead of a few families and companies owning all the wealth in this country, the people will own it. The poor people will own the airplanes, the railroads, the mines, the forests, and the factories. And the poor will determine who runs all these industries. After all, it is we who work in them and make these few bastards rich. Why shouldn't we run them?

Socialism does not mean that people's clothes and homes will be taken away, No. It means though that new housing will be built by the poor and for the poor. It means that clothes will be free. Why should people have to pay for basic necessities like food, clothing, and shelter? These are the rights of any man, not privileges. Only under capitalism, which is individual ownership of property, can a Puerto Rican mother make 100 dresses a day in a factory and not afford to dress her children well. She has to steal when the foreman is not looking or come to the YOUNG LORDS Free Clothing Drive.

If we don't educate our people to socialism now through theory and practice, after armed struggle ends in the u.s. Puerto Ricans will start counter revolutionary activities because they will have found that their government is socialist. Out of fear of a word, they'll fight and die without even having understood why.

D. We must teach our people to make sacrifices and to be self-reliant.

There is no battle won without sacrifice. Albizu Campos once said, "Our nation is valor and sacrifice." The people will win in Puerto Rico and in amerikkka, but it will not be easy. Are we willing to sacrifice our sons, our daughters, our wives, ourselves to the revolution? What do we say to our children or friends when they say they want to join the YOUNG LORDS PARTY? Do we scream, cry and reject them, or do we embrace them for having become warriors?

We have the most precious sacrifice, our lives, because we don't have any money, nor do we own property. We have nothing to lose but our chains and everything to gain, our island and our communities.

Let us learn to depend upon ourselves for the things we need in a revolution. Even in poverty, you can become soft by being used to the "man" giving you everything. What will happen when the police close the supermarkets or cut the phone lines? I can see the panic now if they stop dope from coming in.

We must always remember that whatever amerikkka controls, she can also end—even our own businesses!

Once we understand why we must struggle politically, we must then figure out how or in what manner to fight. That means taking all those ideas of unity and mobilization of Puerto Ricans and putting them to work, because only through practice will we find out whether those ideas are correct.

The YOUNG LORDS PARTY's example has been that the correct way to struggle is around issues that affect Puerto Ricans' everyday lives. For example, if the system of health care in New York City is not serving our people the way it should be, then we move on the health system. We asked for a tuberculosis truck from the city so that we could test our people since many of them die every year from this disease. We went downtown twice, and twice we were laughed at. So we took it: we ripped it off. The city and the owner of the truck got mad, but we didn't give a damn. It's not their people dying from t.b.—it's ours. We love our people too much to care about how the city feels. We didn't feel we robbed it. Our people work and pay taxes for those trucks, and they deserve to use them fully.

The objective in all of our tactics is to serve our people and to educate them. We definitely served our people. The city tested only 125 people a day with that truck—we tested 325, and before they took all their trucks off New York City's streets we tested over 1,000 Puerto Ricans.

We also educated our people by letting them know that once you've asked nicely for something that's desperately needed and the government says no, take it. We don't care whether it's a school, a court, a jail, a church, or a hospital. Any institution that controls the lives and deaths of our people must be controlled by our people.

For those of us who would criticize the YOUNG LORDS PARTY for not obeying the law, I have 2 basic questions. Who makes the law? And whose interests do those laws serve?

When laws do not serve the people and just help the rich get richer, then we must fight to change those laws, not in the courts which they control, but on the streets which we control.

Waging political struggle does not mean revolutionaries avoid confrontations. On the contrary, that's exactly how we teach the people how to struggle. We may not always win physical victories or institutional victories, but we must always educate the people. The political education is the most important in waging political struggle.

Even when we begin to shoot back at these foreign troops that occupy our communities, we are still in the stages of political struggle because we are educating our people to defend themselves against unjust attack. The people are also educated by the pigs, because they see these scared rabbits start beating and jailing any Puerto Rican in sight. Repression makes a whole lot of Puerto Ricans think twice about amerikkka.

The change from political struggle to armed struggle comes when the Party feels 2 conditions are met. First, it must thoroughly go over its own strengths and weaknesses and those of the Puerto Rican community. Is the Party and the community ready to sustain a long hit-run war with the enemy? The PARTY must feel and know that it will be victorious.

The second condition is that the PARTY must know whether conditions are ripe in amerikkka for armed struggle. How are amerikkka's armed forces deployed? Are more and more people seeing where amerikkka and big business are at?

If both conditions are met then armed struggle must begin. However, we, as revolutionaries, will pick the time and the place to start, not the enemy. And we will follow the advice of General Giap, Minister of Defense of the North Vietnamese Army, ". . . Strike to win, strike only when success is certain; if it is not, then don't strike."

Because the u.s. has more and better guns, we must use urban guerrilla warfare to fight this country on our terms. All of our energies must be concentrated on the military aspect of the struggle. We must find ways of nibbling at her strength, here, there, everywhere in places she would never expect. Urban guerrilla warfare has no front or rear. Wherever the enemy is, is where the battle should be taken.

Armed struggle means a constant offensive in the face of more men and more guns. It does not mean physically provoking the enemy, when the revolutionary party or group has no means by which to cause more casualties on the enemy's side than on theirs. It does not mean that revolutionaries should get so mad that they forget to think and place themselves in a suicidal position. Anger without reason lasts less than a few days in revolutionary struggle and always puts revolutionaries at a disadvantage because they're reacting not creating. The YOUNG LORDS PARTY does not believe in a defense which is trapped in a building or a street or an area. Offense is defense.

The objectives of all revolutionaries should be to keep themselves alive each day getting stronger while the enemy grows weaker. Amerikkkans cannot fight a long war, they have never been able to. We must be careful not to carry their bad traits into battle with us. These bad traits are decisions based on importance or on gaining a quick victory.

The survival of our PARTY and all of our people engaged in warfare will depend on the following:

Mobility,
Flexibility,
Creativity,
Determination,
Boldness,
Invisibility.

Needless to say, without training all of these concepts are wasted ideas. Any revolutionary group must develop an underground, an underground that can hide warriors and arms. Since urban guerrilla warfare will not consist of one massive force fighting another massive force, Puerto Ricans will need places where they can hit, destroy, and hide. Obviously, the underground must also provide the military training for the revolutionary brothers and sisters. It must always be remembered that a few well trained revolutionaries can immobilize an entire city. In East St. Louis, a black community, one political sniper offed several people, white and black. The community never turned him in because they didn't know who he was and because his targets were known to be enemies of the people.

The strategy of all urban guerrillas is to attack the enemy's weakest points in the cities. For example, MIRA, a revolutionary Puerto Rican group that is underground, has been bombing woolworth's in New York City because they are one of the companies exploiting Puerto Ricans, particularly in Puerto Rico, and are very exposed. As the capitalists rush guards to secure those stories bombed, other Woolworths are blown up. Eventually, they will have to put heavy security around all of their stores. But what will they do when the guards start getting offed? Will they then hire guards to protect the guards? And what will happen to their profits?

The enemy must rush troops to defend his most exposed side and at the same time he must guard those interests which are the most vital to the people with money. A perfect example of this is how the Weathermen operate. They'll bomb a weak point in the city, and the police will run to defend it while the FBI harasses innocent people with questions. Meanwhile, the Weathermen are free to bomb a place as vital as police headquarters in New York City. The enemy has to guard both weak spots and his strong points. He can't do two things at once, be everywhere at the same time. He will eventually become too demoralized to fight well. Especially, when he starts to bleed.

Yes, he can surround our communities, but he will only make our job easier because the people who live there will have no choice but to fight or be massacred. But can he surround all oppressed people's communities? If we analyze things correctly, when Puerto Rican communities go up, a lot of other communities should go up too—Black, Asian, and Latino. Sure our families are in danger of being attacked right in their own communities. However, so is the enemy's family. Not only is his family in danger, but also his pocketbook, which he cares about much more. For every Puerto Rican that is brutalized or killed, one of the enemies should be offed in a restaurant where our people wash dishes, in a hotel where our people are the doormen, or on the streets where the majority of our people are.

All tactics change as the people's struggle intensifies, so revolutionaries should not become fanatics about this or that aspect of the struggle.

It is important to understand that urban guerrilla offensives can only occur when all revolutionary groups—Puerto Rican, Black, Asian, White—are clear as to their role and how they participate in bringing the system to a crash. This simply means that eventually all revolutionary groups will have to think beyond the boundaries of their own communities if they want to be victorious.

Armed struggle is the peak of a people's war. It is the phase that signifies the beginning of the end. The YOUNG LORDS PARTY realizes that it will be a long, difficult struggle; but we will win because our people, all oppressed people, are with us. And amerikkka makes our job of recruiting revolutionaries much easier by refusing to change the physical conditions of our people. We will win because of the just nature of our struggle. We will win because of our boldness, our swiftness, and our firepower. We will win because we believe in the strength of the Third World.

ALL POWER TO OPPRESSED PEOPLE!
BE HUMBLE BEFORE THE PEOPLE AND VICIOUS
BEFORE THE ENEMY!

Felipe Luciano
Chairman
YOUNG LORDS PARTY

....

Message from a Revolutionary Compañera

(From the newspaper *Palante*, 30 October 1970, volume 2, number 14)

I address myself to the members of the YOUNG LORDS PARTY and to all Puerto Rican, Latin American, North American patriotic organizations of New York; in short, to all men and women in the new struggle for people's liberation who have made the independence of Puerto Rico their cause, and who will unite in front of the United Nations building the 30th of October to demand the immediate withdrawal of the yanqui invading forces from our land and the recognition of Puerto Rico as a sovereign and independent nation.

I send you my most cordial message of fraternity and gratitude on behalf of the freedom loving people of Puerto Rico, who on that same day of October 30th will be gathered together solemnly in a National Assembly in the town of Jayuya to proclaim and reaffirm the validity of the cry for liberty that we uttered in those mountains on October 30, 1950, exactly 20 years ago.

That 30th of October a general uprising took place in the whole island. There were shoot-out battles in the barrio Macana of Penuelas, in Utuado, Ponce, Arecibo and in front of La Fortaleza, the official residence of the colonial governor in San Juan. In Jayuya, the revolutionaries took over the town, battling the police in their own headquarters, setting fire to the city hall and the federal offices of the u.s.; that is, the post office and the army recruiting office (which at that time was recruiting Puerto Ricans to serve as cannon fodder in Korea). The municipality of Jayuya was under the power of the

(Above) From the newspaper *Palante*, 11 September 1970, volume 2, number 11.

(Right) From the newspaper *Palante*, 25 September 1970, volume 2, number 12.

revolutionaries for three days, under the command of Elio Torresola. Elio is the brother of our martyr, Griselio Torresola, who fell November 1st in front of Blair House in Washington when as a participant in this revolution he went with Oscar Collazo to shoot the president of the u.s.

In Jayuya, the u.s. flags were lowered from all the public buildings for three days and the Puerto Rican flag was raised in a building in the center of the town from where we issued our freedom proclamation with the cry of VIVA PUERTO RICO LIBRE!

The lackey government of the colony under the command of the traitor Munoz Marin mobilized the pigs, the badly named National Guard, and launched it against Jayuya, occupying the town after having bombed and strafed it from its planes. Our people overcome, the lackeys at the service of yanqui imperialism handed over the control of the town to the insular, federal, and municipal functionaries in a public ceremony.

This ceremony which was photographed by the newspapermen is the tacit reminder that our people proclaimed their independence for three days and that it repudiated the intervention of the u.s. in our fatherland.

This struggle of 1950 was nurtured with the blood of our purest men. Once more the sacrifice of our martyrs consecrated our sovereignty; for in that glorious step we reaffirmed our desire to be free, continuing the chronology of our independent republic begun in Lares.

The intervention of the united states in Puerto Rico has been disguised with different names—the last one, the so-called "free associated state." This intervention has been fought against in whatever form the island has been able to, this small island that has known how to rise up, especially in the last 40 years under the inspiration of the hero and teacher Don Pedro Albizu Campos. Puerto Rico has kept up a war for its liberation from the first encounter in 1932 in which Rafael Manuel Suarez Diaz offered his life on the stairs to the capitol building to the recent death of another student, Antonia Martinez, who less than a year ago fell, beaten down by the imperialist's bullets in the University in Rio Piedras, and the burning of the 2000 draft cards in Lares on September 23.

The struggle has had many martyrs and hundreds of Puerto Ricans have suffered imprisonment, which demonstrates our unbeatable determination to reestablish the independence of Puerto Rico which was proclaimed in Lares and Jayuya.

Today Puerto Rico is suffering the most monstruous intervention as our territory is surrounded with land bases and submarine bases with powerful atomic weapons that, because of the smallness of the island, can cause the destruction of all the Puerto Ricans and the total disappearance of the island from the map of the world.

And as if this horrible menace were not enough, genocide is being perpetrated in the most shameless way with a massive house to house campaign to force the women to use a u.s. form of birth control. The plan is to prevent the birth of more Puerto Ricans. At the same time, they stop the advancement of our youth when they recruit them to take them to their deaths in the fields of Vietnam. On the other hand, they have no qualms in firing over the heads of the Puerto Ricans who live on the island of Culebra and the u.s marines have the audacity to ask that the people of Culebra abandon their island because the almighty marine of the biggest empire in the world has decided to use this island as a target for their military practices.

Friends of the demonstration in front of the United Nations, I invite you to prepare a document including these and other violations to the human and political rights of our Puerto Rican fatherland and to present them to all the chiefs of staff of all the countries of the world. I ask you not to stop and to continue picketing periodically the United Nations to demand the liberty of our prisoners of war in the jails of the united states, our patriots—Oscar Collazo, Lolita Lebron, Rafael Cancel, Andres Figeroa, Irving Flores, and Carlos Feliciano.

To all of you gathered there on that day, we say to you, forward, always forward, every day with more faith in the ultimate victory. If on that day or in following days, the United Nations plays deaf to your demand, you Puerto Ricans who are there, come back to our Puerto Rican countryside and let us redouble the fight without mercy and without rest from all the angles and by whatever means necessary until we obtain the liberty of Puerto Rico.

From Bayamon, Puerto Rico, says hello one that was imprisoned for 17 years for only the crime of loving her fatherland.

> Blanca A. Canales

....

Yanquis Own Puerto Rico

(From the newspaper *Palante*, 11 December 1970, volume 2, number 17)

The Young Lords Party is a revolutionary political party, fighting for the liberation of the Puerto Ricans everywhere, inside the united states and on the island. Because two thirds of our people are on the island, it is necessary for us who are here inside the belly of the monster to know more about the conditions in Puerto Rico.

Gloria Gonzales—Field Marshall, Yoruba Guzman—Minister of Information, and I, Denise Oliver—Minister of Finance just got back from a ten day trip to Puerto Rico. In those ten days we tried to see as much as possible and to rap to as many people as we

From the newspaper *Palante*, 30 October 1970, volume 2, number 14.

could. Yoruba and I had never been to Puerto Rico before. We set up better lines of communication so that we will be able to put more articles in Palante about what's happening on the island.

Before we could even get on the plane we were hassled by pigs in the airport who insisted that we were carrying "metal" onto the plane (Yoruba had a nail file). They are very uptight because of the last planes hijacked to Cuba was ripped off by a young Puerto Rican brother wearing a Young Lords Party button. When we got off the plane we were immediately grabbed by a Puerto Rican C.I.C. agent (the Puerto Rican C.I.A.) who looked like he was afraid we were going to shoot him or something. There were agents all over the airport, and we had our own very special pig (a pig with an afro—probably the only pig on the island with a fro) to follow us around. This was our welcoming committee.

The airport was full of gringos and gringas, all running around in sombreros and mumo's, trying to look like "native." Most of the signs in the airport are in english and the people who work there are either Americans or gusanos. We went to a restaurant to eat our first food in P.R. but almost everything was American—hamburgers, coca-cola . . . , except for a few "native specialties" on the menu. As if the Puerto Rican people are savages. The sign on the clock over our heads read, "you have a friend at the Chase Manhattan—all over the Caribbean."

We drove to San Juan and we were greeted by a sign saying "Welcome to San Juan—The oldest city in the united states." All along the highway are signs advertising American garbage—Texaco, Ford, McDonalds Hamburgers. . . . Puerto Rico—Where are you? Puerto Rico is being turned into the "showplace colony" of the united states. American corporations are everywhere, all over the island, using Puerto Rican people as cheap labor. Everything that cannot be sold in the states is dumped in Puerto Rico—plastic palm trees in people's homes instead of the real thing that grows outside, makeup that is not needed, wool maxi-skirts and boots to be worn in 80 degree weather. And the people are brain-washed into buying this shit. The radio blasts American music and advertisements—"radio San Juan—turns me on." We turned it off. You get better service if you speak English, the tourists act like they owned the island and the Borinquenos are just there to be servants and part of the scenery.

But the Condado is a war zone. Any Puerto Rican who values his life doesn't go there after sunset because C.A.L. is bombing everything—hotels, big gringo stores, banks, and they're doing a good job. . . . Right On! The hotels own the beaches, beaches where gringos lie around like red lobsters under our beautiful sun. Our children have to swim in sewers, or in flooded sections of El Cano, Fanguito or Loiza Aldea, where there are no sewers.

People are being brainwashed by the churches and the government. One old lady told Yoruba, "Puerto Ricans should not go to the beaches with the tourists because some dirty P.R. man would probably pinch a gringa's ass, and insult her. The beaches should be segregated because we need the tourist's money." Puerto Ricans—WAKE UP!

Construction is going on all over the island. Everything is built of concrete, ugly little houses that look like boxes, that cost $8,000 to build and sell for $25,000. Built so quickly that they start to fall apart as soon as they are finished, built of concrete owned by ferre the Puerto Rican cement company. Ferre, who gets fat and rich at the expense of the people. Construction workers try to strike but the judges controlled by ferre hand down orders sotpping the strikes.

We drove to the country, to Fajardo, to Manati, to Guaynabo, the beautiful green country full of beautiful people with brown faces and musical voices, and everywhere the earth was rich but everywhere nothing is being planted because all crops are imported from the states. Everywhere the hills and mountains are being eaten up by the mines and the machines to make more cement for ferre's company. Huge petro-chemical plants in Humacao pollute the water and the air with poisonous gases—the same plants that they wouldn't build in the states because of the "harmful" effects of the gasses. El Yunque's beauty is no longer untouched—signs advertise "Your Happy Rain Forest Resturants," and gringos drive all over the mountain in chauffeured limousines, driving the jibaros on their horses off the road.

Drugs are everywhere. ¼ of a million dollars worth of heroin is sold everyday. Prostitution is legal, for all of our people are prostitutes for the American capitalists. Our sisters are forced to sell their bodies to the Americans on the streets and in the factories. The machismo is so strong that there are almost no sisters in the leadership of the independence movement. Where are the Lolitas, the Blancas, the Viscals? Sisters dye their hair blonde to look like gringas and brothers process their hair to look like gringos. There is no such thing as "pelo malo" (bad hair). People wearing afros (very few) wear them because it's a fad. Indian hair is not "pelo muerto" (dead hair). We should be proud of our Afro-Indio culture. We must fight against racism because it is a tool used to divide us. Many Black Puerto Ricans wind up voting for statehood because the only Black Puerto Rican leader was Jose Celso Barbosa (an American puppet), and he was for statehood.

We visited many independence groups. At M.P.I. we rapped with Florencio Merced and visited the headquarters of Claridad. The exploitation is so heavy that M.P.I. pays 4 times as much money to print Claridad than we do to print Palante. We visited P.I.P. (Puerto Rican Independence Party) and Reuben Berrios, the president, drove us all over the island. We talked to old nationalists, and visited Blanca Canales. The Nationalist Party is printing our 13 pt. Program and Platform in their newspaper every issue.

At the Taller Alacran, a political artist's workshop in San Juan, we picked us some new political posters and looked at the footage of a film they are making about Julio Roldan. Julio was buried in Aguadilla and the Taller filmed the march and burial ceremony.

Our people are beautiful, Puerto Rican people have a revolutionary history, Puerto Rico is beautiful. Mar Chiquita is a beautiful beach because it is free of gringos—but how long? How long before the whole island becomes an advertisement for "fun in the sun." "Y you tranquilo" (and I'm cool is now the hip slang of the youth; when it should be "fuego, fuego, fuego, los yanquis quieren fuego" (fire, fire, fire, the Yankees want fire). We cannot "be cool" much longer. We must unite our Nation, on the island and inside the united states, we must pick up guns to defend ourselves and liberate ourselves. We must follow the examples of Lolita Lebron, Albizu Campos, Julio Roldan, c.a.l. and mira. We must struggle against the american pigs and Puerto Rican vendepatrias.

NOSOTROS NO SOMOS "TRANQUILOS"! VIVA PUERTO RICO LIBRE!
DESPIERTA BORICUA DEFIENDE LO TUYO CON ARMAS!

Denise Oliver
Minister of Finance
YOUNG LORDS PARTY

....

Puerto Rican Society: An Analysis

(From the newspaper *Palante*, 5-19 March 1971, volume 3, number 4)

On March 21, the Young Lords Party will begin to reunify the Puerto Rican nation. On that day, we will open our first branch on the island and have demonstrations in Ponce, New York, Bridgeport, Conn., and Philadelphia, Penn. We will begin to unite the 1,500,000 Puerto Ricans who were forced to come to the usa with the 2,700,000 on the island for two goals—national liberation and self-determination.

We will continue the fight of our Taino and African ancestors, of Ramon Emeterio Betances, and of the Nationalist Party to free our people from the chains of slavery to another country. Throughout our history, whenever Puerto Ricans rose up against their hunger, miserable conditions and racism, we have lost. Why have we lost? For many reasons. Sometimes we were not organized enough. Sometimes infiltrators from the police turned us in. Sometimes the organizations did not really speak to the needs of the people.

One reason that has hurt our fight for freedom is that many of our own people have attacked us, sold us out, joined with the very government that has caused us to be poor, suffering and oppressed. People like Celso Barbossa, munoz marin, luis ferre, herman badillo, teodoro moscose, manuel casiano, and others have been the vendepatrias, the lombrices of Puerto Rico. Many times our people have been divided among themselves and the revolutionary organizations did not unify them, because they did not understand how the people are divided in the first place.

In May, 1970, the Young Lords Party studied the divisions in our people, divisions that make us weak. We call this "Analysis of Puerto Rican Society." This is how we are divided in classes. Every Puerto Rican fits into one of these classes. Your class is determined by how you make your living, how you survive everyday in this crazy amerikkkan controlled world:

LUMPEN: Are men and women who are unemployable, on drugs, prostitutes, welfare mothers, people in jail. Most of us never had a chance for a decent life. We are young, poor, there were never any jobs waiting for us, there was no future, so we turned to drugs and crime. The society calls us worthless, good for nothing. But all we are is oppressed human beings. We rob from our own people because we're prisoners, of drugs, or our conditions. We don't bring the drugs into the community, the businessmen and government do to keep us pacified. We are waking up and uniting as a class with the rest of our people to destroy the real enemy—the Yankees.

INDUSTRIAL WORKERS: The majority of the population are workers. We work in factories and in government employment, in sweat shops and petroleum refineries, in construction and in restaurants. We make $40, $60, $100 a week and hardly stay alive, while our bosses make hundreds of thousands off of our hard work. We don't like to get into trouble because we might lose our job, or our project or casserio [public housing] apartment, or our children, might suffer. We are the housewives and working women who are oppressed not just on the job but at home from our own husbands who beat us or mistreat us because they don't know any better. We are afraid of the lumpen because they rob us, but we know that the system forces them into drugs and prostitution. They are our brothers and sisters, compatriots, oppressed by the same enemy. We will join with them to free Puerto Rico, and after the Yankees are kicked out, we will take over and run the factories for the good of all the people.

AGRICULTURE WORKERS: We are the last of the campesinos, who had our lands bought up or stolen by the amerikkkans, who were tricked into slave like migrant labor and shuttled back and forth from the u.s. to Puerto Rico, to pick tomatoes or other crops for the same oppressor. We are not allowed to grow what we want on our lands in Puerto Rico, because the amerikkkans don't buy our food, but instead try to sell us their canned food. We will join with the lumpen and industrial workers for the liberation of our people.

The Petty-Bourgeois are people who don't work for anyone else, but also who don't employ anyone, or very few people. In other words they live off their own labor. There are three main types of petty-bourgeois.

BODEGUEROS: We own our stores or businesses. We have anywhere from 1 to 5 people who work for us. We make enough to live on if we work hard ourselves. But now the amerikkkan chain stores or the Cuban gusanos are running us out of business. If we don't join with the other oppressed classes we will soon be destroyed by the amerikkkans and Cuban gusanos (exiles).

UNIVERSITY STUDENTS: We are mostly middle class, our families are well-off. Some of us, though, come from poor families, but at the university they are working on our

minds trying to make us think middle class. They want us to join white amerikkkan society. We will fight against that. We are Puerto Ricans and we will determine our own lives.
We will use these skills to help our own people, not to oppress them.

PROFESSIONALS: They are the professors, engineers, doctors, directors of poverty
programs, middle level management of amerikkkan business. They are well off, but
under colonialism and racism of the Yankees[, they are] always remind[ed . . .] that they
are spics, not gringos. Some of them will join with the people in the national liberation
war. Many of them, though, will fight against us, and will be alcahuettes [pimps] of the
amerikkkans.

CAPITALISTS AND TRAITORS: These are the few Puerto Rican capitalists, like ferre,
and the big traitors, like sanchez vilella, badillo, hernandez colon, all the politicians and
others whose lives are tied up with the amerikkkan occupation. They are also the thousands of Cuban pigs who were kicked out of Cuba by Fidel. We will kick all of them out
of Puerto Rico to establish a free, independent, and socialist nation.

The lumpen and workers, allied together, will lead the revolution. The students, bode-
geros, and professionals will join with them. Some professionals, vendepatrias and capitalists will be against us. But in the long run, we will win and Puerto Rico will be free.

CENTRAL COMMITTEE

....

Armed Struggle 1

(From the newspaper *Palante*, 7-20 June 1971, volume 3, number 10)

People speak of revolution and many do not understand. Many who speak of it do
not understand what it really is. In a revolution, the sun rises and sets every day, just
like before. In a revolution, the people still have the same needs they always did. But in a
revolution, the sun rises and sets on people who are changing quickly. It rises and sets on
people engaged in a war.

One day, you are a factory worker in a Parke-Davis plant in Carolina, or a garment
worker in New York, or a housewife in Fajardo; one day you are a drug addict on a Philadelphia street, or a prostitute in the Condado. One day you are a brother in a garage in
Watts, or a vendor in the marqueta in Mayaguez; one day you are a high school sister
expelled for pregnancy, or a veteran from the army. And you continue to be that, or you
leave that job and join a movement. But you have changed. You have slowly begun to
understand why all your life you have been suffering, why all your life things have not
been going right, why you have so much hate, frustration, and misery inside of you. And
you become a fighter, a revolutionary, someone engaged in a war. You become a participant in your life. You take your destiny back from the oppressor and begin the long road
toward freedom.

The road to freedom is not an easy one—it's always getting harder. Somewhere along
that road, the oppressor becomes afraid of our unity, of our growing strength. They
become afraid because we are clear about our goals and they are unable to stop us. And
the clubs start swinging, people start screaming, bullets start flying, sirens start blaring,
tanks start rolling, and maybe bombs start falling.

It happens once, twice, three times. It happens sporadically at first, then regularly. It starts spontaneously and becomes organized. It comes fiercely, sometimes, and quietly other times. And little by little, over a period of time, what had been mainly a political struggle, a battle of words, demonstrations, strikes, conferences, newspapers, becomes a battle with arrests, courts, hospitalizations, dead, wounded, orphaned, occupations and retaliations. The political struggle begins to give way to the armed struggle. The political struggle frees the minds of the people, and the armed struggle frees the bodies of the people.

But many people never see the war, never look toward the future, never prepare. The war comes. They are not ready. They die, are arrested. The people are set back. A revolutionary party must look toward the future. The job of a revolutionary party is to plan further than the people can see, to prepare the future conditions and for the future conditions. One of the jobs of a true revolutionary party is to give guidance, education, and organization to the building of a people's army. Without an army a people's movement is like a baby who can cry but can't walk. Without an army, the people are begging for justice; with an army, the people are making sure they get justice. The capitalist fought and killed to get what he has, and will fight and kill to keep it. We must be prepared to defend ourselves.

A war is bloody. A war kills. A war can destroy a nation. But wars are necessary, as long as capitalists exist. The capitalists have been waging war on us all our lives. We must engage in war to eliminate capitalists because they insist on continuing their exploitation, continuing their money-making, their greed, and their oppression. A revolutionary war will end this.

The problem, then, is preparing for warfare, preparing for the time when political methods no longer help the people progress. War will naturally break out as the only way we have to resolve the problems of misery, hunger, and exploitation. Revolutionary war is different from other types of war. In a war, one group or body of people fight to destroy another group or body of people for a reason, usually the basic needs of the group or the specific needs of some of the people.

There are different types of war. Wars differ on why they are being fought and how they are being fought. There are colonial wars, imperialist wars, civil wars, revolutionary wars, religious wars, land wars, etc. And those wars are fought in different ways. There are regular wars, air wars, guerrilla wars, naval wars, etc. The different forms of war depend on the conditions, on the level of technology of the groups, on the number of people, and on the immediate and long-range objectives of the war. There are wars of quick decision, sustained wars, and protracted wars. There are offensive and defensive wars, and combinations of the two. And there are good wars and bad wars, just wars and unjust wars, wars of oppression and wars of liberation.

But in all wars, the goal is the same, preserve oneself and destroy the enemy.

All revolutionaries, at some point or another have to confront the problem of war. First, will they fight it or not? If they do not, we move backward and not forward. If they do, they must decide on the nature and forms of the war. If they understand that only through war can we resolve the problems that we can't resolve through peace, that only through war can we assure peace in the future, then they set about the work.

In Puerto Rico, no one has ever believed that we could defeat the united states in a war. Betances believed the Puerto Rican people could defeat Spain in war. The great patriot, Ramon Emeterio, developed a policy, a plan, to establish the Republic of Puerto Rico and defeat Spain militarily.

The plan put too much emphasis on technology and not enough emphasis on the people (the ones who will take part in the war). It showed that Betances had an understanding of the skill of a certain type of war, the type of war Spain had been fighting for years, and had taught him to fight. It showed that he at least had a basic understanding of the conditions of Puerto Rico, where the people were strong and the Spanish were weak. But because it assumed that all the people were educated and prepared to fight for independence, the plan failed. An armed struggle without the people involved is not a revolution; it's a "coup," a change of powers from one group of professional politicians to another. What we need in Puerto Rico, what we need in the united states, what all people who are oppressed throughout the world need are long thorough revolutions that put the people in power. Revolutions that give the people the power to control their own lives.

When the united states invaded Puerto Rico, Cuba, the Philippines, and Hawaii in the 1890's, it established military control [illegible] easiest in Hawaii and Puerto Rico and [illegible] in the Philippines and Cuba. Both Hawaii and Puerto Rico, in addition to being [illegible] economically and politically became important military bases for the [illegible] expansion of Europe's stepchild, amerikkka.

QUE VIVA PUERTO RICO LIBRE!

Juan Gonzalez
Minister of Defense
YOUNG LORDS PARTY

....

Armed Struggle 2

(From the newspaper *Palante*, June 1971, volume 3, number 11)

Because the revolutionary movement in amerikkka and in Puerto Rico is young, the revolutionary organizations have a bad understanding of what armed revolution is about. In Puerto Rico, the Revolt of Jayuya in 1950 at least gave our people a sense of what armed struggle, if not revolutionary warfare, is. Because many revolutionaries do not understand the importance of armed struggle, they don't study the revolutions of other countries. Those people will die. Worse, they will fail.

Don Pedro and the Nationalist Party never really believed that we could defeat the united states in Puerto Rico. The armed actions of the Nationalist Party were always either self-defense or symbolic acts of armed propaganda. Oscar Collazo's act of protest at the Blair House, Lolita Lebrón's commando act in Congress in 1954, even the Revolt of Jayuya were symbolic acts which the Nationalists hoped would force the united states to grant independence to our country.

It took the victories of the Cuban Revolution and the Vietnamese Revolution for our independentistas to even begin thinking about true armed struggle. And to this day, many Puerto Ricans do not believe we can survive in a war against the united states. The activities of the Armed Liberation Commandos (CAL) or the Movement for Puerto Rican Independence (MPI) are based on making life impossible for the amerikkkans through sabotage and political activities respectively—not in a firm belief that should the united states continue its domination of our country that we can defeat it in a war of national salvation.

The battle of the Nationalists was a romantic but heroic fight of brave men and women against the yanquis. But they armed themselves with pistols—with .45's and .38's, with .22's. They were open targets for the Puerto Rican lombrices and amerikkkans.

The revolt of Jayuya was planned only a few days before the outbreak. It was a response to a repression that Muñoz Marín, the traitor governor, had been planning along with secretary of war, jordán. The Nationalists were not prepared for the confrontation. The plan called for seizing the police headquarters in about ten towns, seizing the extra arms, then moving quickly to the center of the island, around Utuado, Jayuya, for guerrilla war. No account was taken of the state of the people at the time, of the military capabilities of the amerikkkans and Puerto Rican lombrices. At the last moment, Don Pedro changed some of the leadership of the attacking groups. Raimundo Pacheco, Olga Viscal and their group attacked the Fortaleza in San Juan after a foul-up in finding their stored weapons; and Raimundo along with four others died. Blanca Canales, Elio Torresola, and Carlos Irizarry were the only group actually able to capture a town, Jayuya. Juan Jaca Hernández and his group in Arecibo never made contact with the Jayuya group. 2000 were arrested and many killed. The Nationalists were not prepared for the insurrection; the enemy was.

The Nationalist Party had based too much of its concrete support on middle class and well-to-do independentistas. When the armed struggle begins to broaden, those classes of people will become more and more afraid, less and less helpful, because they have the most to lose. A revolutionary war can only be founded on the poorest and most oppressed who have everything to gain and nothing to lose—the popular classes.

How does a struggle change from a political struggle into an armed struggle? Take the example of the liberation war of Guinea-Bissau under the leadership of Amilcar Cabral. In September, 1956, after years of portuguese colonialism, Amilcar Cabral and others formed the PAIGC (African Independence Party of Guinea and Cabo Verde Islands). They began organizing among the people, mostly in the metropolitan area. In August, 1959, three years later, the portuguese killed 50 workers in a strike in the city of Pijiguiti. It was then, for the Party, that the political struggle began to give way to the armed struggle. Cadres were sent into the countryside to begin the military war. In 1960, a school was started by Cabral at Conakry for the training of guerrillas. Since then, there has been a continuous war and political mobilizing of the people. Schools, hospitals, and factories have been set up in liberated zones as the war continues. Each day the PAIGC liberates more and more territory until most of the land is already controlled by the people. In Guinea-Bissau, the Liberation forces can control territory because the military might of portugal is weak compared to england, france, or germany. Guinea-Bissau is far from portugal's center, and portugal itself is economically and politically a weak colonial oppressor.

The work that the Liberation forces have done in educating the people in concrete ways about their oppression, in training new revolutionary leaders, in publicizing their cause to the peoples of the world, have been key to their success.

The development of the People's Liberation Army of Vietnam was somewhat different. It was the takeover of Vietnam by japan, World War II, that created the conditions out of which came the revolutionary movement. The Vietnam Workers Party was organized in 1930 with 211 members. Other Nationalist organizations had developed during french colonialism, but none could mobilize the masses of the people. During the 1930's revolts of peasants and workers occurred all over Vietnam and it was during that period that leaders like Vo Nguyen Giap first were involved in activities. But throughout that period the Party was controlled by the French Communist Party (like the Socialist Party of Santiago Iglesias was controlled by the Amerikkkan Socialist Party) and was not speaking to the needs of the Vietnamese people, but more to the needs of the french communists.

Ho Chi Minh for all this period was outside the country, in China, in the soviet union, in europe. He would give direction and advice to the Central Committee through letters and articles. In 1939, the Party was banned by the french and repression set in, sending Giap and Pham Van Dong out of the country and killing many good members. The french administration collaborated (cooperated and worked with) with the japanese to set up fascism. In September, 1940, as japanese troops began to move into Vietnam, the Montagnards, a national minority, of Bac Son Province revolted. Other nationalist uprisings followed. Just on the other side of the border, in China, the Central Committee met. They began to organize the first military force of the Party. But in 1941, there was another meeting of the Central Committee that Ho attended. He pushed the idea that a broad patriotic front, the League of Independence of Vietminh (Vietnam) should be organized, that all the different classes of people who were being oppressed by the french and japanese should be united in a war of national salvation. Since it began in 1930, the Party had believed in armed struggle; but in 1941, it was decided the time to begin was there.

¡QUE VIVA PUERTO RICO LIBRE!

Juan González
Minister of Defense
YOUNG LORDS PARTY

....

Armed Struggle 3

(From the newspaper *Palante*, 4-18 July 1971, volume 3, number 12)

General Vo Nguyen Giap is an amazing revolutionary. Unknown to most Puerto Ricans and poor people, he is the leader of the Vietnamese People's Liberation Army. He learned through many years that the ways of thinking and principles of revolutionary war are different from other types of war. He wrote:

"Guerilla war is the war of the broad masses of an economically backward country standing up against a powerfully equipped and well-trained army of aggression. Is the enemy strong? One avoids him. To his modern armament, one opposes a boundless heroism to vanquish either by harassing or by combining military operations with political and economic action; there is no fixed line of demarcation, the front being wherever the enemy is found.

In the war of liberation in Vietnam, guerilla activities spread to all the regions temporarily occupied by the enemy. Each inhabitant was a soldier, each village administrative committee a staff.

The people as a whole took part in the armed struggle, fighting according to the principles of guerrilla warfare, in small packets, but always in pursuance of the one and same line, and the same instructions, those of the Central Committee of the Party, and the government."

During 1941, the Party began to organize armed self-defense units in Cao Bang province. This was preparation for the later building of the People's Army. Says Giap, "Many pamphlets such as Guerrilla Tactics, Experience in Guerrilla Warfare in China, Experience in Guerilla Warfare in Russia, were written by Uncle Ho (Ho Chi Minh) and lithographed with the aim of propagating (spreading) military knowledge among the people. They were much appreciated and avidly read by members of self-defense units and associations for national salvation."

In 1943-44, terror and repression by the government spread. The people formed anti-terror committees. Local oppressors were killed. Small uprisings broke out. The Central Committee, meeting in July 1944, decided to start armed insurrection. But Ho returned from abroad and said it was not yet time. Not enough political work had been done in other parts of the country. He suggested, instead, that Giap begin organizing the Armed Propaganda Unit for Liberation. He said that the people first had to pass through the transition from political to armed struggle by a force that educated them through armed actions. On December 22, 1944, 34 comrades formed the Propaganda Detachment. 6 months later, it had become an army of 10,000. The great victory of Dienbienphu (where French forces were defeated), the victories of the Tet offensive of 1968 (in which the amerikkkan embassy in Saigon was attacked), are 2 examples of the thousands of victories won by the Vietnamese People's Army.

In China, the development of the revolutionary army went a whole different way. In 1927, Mao was heading a peasant's league in a country of China called Hunan. There were over 1,000,000 peasants in the league. The Chinese Communist Party, formed in 1921, was trying to serve and protect the workers and peasants of China.

When the Japanese invaded China, the Nationalist Party of China, the Kuomintang, had allied with the Communists to fight the Japanese invaders. But in 1927, Chiang Kai Shek, head of the Nationalist Party, pulled a coup. Mao was a leader of the peasants along with Chu Ta. They founded a broad army some months later called the 4th Army. Throughout the revolutionary wars of China, hundreds and thousands and millions of men were involved in the 4th Army and 8th Route Army. The Chinese war was a mobile war, with guerrilla units fighting behind enemy lines, and the regular army units fighting in liberated base areas.

Liberated areas were possible in China, especially during the war against Japan, because China was large and semi-colonial. It had very little modern communications or transportation. The Japanese were limited in resources and men and could not control all of China. They were doomed to lose. And after they were destroyed, the puppet soldiers of Chiang Kai Shek were defeated in a 3-year war from 1946-1949.

The wars were not easy. There were setbacks and revivals, setbacks and revivals. The revolution of 1924-27 was betrayed by Chiang Kai Shek. The revolution of 1927-1935 passed through hard times where the Red Army and the Party were reduced from hundreds of thousands to a few thousand. At that time in the world there were only three revolutionary armies—the Red Army of the Soviet Union, the Loyalist Army of Spain, and the

Red Army of China. With the invasion of China by Japan, a United Front between the Kuomintang and the Chinese Communist Party was formed to fight the Japanese. And after the defeat of the Japanese, the final Civil War against the Kuomingtang destroyed Chiang Kai Shek and his amerikkkan supporters. By the time of the Civil War, there were liberated areas that contained some 100,000,000 people where land reforms and socialist living were beginning.

The Chinese and Vietnamese revolutions are the most thorough going revolutionary wars ever fought by poor and oppressed peoples. By comparison, the civil war of the united states, the American revolution, the revolt of Jayuya or El Grito de Lares are firecracker battles. Because they were protracted wars—wars that last for a very long time—they created tremendous changes in the way of life and way of thinking of the people. Whole generations knew no other way of life but war for liberation. The wars were to establish peace but a peace without oppression, a peace without misery, a peace for everyone, not another truce between rich and poor. We know that if you want peace, you have to fight for it.

ALL POWER TO OPPRESSED PEOPLE!
QUE VIVA PUERTO RICO LIBRE!

Juan Gonzalez
Minister of Defense
YOUNG LORDS PARTY

....

On Our Struggle

(From the newspaper *Palante*, 16-29 August 1971, volume 3, number 14)

The following is a speech given by our Minister of Defense, Juan Gonzalez, on July 25, 1971, anniversary of the u.s. invasion of Puerto Rico through the bay of Guanica. Among the participants in the Guanica Commemoration were: MPI, PIP, FUPI, JIU (University Independentist Youth), Socialist League, SMO (Committee to End the Draft), Nationalist Party of Puerto Rico, YLP. About 2,000 persons attended the rally.

Companeros and companeras.

July 25th should be and will be a day of national protest. On July 25, 1898, the war began—the new war of resistance against the new enemy of the Puerto Rican people—the united states. We, the Young Lords Party, unite with the other companeros and companeras who fight for the liberation for the Puerto Rican Nation.

The Nationalist Party of Puerto Rico was the first party to raise Guanica, to protest the invasion of the gringos as should be. In these as in many of the struggles for freedom of our people, the Nationalist Party was at the vanguard of its time. The Young Lords Party follows the example of Don Pedro Albizu Campos and the Nationalist Party and declares that for us Guanica is a day of national protest, and will be a day of national protest until we drive the Puerto Rican lombrices like ferre, the Cuban gusanos, and yankee amerikkkans into the sea.

I want to speak a little bit about how we arrived, how we all arrived here today. I'm going to say it in a not well prepared way. I'm not a speaker—besides, it's time that the people stop looking for speakers, for very prepared leaders—lawyers, professors, doctors, whatever. It's time that the poor look for [sic] ourselves as leaders. It's time that the universities take their place behind the poor in this struggle.

The struggle did not begin yesterday, nor in 1898, nor in 1868. The struggle began since the time in which human beings have been in this world, looking for a way to survive against the forces of nature. We united in societies and, little by little, the societies developed until different types of persons began to oppress parts of society. Societies developed in conflict, class conflicts: the majority, the poor, looking for a way to meet the five basic needs—clothing, food, shelter, mental satisfaction and reproduction. Without reproduction, without the continuation of human beings, there is nothing. The minority, the rich, met their basic needs but took too much of control—of slaves, of women, of land, of factories, of other countries. Humanity passed through different stages, with the majority always searching for those five basic needs, and the search for those needs is called the history of humanity.

In Borinquen, the Tainos were the first to resist; at first, the Caribs invaded but they never gained control of the land. After a while came the Spanish—who were looking for gold and silver and were willing to enslave or kill anyone who tried to stop them. The Tainos dealt with the European invaders but the superiority of arms of savages like Ponce de Leon, conquered them. Genocide against the Tainos was almost complete.

To meet its needs as an empire, spain decides to import Africans, to buy human beings kidnapped from the nations of Yoruba, Ghana, Nigeria, Songomy, human beings with their own history, their own culture, their own way of being. Millions of slaves were brought to all the ports of the Americas—Port au Prince, San Juan, Havana, Charleston, New Orleans, Veracruz. Millions died on the trip. And for what? To work as domestics, to cut cane for an absent owner. When they arrived in San Juan, a priest who would give them their Christian faith, a carimbo (branding iron) to register slaves, and a whip, just in case the slave didn't like the Christian treatment, were waiting.

Slavery is the most disgusting reality in the history of Puerto Rico. From slavery, from the riches of free labor for centuries by African men and women, comes the money of what is left of the old rich families of Puerto Rico.

But resistance continued and the triumphant Haitian Revolution, the first armed success of the slave class, raises the consciousness of all the Africans in the Americas. In Puerto Rico, although the slave class never grew to more than 10% of the population, half of the population was and is free Blacks—men and women of enslaved families, and the reality of racism brought by the Spanish, remains in the Puerto Rican culture and thinking. The amerikkkans made racism even twice as bad, to the point that now our people forget our African and slave roots.

The Revolution of Lares, more than an uprising for independence, was a rebellion against slavery.

The new slavery arrived with the amerikkkans and the only ones in this century who truly confronted that empire was the Nationalist Party of Puerto Rico, and for a time, the Socialist Party. Don Pedro was the defender of our nationality. Don Pedro assured with his struggle that at a later time in the future, men and women, poor and humble, capable of liberating Puerto Rico, would arise.

When it became obvious that the Nationalist Party was winning support among the people that were fed up with the amerikkkan presence, they tried to kill them. When the Nacionalistas responded courageously, when the Nacionalistas showed themselves to be the new defenders, the yankees prepared their new plans. This came at the time when the world depression created unemployment and many workers were rising up in struggle. The Yankees decided to force one-third of the population, after taking their land away from them, to go to New York, Chicago, Philadelphia to enslave us in the factories of the garment and light industry of the eastcoast of the u.s. Why did my mother and father leave La Cantera in Ponce to go to New York? Why did so many of our people leave? Because there was no work, there was no future. The amerikkkans found themselves a traitor, luis munoz marin, to come and convice our people that they should wait for their freedom, while he sent the rest of our people to New York with the amerikkkan dream— that did not exist, that has never existed. Already by 1960 they had accomplished what we call the division of the Puerto Rican Nation. We are a divided nation. How many of us don't have relatives in some part of the united states? How many of us have spent a couple of years working hard to return with memories of racism, brutality, robbery? The reality now is that the nation does not exist only in Puerto Rico. That is why a Puerto Rican revolutionary party can rise in New York and Chicago, in the third of the nation that went through the greatest suffering since the time of slavery—the suffering of grow- ing up in another country, of working in another language, of feeling inferior and sec- ondary, of feeling even greater racism than in Puerto Rico.

Many independentistas who write or speak about Puerto Rico, fail to mention these two realities that are vital in order to understand our history—the period of slavery, dur- ing which one part of our nation treated another part as if they were not human; and the division of the nation when the yankees deceived us and forced us to go the u.s. But it's understandable why the independentistas have not written nor have spoken about these realities. The majority of the leaders up to this point have been from very smug classes—intellectuals, almost never afro-boricuas who have felt the racism, not the vic- tims of migration—because few of the middle class left Puerto Rico—only the jibaros and jibaras, the workers, tried to find a new life.

But we the poor feel the division of the nation everyday. We feel the divisions within our nation.

The Young Lords Party rises in Chicago and later in New York as a gang trying to defend ourselves against amerikkkan oppression. Little by little we change our under- standing and a revolutionary thinking begins to develop. We realized that only with the liberation of Puerto Rico and self-determination inside the united states is it possible to end all the daily pain and suffering with the rats, the poverty, the sicknesses, the unem- ployment, the slavery inside the factories, the lack of adequate housing.

And we fight in New York, we fight in Bridgeport, in Philadelphia, against garbage in the streets, the conditions in the hospitals, against the hypocrisy of the churches. We arrived at the point, last year, when we decided that the solution to our problem did not exist only in the united states but here, in our island. We planned to return. We planned to unite the nation that has been divided for these past thirty years. Like Don Pedro said in Lares after 10 years in prison and in exile, "I have never been absent from Puerto

Rico." This is the reality of the million and a half Boricuas in the ghettoes of the united states. In our hearts, in our oppression, we are still Puerto Ricans of poor class—workers, campesinos and campesinas, lumpen. (The lumpen are the thousands and thousands of our people for whom the system has no use. It does not offer them jobs, future, nothing. They are the drug addicts, the prostitutes, the prisoners in jail—the wretched of the earth. The whole system and the rest of society turn their backs on them. In our Party we have many lumpen who are now producing for their nation. The Party organizes and educates lumpen and we see the small lumpen class as part of the exploited and oppressed masses of this country. There is no suffering more painful than the sickness before that fix, than that slavery to scag. We believe that an alliance of all the popular classes under the leadership of the workers, will win the national liberation of Puerto Rico and self-determination in the united states.)

Our Party, then, spouts up by force. We did not grow because we had read many books, or because we went to the university, or because we had an understanding of good organization. We arose because we were tired of oppression, and by force we built a revolutionary party. It took hard struggle—many didn't know how to read and write. Many of us did not know how to speak our language well. We had never studied or analyzed. But little by little, we learned. Little by little, we began to read, to study, to learn our language. And we always practiced serving the people and defending the people. When professional leaders, the politicos, came to visit us, we would always remember that we were from the people, that our practice was always among our people, and we told them and we're going to tell them: "The revolution is not made in a restaurant, it's not made in La Taona, its made in the factory, it's made on the street, it's made in the countryside, it's made with the people. The revolution is not made in the metaphysical (make-believe, dream) world, it's made in the material (real) world."

Due to our roots, we are going to commit political mistakes, organizational mistakes but we are always willing to listen to criticisms and correct our mistakes. When we established the Party on the island, we were expecting to enter the struggle here in an atmosphere of comrades. Instead we found the rejection of the same independentistas who were supposedly companeros and companeras. They treated us like a certain rare animal, but they offered little in terms of help. Only the Nationalist Party of Puerto Rico and the Revolutionary Committee of Workers gave us a welcome and help.

This is a very serious criticism for anyone who calls himself or herself independentista, not helping companeros and companeras in time of need. But in spite of all that, we established ourselves, in El Cano in Santurce, and in Callejon Fuerte in Aguadilla, and we won the support of our people little by little, day by day. Lombriz ferre and his gang, the cic, increase their repression everyday. But this makes us stronger because if the enemy attacks, we are doing something good. We say to all rentas, agents and police, "Be careful, the tables are going to turn around."

The movement for national liberation grows everyday—the occupation of lands like Carolina headed by PIP, the struggle against the mines of MPI, the bombs of CAL and MIRA, the historic example of the Nationalist Party—are all part of the same struggle. The only thing missing was more discipline, the kind of discipline of iron. When an individual submits to the discipline of an organization and that organization prepares itself

Denise Oliver speaks at a rally on 110th Street in East Harlem, in late 1969. Photograph courtesy of Hiram Maristany.

Woman holds Puerto Rican flag at a rally at the United Nations in October 1970. Photograph courtesy of Hiram Maristany.

Funeral procession for Julio Roldan in October 1970. Photograph courtesy of Hiram Maristany.

Young Lords and others block streets during the summer 1969 "garbage offensive." Photograph courtesy of Hiram Maristany.

Young Lords march in unison sometime in the early 1970s. Photograph courtesy of Hiram Maristany.

Young Lords sold newspapers as a fundraiser and information source for the organization. This photograph includes the June 5, 1970, issue of *Palante*. Photograph courtesy of Hiram Maristany.

Felipe Luciano addresses a crowd in front of "the People's Church" in East Harlem in 1970. Photograph courtesy of Hiram Maristany.

The fact that they were struggling for revolution does not mean Young Lords did not have fun. This young woman is caught off guard by the camera at a rally sometime in the early 1970s. Photograph courtesy of Hiram Maristany.

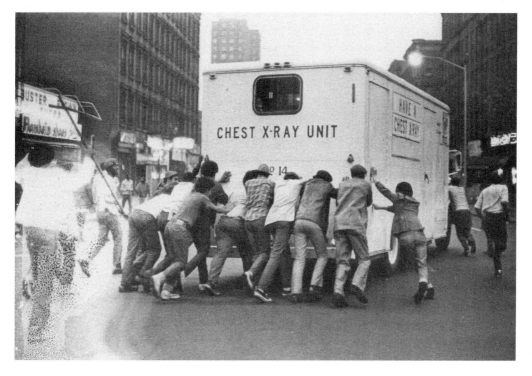

Young Lords "liberate" an X-ray truck to test for tuberculosis in East Harlem in June 1970. Photograph courtesy of Hiram Maristany.

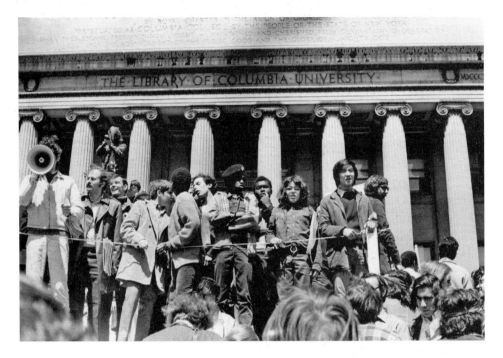

Young Lords and others at a rally in front of the Columbia University library in 1969. Photograph courtesy of Hiram Maristany.

for the time when every Boricua is going to deal, we'll throw the Puerto Rican lombrices, the Cuban gusanos, and the yankee amerikkkans off our land.

VIVA PUERTO RICO LIBRE!
FREE CARLOS FELICIANO!

Juan Gonzalez
Minister of Defense
YOUNG LORDS PARTY

....

YLP on Elections

(From the newspaper *Palante*, December 1971, volume 3, number 19)

During the last few months, there has been an important debate going on in Puerto Rico and in the Puerto Rican colony inside the united states, the debate among all the political organizations fighting for independence and national liberation of our people. That debate is over the proposal of the Movement Pro Independence for a United Front between itself and the Puerto Rican Independence Party. The political commission of MPI and the national committee of PIP announced that they had opened discussions over the possibility of united work for the 1972 elections.

In addition, the MPI announced sometime ago, that they were in the process of transforming into a Socialist Party in their next national assembly.

The Puerto Rican Independence Party was founded in 1947. From its beginning, the party chose the electoral road—participation in the colonial elections—as its principal road for achieving independence. The Movement Pro Independence founded in 1959 as a split off from PIP, and with youth just graduated from the Federation of University Students for Independence, chose the road of a mass political movement. For many years the MPI maintained the belief that the elections in Puerto Rico were illegal. MPI led electoral boycotts in 1960, 1964, 1968.

MPI followed the principles and words of Don Pedro Albizu Campos and the Nationalist Party who said, "if the elections were good for Puerto Rico, there would be no elections."

We in the Young Lords Party also follow the teachings of Don Pedro. We know that since the amerikkkan invasion of Puerto Rico in 1898, the united states has controlled the press, radio, television. They control the schools. Every day, our people are bombarded with more and more amerikkkan propaganda. More than 25,000 amerikkkan troops occupy our territory. With those forces of repression, it is impossible to talk of free elections.

As the National Liberation Front of Vietnam says—first, the amerikkkans should get out, then we will be able to have free elections.

With the division in our nation between the rich who have millions to launch electoral campaigns, and the poor who hardly have enough money to live decently, we can't talk about free elections representative of the interests of the majority of the people.

Everyone knows that in Puerto Rico, even with the "electoral vote," that uncle sam runs the show, uncle sam is the boss of all the working people of the world. And no boss ever permits his slaves even a little bit of power.

Our people have experience with crooked politicians full of empty promises. In the 1940's, luis munoz marin and the slogan "Bread, Land, and Liberty." Where is the bread? Where is the land? Where is the liberty? munoz marin was for independence, until he got into office. Then he became a traitor, and a rich man.

Puerto Ricans inside the united states have much experience with crooked politicians, who look only for fame, money, and power. We believed their honeyed promises in the past, that was how lombricas like badillo were elected: traitors who do nothing to change our conditions of racism and poverty.

That is why earlier, in 1938 the Nationalist Party had established its principle of cooperation with the colonial government. The Puerto Rican Independence Party tries to deny our history and the people's experience with colonial elections. Since 1947, the leaders of PIP tried to convince our people that through elections we could win independence. While Concepcion de Garcias, the President of PIP was talking about democratic means, the amerikkkan government and colonial government of munoz marin was killing Nationalists in the streets, jailing Don Pedro Albizu Campos, and persecuting all independentistas.

Now, the new PIP says that participating in the elections are only a tactic against the amerikkkan government. But elections have been a "tactic" of PIP leaders for the last 20 years. Meanwhile, the united states divided the Puerto Rican nation, forcing one million Puerto Ricans to leave Puerto Rico to live and slave in the ghettos and factories of the united states. Meanwhile, thousands of Puerto Ricans died in the amerikkkan invasions of Korea and Indo China.

Even MPI, that for years had raised a political stand of boycotting the elections, is now talking about going to the elections in 1972, in a United Front, would be a progressive move—if that United Front raised the struggle against our oppressors to a stronger level. But a United Front to go to the elections would be a step backward for our people. We can't fool ourselves, nor can we fool our people. We have the example of the socialist party and Santiago iglesias pantin's treason of the interests of working class Puerto Ricans. We do not need any more experiences with the vote, no more foolery.

With all their good intentions, the leaders of PIP and now the MPI are incorrect when they choose the electoral road. Only the road of a mass revolutionary movement that participates in a protracted struggle against the Cuban gusanos, Puerto Rican lombrices and yankees, can win our liberation and end the oppression by the rich of the poor.

The vote is a trick that every four years divides the Puerto Rican family. A slave cannot vote until he or she is free. Down with the amerikkkan trickery.

VIVA PUERTO RICO LIBRE!
THE WORKPLACES BELONG TO THOSE WHO WORK THEM!

Juan Gonzalez
Minister of Defense
Central Committee
YOUNG LORDS PARTY

7

On Women in the Revolution

When the New York Young Lords organization was founded in the summer of 1969, it filled a need for progressive Puerto Rican activism that had been created when the first generation of militants was driven underground by McCarthyism in the 1950s. In the beginning, however, some of their goals vis-à-vis gender equality were not yet being enacted. Women in the Lords confronted their male leaders with a simple demand: start promoting women's equal agency in the revolutionary struggle. The selections in this chapter explore the various ways in which the Young Lords publicly articulated their demand for equality and their critique of a dominating masculinity known as *machismo*.

....

Women's Oppression: Cortejas

(From the newspaper *Palante*, 22 May 1970, volume 2, number 3)

It is a well known fact that in our Puerto Rican culture married men are encouraged to have a woman on the side, or what we call "una corteja." It is a fact of our society that we try to hide, yet it is there and is clearly oppressive to our women. The wife is there to be a home-maker, to have children and to maintain the family name and honor. Therefore she must be "pure" for the rest of her life, meaning no sexual pleasure. The wife must have children in order to enhance the man's concept of virility and his position within the Puerto Rican society. La corteja becomes his sexual instrument. The man may set her up in another household, paying her bills. The man may have children with this women, but they are looked upon as by-products of a sexual relationship. Both women must be loyal to the man. Both women are exploited, neither being allowed to develop as total human beings and being forced into dependency on a man for status. Also both sets of children grow up very confused and insecure and develop negative attitudes about the role and function of women as well as a messed up concept of what manhood is.

We know that under capitalism, manhood is defined according to the amount of money a male has. Puerto Ricans, since they are exploited by capitalists, have no money, and as a result no status or prestige. As Eldridge Cleaver puts it, our men are "deballed." Since they can't prove manhood economically, they try to do it sexually at the expense of their women.

We say that for our men to have a corteja is oppressive to women. The 10th point of the YOUNG LORDS ORGANIZATION Platform states: "WE WANT EQUALITY FOR WOMEN. Machismo must be revolutionary and not oppressive." The exploitation of Puerto Rican women on the part of Puerto Rican men must stop; Puerto Rican men must realize that machismo is an extension of capitalism and must be gotten rid of. Puerto Rican women must realize that the main oppressor is u.s. capitalism. As Puerto Rican people, we must not allow this racist decadent system to rule over our lives because it destroys us. Therefore, we must destroy it first. We have to control our own destinies and determine our lives in order to be free to create a new and equitable system for women and men. Our people must pick up the gun and say to the pig, Basta ya!

FORWARD SISTERS IN THE STRUGGLE!

MACHISMO IS FASCISM!

SELF-DETERMINATION FOR ALL PUERTO RICANS!

Connie Morales
Education Ministry
YOUNG LORDS ORGANIZATION
Bronx Branch

....

Revolutionary Sister

(From the newspaper *Palante*, 19 June 1970, volume 2, number 5)

On October 29, 1950, in the town of Jayuya, a group of Puerto Rican nationalists were meeting to discuss and decide on a plan of action. The Nationalist Party of Puerto Rico was undergoing a great deal of repression. They knew that orders had come down from Washington to arrest the members of the Nationalists Party and destroy, once and for all, the only source of opposition to amerikkkan colonization of Puerto Rico. The patriots of Jayuya arrived and as the meeting began, the room became filled with an air of tension and an uneasy silence was felt by everyone present.

A small, medium-build woman presided over the meeting, and all attention became focused upon her. A soft-spoken woman, Blanca Canales possessed those qualities of Puerto Rican womanhood at its highest level—courage, dedication, and moral strength. Though her physical appearance gave the impression of a delicate and fragile person, Blanca maintained the inner control to remain calm in the most crucial times and take command of the situation. She along with Carlos Irizarry, Elio Torresola, and Mario Irizarry, were the principal leaders of the revolutionary movement in Jayuya. Together, they determined the political direction and military tactics that would take place in the few remaining hours.

At 4:00 a.m., October 30, just before daybreak, Blanca Canales with 30 other patriots (from the ages of 13 to 25 years) rode down the mountain of Barrio Coabey into the town of Jayuya, opened fire and attacked the jailhouse. One policeman was shot and killed. As the patriots continued to shoot, return fire began. "Chevere," a 14 year old nationalist, was shot in the head, fell to the ground dead, his brains exposed. Carlos Irizarry, commander of the nationalist forces, climbed to the steps of the jailhouse, urging the rest of his men forward. From the sentry outpost, a policeman shot at Carlos, and the bullet entered down into his shoulder through his hip. He stumbled and fell to the ground. His brother, Mario Irizarry, saw his brother collapse, but remained stationed at his post giving cover for the men going ahead. They rushed to the door and with more exchange of fire, the nationalists captured the jailhouse and raised the flag of Puerto Rico. Blanca Canales, armed with a pistol, proved herself a true revolutionary and fighter for the freedom of her people. Once inside the jailhouse, she took charge of the political leadership of the liberation forces. For two days, the nationalists occupied Jayuya while in the nearby towns of Utuado and Panuelas, similar uprisings against the imperialist united states' control of Puerto Rico were happening.

For two days, the national guard sent planes to bombard the town of Jayuya. They came with tanks and heavy arms equipment; and after constant gunfire, the remaining nationalists fled into the mountains. Blanca Canales was captured in Utuado and was tried for conspiracy to overthrow the amerikkkan government. It is absurd that anyone struggling for freedom and liberation should be tried and sentenced by the very fascist government that oppresses him. Blanca was sentenced to 18 years in federal prison, 10 years of which she spent in Olderson, West Virginia and 8 years in Vega Alta, Puerto Rico.

All during her imprisonment, Blanca remained firm to her beliefs; she has never once regretted her actions for the liberation of Puerto Rico. She was released in December, 1968, and is now in Puerto Rico, still very active in the Nationalist Party.

What must be remembered about Blanca Canales is that she lived the teachings of Don Pedro Albizu Campos. For Blanca, nationalism (the pride of being Puerto Rican) was as strong as her belief in the Bible. Her life was dedicated totally to the struggle for the independence of Puerto Rico.

What must be learned from the revolutionary example of sisters like Blanca Canales, Lolita Lebron, and Carmen Perez is that we, as Puerto Ricans, must never for a moment forget that we are Borinquenos, that there have been hundreds of men and women who have died and been imprisoned fighting for the land which is ours. Point 12 of the YOUNG LORDS PARTY's 13-Point Program states: "We believe armed self-defense and armed struggle are the only means to liberation." There is no country in the world that has gained liberation without bloodshed. This is a historical fact—until Borinquenos physically resist the colonization of Puerto Rico and the genocide of Puertorrinquenos, we will continue to live under the fascist government of amerikkka. Borinquenos, awaken! As Malcom X once stated, "The price of freedom is blood; if blood frightens you, then freedom frightens you."

DESPIERTA BORICUA, DEFIENDE LO TUYO!
QUE VIVA PUERTO RICO LIBRE!

Myrna Martinez
Ministry of Defense
Officer of the Day
YOUNG LORDS PARTY

....

Sterilized Puerto Ricans

(From the newspaper *Palante*, 28 August 1970, volume 2, number 10)

Genocide is being committed against the Puerto Rican women! In no other nation has sterilization been so prevalent as a means of genocide against an oppressed people. Why Puerto Ricans? First, the united states needs Puerto Rico as a military stronghold to maintain "political stability" and control in the rest of Latin America. Second, Puerto Rico is the fourth largest worldwide consumer of amerikkkan goods and yields massive profits to amerikkkan capitalists. Also, Puerto Rico supplies fighting men and a cheap

labor pool, both necessary to u.s. capitalism. One way to control a nation of vital importance is to limit its population size. The u.s. is doing exactly this through sterilization.

The practice of sterilization in Puerto Rico goes back to the 1930's when doctors
pushed it as the only means of contraception. As a result, throughout the island, Puerto
Rican women of childbearing age were sterilized. In 1947-1948, 7% of the women were
sterilized; between 1953-1954, 4 out of every 25 Sisters were sterilized; and by 1965, the
number increased to 1 out every 3 women. This system was practiced on Sisters of all
ages. But, since 1965, the trend has been to sterilize women in their early 20's when they
have had fewer babies. This is especially true among lower class Sisters where future revolutionaries would come from. Committing sterilization on young Puerto Rican mothers with fewer children means that the u.s. is able to significantly reduce and limit the
Puerto Rican population in a short period of time.

Genocide through sterilization is not only confined to the island of Puerto Rico. It is also
carried out within the Puerto Rican colony in the u.s. In El Barrio, sterilization is still practiced as a form of contraception among women, especially young Sisters. One out of four
sterilized women in El Barrio has the operation done when she's between 20 and 30. But the
system justifies the shit saying the Sisters go to Puerto Rico to get it done. Yet the evidence
says that over half the Sisters get the operation done right here in New York City and are
strongly encouraged by their doctors to do so. Again, sterilization in the early reproductive
years of a woman's life limits the Puerto Rican population substantially and permanently.

Sterilization is also a form of oppression against Puerto Rican women. We are
oppressed by our own culture that limits us to the roles of homemaker, mother and
bearer of many children which measures male virility. We have been made dependent
on family and home for our very existence. We are used by u.s. corporations to test the
safety of birth control pills before placing them on the market for sale. Our bodies are
used by capitalists for experimentation to find new moneymaking and genocidal gadgets.
We are prevented from getting adequate birth control information and legal abortions.
As a result, one out of every four Sisters who try it die from self-induced abortions, giving Puerto Ricans the notoriety of having the highest death rate casualties from abortion
than any other group. Sterilization is just another form of oppressing us.

Sterilization is irreversible and as such the u.s. can control the Puerto Rican population. Sterilization once done cannot be undone. We must stop sterilization because we
must leave the option open to ourselves to control the Puerto Rican population. Our
men die in Vietnam, our babies are killed through lead poisoning and malnutrition, and
our women are sterilized. The Puerto Rican Nation must continue. We must open our
eyes to the oppressor's tricknology and refuse to be killed anymore. We must, in the tradition of Puerto Rican women like Lolita Lebron, Blanca Canales, Carmen Perez, and
Antonia Martinez, join with our Brothers and together, as a nation of warriors, fight the
genocide that is threatening to make us the last generation of Puerto Ricans.

STOP THE GENOCIDE! OFF THE PIG!
NO MORE STERILIZATION OF SISTERS!
QUE VIVA PUERTO RICO LIBRE!

Iris Morales
Ministry of Education

GENOCIDE!

PUERTORRIQUEÑAS ESTERILIZADAS

From the newspaper *Palante*, 8 May 1970, volume 2, number 2.

An Interview with Blanca Canales

(From the newspaper *Palante*, 25 September 1970, volume 2, number 12)

On August 15, two members of the Central Committee of the YOUNG LORDS PARTY (Juan Gonzalez and Juan "Fi" Ortiz) went to Puerto Rico, on the first official trip of the Party, with the purpose of establishing communications with other progressive groups on the island. One of the groups we visited was the Nationalist Party.

We had an interview with Blanca Canales, one of the leaders of the 1950 rebellion. Dona Blanca was a social worker then, which put her in touch with many of the social problems of the island, problems which were then, as well as they are now, symptoms of yanqui colonialism in Puerto Rico.

Dona Blanca became a disciple of Don Pedro Albizu Campos in the early 1930's. She met Don Pedro while she was attending the University. She soon found that she was spending every free minute in his class. Visitors would come from every part of the island to hear and learn about such subjects as government, economics, mathematics and languages. Dona Blanca remembers that Don Pedro always caused a great sensation among the people where ever he went. His passion and love for Puerto Rico, became the passion and love of all his followers. The men and women who followed Don Pedro into the Nationalist Part felt and experienced the same love for their people and their island, as the Young Lords Party does now. An all consuming love that would drive us to fight and to die, to see our people free and our island liberated.

Following below, are some questions we asked Dona Blanca Canales during our interview.

QUESTION—Where were you born and how was life when you were younger?

I was born in Jayuya. My father was the Mayor of the town. I spent the first 13 years of my life at home, when I graduated from the eighth grade my parents sent me to high school in Ponce, from where I went to the University of Puerto Rico where I received my Bachelors. My parents taught me the history of my country—they always believed Puerto Rico should be free and independent.

The schools I went to only taught yanqui history. You know stuff like George "I never a told lie" Washington, Bunker Hill, Lincoln freed the slaves. The schools were run by yanquis and vendepatrias and they discouraged the teaching of Puerto Rican history. But I had a teacher once, Carmen Maria Torres, who used to smuggle into the schools books on Puerto Rican history and she would spend time telling us about Puerto Rican heroes like Betances, and the revolution in Lares on September 23, 1968—I felt re-born.

Coupled with the stories my mother used to tell me about my grandfather who was also a revolutionary involved in the uprising in 1868, you can understand how I developed such a fierce love for my country and a desire to see it free and independent.

QUESTION—From your own point of view, what was the tactical purpose of taking the police station in Jayuya?

This is a question of . . . how do you say it now . . . of 50 thousand dollars. This is a long history in the sense that to talk about it one would have to explain how we gradually prepared and armed ourselves during the years and how we had thought of the type of revolution we would carry out and what things would be able to be done. Then when October 30 came of which I would like to speak more and not only answer the question.

Before the 30th, Don Pedro had informed us of the fact that they had been arresting Nationalists all over the island and that we had to commence the revolution. We knew that we would not be victorious but we had to hit our oppressor hard to show our determination to struggle for the independence of Puerto Rico, to the other countries of the world.

We realized we were already in the midst of a revolution when we heard that the headquarters in Arecibo had been attacked and that shooting had begun among the Nationalists and the police. We thought it best to take advantage of the time and liberate the town of Jayuya. At that time there were only four police at the headquarters. It was pretty easy; to hit them unexpectedly was best. The troops that we gathered on the farms were led by my cousin and companero, Elio Torresole and Carlos Irrizary.

We sent these troops to attack the headquarters at noon and there and then the shootout began. We ran out of bullets and then seized the headquarters with molotov cocktails. One policeman died and the others escaped. In the meantime I was in the middle of the town, next to a hotel. I raised the flag of Puerto Rico and screamed "Viva PUERTO RICO Libre" to establish the fact that we had proclaimed the Republic.

The town of Jayuya united, some applauded us, some cried and screamed and others stood around in admiration.

QUESTION—You were in jail for many years. How did they treat you in jail as a political prisoner, especially in relation to the other prisoners?

I was in jail for 16 years and 10 months, almost 17 years. The empire does not give recognition to the political prisoner. I was treated like a common prisoner. During the first eight months I was incommunicado. Perhaps I can say that because of my age—I was 44 years old when I was first incarcerated—I was able to relate well with the other prisoners.

First they took me to the united states. They kept me at the Augusta Reformatory for 5 1/2 years and then brought me back to Puerto Rico. The only well treated prisoner is the stool-pigeon, all others were treated badly. In fact we didn't even have the right to talk. Time and time again they tried to destroy my revolutionary spirit and to do away with the love I had for my country and the right to fight for her.

QUESTION—Being in the southern part of the united states, were all the prisoners black?

There was racial separation in jail. In one section the white prisoners, in another section the Black prisoners; I was placed with the whites. After a few years they passed an integration law in the jail. The white prisoners refused to abide by that law. I and a group of white communist prisoners decided to struggle against this racism and show those people some decency and the reality that we are all the same. We were the first to integrate. From then on, united with my Black companeras, I enjoyed the best years I had to do in that prison.

QUESTION—What is the role of the woman in the revolution?

The role of the woman is as important as of the man. The revolutionary woman must act accordingly with the demands of the revolution, be it to arm herself, educate her people or whatever is necessary.

QUESTION—What do you think of the contemporary independence movements?

I believe that all of today's movements are important. What is needed is unity to achieve the independence of our nation. Some times posters, other times fires, strikes, votes, all that is necessary. My hopes lie with the youth, because you have the ability to carry the word onward.

....

Young Lords Party Position Paper on Women

(From the newspaper *Palante*, 25 September 1970, volume 2, number 12)

Puerto Rican, Black, and other Third World (colonized) women are becoming more aware of their oppression in the past and today. They are suffering three different types of oppression under capitalism. First, they are oppressed as Puerto Ricans or Blacks. Second, they are oppressed as women. Third, they are oppressed by their own men. The Third World woman becomes the most oppressed person in the world today.

Economically, Third World women have always been used as a cheap source of labor and as sexual objects. Puerto Rican and Black women are used to fill working class positions in factories, mass assembly lines, hospitals and all other institutions. Puerto Rican and black women are paid lower wages than whites and kept in the lowest positions within society. At the same time, giving Puerto Rican and Black women jobs means the Puerto Rican and Black man is kept from gaining economic independence, and the family unit is broken down. Capitalism defines manhood according to money and status; the Puerto Rican and Black man's manhood is taken away by making the Puerto Rican and Black woman the breadwinner. This situation keeps the Third World man divided from his woman. The Puerto Rican and Black man either leaves the household or he stays and becomes economically dependent on the woman, undergoing psychological damage. He takes out all of his frustrations on his woman, beating her, repressing and limiting her freedom. Because this society produces these conditions, our major enemy is capitalism rather than our own oppressed men.

Third World Women have an integral role to play in the liberation of all oppressed people as well as in the struggle for the liberation of women. Puerto Rican and Black women make up over half of the revolutionary army, and in the struggle for national liberation they must press for the equality of women; the woman's struggle is the revolution within the revolution. Puerto Rican women will be neither behind nor in front of their brothers but always alongside them in mutual respect and love.

Historical

In the past women were oppressed by several institutions, one of which was marriage. When a woman married a man she became his property and lost her last name. A man could have several wives in order to show other men what wealth he had and enhance his position in society. In Eastern societies, men always had several wives and a number of women who were almost prostitutes, called concubines, purely sexual objects. Women had no right to own anything, not even their children; they were owned by her husband. This was true in places all over the world.

In many societies, women had no right to be divorced, and in India it was the custom of most of the people that when the husband died, all his wives became the property of his brother.

In Latin America and Puerto Rico, the man had a wife and another woman called la corteja. This condition still exists today. The wife was there to be a homemaker, to have children and to maintain the family name and honor. She had to be sure to be a virgin and remain pure for the rest of her life, meaning she could never experience sexual pleasure. The wife had to have children in order to enhance the man's concept of virility and his position within the Puerto Rican society. La corteja became his sexual instrument. The man could have set her up in another household, paid her rent, bought her food, and paid her bills. He could have children with this woman, but they are looked upon as by-products of a sexual relationship. Both women had to be loyal to the man. Both sets of children grew up very confused and insecure and developed negative attitudes about the role.

Women have always been expected to be wives and mothers only. They are respected by the rest of the community for being good cooks, good housewives, good mothers, but never for being intelligent, strong, educated, or militant. In the past, women were not educated, only the sons got an education, and mothers were respected for the number of sons they had, not daughters. Daughters were worthless and the only thing they could do was marry early to get away from home. At home the role of the daughter was to be a nursemaid for the other children and kitchen help for her mother.

The daughter was guarded like a hawk by her father, brothers, and uncles to keep her a virgin. In Latin America, the people used "duenas" or old lady watchdogs to guard the purity of the daughters. The husband must be sure that his new wife has never been touched by another man because that would ruin the "merchandise." When he marries her, her purpose is to have sons and keep his home but not to be a sexual partner.

Sex was a subject that was never discussed, and women were brainwashed into believing that the sex act was dirty and immoral, and its only function was for the making of children. In Africa, many tribes performed an operation on young girls to remove the clitoris so they would not get any pleasure out of sex and would become better workers.

The Double Standard, Machismo, and Sexual Fascism

Capitalism sets up standards that are applied differently to Puerto Rican and Black men from the way they are applied to Puerto Rican and Black women. These standards are also applied differently to Third World peoples than they are applied to whites. These standards must be understood since they are created to divide oppressed people in order to maintain an economic system that is racist and oppressive.

Puerto Rican and Black men are looked upon as rough, athletic and sexual, but not as intellectuals. Puerto Rican women are not expected to know anything except about the home, kitchen and bedroom. All that they are expected to do is look pretty and add a little humor. The Puerto Rican man sees himself as superior to his woman, and his superiority, he feels, gives him license to do many things—curse, drink, use drugs, beat women, and run around with many women. As a matter of fact these things are considered natural for a man to do, and he must do them to be considered a man. A woman who curses, drinks, and runs around with a lot of men is considered dirty scum, crazy, and a whore.

Today Puerto Rican men are involved in a political movement. Yet the majority of their women are home taking care of the children. The Puerto Rican sister that involves herself is considered aggressive, castrating, hard and unwomanly. She is viewed by the brothers as sexually accessible because what else is she doing outside the home. The Puerto Rican man tries to limit the woman's role because they feel the double standard is threatened; they feel insecure without it as a crutch.

Machismo has always been a very basic part of Latin American and Puerto Rican culture. Machismo is male chauvinism and more. Machismo means "mucho macho" or a man who puts himself selfishly at the head of everything without considering the woman. He can do whatever he wants because his woman is an object with certain already defined roles—wife, mother, and good woman.

Machismo means physical abuse, punishment and torture. A Puerto Rican man will beat his woman to keep her in place and show her who's boss. Most Puerto Rican men do not beat women publicly because in the eyes of other men that is a weak thing to do. So they usually wait until they're home. All the anger and violence of centuries of oppression which should be directed against the oppressor is directed at the Puerto Rican woman. The aggression is also directed at daughters. The daughters hear their fathers saying "the only way a woman is going to do anything or listen is by hitting her." The father applies this to the daughter, beating her so that she can learn "respeto." The daughters grow up with messed up attitudes about their role as women and about manhood. They grow to expect that men will always beat them.

Sexual fascists are very sick people. Their illness is caused in part by this system which mouths puritanical attitudes and laws and yet exploits the human body for profit.

Sexual Fascism is tied closely to the double standard and machismo. It means that a man or woman thinks of the opposite sex solely as sexual objects to be used for sexual gratification and then discarded. A sexual fascist does not consider people's feelings; all they see everywhere is a pussy or a dick. They will use any rap, especially political, to get sex.

Prostitution

Under capitalism, Third World women are forced to compromise themselves because of their economic situation. The facts that her man cannot get a job and that the family is dependent on her support mean she hustles money by any means necessary. Black and Puerto Rican sisters are put into a situation where jobs are scarce or nonexistent and are forced to compromise body, mind, and soul; they are then called whores or prostitutes.

Puerto Rican and Black sisters are made to prostitute themselves in many other ways. The majority of these sisters on the street are also hard-core drug addicts, taking drugs as an escape from oppression. These sisters are subjected to sexual abuse from dirty old men who are mainly white racists who view them as the ultimate sexual objects. Also he has the attitude that he cannot really prove his manhood until he has slept with a Black or Puerto Rican woman. The sisters also suffer abuse from the pimps, really small time capitalists, who see the women as private property that must produce the largest possible profit.

Because this society controls and determines the economic situation of Puerto Rican and Black women, sisters are forced to take jobs at the lowest wages; at the same time take insults and other indignities in order to keep the job. In factories, our men are worked like animals and cannot complain because they will lose their jobs—their labor is considered abundant and cheap. In hospitals, our women comprise the majority of the nurse's aides, kitchen workers, and clerks. These jobs are unskilled, the pay is low, and there is no chance for advancement. In offices, our positions are usually as clerks, typists and no-promotion jobs. In all of these jobs, our sisters are subjected to racial slurs, jokes, and others indignities such as being leered at, manhandled, propositioned, and assaulted. Our sisters are expected to prostitute themselves and take abuse of any kind or lose these subsistence jobs.

Everywhere our sisters are turned into prostitutes. The most obvious example is the sisters hustling their bodies on the streets, but the other forms of prostitution are also types of further exploitation of the Third World women. The only way to eliminate prostitution is to eliminate this society which creates the need. Then we can establish a socialist society that meets the economic needs of all the people.

Birth Control, Abortion, Sterilization = Genocide

We have no control over our bodies, because capitalism finds it necessary to control the woman's body to control population size. The choice of motherhood is being taken out of the mother's hands. She is sterilized to prevent her from having children, or she has a child because she cannot get an abortion.

Third World sisters are caught up in a complex situation. On one hand, we feel that genocide is being committed against our people. We know that Puerto Ricans will not be around on the face of the earth very long if Puerto Rican women are sterilized at the rate they are being sterilized now. The practice of sterilization in Puerto Rico goes back to the 1930's when doctors pushed it as the only means of contraception. In 1947-48, 7% of the women were sterilized; between 1953-54, 4 out of every 25; and by 1965, the number had increased to about 1 out of every 3 women. In many cases our sisters are told that their tubes are going to be "tied," but are never told that the "tying" is really "cutting" and that the tubes can never be "untied."

Part of this genocide is also the use of birth control pills which were tested for 15 years on Puerto Rican sisters (guinea pigs) before being sold on the market in the u.s. Even now many doctors feel that these pills cause cancer and death from blood clotting.

Abortions in hospitals that are butcher shops are little better than the illegal abortions our women used to get. The first abortion death in NYC under the new abortion law was Carman Rodriguez, a Puerto Rican sister who died in Lincoln Hospital. Her abortion was legal, but the conditions in the hospital were deadly.

On the other hand, we believe that abortions should be legal if they are community controlled, if they are safe, if our people are educated about the risks and if doctors do not sterilize our sisters while performing abortions. We realize that under capitalism our sisters and brothers cannot support large families and the more children we have the harder it is to support them. We say, change the system so that women can freely be allowed to have as many children as they want without suffering any consequences.

Day Care Centers
One of the main reasons why many sisters are tied to the home and cannot work or become revolutionaries is the shortage of day care centers for children. The centers that already exist are over-crowded, expensive, and are only super-baby-sitting centers. Day care centers should be free, should be open 24 hours a day, and should be centers where children are taught their revolutionary history and culture.

Many sisters leave their children with a neighbor, or the oldest child is left to take care of the younger ones. Sometimes they are left alone, and all of us have read the tragic results in the newspapers of what happens to children left alone—they are burned to death in fires, or they swallow poison, or fall out of windows to their death.

Revolutionary Women
Throughout history, women have participated and been involved in liberation struggles. But the writers of history have never given full acknowledgement to the role of revolutionary women. At the point of armed struggle for national liberation, women have proved themselves as revolutionaries.

MARIANA BRACETTI was a Puerto Rican woman who together with her husband fought in the struggle for independence in Lares. She was called "el brazo de oro" [golden arm] because of her unlimited energy. For her role in the struggle, she was imprisoned. She sewed the first flag of El Grito de Lares.

Another nationalist woman was LOLA RODRIGUEZ DE TIO, a poet who expressed the spirit of liberty and freedom in "La Borinquena." Besides being a nationalist, she was a fighter for women's rights. She refused to conform to the traditional customs concerning Puerto Rican women and at one point cut her hair very short.

Only recently, a 19 year old coed, ANTONIA MARTINEZ, was killed in Puerto Rico in a demonstration against the presence of amerikkkan military recruiting centers. She was murdered when she yelled "Viva Puerto Rico Libre!"

SOJOURNER TRUTH was born a slave in New York around 1800. She traveled in the north speaking out against slavery, and for women's right. She was one of the most famous black orators in history.

KATHLEEN CLEAVER is a member of the Central Committee of the Black Panther Party. The Black Panthers are the vanguard of the Black liberation struggle in the united states. Another Panther sister, ERICA HUGGINS, is imprisoned in Connecticut for supposedly being a member of a conspiracy. She was forced to have her child in prison, and was given no medical attention while she was pregnant. Her child was later taken away from her because of her political beliefs.

ANGELA DAVIS is a Black revolutionary sister who is being hunted by the f.b.i. and is on their 10 most wanted list because she always defended her people's right to armed self-defense and because of her Marxist-Leninist philosophy.

In other parts of the world, women are fighting against imperialism and foreign invasion. Our sisters in Vietnam have struggled alongside their brothers for 25 years, first against the French colonizer, then against the japanese invaders, and now against the amerikkkan aggressors. Their military capability and efficiency has been demonstrated in so many instances that a women's brigade was formed in the National Liberation Front of the North Vietnamese Army.

BLANCA CANALES was one of the leaders of the revolution in Jayuya in 1950.

LOLITA LEBRON, together with three other patriots, opened fire on the House of Representative in an armed attack in 1954, bringing the attention of the world on the colonial status of Puerto Rico. She emptied a 45 automatic from the balcony of the Congress on to the colonial legislators. She then draped herself in the Puerto Rican flag and cried "Viva Puerto Rico Libre." The result was 5 legislators shot, and one critically wounded. She was imprisoned in a federal penitentiary and sentenced to 50 years. She is still in prison for this heroic act of nationalism.

LA THI THAM was born in a province which was constantly bombarded by u.s. planes. After her fiance was killed in action, she sought and got a job with a time bomb detecting team. She scanned the sky with field glasses and when the enemy dropped bombs along the countryside, she would locate those which had not exploded and her teammates would go and open them and clear the road for traffic.

KAN LICH, another Vietnamese sister, fought under very harsh and dangerous conditions. She became a brilliant commander, decorated many times for her military ability. Her practice to "hit at close quarters, hit hard, withdraw quickly" proved to be valid.

The Central Committee of the Young Lords Party has issued this position paper to explain and to educate our brothers and sisters about the role of sisters in the past and how we see sisters in the struggle now and in the future. We criticize those brothers who are "machos" and who continue to treat our sisters as less than equals. We criticize sisters who remain passive, who do not join in the struggle against our oppression.

We are fighting every day within our PARTY against male chauvinism because we want to make a revolution of brothers and sisters—together—in love and respect for each other.

FORWARD SISTERS IN THE STRUGGLE!
ALL POWER TO THE PEOPLE!

Central Committee
YOUNG LORDS PARTY

....

World of Fantasy

(From the newspaper *Palante*, 29 January 1971, volume 3, number 2)

Television is used to brainwash and confuse our nation here and on the island. The programs shown provide false images and ideas that do not relate to the reality of oppression of Puerto Ricans, especially sisters.

These lies come in many forms. One way is through the novellas (soap operas) that are shown on t.v. These novellas are geared towards our sisters in the Puerto Rican Nation. They are supposed to be a source of "entertainment" and are used to make us sisters passive to our daily oppression. The stories revolve around upper middle class people, racism, sexism (male chauvinism–female passivity) and religion, all of which are products of the capitalist society and all designed to enslave us and our minds.

The racism scene usually involves a young couple, one of whom is Black. The problems develop when they want to get married—they know that their family will not accept the Black person. What happens to a sister who looks at a program like this? It will create racist attitudes and we begin to think that being Black is not good and that somehow the best thing to be is white.

Television, especially novellas, also condition us to the roles that we have to play as "man" and as "woman." This is what is called sexism. The model families sold to us in these novellas define for us how we're supposed to act and what we're supposed to do.

For example, you have the typical mother who cooks, cleans, washes, shops, takes care of the kids, etc. The typical father, who works, is out all day and the typical children want to be just like their mommies and daddies. The man is the "head of the house" and the bread winner. He comes home from work and expects to have his dinner ready and see the house spotless. The wife, of course, is loving, fragile, and if her husband has another woman on the side, she is patient and understanding, because after all, he is a "man." When our sisters watch these novellas, they make us passive to oppression as Third World People and to our oppression as women. We accept our brothers' male chauvinism because we are taught that that is what a man is.

Taking another example, let's say that on t.v. there's a story where one of the children becomes ill. The doctors can't find the cause of the illness. There's no medicine that can help. Then an elderly woman comes to visit and stays with the child for a while. Within a matter of days, the child miraculously recovers. The doctors, bewildered, want to know what the old woman did to cure the child. The woman pulls out a statue of the virgin mary or jesus christ and says that through her faith in god, the child was cured and that we should all slave very hard because someday a savior will come who will lead us to a new kingdom. Religion is another way that we are kept pacified.

The people that are shown to us in these novellas are upper-middle-class people. They are the ones who own their own houses and cars. The husband is a doctor or lawyer or he owns his own business. Their children go to private schools. The reason these people are shown to us is so we can think that our problems and their problems are the same. We become involved in these stories and we begin to sympathize with these people and we try to act like them, forgetting ourselves and most importantly, our people and the reality of our oppression.

But these novellas are not real. They don't show us the truth of our oppression and how we live. They don't show us how in a capitalist society, poor people work hard and

From the newspaper *Palante*, 29 January 1971,
volume 3, number 2.

yet barely survive, while a few play in all the riches of our island and the world. T.V.
is used as a tool to sell us lies and to try to make us believe those lies. It shows nothing of how our sisters die of abortions forced upon us because in the land of plenty, we
can't "afford" another human life. It shows nothing of how doctors tell us to take the pill,
making us believe that it is safe, when in fact, they were using us as guinea pigs and all
the time making us sterile. It doesn't show how hard we work and yet how little paid.
It doesn't show the housing conditions we are forced to live in. It doesn't show how we
work all day in a factory only to return home at night to a husband who either is drunk,
out all the time, or beats us constantly. Television is unreal but our oppression isn't.

In a socialist society, television will be put to better use. It will be used to serve our people by having educational programs for example. Programs where our people can be taught
to read and write. Programs that show us what is really happening in the world around us,
not like the television now that shows us only what the rich capitalists want us to know.

In this society, being Third World and being a sister means that we are oppressed
not only by the society but by our own brothers. This is what we call the Triple Oppression—because we are oppressed because we are Third World, because we are sisters, and
because we are poor. This system, through television, tells us that that is the way that it
is supposed to be. Sisters, they say, are supposed to be weak and inferior while brothers are strong and superior. This society has in the past succeeded in making us think
that we're all inferior. Brothers have directed their frustrations into themselves and have
taken it out on sisters. Sisters have directed our frustrations into ourselves, developing
self-hatred. We must stop competing with each other, trying to be like somebody on t.v.
and we must look for ourselves as what we are, how we live, and where we stand.

For now, sisters and all oppressed people are moving. We know that in this society there is no freedom. The 5th Point of the Young Lords Party Program and Platform says that "We want equality for women. Down with machismo and male chauvinism." The Young Lords Party also is fighting for the "liberation of all Third World People" (as stated in our 3rd Point of the Program). We are going to fight for our liberation and the liberation of all oppressed people, and we know that there is power only in unity.

REVOLUTION WITHIN THE REVOLUTION!
ALL POWER TO THE PEOPLE!
ALL POWER TO THE SISTERS!

Jenny Figueroa
Ministry of Information
YOUNG LORDS PARTY
Lower East Side Branch

....

Madame Dinh

(From the newspaper *Palante*, 19 February 1971, volume 3, number 3)

In Vietnam the people have shown the strength of a unified people's army in defeating first the French and now the u.s.a. One sister who has come to the forefront of this struggle is Madame Nguyen Thi Dinh who is presently the vice commander in chief of the Armed Forces of Liberation of South Vietnamese.

Nguyen Thi Dinh, the youngest of 11 children, was born to a poor peasant family in the province of Bentre. As young as age 14, she joined in the fight against rich peasants and the french colonizer in an insurrection that took place in 1930. Heavy repression came down on her family and one of her brothers was jailed. When he got out of jail he began teaching her more about political matters. Then at the age of 16 she became a messenger for the revolutionary movement fighting against the french.

Again in 1939, repression came down very hard on the revolutionary movement. All known cadres (revolutionaries) and even poor peasants who were not involved in revolutionary activity were arrested and tortured. Madame Dinh's husband was jailed that year, only two years after their marriage. He died in prison without her ever seeing him again. A year later, she was imprisoned and her 6 month old baby was taken away from her. She was brutally tortured trying to get her to confess to subversive activities against the government, but she wouldn't speak. At the time she was arrested, 1,000 prisoners including 100 women were also arrested, most of them not knowing why. Madame Dinh took it upon herself as a revolutionary to educate all the sisters and brothers, showing that a revolutionary organizes and educates the people wherever she or he is at.

In 1943, she suffered a severe heart ailment. The oppressor in political activity released her from prison. However, she was constantly watched and was unable to travel outside the village. Any friends she made contact with were arrested. Finally, she went to work with the Viet Minh in 1944, and in 1945 she took her part in a popular insurrection against the french and the rich peasants. After the insurrection, the war of resistance began on Sept. 23 (the anniversary of our Grito de Lares when we began our struggle as Puerto Ricans against the spanish colonizer).

In 1946, Madame Dinh was sent to Hanoi to report on the revolution in the south. There she saw Ho Chi Minh. After completing her mission, she was sent to publicize the revolution. She went from village to village bringing the revolution to the people. Then Nguyen Thi Dinh led the armed uprising in the province of Bentre and was in charge especially of the military aspects. This is important because many people although they recognize the need for sisters in revolutionary struggle doubt the military capabilities of women. She continued her political work in this province and became one of the leaders. By 1960 in the struggle against the u.s.a. she became the first secretary of the revolutionary organization in her native province. By the end of 1961, she became vice president of the National Liberation Front. In 1964, she became a member of the central committee of the National Liberation Front as vice president of the military chief of staff of the National Liberation Front and president of the women's committee.

It is important for us to know the history of third world women who fought and are fighting for the freedom of our peoples. We usually don't know anything about them because even today people believe women have no role in revolution. Yet sisters all over the world and especially the vietnamese have shown that revolution is the duty of both men and women.

FORWARD SISTERS IN THE STRUGGLE
PONCE-MARCH 21ST ROMPE CADENASI

Iris Morales
Young Lords Party
EL BARRIO Central Hdqrs.

....

Abortions

(From the newspaper *Palante*, 19 March–2 April 1971, volume 3, number 5)

A sister we know went to a clinic where they perform D'n'C (abortion that's performed up to the 12th week of pregnancy by means of a suction machine that pulls the fetus from the womb).

"You're 18 weeks pregnant. We can't do it here. You'll have to go to a hospital for a saline induction," the doctor said. (A saline induction is an abortion performed after the 12th week of pregnancy where the woman is injected with a saline solution that induces labor as in normal birth.)

She went to a hospital where a Puerto Rican attendant directed her to the abortion ward adding, "That's where they kill babies!" There another doctor estimated that she was 14 weeks pregnant and would have to return when she reached her fourth month salting out.

The sister returned and was sent to still another hospital where a long line of women waited with $400 in hand to pay in advance for their abortions. Since she had no money, she was sent to another hospital, a city hospital, where a doctor examined the sister and said that she was 6 1/2 months pregnant and that it was "too late." The sister returned home to her other children and her unemployed husband to do more hustling to allow her future child to survive when she gives birth. In a certain sense, she went home relieved because, being a Puerto Rican woman, she knew that for her entering an abortion clinic in a New York City hospital was either risking her life or the possibilities of ever being pregnant again. And she was scared!

The case of the sister is no different from that of other Third World (Puerto Rican, Black, Chicano, Asian, Native American) women who face the situation of choosing between the risk of an abortion from a racist hospital administration, or of inventing new ways of hustling to clothe, feed, and shelter an addition to her family.

In Puerto Rico, the amerikkkan government has been pushing sterilization as the only means of contraception since the 1930's with the result that by 1965, ONE OUT OF EVERY THREE WOMEN WERE STERILIZED. The Puerto Rican woman was also used as a guinea pig for the contraceptive pills that were tested on the island for 15 years before being sold in the u.s. market, while even now these pills are believed to cause cancer and death from blood clotting. In a San Juan slum known as El Cano de Martin Pena, one out of every eleven children born dies before he or she is 1 day old. While one out of every four women in Puerto Rico dies from self-induced abortions.

If a Puerto Rico woman decides to have an abortion, the Church that charges her around $3 for a baptismal certificate but that won't feed her children, tries to make her feel guilty. The man who gets drunk and beats her while she's pregnant and tells her that he doesn't want to be a "chancletero" [lowlife] makes her feel guilty. And the "welfare" department tells her that it's going to be rough if she doesn't have an abortion.

The government forces us to live like roaches, always in the garbage. When we can't produce in the sweat shops to make them more money because of the high unemployment rates; when we can't buy their junk because they won't give us credit to legalize the rip-off; when we're no longer of any use to them and become a threat of possible revolutionaries, they exterminate us like roaches.

So we have the Third World woman holding on to her pregnant body, watching her already born children nibble on lead paint in place of food, watching the rats that gather worrying about having her insides zipped up during an abortion.

Point Number 6 of the Young Lords Party 13 Point Platform and Program states "We want community control of our institutions and land." This means that we want institutions, like hospitals where sisters go to have abortions, to be under the control of our people to be sure that they really serve our needs. Until we struggle together to change our present situation, women will not be allowed to have the children they can support without suffering any consequences.

QUE VIVA! PUERTO RICO LIBRE!

Gloria Colon
Ministry of Education
Central Headquarters
YOUNG LORDS PARTY

....

Position on Women's Liberation

(From the newspaper *Palante*, May 1971, volume 3, number 8)

Puerto Rican, Black, Asian, Native American and other Third World Women (women of color) are becoming more aware of how we have been especially oppressed. Women have historically been at the bottom of the ladder; under capitalism, this has been intensified so that we are oppressed three ways. First, we are oppressed as Puerto Ricans, Blacks, Chicanas, Native Americans or Asians (Third World People). Second, we are oppressed as women. Third, we are oppressed by our own men who have been brainwashed by this capitalist system into believing a whole set of false, empty standards of what manhood is supposed to be—machismo. The Third World Woman thus becomes the most oppressed person in the world today.

Whenever there is oppression a movement develops to end that oppression. Third World Women have been and are still being oppressed, and therefore, there is a movement of liberation. Third World Women have always struggled in many different ways. This struggle, however, should not be confused with the Women's Liberation Movement. There are many differences—differences in the background of the women involved and differences about how best to end the oppression of women.

The Women's Liberation Movement is made up of many different groups. But, the mass media has focused most of its attention on the counter-revolutionary parts of the Women's Movement. These women are middle class and upper class women whose efforts are directed against the freedom of all people, such as the National Liberation of Puerto Rico and self determination for Puerto Ricans in the u.s. They believe that the greatest contradiction (conflict) in the world lies between men and women. This counter culture-revolutionary part, or the right-wing of the women's movement, believes that even if there were socialist revolutions all over the world, women would still occupy a secondary (inferior) place in that new society. The right wing in the women's movement says all women are sisters and all men are enemies. Yet, this is only one part of the woman's movement.

In the Young Lords Party we disagree with the analysis made by the right wing. We feel that the greatest conflict in the world today lies between capitalism (and capitalism's invasion of other countries, imperialism) and socialism, and people's drives to bring socialism to their countries, to their lives. We believe that the new society we are talking about will not come about by women separating themselves from men, but through sisters and brothers struggling with one another, working together, to deal with the negative things inside all of us. For sisters, this feeling that we are supposed to be passive towards brothers, you know, let them run things; with brothers, this feeling that we are supposed to be superior or better than sisters, you know, acting out those macho roles. The Party knows that Puerto Rican, Black, and other Third World Women make up over half of the Revolutionary Army; in the struggle for the liberation of Puerto Ricans, sisters and brothers must press for the equality of women—the women's struggle is part of the Revolution within the Revolution.

What is a man? What is a woman? Non-consciously we believe a man is strong, aggressive, hairy, decisive, hard, cold, firm, and intelligent. Non-consciously a woman is weak, timid, smooth, soft-spoken, scatter-brained, soft, warm, dumb, and loving. Both of these sets of descriptions are a result of the way we have been trained non-consciously. From the time that we are born, we are taught by our parents and by society to be a "man" or a "woman" and to live up to those false characteristics we are supposed to have. These personality traits are part of the way we are supposed to be.

See, originally in the Party—we didn't understand these concepts. We knew that brothers were messing over sisters and we said machismo and male chauvinism must be eliminated. We did not understand that brothers were acting out the roles that this society had assigned to them. Brothers have trouble understanding why some of the ways they related to sisters was wrong because they had been taught to be this way. We said "But that's the way a man is supposed to be."

On the other hand, we would criticize our sisters for being passive and allowing men to mess them over. We did not understand that everything in a woman's experience in this society conditions and prepares us to be shy and timid. Everything in a woman's experience conditions us to accept leadership from men and to accept our roles as someone who cooks, sews, and takes care of children.

The right wing in the women's movement says men are evil and can't be changed. Babies are not born oppressors. Therefore, our major enemy is capitalism rather than men.

But there ain't no doubt about it, there are a few rich men who control this planet. They are our enemies. Not because they are men, but because they are capitalists. Some of the rulers are women (and some of them are in the right-wing women's movement). They are also our enemy, not because they are women, but because they are capitalists.

There is a center position in the women's movement. These are liberals, reformers, who merely demand "more rights" for "women." There is a left-wing, and the best of these women are revolutionaries who understand who the real enemy is. But both the center and the left wing made no attempt at stopping the right, or exposing them for what they are—pigs, agents and supporters of the enemy. They must do so now.

The progressive, must see that most of the right wing in the women's movement are white, and their racism is being reinforced heavily against Third World People, brothers and sisters.

We reject those women's groups that turn their backs on socialism because they say it was created by men, or they reject the groups like the YLP who have discipline because they say discipline and structure is a man's thing. We support those groups that are anti-capitalist, anti-imperialist, and see the fight for women's liberation as part of the fight for socialism.

All oppressed people together will make the Revolution within the Revolution and end all kinds of oppression.

UNIDOS VENCEREMOS!
FORWARD SISTERS IN THE STRUGGLE!

Central Committee
YOUNG LORDS PARTY

....

Sexism

(From the newspaper *Palante*, June 1971, volume 3, number 11)

How painful it is to see our people in suffering and misery.

Seeing brothers and sisters shooting up because society doesn't give them any other alternative. Seeing brothers and sisters sweating blood in the factories of Carolina, New York, or in Fajardo, without getting paid enough to live decently. That the Jibaro or Jibara have to buy pineapple juice in cans because their hands are no longer used to grow food. It is also painful to see our sons leave home never to return because they have to go fight a war that they don't understand, that we didn't start.

This is the sad state that the Puerto Rican Nation is in. Those responsible—the yanquis. Our answer is to struggle, united, united in the struggle to get these pirates, thieves, criminals, out of our island.

But there are still things, problems, obstacles that don't let us unite in order to reach our goals. We are still divided and at times, we don't understand why. One of these divisions is the division between men and women. Let's see where this division came from.

The development of human beings has been a history of struggle to live and to survive. We need food, clothing, housing, and ample time to develop our minds. We learned to use our land to grow food, use trees to make houses, to kill animals to make clothing.

But there is still something that I didn't mention but that has great importance in this process of survival. This is reproduction. The man and the woman in their coming together reproduced—this being one of the great contributions of humanity to humanity. But as we grew, we needed more of the basic necessities.

From this came the first division of labor. We were divided into men and women. The men did one thing and the women another. The man would hunt, fish, discover new worlds; while the woman would stay home and take care of the children and take care of the agriculture.

Since the man would come and go and see new means of production (clothing, food, etc.), less importance was paid to reproduction. Production became the important thing. The woman, who did not participate in the majority of production, became a secondary human being. The man began to see himself as strong and intelligent. The woman began to see herself as stupid, weak, and began to feel inferior. Throughout the ages, this problem still has not been resolved. From this came sexism.

Nowadays, the brothers want to prove they are "machos." They see a sister and think of her as a sexual object. They whistle, call her "mami" and tell her how "fine she is." If the sister doesn't want to be treated like this, she stops being "feminine." Or when a brother and a sister marry, the sister becomes property, to cook, iron, wash dishes, to be the household slave. Or when a sister is a prostitute, selling her body as the only way to survive, she has to take beatings from amerikkkan soldiers and from the pimp. These abuses are immense. This is machismo.

On the other hand, the woman has learned to accept that she is a sexual object, ironer, and cook, and that she isn't worth anything! This is passivity.

Meanwhile, the yanquis laugh because our nation is divided in half. Brothers and sisters keep themselves weak and don't struggle against their common enemy.

The worker or lumpen isn't guilty of the misery we live in. It isn't the fault of the women lumpen or workers that there aren't any jobs or adequate living facilities. We have to stop being "machos." This won't free our nation. We have to stop being passive. We must struggle against believing we're weak, stupid, or better than other sisters. We have to feel proud that in 1954, a sister named Lolita Lebrón knew how to defend the rights of Puerto Ricans.

The problems between men and women have to end; and in being united, we will fight together against the real enemy.

This is not a question of women's liberation. This is for National Liberation. To achieve it, we need unity—unity of Puerto Ricans on the island and Puerto Ricans in the u.s.—a lumpen-worker alliance.

UNITY AMONG ALL OPPRESSED PEOPLE!
FREEDOM FOR LOLITA LEBRON, ANGELA DAVIS NOW!

Gloria González
Field Marshall
YOUNG LORDS PARTY

....

Women in a Socialist Society

(From the newspaper *Palante*, 31 March–14 April 1972, volume 4, number 7)

> How sad it is to be a woman!
> Nothing on earth is held so cheap.
> Boys stand leaning at the door
> Like gods fallen out of heaven.
> Their hearts brave the four oceans.
> The wind and dust of 1000 miles.
> No one is glad when a girl is born:
> By her the family sets no store.
> —Fg Hsuan

> Times have changed, and today men and women are equal. Whatever men comrades can accomplish, women comrades can too.
> —Mao Tse-Tung, 1964

China in 1935 was a country of the very rich and the very poor. The rich had houses, land, cattle, and sent their sons and daughters to the best schools; while at the same time the working people were so exploited and so poor that even though they worked farming the land from sunrise to sunset, people still had little clothes, their homes were made from adobe (dirt), and there was so little food (the rich took most of the crops) that people ate leaves of the trees and every couple of years, one-third of the people would die from starvation.

Even though all the people suffered, the women suffered even more—nobody wanted girl babies, a lot of times girl babies were killed by their parents, women were sold to their husbands, marriages were arranged by the parents. Once you were married, you weren't allowed to leave the home, but had to spend the whole time serving the husband, in-laws, and children. You could only speak when spoken to, your feet were bound, on purpose, so you couldn't walk far, and the bones were broken.

But as the poor and working people in China fought against the rich Chinese and the Japanese (who were invading the country), little by little, men's attitudes and ideas about women began to change and everyone started to see how men and women should be on an equal level at home and in the workplaces and not one sex above the other. It was a long, hard struggle and it still continues.

China in 1972—working people control the hospitals, schools, factories, police, transportation, manufacturing—everything. Everyone works to improve society for everyone, not just for the benefit of the few. And working women are playing an important role—they are in the 'revolutionary committees' that run the cities; in the army, navy, air force, in the Taching oilfield large numbers of women workers work in oil-refining and extracting (taking oil from the earth); there are women electricians that work with wires and cables 30 meters above the ground: women workers in a province named Heilungkiang built a 110 meter long concrete bridge for transporting timber; women took part in digging a 1,200 meter long pipeline that brought water to a village; in Peking women work in a factory that makes high-precision equipment for furnaces, in short, women work in all fields—farming, water, conservation, construction, forestry, fishery, meteorology, medicine, teaching, engineering, technology, geology, to name only a few! There's equal pay between men and women for equal work; the retirement age is usually 50 with 50%-70% of your former wage as pension. Pregnant women get 56 days of maternity leave with full pay and all the workplaces have child care centers. Many women factory workers get sent to school to get an education to learn more than one skill.

But still, the Chinese people understand that the main problem is imperialism, that [is the] economic system we have in the u.s. and all of its colonies, such as Puerto Rico and Hawaii. Capitalism: where the few rich control the lives of the majority, poor and working people. We all have to change the way that we were taught to act, think and do things, and the oppression of women is just one thing of many that has to stop.

At the same time, there cannot be any real equality between the sexes or an end to racism, wars, and bad working conditions, until the rich people who control us now are crushed, and we, the poor and working people, are in total control.

POWER TO ALL POOR AND WORKING PEOPLE ALL OVER THE WORLD!
FORWARD SISTERS IN THE STRUGGLE!

WOMEN'S UNION
YOUNG LORDS PARTY

8

The Garbage Offensive

Garbage collection was a significant problem in communities such as El Barrio/East Harlem. Streets were littered with debris of both the conventional (waste paper, food, plastics, etc.) and unconventional (cars, tires, glass, sinks, etc.) kinds. The first issue the newly formed New York Young Lords mobilized around was garbage collection. Rather than simply petition the city for better service, the Young Lords started cleaning up the community themselves. When the city continued to deny regular garbage collection services or the resources for the Lords to take care of things on their own (brooms, trash bags, etc.), the Young Lords and community members repeatedly blocked the streets with burning debris. The selections in this chapter help illustrate, through words and images, the ways in which the Young Lords sought material transformations in their community around the issue of garbage collection.

....

Young Lords Block Street with Garbage

(From the newspaper *Young Lords Organization*, 1969, volume 1, number 4)

In a display of community strength and support of the YOUNG LORDS ORGANIZA-TION, the people of East Harlem (El Barrio), and the YLO closed the streets of Third Ave. from 110th, across to 112th and down to Second Ave. on Sunday, July 27.

For two weeks previously, the YOUNG LORDS had been cleaning garbage from the streets and into garbage cans to show the people that the department of garbage (Lindsay's department of sanitation), or D.O.G., does not serve them. At first, communication with the people was slow. Then, as the barriers broke down and everyone got their thing together, the people saw that even a nothing department like D.O.G. looks upon Puerto Ricans and Blacks as though they are something lower than garbage. These dogs at D.O.G. have forgotten that they must SERVE THE PEOPLE. And it all blew up on Sunday.

By July 27, the original operation had grown to such a large number of people, not just including LORDS, that the brooms and shovels we were using were not enough. So four LORDS—the Deputy Minister of Finance, Information and Education and an information photographer—went to the nearest D.O.G. hole at 108th St. After some Bureaucratic Bullshitting they steered us to the D.O.G. hole at 73rd St. Dig it! Two miles away, while a hole is sitting three blocks away.

After playing the man's game of red tape, the LORDS brought it all back home. We ran it down about what happened and a course of action was developed. As fast as it takes a streetlight to change, all the People—Lords, mothers, Li'l Lords—placed cans of garbage across Third Ave. at 110th St. The pigs, who have been eyeing the LORDS for the past few weeks in New York, came to the scene in a matter of seconds. Sources on the blocks say the pigs had trucks waiting a few blocks away.

But the pigs found out that the spirit of the people is greater than all the man's pigs. At least 1,000 Puerto Ricans turned out to cheer the LORDS on as they woofed the pigs to their pens. Brothers and Sisters on 111th and 112th caught that old revolutionary spirit, last seen in '66, and blocked their streets, too.

When a garbage truck finally did show, the man vainly tried his game once more. For all those streets filled with garbage, D.O.G sent one Puerto Rican Brother. The people wouldn't fall for this cheap trick, and finally two white garbage men patted the junk into place while the brother hustled it into the truck. Afterwards a rally was held at 112th St. The cats in the street agreed to that.

> The streets belong to the People!
> The moon belongs to the People!
> Power to the People!
> PALANTE!

> Yoruba
> Dep. Minister of Information
> New York State YLO

....

El Barrio and YLO Say No More Garbage in Our Community

(From the newspaper *Young Lords Organization*, 1969, volume 1, number 4)

East Harlem is known as El Barrio—New York's worst Puerto Rican slum.

There are others—on the Lower East Side, in Brooklyn, in the South Bronx, but El Barrio is the oldest, biggest, filthiest of them all. There is glass sprinkled everywhere, vacant lots filled with rubble, burnt out buildings on nearly every block, and people packed together in the polluted summer heat.

There is also the smell of garbage, coming in an incredible variety of flavors and strengths.

For weeks the YLO had been asking the Sanitation Dept. for brooms and trash cans so they could clean up the streets and sidewalks of El Barrio. The city ignored the request. Finally, on Sunday, August 17, the community rebelled.

All the rubbish that had accumulated along East 110th St. was dumped into the middle of the street. At 111th and Lexington Ave., the people turned over several abandoned cars and set them afire.

Hundreds of nervous cops arrived on the scene. When they dragged Ildefenso Santiago out of his car and took him to the precinct house, reportedly on suspicion of burglary (they found a screwdriver in his car), the people retaliated by filling the streets with more trash, cars, old refrigerators, and any thing else they could find. It began to look like a repeat of the 1967 summer riot in which at least two people were killed and scores injured in street fighting with cops.

At this point, members of the YLO stepped in to work with the people. They organized a march to the precinct house where Santiago was being held. Chanting "Viva Puerto Rico!", "Power to the People!", and "Off the Pig!", nearly 300 people marched to the 126th

AMERIKKKA

THE
BEAUTIFUL

From the newspaper *Palante*, 16 October 1970, volume 2, number 13.

St. police station to demand Santiago's release. Within half an hour, he was free, and the crowd carried him back to his car on their shoulders.

"It was a victory for the people," said Felipe, chairman of YLO, at a rally the following day. "They've treated us like dogs for too long. When our people came here in the 1940's, they told us New York was a land of milk and honey. And what happened? Our men can't find work. Look at them. They sit around and play dominos because they can't get a decent job. Our women are forced to become prostitues. Our young people get hooked on drugs. And they won't even give us brooms to sweep up the rubbish on our streets."

The YLO has issued a set of demands: regular collection of trash; at least ten brooms and trash barrels per block; the hiring of more Puerto Ricans by the Sanitation Dept; and higher starting pay for sanitation workers.

The next day, the New York Post reported the incident, obscured the main point of the protest by saying the people acted as a result of "misunderstanding" about Santiago's arrest. In fact, the people of El Barrio have said that they will no longer tolerate the city's neglect of their needs. They are taking matters into their own hands.

The way Felipe put it at the rally was that we're building our own community. "Don't fuck with us. It's as simple as that."

9

Health and Hospitals

Adequate health care for the poor was one of the chief demands of the Young Lords. Faced with a health-care crisis on various fronts, the Young Lords (together with the Health Revolutionary Unity Movement) started lead poisoning and tuberculosis testing programs, took over Lincoln Hospital in the Bronx, and demanded equal treatment of all "Third World" peoples. Articles in this chapter cover the principles of their health program, describe the theoretical and historical rationales used in advancing their arguments, and document specific health initiatives the Young Lords launched in their communities.

....

Ten Point Health Program

(From the newspaper *Young Lords Organization*, January 1970, volume 1, number 5)

We want total self-determination of all health service at East Harlem (El Barrio) through an incorporated community-staff governing board for Metropolitan Hospital. (Staff is anyone and everyone working in Metropolitan, except administrators.)

We want immediate replacement of all Lindsay and Terenzio administrators by community and staff-appointed people whose practice has demonstrated their commitment to serve our poor community.

We demand an immediate end to construction of the new emergency room until the Metropolitan Hospital Community–Staff Governing Board inspects and approves them or authorizes new plans.

We want employment for our people. All jobs filled in El Barrio must be filled by residents first, using on-the-job training and other educational opportunities as bases for service and promotions.

We want free publicly supported health care for treatment and prevention.

We want an end to all fees.

We want total decentralization of health—block health officers responsible to the Community-Staff Board should be instituted.

We want "door-to-door" preventative health services emphasizing environment and sanitation control, nutrition, drug addiction, maternal and child care and senior citizen services.

We want education programs for all the people to expose health problems—sanitation, rats, poor housing, malnutrition, police brutality, pollution, and other forms of oppression.

We want total control by the Metropolitan Hospital Community-Staff Governing Board of budget allocations, medical policy, along the above points, hiring and firing and salaries of employees, construction and health code enforcement.

Any community, union, or workers organization must support all the points of this program and work and fight for them or be shown as what they are—enemies of the poor people of East Harlem.

POWER TO THE PEOPLE!
QUE VIVA EL BARRIO!
FREE PUERTO RICO NOW!

New York State Chapter
Young Lords Organization

....

Revolutionary Health Care Program for the People

(From the newspaper *Young Lords Organization*, January 1970, volume 1, number 5)

Mingo El Loco was a brother off the block who helped out the Young Lords Organization every once in a while. He would loan the Organization his car, would help pass out our literature, would recruit for us. A few weeks ago Mingo was stabbed by another brother. It happens all the time in the street. Our people are always killing each other off instead of fighting the enemy—the pigs, the businessman, the politician.

The ambulance was called. For one hour it didn't come. Meanwhile the pigs arrived. Mingo was dying on the street, but the police did nothing. Finally, the people tried to take him to the hospital in their own car. He died on the way to Metropolitan.

People dying because of ambulances that arrive late, or in emergency rooms of city hospitals while they wait for hours, happens often. The people have become used to butcher health care and resigned to the fact that they'll never be decently treated by the health system.

But the Young Lords, after Mingo's death, began to investigate health in New York and we have begun a program to organize the people—community and workers—to demand decent health care.

As we talked to dozens of sympathetic doctors, nurses, medical students, maintenance, clerical and laboratory workers in Metropolitan Hospital, we began to understand more and more about health oppression.

—We learned that many of the diseases that our people die of could be simply cured or even prevented with correct mass health programs which the hospitals do not have. For instance, thousands of children become sick or die because of lead poisoning, from eating fallen plaster in ghetto buildings. A mass lead-poison detection program could save the lives of thousands of our children. Anemia, tuberculosis, bad nutrition, upper respiratory infections, could be stamped out with mass health programs that go out to the people, into the homes and communities, instead of waiting for a patient to come in to the hospital with the disease already in advanced stages.

—We learned that doctors were making $60-70 thousand a year because poor people have to have health care. That their organization, the fascist American Medical Association, for years has been trying to keep the number of medical schools down so that doctors could charge higher fees.

—We learned that the drug companies, like Upjohn, Park and Davis, etc., not only push many useless or harmful drugs just for profit, but that they have much influence in Washington and state legislatures over medical bills. Many times officers of these companies sit on the boards of private hospitals and help determine the policy that has been mistreating our people for years.

—We learned that there are things called health empires: medical schools and private hospitals that through affiliations (contracts with the city) operate and run city hospitals. In New York, for instance, Columbia controls Harlem Hospital, Albert Einstein controls Lincoln Hospital, Beth Israel controls Gouverneur Hospital, New York Medical College controls East Harlem's Metropolitan. These affiliations end up helping the medical school much more than the municipal hospital. For instance, interns and medical students have much more practice and experience in the city hospital, because in the private hospital, patients are treated by their own doctor and refuse to be treated by students. The poor people who come to the city hospitals are used as guinea pigs, sometimes, for new treatments, methods, new medicines that will then be used on the rich. The priorities for the medical schools are training and research. The needs of the people are for mass, quality free health care. The two are often antagonistic in our society.

—We learned that in our communities, control of health must be taken out of the hands of drug companies, avaricious professionals, pig politicians, and racist administrators and put in the hands of the people. That is why we demand

COMMUNITY WORKER CONTROL

FREE HEALTH CARE

MASS HEALTH SERVICE.

The Young Lords have developed a Ten-Point Program of Health that explains what we want, the minimum necessary for our people—for Puerto Rican, black and poor white oppressed peoples. We have joined with revolutionary workers in other parts of the city, with the Health Revolutionary Unity Movement at Gouverneur Hospital on the Lower East Side, with the Lincoln Hospital workers in the South Bronx, with the Black Panther Party Free Health Clinics in Staten Island and Brooklyn. We are building a city-wide revolutionary health movement that will shake the city to its rotten pig core.

The revolutionary health groups have also begun forming an alliance with radical medical students and professionals around a week of activities in February, 1970—People's Health Week, which will attempt to have teach-ins, demonstrations, and mass health programs, and educate the people about the difference between capitalist medicine and socialist medicine, between medicine that oppresses the people and medicine that serves the people.

By becoming involved in Breakfast Programs, Clothing Programs, Health Programs, the Young Lords are demonstrating to all Latin and other oppressed peoples that we truly do serve and protect. Wherever the people suffer and resist oppression, we are there to aid, shape and lead their struggle.

Long Live Boricua
Long Live Independent Puerto Rico
Free Health Care for Everyone
Hands off Cha Cha
Venceremos

YOUNG LORDS ORGANIZATION
New York State Headquarters

....

HRUM: Health Workers Organization

(From the newspaper *Palante*, 22 May 1970, volume 2, number 3)

The Puerto Rican and Black workers in the Human Services is known as an assistant, assistant to the teacher, the assistant to the welfare investigator, and in the hospitals we are the assistants to the doctors, nurses, social workers, etc.

As assistants (sophisticated word for slave) we are totally oppressed and unfortunately at the same time we assist in the oppression of our people.

Eighty per cent of the hospital workers are Puerto Rican and Black—residents of the poorest communities. As Puerto Ricans and Black workers in the emergency rooms and clinics, we see what oppression in the hospital is like, the inferior medical attention our neighbors are subjected to or obligated to accept. The worker also gets the same treatment. The enemy effectively divides the people and the worker finds himself each day divided more and more into two categories: the worker that identifies with the hospital and defends the oppressive, abusive and racist thieving doctors; the worker that does not turn his back on his people and defends the patients and his co-workers above everything else.

The newly formed Health Revolutionary Unity Movement is in the second category. The organization was formed for two reasons: we know that the health system will not change unless we push that necessary change. The unions 1199 and District Council 37, even though progressive in the question of salaries, do not fight against the conditions imposed on the workers nor the quality of the medical services our people are receiving.

Many struggles have risen in the hospitals by revolutionary Puerto Rican and Black workers. During one of these struggles less than a year ago in Lincoln Hospital, the workers took over the mental health services demanding community control of the services. Also in a dump of a clinic in the Lower East Side, the Governeur Clinic, a similar struggle was waged.

Although the struggles have not triumphed significantly they have helped us to learn self-organization.

The organization is composed of Puerto Rican and Black workers of Metropolitan, Lincoln, Governeur hospitals and NENA Health Center among many others.

We insist that the time has come to act against a system that enriches itself at the expense of our people.

So that our struggle can be effective, we must make clear our purposes. That is why the Health Revolutionary Unity Movement uses the 10-Point Program as their principal guide. Our efforts have been demonstrated with the educative newspaper "For the People's Health." In addition, we work in complete solidarity with the organizations that have shown their commitment to serve and protest the exploitation and oppression of our people, such as the Young Lords Organization and the Black Panther Party.

In the next edition of "For the People's Health" we shall announce our first general meeting. We invite all workers to attend and in that way join the Health Revolutionary Unity Movement.

In unity, there is strength! The same enemy of Cambodian people is found in the hospitals.

THE HOSPITALS BELONG TO THE PEOPLE!
VIVA PUERTO RICO LIBRE!

Gloria Cruz (field worker—Governeur Clinic)
Health Ministry
YOUNG LORDS ORGANIZATION

....

Socialist Medicine

(From the newspaper *Palante*, 5 June 1970, volume 2, number 4)

Every Saturday, the YOUNG LORDS PARTY goes door to door in El Barrio and the South Bronx, testing for tuberculosis. Even though t.b. has been eliminated among the rich, the middle classes, and white people in general, it is alive and spreading in the Puerto Rican and Black colonies of amerikkka, the "richest" country in the world.

Tuberculosis is known as a disease of oppression, just like lead poisoning, anemia, malnutrition, etc. It comes from being so oppressed by the man that we cannot get jobs that pay enough, houses that shelter us right, or hospitals to care for us; it comes from not being able as a nation, as Borinquenos, to control all these things; it comes from being poor, oppressed, and powerless.

During the last 3 months, in El Barrio, and the last month in the South Bronx, we have given over 800 tests for tuberculosis. One out of every three people tested has had a positive reaction. Why aren't the hospitals doing anything to prevent t.b. in our communities? Because the hospitals do not serve the needs of our people. They exist only to make a profit. Hospitals are only interested in hospitalization (which costs in the hundreds per day), lab tests and medicines. All of which they can charge a lot for. But, as the YOUNG LORDS PARTY has shown, all that is necessary for t.b. testing is a few hours work and dedication.

We live in a country that makes proper health care a luxury only rich people can afford. Heart transplants and brain surgery are done on rich people; t.b. preventive medicine is not done on Puerto Ricans and Blacks because this capitalistic system wants to make the rulers live longer and let the spics and niggers die off as quickly and quietly as possible.

The racism of the health empire must be exposed. It is in every area of medical service. Puerto Ricans have had "drug problems" for many years, but it wasn't until a few white kids in the suburbs started getting strung out, that the health empire "discovered" drugs, and a big stink was made in the press. This is like Columbus "discovering" Puerto Rico. The 70,000 Taino Indians had always been there, but just like the drug problem, until the man feels it directly, in his pocket or in his home, it doesn't exist and he doesn't give a damn.

Point 5 of the YOUNG LORDS PARTY 13-Point Program and Platform states "We want community control of our institutions and land," and Point 13 says "We want a socialist society." In a socialist society, the institutions like the hospitals are controlled by the hospital workers and the patients. Also under socialism they extend their services out to the people visiting them in their homes and setting up Free Health Clinics in every block. This type of service which keeps people from getting sick in the first place is called preventive medicine. Although doctors admit it is needed, preventive medicine will never be done in amerikkka, as it is today because it is a capitalist society. Capitalists run hospitals and make money out of Puerto Ricans being sick and if there's no money, they're out of business. Socialists are concerned with keeping people healthy, not with making money.

As long as we don't control institutions like the hospitals we will continue to die of disease like t.b. and receive poor or no health services in general. We must begin to fight together as a people to take over all the institutions that control our lives, by taking the central power that protects the capitalist hospitals, the state. Pig administrators who run hospitals and profit from other people's suffering must be put up against the wall. As long as pigs like these are in our communities, they will continue to use (exploit) us.

The YOUNG LORDS PARTY will continue to serve our people through our Preventive Medicine Programs, and we will at the same time continue to expose the way in which the institutions in our communities exploit us. The YLP will fight until hospitals, police, schools, etc. are run by the people, especially those who work in and are affected by these institutions.

FREE HEALTH CARE FOR ALL!
LIBERATE PUERTO RICO NOW!

Carl Pastor
Ministry of Health
YOUNG LORDS PARTY

....

The Fight against Prospect Hospital

(From the newspaper *Palante*, 19 June 1970, volume 2, number 5)

Many of our people believe that hospitals and professionals in the hospitals really want to help them. But more and more people are beginning to realize that the only interest that hospital heads have is how much money they will be able to make out of every patient they see. This exists especially in a hospital in the South Bronx named Prospect Hospital. The majority of the people in the South Bronx have never been treated or examined in this hospital for a number of reasons, but mainly because not so many people have Medicaid or money, so they don't get treated for illnesses. It is just like the other corporations in our communities like A&P, John's Bargains Stores, Key Foods, etc.

If you don't have the money or a credit card, you can't buy. (If you don't have money or a Medicaid card, likewise, you can't be treated.)

The YOUNG LORDS PARTY has started a series of preventive medicine programs in the South Bronx, and detecting tuberculosis is the main program we have now. When we go door to door on Saturdays, we give our people a tuberculine test. Three days after the test is given we go back to those families we tested to check if the test is positive or negative. If the test is negative, the person is okay. If the test is positive, then the person needs a chest x-ray. The chest x-ray tells if the person has tuberculosis or not. If the person has tuberculosis, he will be treated for it. This is what Prospect Hospital should be doing, treating the people in the community for sicknesses that are caused by the living conditions in our neighborhood.

About a month ago, three brothers from the YOUNG LORDS PARTY went to Prospect Hospital to talk to the pig administrator silverman and his flunky freeman. The three YOUNG LORDS explained how our people are dying of tuberculosis every day and that if Prospect Hospital allowed the YOUNG LORDS to use the hospital's x-ray machines, many lives would be saved. For a whole month these pigs said "no" to us. To them it wouldn't be right to let us use the x-ray machines since they wouldn't be making a profit out of it.

Prospect Hospital planned a health fair in order to create a good image, since we were letting our brothers and sisters on the street know where this hospital was really at, and they were worried and felt threatened. So on Thursday, June 4, 1970, at 10 a.m., we went again to talk to silverman and freeman, the administrators. This was the fourth time we went to these pigs to demand what is the people's. This time their answer was not "no" but "yes," because they were scared about their image. We should all understand that they don't really want us to use the x-ray machines. The reason they are letting us use them is not because they love the Latino and Black community, but because the PARTY and our people backed silverman and freeman up against the wall.

The YOUNG LORDS will not stop putting pressure on Prospect Hospital. What we want is not just access to Prospect Hospital's x-ray machines; we want access to Prospect Hospital. Point 5 of the YLP 13-Point Program says: "We want community control of our institutions and land."

> HOSPITALS MUST SERVE OUR PEOPLE!
> LIBERATE PUERTO RICO NOW!
>
> Carlito Rovira, Ministry of Health
> YOUNG LORDS PARTY
> El Barrio Branch

....

Think Lincoln

(From the newspaper *Palante*, 3 July 1970, volume 2, number 6)

In July 1970, Lincoln Hospital will be the victim of the greedy businessmen who make money from the illnesses of the people of the South Bronx. Because of the cutbacks in federal money going to social service programs, the controlling Einstein Medical College empire will have less money to spend on its many hospitals, and Lincoln will be the hardest hit. The Einstein empire will have to redistribute its funds and this will affect worst the Department of Medicine, Section K, and the Emergency Room at Lincoln.

DEPARTMENT OF MEDICINE:
There is a six month job freeze in the Department of Medicine making it impossible to replace the 5 specialists, including 2 heart specialists and 1 kidney specialist, who have resigned. A vicious cycle of poor health care may result from this because some of the medical students who will be losing their teachers, when the specialists are not replaced, are threatening to leave.

SECTION K:
The redistribution of funds will also hit Section K at Lincoln. Section K is the screening clinic. People come here from the street or are referred by departments inside or outside the hospital. In Section K a patient's illness is diagnosed and he is then sent to the specialty clinic that can give him the treatment he needs. Because of the budget changes, Section K may have to cut out all evening and weekend hours. This means that during the daytime hours the already overcrowded Section K will be even more packed with patients who will have an even longer wait than before.

EMERGENCY ROOM:
The budget changes that will affect Section K will also affect the Emergency Room. Patients who ordinarily are seen in Section K will have to be sent to the Emergency Room on weekends and in the evening if Section K is closed during these times. The Lincoln Hospital Emergency Room is now the second busiest in the nation. It won't be able to stand the strain of any more patients. It isn't able to handle the present patient load, but with Section K patients in addition to its normal load, the medical care will be even worse than before.

When Dean Scheinberg, the dean of Einstein Medical School, was asked about the changes in spending in the Einstein empire, he said that the money had to be taken either from Jacobi or Lincoln, and they wouldn't take it from Jacobi, so Lincoln would have to suffer.

As a result of these drastic changes a group of community people, Lincoln Hospital workers, HRUM (Health Revolutionary Unity Movement), and the YOUNG LORDS PARTY came together to form the Think Lincoln Committee (TLC). TLC committed itself to fighting for better health care for the people who are forced to go to Lincoln Hospital for services. The group began to build consciousness among the people, through leafleting, putting up posters, and generally talking to people in the community and hospital. The response of the people of the South Bronx was that it was about time that butcher shop Lincoln was changed into a hospital to serve the people.

After hearing many complaints, the TLC set up a patient-worker complaint table in the Emergency Room. Before long, the complaints of the horrible treatment of our people began to pour in.

The TLC members began to move on each complaint by helping people as they registered at the desk, in the Emergency Room, by confronting the hospital administrator, and by making demands on the hospital that would insure better service for our people.

The five major demands of TLC are: 1) Doctors must give humane treatment to patients. 2) Free food must be given to patients who spend hours in the hospital waiting to be seen. 3) Construction on the new Lincoln Hospital must start immediately. 4) There must be no cutbacks in services or in jobs in any part of Lincoln Hospital. 5) The immediate formation of a community-worker board which has control over the policies and practices of the hospital.

Because of our activities, the atmosphere of the hospital has changed considerably. The workers are beginning to be concerned about patients' rights and patient care. They are also beginning to fight with the TLC and other active groups around the issues that we have brought to the attention of the people.

The TLC will continue to struggle day and night to bring decent health care to the people of the south Bronx.

THINK . . . LINCOLN!

LINCOLN HOSPITAL MUST BELONG TO THE PEOPLE!

HEALTH WORKERS DEFEND PATIENTS!

PATIENTS DEFEND HEALTH WORKERS!

Cleo Silvers

Danny Argote

THINK LINCOLN COMMITTEE

....

TB Truck Liberated

(From the newspaper *Palante*, 3 July 1970, volume 2, number 6)

Everyday, Puerto Rican people are faced with the same deadly health problem—tuberculosis—a disease that affects our lives and a disease that can be prevented. The reason that t.b. isn't being prevented is that preventing diseases like t.b. cuts the profits of the capitalists that run the city hospitals. Therefore, the hospitals don't work on preventing these diseases.

The YOUNG LORDS PARTY has always said that the time will come when the people take over all the institutions and machinery that control and exploit our lives. On June 17, the YOUNG LORDS PARTY put this idea into practice. On this day, we liberated an x-ray truck from the politicians that had been using the truck only for propaganda purposes that serve their own interests and profiteering businessmen that only think about making money.

The truck was seized only after members of the YLP had gone to the Tuberculosis Society several times asking them for the use of the truck. Each time, the request was refused. By refusing us, they made it clear that they aren't concerned with the health of our people. These trucks have been seen in our community only on a very limited part-time basis. We realized that the reason our people didn't use it was because the people running the show prior to the LORDS were outsiders who couldn't relate to our people, our language, and our customs. They never made any real attempt to get the people to use the x-ray facilities.

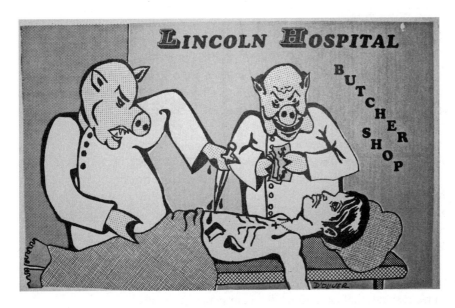

From the newspaper *Palante*, 17 July 1970, volume 2, number 7.

In the three days that we have had the truck, we have already tested 770 people. According to the technicians, the usual amount of people taken care of in the same amount of time is about 300. So, as far as the YOUNG LORDS PARTY is concerned, this truck rightfully belongs to the people!

The last point of our 13 Point Program and Platform states that "We want a socialist society." Under a socialist society, medical services are extended outside of the hospital by setting up clinics in all communities and by visiting people's homes. This type of medical service is called preventive medicine. Although doctors admit it is needed, preventive medicine will never be done in amerikkka as it is today, because in the capitalist society in which we live, capitalists run health services in order to make more money, not to improve health care. The sicker we are, the more money the capitalist makes. The YOUNG LORDS PARTY believes that health care should be a right for all people not a privilege. That is why we put the x-ray facilities in the hands of the people.

The Ramon Emeterio Betances Free X-Ray Truck now belongs to the people. It will be on the streets 7 days a week, 10 hours a day. This truck is here to service the needs of our people.

ALL POWER TO THE PEOPLE!
FREE HEALTH CARE FOR ALL!
LIBERATE PUERTO RICO NOW!

Carl Pastor
Ministry of Health
YOUNG LORDS PARTY

....

Murder at Lincoln

(From the newspaper *Palante*, 31 July 1970, volume 2, number 8)

Our people are being killed every day. The facts are cold and real. Drug addiction, inadequate housing, and inferior medical services all contribute to the slow killing off of our people. Another very specific way that genocide is being committed is through the limiting of our population.

When drug companies came out with the million-dollar birth control pill, they tested it in Puerto Rico. As a result of years of experiments and quack operations (tying of tubes, cutting of tubes), one out of every three sisters of child bearing age on the island is sterilized. Those sisters that they have not been able to sterilize are on pills, loops and all sorts of jive methods to keep us from bearing warriors that will join the fight for our liberation.

Just recently, on July 1, 1970, a new plan for the limitation of our population was passed—the abortion law. Under this new method we are now supposed to be able to go to any of the city butcher shops (the municipal hospitals) and receive an abortion. These are the same hospitals that have been killing our people for years.

Already the first abortion death has occurred at Lincoln Hospital, butcher shop of the South Bronx. Carmen Rodriguez, 31, went to Lincoln seeking an abortion. She suffered from many of the diseases that afflict all oppressed people. She was at one time addicted to drugs; she suffered from asthma, anemia, and a severe heart condition. With all these health problems, she was sent to the operating room without her medical history chart even being checked. She was injected with a medication for asthma; however the type of medication used is the worst possible for a patient with a heart condition. But how would they know? They never bothered to check her chart. The punk that was treating her was a student. Lincoln is "affiliated" with Einstein Medical school which assigns inexperienced students to learn medicine by practicing on our people. He continued to give her this medication until finally her heart stopped. Then, they proceeded to open her chest up, but by then it was too late—her brain had been damaged. Carmen's brain stopped functioning on July 17. Although she was dead, the hospital tried covering it up until July 20 when her heart muscle stopped beating. Doctors have recently decided that death occurs when the brain stops.

This death was no accident. Carmen died because amerikkka is killing our people.

Carmen was forced to go for an abortion because under this capitalist system that which is our right—food, clothing, and shelter—is kept from us. Instead we become the drug addicts, the prostitutes, the ill, and the hungry. What choice does a sister have when she is pregnant, thinking of providing for her child? Will he or she grow up to be a junkie or maybe die in the wars created by amerikkkan greed and madness? We know there is but one choice. Armed self-defense and armed struggle are the only means to liberation (Point 12 of the YOUNG LORDS PARTY 13 Point Program).

We will continue to fight for our liberation. We will continue to serve and protect our people in the hospitals, on the streets, everywhere. We know that the realities of oppression will continue to force our sisters to seek these abortions, and so we will continue to educate that this genocide will only stop when we rise up against our oppressors.

DESPIERTA BORICUA OR WE WILL BE THE LAST GENERATION
OF SPICS ON THE FACE OF THE EARTH!
LIBERATE PUERTO RICO NOW!
VENCEREMOS

Gloria Cruz
Health Captain
YOUNG LORDS PARTY
National Headquarters

SEIZE THE HOSPITALS!!

....

Lincoln Hospital Must Serve the People

(From the newspaper *Palante*, 11 September 1970, volume 2, number 11)

The struggle for better health care at Lincoln Hospital in the South Bronx continues.

Lincoln Hospital has an abortion waiting list of over 300, but provision has been made for only 3 abortions a day. This means that many of our sisters will be in advanced stages of pregnancy when the abortion is performed; this makes the abortion more dangerous. In addition, these operations are not even performed in a well equipped, sterile operating room, but rather in a small room that had previously been used as a storeroom. The man responsible for this inefficient program is j.j. smith, head of obstetrics and gynecology. He is the man whom we hold directly responsible for the needless death of Carmen Rodriguez, a sister who was killed because she was injected with salt solution that stopped her heart during an abortion. The doctor that was performing the abortion didn't even check her chart before administering the injection; if he had, he would have seen that she had a heart condition and couldn't be given that type of injection.

The first time smith was confronted with the inefficiency of his department and examples of how he was failing to provide desperately needed services, he promised to begin doing his job. As soon as the pressure was turned off, he lay right back on his ass, and services continued as usual—nothing being done for our sisters. But the people learned a lesson. They understood that the people who have to suffer this service have the right to demand that an inefficient butcher be thrown out. And that's what happened. Because j.j. smith wasn't doing his job and wasn't running a program that met the needs of our people, he was fired by the community and concerned workers.

In the meantime, lacot, head administrator of the hospital, moved against all the workers and community people that had been working to improve conditions in Lincoln. He got an injunction from the courts saying that workers could not meet to discuss problems of poor health care. In this out-front anti-labor move, lacot said workers no longer had the right of freedom of speech or assembly. He also said that no posters or leaflets would be allowed in the hospital, but he permitted a group of nurses who oppose community control to meet and pass out leaflets whenever they wanted. The injunction also said that any member of the YOUNG LORDS PARTY, the Health Revolutionary Unity Movement, or the Think Lincoln Committee that entered the hospital would be arrested.

It went further though to say that any "John Doe" or "Jane Doe" could be prevented from entering the hospital. With helmeted riot police and plainclothes detectives around to enforce this injunction, lacot has given himself the power to bar any member of the community he wants from entering the hospital—he has created a police state where we wanted to create a People's Hospital.

On Thursday, September 4, the people of the South Bronx fought back and staged a large rally outside Lincoln Hospital. Over 200 people heard speakers from the YOUNG LORDS PARTY, the Black Panther Party, HRUM, TLC, the Unity Movement, Women's Liberation, and Youth Against War and Fascism, pledge their support to continue the struggle to return Lincoln Hospital to the people. The people at the rally demanded:

1) Reparations for the death of Carmen Rodriguez.

2) An end to the injunction and the denial of the people's right to determine the kind of health care they want and need.

3) A People's Tribunal to put Lincoln Hospital on trial and make the people who run this hospital answerable to the people they are supposed to be serving.

4) A general strike of workers.

Nobody but us is going to worry about our people and whether they live or die especially not people who live a million miles away and go home to clean, lily white communities where they don't know what it is to sit hours in hot, dirty rooms waiting to be treated. j.j. smith and the crew that run Lincoln Hospital neither understand nor care what kind of health services we receive. They have made that clear by their practice, everybody in the South Bronx knows that Lincoln Hospital is a butcher shop. So we say it is in our power to remove these inefficient, uncaring dogs and replace them with people who understand that their job is to serve the people and be accountable to them, people who really understand that health care is a right, not a privilege!

ALL POWER TO THE PEOPLE!

SEIZE THE HOSPITALS—RETURN THEM TO THE PEOPLE!

Health Ministry
YOUNG LORDS PARTY

....

Seize the Hospitals!

(From the newspaper *Palante*, 11 December 1970, volume 2, number 16)

For years Lincoln Hospital has been the scene of a continuing fight for better health care. In March, 1969, a group of mental health workers with the help of the Black Panther Party took over the Mental Health Center. In the summer of 1970, the Young Lords Party along with the Health Revolutionary Unity Movement (HRUM) and the Think Lincoln Committee took over the Nurses' Residence of the hospital. In the most recent action on November 11, HRUM and the South Bronx Drug Coalition took over the sixth floor of the Nurses' Residence. This action was taken to: 1) Implement a drug program that would serve the community effectively and be run by the community, 2) Provide an educational program that would teach the true nature of our oppression and the connection between capitalism, dope and genocide, and 3) Demonstrate the need for a drug program at Lincoln since the South Bronx has a total of 40,000 drug addicts and Lincoln has facilities to deal with at the most 40.

At noon on November 11th, about 35 addicts along with workers from the hospital and community people sealed off the sixth floor and began to implement the drug program. Physicals were given by doctors that had volunteered their time. Beds were assigned, and medicine was given out.

In the meantime, negotiations were going on in the office of the hospital administrator, Lacot. Lacot took the typical anti-people position. His response to the valid community demands was "No program," and he ordered the people out of the hospital. At 4:00 p.m. Lacot and about 40 helmeted police in riot gear came to the sixth floor (which is only used as sleeping quarters for doctors on call) and ordered the people off the floor or be arrested. When the police finally managed to get past the barricade, 15 people were arrested. These people were put in jail because their interest was in saving the lives of their people.

We have to understand that this action as well as all others was taken after people saw a problem in the community, asked for help and were refused by the hospital. Not until people take positive actions (which are sometimes called "illegal" by the real criminals) does the administration attempt to do something. It has always been this way. This situation was no different. Not until the community and workers got together and took over the sixth floor and were arrested did puppet Lacot (he is only the mouthpiece for the hospital corporation that really controls Lincoln) attempt to throw a program together. What happened in this program run by the hospital was that addicts weren't getting medicine, were going around sick, and had to go through a whole irrelevant run-around. Finally the program was closed down because of mismanagement.

We must begin to ask questions about all the things that affect the lives of Puerto Rican and Black people. Who can better determine what's best for ourselves than us? If this is the richest country in the world, why is it that this country is 13th in the world in health care? Why is it that we have to live in housing that is not fit for animals? Why do we have to be subjected to an inferior school system? Why is it that the jails are filled with Puerto Rican and Black people? Is it that we are a criminal people? Or is it the conditions that create the problems?

We must begin to realize that we live in a system that does not concern itself with the lives of the majority of our people (who are poor), but rather only cares about how it can obtain more wealth for a few money-hungry businessmen. This country can only exist by exploiting and killing other people, mostly Third World people, like it's doing in Vietnam, Puerto Rico and all other colonies inside and outside the united states.

We must begin to create struggle everywhere we go, not only in the hospitals but in all institutions that control the lives of our people. We must make them more responsible to our needs.

ALL POWER TO THE PEOPLE

Carl Pastor
Field Lieutenant
YOUNG LORDS PARTY
Lower East Side Branch

10

The People's Church

Based on (a) their platform commitment to "community control" of local institutions and land and (b) the leadership of the Chicago branch of the organization, the New York Young Lords twice seized a conservative local church in
the middle of El Barrio. Located at the intersection of 111th Street and Madison
Avenue, the First Spanish Methodist Church was taken over (the Young Lords
claimed) because it refused to serve its community or provide the Young Lords
with space to run some serve-the-people programs. The church was taken over
a second time after the alleged suicide of a Young Lord while he was being held
in the notorious Manhattan detention facility "The Tombs." Selections in this
chapter document why the Young Lords took over the church and renamed
it "The People's Church," why it was taken over a second time, and what they
thought the relationship is/should be between "the people" and "the church."

....

The People's Church

(From the newspaper *Palante*, February 1970, volume 2, number 1)

Two weeks after the church was taken from the people we returned for a second time
to find the 11 o'clock service was changed to 3 o'clock and that you needed a ticket to
pray. Reverend Humberto Carazana mobilized all his Cuban exiled friends (gusanos) to
pose as members of the community in the eyes of the people. A week later, we returned
and found the same situation, more gusanos, more cops and more refusals. They refused
to take clothes from us to distribute to the community. They refused to even talk to
us. We were not even allowed to enter the church or even be on the same side of the
street. The cops surrounded the people as we pleaded with the gusanos to open up to the
community.

On Jan. 31, we met with Herman Badillo, a Puerto Rican who had remained quiet
during the entire church occupation, and the Reverend Carazana who appointed Badillo
moderator for the negotiations.

There was supposed to be a series of five meetings. During these meetings all the court
cases were to be stopped. The two meetings that we had did not resolve anything because
the church kept on insisting that they did not have to open up to the community if they
did not want to. The church handed us a proposal that was meaningless because they
refused to include the community in any of the programs. Their day care center is a thing
for only 35 children in that huge space that they have. They are also going to pick some
buildings from East Harlem and advise the people of their "rights."

We all know that that is not going to help the horrible conditions that our people are
living in. Their drug addiction program is a program that will take you off drugs and

return the addict to "God." We told them that there is no point in talking anymore until they realize that they cannot turn their back on the community if they expect to have a church in that community. They decided to go on with the programs even if the negotiations did not continue, and they are not going to continue.

We have been very flexible with the church. We stopped going to the church so that we could talk things out, and we said that the liberation school was negotiable. They refuse to give the people anything.

We are going back to the church. We will continue to go back until that church is the People's Church, as it stands now those gusanos are occupying the people's church. The entire Methodist structure will be under scrutiny. The entire structure will not be safe until they respond to the needs of the people!!

> VOLVERMOS!!
> Todo Poder al Pueblo!
>
> Juan "Fi" Ortiz
> Minister of Finance
> N.Y. State—Y.L.O.

....

Interview with Yoruba, Minister of Information, Young Lords Organization, Regarding Confrontation at the First Spanish Methodist Church in El Barrio (Spanish Harlem)

(From the National Council of the Churches of Christ in the United States of America Communication Center file on the Young Lords, 1970)

Q. Why was the First Spanish Church chosen to present your demands that they serve the community? Will you make similar demands of other community churches?

A. The First Spanish Church was chosen because it was right smack dead in the center of El Barrio. It's a beautiful location right in the middle of the community that has consistently closed itself up to the community. It's only open for a few hours each week and for the rest of the week it turns into one big brick that sits on 111th St. and Lexington. It's not just the Young Lords or our political beliefs that they responded to—they don't even deal with the anti-poverty organizations in the community.

Most of the other churches like St. Cecilia's and Good Neighbor and some of the Catholic churches have some kind of program. They could do a little more brushing up, be a little more effective, but at least they try, they have something—they have kids come and play in the gym, they have head start programs or something. This church used to have 40–50 young people in the church. Now they've lost all their young people—their own sons and daughters. This church has been around for about 10 years. They had a gym and then there was a fire and they rebuilt the church and had a gym in there. They had a basement and a sub-basement and then took it out a few years ago.

The young people started coming back when we started doing our thing in the church and there's a conflict going on in the church now between the young people and the board of directors. The young people are also put off by us, but they know there's nothing wrong with breakfast programs, so they've been helping us a lot.

Q. On Sunday you made a statement that you were unarmed and if the police came in they would be killing innocent people—are you always unarmed?

A. We believe that eventually we will have to arm ourselves, and the people will have to arm themselves, when we make our move for liberation. Right now that's not a probability—that would be suicidal at this point because what we are right now is a propaganda unit. We're educating the people to what it is to be born in Kenya, what it is to be Puerto Rican, and also to the contradictions in the society. We don't need guns to do that. We don't have any guns in this office—to do so would be to invite the police to come in to have a massacre, to have a riot.

We know they have their agents, their spies. They've been checking us out. They know darn well we don't have any guns, but they're just trying to be funny. Last Wednesday at 3:00 p.m. they surrounded the office with 150 police and out here on Madison Ave. police cars lined up. They were on the rooftops across the street and they just sat there for 15 minutes, just checking us out. It was to intimidate us, to have us provoke something. The people came out into the street and were behind us. They asked what are they here for and we told them what they were here for. Our explanation made a connection with what happened to the Black Panther party a week before and the people said "Why? You haven't hurt anybody."

So it's obvious that what's going down is just this mad provocation and that's the only conspiracy. There's a trial in Chicago they call the "Conspiracy 8" but the only conspiracy in this country is that of a small ruling class that just puts down poor people and that's the conspiracy that we just want to move out of the way.

Q. Do you think that the concept of reparations as expressed by James Forman is a valid one for Puerto Rican people?

A. James Forman's basic concept is that the churches have been a helping hand and a willing partner in the oppression of black people. This also holds true for Puerto Rican people, especially the Catholic church since most Puerto Ricans are Catholic.

The other issue that has been brought us is that organized religion has got to respond to the needs of the people. Now the Board of Directors and members of that church say that we imposed ourselves on them by speaking up and asking for space during their service. We say that they have imposed themselves on the community by putting their church in the middle of their community and then not opening their doors to the people. That's the true imposition that they fail to see. Some other people and the press just like to play up this thing that we disrupted the service. We were upholding an ancient Christian tradition since the time of Paul, that says anybody that comes to a service has the right to speak up. In true Christianity the rights of the minority have always been respected.

There are certain people in organized religion who have become established that feel that theirs is the only way to serve God, to serve the people. That's not quite right. The contradictions of an organized religion that can permit someone like Cardinal Spellman to bless the troops before they go out and commit something like the Song My massacre makes it obvious that there is no separation between church and politics.

We know that within the church there's a small revolution going on—Ivan Illych in Mexico is a beautiful brother who's taking care of a lot of business and educating the people and exposing the contradictions that exist in capitalism. Camilo Torres died in Latin America for what he believed in, so there are some. The hierarchy of the church has got to come down from up there in the sky and see what's happening with the people.

Q. Can you tell me what is your relationship with the Black Panthers and the Patriot Party?

A. You see, if we're attacked we're going to defend ourselves. Huey Newton brought that principle up and it's true. Anybody in the street knows that for a long time our people have been beat, we've been brutalized, killed, raped and the only way we're going to stop that is by defending ourselves. Now the police came into Fred's home and murdered him in his bed in Chicago. They claim that he attacked first, which is a lot of nonsense. Or that raid in Los Angeles—they claim the Panthers came out and started shooting. There's 300 police surrounding the office and right away the Panthers are going to start shooting at the 300 policemen. Why? Because they're crazy. That doesn't make any sense.

The police obviously provoked that whole thing and started it. If you just sit there you're going to get wiped out, and if you're going to go down you might as well take somebody with you—you've got to defend yourself. That's human instinct, survival instinct.

The Rainbow Coalition consists of the Patriot Party, Young Lords Organization and the Black Panther Party. If you're not familiar with the Patriots, that's a revolutionary white organization. We call it the Rainbow Coalition because it's a rainbow of cultures and colors. We also say there's a rainbow existing in the Puerto Rican community because Puerto Ricans can be as dark as I am or have blonde hair and blue eyes—Puerto Ricans come out all different ways. But this was done mainly to educate the people. It is a revolutionary force in America today.

The Young Lords Organization is a revolutionary force moving the Latin community, the Black Panther party is moving the black community and the Patriots are beginning to move the poor white community. By us getting together and working together in this Rainbow Coalition the people that see that, that blows a lot of their racism that's been instituted by the man. The lying politicians can't use arguments that we're really racist, because if we're all working together it's got to be something more.

What we relate to is class struggle. We're not interested in struggle between races or between ethnic groups. So that's the main purpose of the Rainbow Coalition—it's for purposes of education. It's also a defense and information coalition. If anything comes up with the Panthers, the Lords and the Patriots are going to go down also, and the same way for all three groups.

When we were involved in the church offensive or some of the other things that we've been involved in, we've received help and support from the Panthers and Patriots. The Panther 21 trial is coming up December 18th and a demonstration is taking place. We'll be down there at the rally along with the Patriots.

Q. Do you study revolutionary thinkers such as the Panthers do Mao's Little Red Book?

A. A revolution has to take a sense of what was done before and then improvise on what's happening in his own situation. Obviously the Chinese revolution is not going to take place in the U.S. The U.S. is not an agricultural society, but it's a highly advanced technological society. Something new under the sun is going to be done for the Second American Revolution. However there's a lot of similarity in what's gone down in other revolutionary situations. Lenin read Marx and Mao read Lenin and Marx, and Castro at first didn't read them and then he found out that what they were saying was exactly the same thing that he was saying—then he decided to check them out. And that's what's happened with us. We read everybody—we read Nat Turner, Frederick Douglas, Betances and Campos—Puerto Rican revolutionaries. Puerto Ricans have had a long history of revolution. They fought against Spain and now they're fighting against the U.S. I hate somebody that makes the same mistake twice, especially when there's no reason for it, because people wrote the earlier ones down. Yet, if you don't take any short cuts, with things so rough already, you're in bad shape. So we read some Mao, Marx, Lenin. We don't let that govern us, we don't put them up as gods. They're revolutionaries just as we are and I respect them for that. We're going to have to do something a little different, that's why they in turn respect us.

Q. Do you also consider Christ as a revolutionary?

A. David Kirk from Emmanus House sent us a telegram when the police rioted a week ago Sunday in the church. It read that if Christ was alive today, he would have been a Young Lord. That's true. We believe that. We also believe that if Christ came back today, they'd crucify him again.

Christ was saying a whole lot. The Bible is used as an instrument of oppression in the hands of the imperialists. They teach only the parts of the Bible that will mollify the people, keep them down, you know, turn the other cheek, be cool, be humble, slow up, wait. They don't show you the parts like when things were going bad in the temple, Christ went in and threw them out and he wasn't non-violent—he was a pretty violent cat when he had to be.

You don't go back into the days of the Old Testament when everybody was doing in everybody else—jacking everybody else up. They were fighting in the name of the Lord—a Holy War which they fought with righteous feeling. And that's why we've got Christ right up there next to Mao—he was a heavy cat.

Q. Do you include any education such as Puerto Rican history in your program?

A. We're primarily a propaganda unit, a teaching agency. At this stage of the revolutionary struggle we're educators with the true history of Puerto Rico and what it means

"IF CHRIST WERE ALIVE TODAY HE'D BE A YOUNG LORD."

From the newspaper *Palante*, 31 July 1970, volume 2, number 8.

to be Puerto Rican as our curriculum. We also expose the contradictions that exist in America and why, contrary to opinion, they're never going to make it in the system.

We have political education classes, in the community. We send our organizers out to knock on doors and with people on the street. The people on the Board of the First Spanish Methodist Church told us that we were Satan, and that if poor people wanted they could educate themselves, and they don't have to play numbers and drink beer. Their idea is that Puerto Rican people dig being poor, and that they made it so why can't everybody else make it. They think that Puerto Rican women on welfare spend their money on beer, they play the numbers and that they really dig the gutter. It took a whole lot to hold our tempers, but their sons and daughters (who were at the meeting between the Board of Trustees and the Young Lords) let them know how we felt.

Q. As it stands now, what charges have been brought against you and what action has been pursued concerning them?

A. On Sunday, December 7, 13 people were arrested—9 Young Lords and 4 supporters. Of these, 5 were hospitalized for injuries received when they were being taken out of the church by the police. The charges against those arrested were felonies—mostly riot in the 1st and 2nd degrees, felonious assault, disrupting a service, conspiracy to disrupt a service—but these have been lowered to misdemeanors. In the hearing Wednesday (Dec. 17) all the complaints had Rev. Carrazana's name on them.

Speech by Felipe Luciano, New York State Chrmn., Young Lords Organization, at the First Spanish Methodist Church in El Barrio (111th St. & Lexington) on Sunday December 21, 1969

(From the National Council of the Churches of Christ in the United States of America Communication Center file on the Young Lords, 1970)

A group of Young Lords and approximately 100 to 150 supporters attended Sunday worship at the First Spanish Methodist Church, scene of confrontations for the past three Sundays over allowing the Young Lords to use the church space for a breakfast program, and to negotiate a daycare center and a liberation school. One of the Young Lords rose in his seat during the service and asked for permission to speak. Most of the parishioners yelled at him to sit down and wait for the service to be over. He did. Most of the parishioners left after the service and did not stay to listen or to say anything. The minister, Dr. Humberto Carrazana, left almost immediately after the service was over. A few members of the lay Board stayed and spoke to the group explaining their position, as well as a young woman representing the young people of the church. The following speech was delivered after all this took place.

Someone asked me if I needed a tranquilizer and I had to tell him no, it's just very, very cold outside, so I'm trembling. Because by law, bail contingency, the 13 defendants (arrested allegedly disrupting the service Sunday, Dec. 7) have to wait outside, 100 ft. away from the church and we have to have permission of the church people before we come in.

It's obvious that the parishioners have not stayed. It's obvious that there's a few members of the Board here—I heard the President of the Board is here. There's some young people here—the young people are in support of us. So, basically, we're talking to ourselves: let's establish that one point.

The parishioners have been consistently intimidated, harassed by the minister and the Board of this church. It can be verified not only by us but by the young people of this church. So they're scared stiff. And let's understand one basic point about our people. We call them our mothers and our fathers because as far as we are concerned they are our people.

The church was built not by outside funds, it was built by their own funds. They worked hard, they're lower middle class now. We all know about the whole American scene of vertical mobility that you move out of the problems of the ghetto, you move out of that sensitivity that you once had into another whole socio-economic area, into a whole different area, you play a different role. And this is one of the things that have not been put down to the parishioners—that they are our mothers and fathers and we understand the problems that they have.

The reasons that they have given us for not having us in the church [are] that we are satanic, we are a devilish influence in the community, we are communism in disguise, all of that superficial jive. There has been no substantive reason as to why we can't have the space. That has to be understood by everyone. There has been no substantive reason why the Young Lords cannot operate a community program in cooperation with the church.

Legally, the church is tax exempt. Any tax exempt institution is run by the people. The people should be allowed to use the space. They have no right to close the doors to any group of people, whether they be anti-poverty, revolutionary, or whatever the case may be, they have no right to close their doors.

Another thing that has been a bone of contention. The one who has the final authority as to who uses the space in the church is Dr. Carrazana himself. It is not the Board of Directors, it is not the parishioners. This is stated specifically in the Methodist bylaws (the Book of Discipline). We got this verified by someone in the National Council of Churches and some of our ministers looked at that passage. This passage was put in because a lot of white ministers were allowing black kids to use their gyms and their facilities inside the church and the parishioners and the Board of Directors got uptight about it. So that it is only the minister who has the final authority, not the parishioners, and not the Board of Directors—even though I am in total agreement with the argument that they should have some say in terms of what happens in their church. But legally, in terms of their ritual, which they've been hitting us with all the time, it is the minister and he has been the one, Dr. Carrazana himself, who decides.

We hold no malice towards the parishioners of this church. All of us young Puerto Ricans have grown up with the same kinds of attitudes from our mothers and fathers—the same racism, the same narrow-mindedness, the same lack of perspective in terms of what's happening outside. We've all grown up with this ritual. I, myself, grew up in a Pentecostal church. You talk about strictness—you ain't seen strictness till you grow up in a Pentecostal church. So that it's not unusual for us to go through this. What *is* unusual is the fact that they are going to turn their back on babies. They are going to turn their back on young people who are saying to them, yes, we agree, you are our mothers and fathers, yes, we want to work in cooperation with you. We do not want to take over this institution. It would be ridiculous for us to talk at this point about taking over this institution. That's jive! Understand that! We're only asking for space. Not money, we're not asking for any kind of financial assistance from the state, the Federal Government, or them. We already have a working relationship with the merchants in our community. They are willing to get us food. We want a daycare center, and we even told them that that is negotiable. We can understand how people can get uptight about the fact that you *may* be teaching Marxism-Leninism in a church. That is negotiable. We are only asking for space, that is non-negotiable, for the breakfast program.

One of our ministers puts it right to the point, very concisely, when he says that not only are we threatening their images, but we are threatening the organized form of religion in this country. What we are doing is showing the contradictions of how organized religion oppresses our people. The people here are following not the spirit of the Law, but the letter of the Law. This can be verified by many passages in the New Testament. When Christ was walking through a cornfield, he took some corn and put it in his mouth and the pharisees, the hypocrites, came up and said, "Rabbi, what are you doing, it is the Sabbath." And he said, "Yeah, Jim, but I'm hungry."

It has to be understood that anybody who's been brought up in El Barrio is a Bible scholar—it was forced down our throats. It has to be understood that Christ, in that service, was a revolutionary. It's because of this that he was killed. Christ used to call the Pharisees and Sadducees, who were the elders of the tribe of Israel at that particular time, which by the way, was under Roman control, so it was a colony, Palestine was, he called them hypocrites, he called them every other name in the book. Man, he didn't have as much patience as the Young Lords are having. He actually went into a church and beat them! And you talk about us being violent! He told them, get out of here you moneylenders, you are filth! All you are thinking of is filthy lucre, you are not thinking about the spirit of the Law.

It has to be understood that we may not advocate a worship in a God. Our god is our people. That is my god. That is my religion. And so I don't care how many plain-clothesmen they have around, even though we've told them to get out. I don't care how many threats there have been against our people—and there have been threats to our lives, to our wives, and everything else. There have also been beatings on this same block. The tension, man, the tension, is unbearable. When all you're doing is asking for basic reforms! Not even revolutionary, but *basic* reforms, and what you do is get killed!

So that in a sense, what we are doing is much more Christian, much more broth-erly, than anything that any church—not only this church—but any church in this coun-try is doing. It is no mistake that they killed Martin Luther King. It is no mistake. He stepped out of his realm of organized religion and said the Vietnam war is genocidal, it is immoral. And began to mobilize and organize people to focus on that issue. And they killed him. And they will kill anyone, and they'll harass anyone who in any way ques-tions the mainstays of this society. You hit the jugular of America, like Malcolm did, and you will die. And we understand that. But that's not going to faze us.

This church is just a symbol. The people built it almost with their own hands—we understand that. But it is a symbol of the oppression that our people are going through. A symbol of the narrow-mindedness that doesn't allow them to look out on the fresh air and see faces. I've explained this many times. Revolutionaries, at least our group, are not a death force. We are a life force, we don't believe in death. We don't want to go to jail. We don't want to die. I will talk to *anyone* whose interest is helping the people. I even went down to the College of Criminal Justice and talked to cops themselves because I believe that everyone has the potential for being human—not Puerto Rican, not white, but human. Without that belief revolutionaries cannot survive. Commit suicide, Jim, unless you believe in that basic goodness in man.

So that in this kind of a confrontation, there can be no noncommitment. One can't be noncommittal about it. Eldridge Cleaver said Jim, you're either part of the problem or you're part of the solution. So that I have to impress it on your minds how important it is, the problem of this church. And how important it is that we continue to come back Sunday after Sunday. One thing these people cannot say is that we've been discourteous. One thing is that we've washed away all the illusions they have about revolutionaries, these images of fuzzy gorillas walking around using Thomson machine guns on people. We've made it very clear that we're not out for armed confrontation with the police—it's suicidal at this point. We can dig that. We've made it a point that we don't have drugs in the office or any other of that silliness. That's what the Young Lords are about.

And so we're going to come back—we need your support—time, and time again. And we are going to batter down the doors of their consciences until they understand. It was done on December 7, when blood was spilled from here all the way to the back of the church—all the way. Already some people have given in. One sister came up to me and asked my forgiveness for hitting me one time when I got up to speak—that was before the police came in and started beating us. And I said of course. We hold no malice towards anyone—we just want them to open up.

The problems of this world, much less El Barrio, will not be solved by people being adamant, being like stones. They will be solved when you are open, when you are flex-ible, when you are receptive in some way. When there is some give and take, which is the only way that people learn. All we are asking for is for them to allow *our* babies—not mine, our babies—call it socialism if you want—to allow our babies to come inside and eat a hot breakfast. To have our babies understand the nature of imperialism, understand the true nature of their country, Puerto Rico, understand the independence movement in Puerto Rico. We have Puerto Rican children who don't know who their revolutionary heroes are, who don't know their language, who don't know their culture, and we will die. I do not want to become an ethnic group that in some way will be assimilated into America. Hell NO! Never! We will stay Puerto Rican! We will continue to speak our language! We will continue to fight and die if necessary for our people.

It's more important that we understand the importance of this institution. This is a symbol, people. And it must be won over. Che said, it may sound corny but a revolutionary is guided by true feelings of love. And I believe that. It's going to take us time, but we're going to listen, no matter what they throw at me. I'm too hardened by broken arms and stitches in my head to be hardened by some words (Felipe bears a cast on his right arm and a patch on his head as a result of the confrontation Dec. 7). I'm going to listen to all of them—I'm going to listen to Iram, I'm going to listen to Carmen, I'm going to listen to all the young people in the church. But I will be firm. The Young Lords will not be moved. We may lose your support, we don't know. What happens is that with the first fires of enthusiasm everybody is in the church, and then as time begins to pass, support begins to peter out. But we're going to stay here. We want you here because it's going to keep us from getting killed. *You* are going to keep *us* from getting killed. And don't take it lightly.

I don't know, and this may not be a revolutionary statement, but I don't know how I'll be able to live if one of our people is killed. I don't know. What do you tell a mother whose 15-year-old boy, who is a member of the Young Lords, is killed by a 38 Smith-Wesson bullet. What do you tell her? He died for the revolution? It may be existential, but think about it. What do you tell her? I may feel it, but she doesn't. All she feels is the loss of a son. That's why we want you here. That's why we want many more people here. That's why we want the pressure on this church, on this institution. And so anyone here who has contacts, begin to use them, I don't care what level you are, I don't care what your commitments are—begin to use them. The Young Lords office needs money, it needs help, it needs paper, it needs stencil machines, mimeograph machines, we need God knows how many things. Only you can help us.

Getting back to our problem—we are going to keep coming back here. Because when we say "all power to the people" we mean it. It's not a trite phrase for us. When we say "I am a revolutionary" we mean it. Fred Hampton meant it. And we're going to make sure that that commitment to people stays solid. It has to be understood that the reason they're vamping on us is because the police department, the state department, city government and the federal government do not want a Latin vanguard to arise in this country. We've been traditionally docile and faggoty. But, you see, the faggots have died. They've died in our culture. A lot of us have changed our names. The old people have died. We have shed off the old clothing. We are going to make the "new man" that Che talked about. We respect the struggles that our people have had in the past—all Latins, whether they be in Puerto Rico, the Dominican Republic, Mexico. We respect the struggles. But we're going on.

And we're *not* only reacting. There's a way now in the movement that any way the 'system' pushes you, you react in the opposite direction—you never think, you're never creative. And so you end up in a suicidal path where you can't move out. No, we're going to be creative, you see. Because one of the things is passion helps, as Fanon says, passion helps, but you know, reason is invaluable. And we are going to think about it. We're not hotheads. We're going to sit down and think. We sit down all the time and talk. We're going to think about it. We're going to stay too.

The United States Government—and it is a conspiracy, on the part of all city officials and everyone else, to mollify, to emulsify any Latin bag. Look, Jim, they're having enough trouble with the niggers—no more trouble with the spics, because they know that when there's trouble with the spics, it's all over. In '67 when the riots occurred in El Barrio—and let this be understood, it didn't last 4 days like in black Harlem, it only lasted one day—and hundreds of thousands of dollars were poured into El Barrio, to the extent that now we have three anti-poverty agencies per block, and ain't nothing being done.

We Puerto Ricans are a very emotional people, most Latin people are, and we will take things up to a point, and then we get into our Bogart bag. That has to be understood about Puerto Ricans. See, Puerto Ricans are crazy. And we have a saying, that a Puerto Rican will throw you up in the air when he gets mad, swish you with a knife fifteen times and not miss once. So let it be understood that we are nice, but we can also be very firm.

The conspiracy is evident, they want to chop us up. They don't want to let Puerto Ricans, they don't want to let New Yorkers or anyone else think that Puerto Ricans can think. You see, we [can] think. We've had thinkers for centuries, from Betances all the way up. We are a tribal people, and we know what's happening. So understand that this conspiracy is very related to you—I don't care who you are. But understand, when the repression hits, it may hit me, and then what the system tries to do is to isolate you from the masses of the people and then begins to knock you down as they did with the Panthers. But understand that in killing me, the next one is you, and you. The next one—you may be liberal, liberal radical, radical-revolutionary, whatever the case may be, but YOU WILL BE NEXT, JIM. You will be next. And don't take it lightly. Twelve million people in Germany—six million Jews and six million nationals had to understand the hard way. That is not going to happen here.

I'll finish with a poem. It's dedicated to El Jibaro, who in Puerto Rican folklore is the cane cutter. He's that mixture of Indian, Black and Spaniard on which a lot of our history is based. He's the man who fought in the mountains with Campos. He's the man who today is dying in the mountains of Puerto Rico because he gets $7.50 a week for cutting cane.

....

Report Given to Rev. Pablo Cotto by Iris Luciano

(From the National Council of the Churches of Christ in the United States of America Communication Center file on the Young Lords, 1970)

The following is a report given to Rev. Cotto by Mrs. Luciano, wife of Mr. Felipe Luciano, Chairman of the Young Lords Organization, here in New York on Sunday, December 28, 1969, 7:30 p.m. at 1678 Madison Ave., near 111th St., Office of the Young Lords Organization in New York City.

This morning after the worship service, the Young Lords Organization took over St. Paul's Methodist Church Spanish at 111th Street and Lexington Ave. Television and newspapers published the event. On Monday, Dec. 22 at a ministers' meeting to look into the situation, I was asked to present my views and I was rudely interrupted and had to walk out of the meeting. I was trying to say that there existed a very real situation which required immediate attention. Also that I believed in dialogue and that I recommended that talks with this group should be encouraged with the view of looking into the program that they were suggesting to see if the church could involve them in projects for the community. At this moment I was interrupted and accused of being a communist. I walked away. The police were outside, probably ready to arrest someone.

On Sunday, the unexpected, by the minister and the congregation who had not been willing to listen, took place. The Young Lords were back attending the morning service, as they had done for seven consecutive Sundays. At the close of the service one of them stood and asked permission to address the congregation. Denied permission they took over the building. After simple negotiations they allowed those who wanted to leave the building, mostly members of the congregation, to do so.

HOW IT STARTED:

Seven weeks ago the organization wrote a letter to the head of the church organization asking the following:

1. Space for a hot breakfast program for children of the community. The Young Lords would provide everything. All they asked for was space during week days when the building was closed and not in usage.
2. Space for a day care center to be established for the people of the community.
3. A liberation school where they would teach special courses according to their philosophy. They did not ask for money.

This letter was ignored. Never answered. The only answer given by the minister and by the president of the Board of Directors was "No." No explanation to it.

At this juncture the group started attending services on Sundays and asking for the opportunity to explain the program to the congregation. Not allowed to do this they attended coffee hours after services, distributed leaflets, engaged the minister and members of the congregation in conversation, but to no avail. Everything was negative.

They persisted in visiting services on Sundays. On December 7, they attended service not expecting difficulty. This was supposed to be testimonial Sunday when people present were allowed to speak during the service. Mr. Luciano tried to speak and was stopped abruptly. To their surprise there were both uniformed cops and plainclothesmen from the police department in the congregation this Sunday. A detachment of additional cops showed up inside the church and started swinging on all sides. It resulted in a riot where eight people were hurt (some were hospitalized), 13 were arrested, five of them women. One girl had 21 stitches taken.

Felipe Luciano had an arm broken and eight stitches. Some were taken to hospitals for treatment and then to jail "tombs" waiting for a hearing which took place around midnight.

The minister had sought legal help while the accused had not had a chance to do so. Charges were filed against them on inciting to riot, criminal trespass and assault.

Cops continued harassment upon members of the organization during the week. Two among these cops are Puerto Ricans. A young man, Ramon, was assaulted by the cops out in the street. When his brother tried to come to his help, he was also attacked. Police tried several times to force the doors of the office of the organization. They went to the place where Mrs. Luciano works asking for information. The former charges were lowered to misdemeanors after certain developments. Those arrested were freed on bail provided by themselves.

Sunday, December 21, back in the service at eleven. This time they had with them a lawyer, a doctor, newspaper people and a number of community people. Around 250 people, all together. In the congregation this Sunday were ministers and other representatives from other churches. While the church had agreed to have an answer ready for this Sunday, no such answer was given. They said they would not even meet to discuss the situation at all. At this the youth of the church became infuriated and started to express themselves. Negotiations with the Board had produced no positive answer. The youth of the church were arrested in support for the program of the Young Lords.

At the close of the service this time the group expected the minister and members of the Board at least to stay and talk to them. Instead, they all left.

Monday, December 22, the ministers met at the church. In the introduction to this report there is an explanation of what took place. The group of ministers present at that particular meeting were radicals not willing to talk on anybody else's terms but their own.

Sunday, December 28.

The day of the takeover. The New York Times, as well as the "El Dario La Prensa" on their Monday editions have [a] complete report on this. Also T.V. and radio. Members of the church were allowed to leave the building. Around 100 youth belonging to the Young Lords Organization are occupying the building. Entrances have been nailed from the inside. The church is trying to get an injunction. Other people chanted hymns outside. This time the police did not enter the building nor take any drastic action. They were around the building. Again the leaders of the church were approached but were negative, as always.

The Young Lords is a volunteer organization. It has no funds. There are no salaries paid to anybody. The Lawyer's Guild of New York is providing legal help. Who are the leaders of the New York chapter?

Chairman—Mr. Felipe Luciano
Minister of Information—Mr. Pablo Guzman (Yoruba)
Minister of Health and Education—Mr. Juan Gonzalez
Minister of Defense—Mr. David Perez
Minister of Finance—Mr. Juan Ortiz (Fi)

The above report was given to me voluntarily and without reservations. I had no difficulty in entering the office neither in contacting the leaders who were there. I identified myself and made myself available for whatever they thought I could do to help. I was treated with courtesy and respect, all the contrary to what I received from the ministers. I was told that all they wanted at the moment was space for their proposed breakfast program. The other demands would be discussed later on. They are still ready for talks with anybody who may show interest in helping solve the situation.

Pablo Cottô
December 29, 1969

Julio Roldan People's Defense Center Opens in the People's Church

(From the newspaper *Palante*, 30 October 1970, volume 2, number 14)

Hundreds of people rushed through the doors of the People's Church on Sunday night, October 18. Over a thousand others stood outside waving Puerto Rican flags, chanting their support, and promising that the murder of Julio Roldan would be avenged. Ten months before, the YOUNG LORDS PARTY and the people of El Barrio had taken over the church on 111th Street and Lexington Avenue, but this time was different. This time we weren't leaving. This time our demands would be met. This time we were armed.

Everyone is dissatisfied with the official reports given by the Department of Corrections on the number of Puerto Ricans found dead in their cells in recent years. But every attempt to investigate the prison system has been turned down. Our people are arrested on phoney charges, held on high bails (which only the rich can pay), and are beaten and murdered in their cells. In taking the church, we checked out this situation; and we made these two demands:

1) That the Methodist Church and other churches give a $150,000 grant to YOUNG LORDS PARTY so that we can set up a legal defense center for the community in the People's Church.

2) That the city immediately allow the clergy to investigate the conditions of the prison system, especially the murders of Julio Roldan, Jose Perez, and three of the negotiators at the Queens House of Detention uprising on October 1.

Reverend Velasquez, pastor of the People's Church, recognizes the problems of our community and has said that he opens the church to the community and endorses our demands. Lawyers, law students, community people and members of the PARTY have already set up the Julio Roldan People's Defense Center.

We ask that the families of people in prisons or detention centers come in and give us information about the condition of their relatives in prison so that we can document their cases in order to bring pressure against the prison system and get information from the outside to them. We also want to document the cases of all brothers and sisters who have been in prison and have experienced police brutality.

The Julio Roldan People's Defense Center will also be offering draft counseling to those brothers who don't want to go into the army. In Puerto Rico, brothers do not have to serve in the army because a strong case has been made in the courts and a strong anti-draft movement has developed. We are trying to do the same thing here. We will also be giving out information about Puerto Ricans who have been jailed here in amerikkka for fighting in the liberation struggle: Carlos Feliciano, George Robles, Oscar Collazo, Martin Sostre, Lolita Lebron, and we will be setting up a committee of people from the community to educate people about these cases and to raise money for their defense.

Finally, we will be setting up a community bail fund, because we know that most of our people cannot afford to bail their relatives out of jail.

We have liberated the People's Church again, and this time we are armed. We know that our demands are righteous, because they come out of the needs of our people. Puerto Ricans and Blacks must have some revolutionary structure to help them battle this corrupt and racist prison system. We are armed because we have seen that the government won't hesitate to kill Puerto Ricans fighting for their rights. We are armed because we must defend ourselves, and we advise all Puerto Ricans and Third World people to begin preparing for their defense. The u.s. government is killing us, and now we must defend ourselves or die as a nation.

LIBERATE PUERTO RICO NOW!
THE PARTY GUIDES THE GUN!
LONG LIVE JULIO ROLDAN!

Richie Perez
Information Captain
YOUNG LORDS PARTY

....

Armense para Defenderse

(From the newspaper *Palante*, 30 October 1970, volume 2, number 14)

In January 1969, the Young Lords Organization began to organize the Puerto Ricans of Chicago to fight against the rats, the roaches, the police, the conditions we live in—to fight for the freedom of our people. On July 26, 1969, the YOUNG LORDS were organized in New York and followed the example of Cha Cha Jimenez, now underground, in fighting for the liberation of Puerto Rico and our people in this country.

On April 4, 1969, Young Lord Manuel Ramos was shot down in the streets of Chicago by a pig. That murderer was never tried, and he still walks the streets. And last week, October 16, 1970, Young Lord Julio Roldan, 34 years old, was killed, hanged in the Tombs, the rathole prison of New York City, by Correction guards.

The murder or "suicide" of a Puerto Rican or black in the prisons of amerikkka and Puerto Rico is not unusual. For years our people have been dying mysteriously in those detention camps. For years revolutionaries, servants of the poor, fighters for freedom, have been killed in the streets, houses, mountains. For years our people have been killed by the yanqui. We die from pneumonia in unheated apartments; we die from sterilization and unsafe abortions; we die from police bullets; we die from overdoses; we die as a nation from the destruction of our culture, language, history; we die from garbage, anemia, hunger, in a thousand and one different ways. We die because we are poor, because we have no power, because the rich politicians and businessmen see nothing but money, profit, killing for themselves.

For almost two years the YOUNG LORDS PARTY has been fighting all the institutions that oppress us—garbage conditions, hospital care, police brutality, the churches not serving the poor. And every time we marched, every time we seized a building, every time we sat in, nothing changed. Anthony Imperiale still runs Newark with a fascist fist. Philadelphia Police Commissioner Bozo Rizzo attacks the Puerto Rican and Black community at will. Lincoln Hospital continues to butcher our people with indecent health care. The garbage remains in our Brownsvilles, Lower East Sides, Kannecot Copper Company is preparing to steal more of our land and resources through its copper mining in Utuado. Ramey Air Force Base with its nuclear weapons and B-52's is destroying our town of Aguadilla. Culebra and Vieques are disappearing under a Navy bombing. We fight, we protest, we demonstrate. Nothing changes.

Our nation is a colony. Whether in Bridgeport or Fajardo, we are controlled by the yanqui. We are his tool, his slave. That is why on October 18, when 2,000 people from El Barrio marched in Julio Roldan's funeral, we seized the People's Church for the second time. This time, though, we took the church with arms, with shotguns, rifles, everything we could find, and prepared to defend it.

We said, two LORDS are dead. We are not going to wait for the third, the tenth, the twentieth. Thousands of Puerto Ricans have died, murdered by amerikkka. We can't stand by anymore. This government, instead of protecting us, kills us. We have no choice at this time, but to pick up those guns and say to all of our nation—ARM YOURSELVES TO DEFEND YOURSELVES.

We were not born violent. We do not enjoy killing. We just want peace and freedom. But our daily lives are violent. This country is violent. The enemy leaves us no choice. Either we sit by, saying "ay bendito" as our nation dies, or we stand up, organize, prepare for the revolution we know is coming.

We are at the stage of armed self-defense. The YOUNG LORDS PARTY is not going to begin shooting down police in the streets or bombing places. We are just going to defend ourselves from murder. And our people will do the same.

Point 12 of our 13 Point Program says, "We believe in armed self-defense and armed struggle as the only means to liberation."

We are beginning to put that point into practice. We are preparing for the day when the whole Puerto Rican nation will rise up to get the yanqui off our backs. The YOUNG LORDS PARTY will organize our people, educate them, prepare them. And in the future, a People's Army will arise, like CAL, like MIRA, to lead that armed fight. All we are doing is educating. Education is the first step in revolution. And armed self-defense is the first step of education for armed revolution.

The People's Church will be remembered as the third time in our history that Puerto Ricans resorted to guns to get justice. First was El Grito de Lares and Betances. Second was Don Pedro and the Nationalist Party. Third is the YOUNG LORDS PARTY.

The first two failed, but they were examples for us, made us proud to be Puerto Ricans. Our march to the United Nations on October 30 is in commemoration of Jayuya and that fight of Don Pedro. We are the sons and daughters of Don Pedro, Elio Torresola, Blanca Canales, and Oscar Collazo.

The future is ahead. We have no more illusions. The people are forging unity. The enemy is paralyzed. The Puerto Rican nation is awake. The road is long and hard. We are young but we are determined. Love for our people guides us. Hatred of oppression drives us. We will not turn back.

VICTORY OR DEATH!

Juan Gonzalez
Minister of Defense
YOUNG LORDS PARTY

11

Social Justice Programs

The Young Lords were committed to fighting for social justice on all fronts. Like the Black Panthers, they ran various clothing and food programs to serve the poor people of their communities. They were stalwart antidrug advocates because they saw first-hand the impact of heroin on the people of their communities. They also made significant demands for prisoners' rights and against prisoner abuse in New York. These essays from the *Palante* newspaper document what programs the Young Lords implemented and why they implemented them.

....

YLO Feeds Children

(From the newspaper *Palante*, 8 May 1970, volume 2, number 2)

In this capitalist society, we are denied certain necessities such as food, clothing and decent shelter. We go to school without eating a hot breakfast and can't concentrate on our own schoolwork as a result. How can we concentrate on doing any learning when our stomachs are growling? We are then told by teachers that we are stupid and can't learn, giving us a defeatist attitude for the rest of our lives.

The YOUNG LORDS ORGANIZATION realizes this, so we have instituted breakfast programs in our communities. One such program is at Emmaus House at 241 E. 116th Street. This Breakfast Program feeds 30 young Brothers and Sisters before they go to school. At this Program, they receive nourishing meals, such as fruit, juice, bacon, and hot chocolate. We do this in order to educate our People as to how a socialist society cares for the basic necessities of a People. The 13th Point of our 13 Point Program states, "*We want a socialist society*" meaning complete liberation, free food, clothing, shelter, education, health care, transportation, utilities, and employment for all.

If the YLO can find hungry children, then people should really question themselves as to why, under this present system, where they have the money to put a man on the moon, people shouldn't go hungry. We realize that the reason for this is that the man is out there for himself, and that he couldn't care if young Puerto Rican and Black Brothers and Sisters go hungry, as long as the man is making his money.

This pig talks of our violence while we are brutalized by his violence, by the violence of hungry children, illiterate adults, and diseased old people. This is why the 12th Point of our Program states that "*Armed Self-Defense and Armed Struggle are the only means to Liberation.*"

The YOUNG LORDS ORGANIZATION is educating our people to the fact that when a government oppresses the People, we have the right and it is our duty, to abolish it and create a new one.

HASTA LA VICTORIA SIEMPRE!
VENCEREMOS!

Connie Morales
Young Lords Organization
Bronx Branch

....

Free Clothes for the People

(From the newspaper *Palante*, 22 May 1970, volume 2, number 3)

The YOUNG LORDS ORGANIZATION has been running a series of Free Clothing Drives. The latest one was held on April 25, 1970, when over 300 mothers came and got clothes and kitchen utensils.

Our cry is a very simple and logical one. Puerto Ricans came to this country hoping to get a decent job and to provide for their families, but it didn't take long to find out that the amerikkkan dream that was publicized so nicely on our island, turned out to be the amerikkkan nightmare.

We live in the worst housing, and have to pay the most rent. We work the hardest and longest under the most inhumane conditions, yet we don't make enough bread to buy clothes for our children to go to school. We have to see our families live on rice and beans and crap all week.

As servants of the people (Revolutionaries), we have committed ourselves whole-heartedly to the development of our Nation of Borinquen and all humanity. We understand that our people can only be educated through observation and participation. The YLO arrived at this conclusion not because we think that people are stupid, but because so many groups or individuals have used us so much—like politicians use workers—that even our own people didn't give a damn about listening to the LORDS' political program. We had to SHOW our people what we were all about, and not TALK so much. After seeing what we were all about by example, our people got involved, at first in El Barrio, in the struggle for liberation. Soon, all Puerto Ricans will join in, because it will take all of us to free ourselves from the mental and physical chains this government has us under.

Our task in the YLO is to make our people conscious of the crimes committed against us by the fascist, racist, money-hungry capitalists. We decided to begin a free clothing program when the Department of Welfare cut the checks to 66 cents a day in New York City and our younger brothers and sisters had to go to school with three year old clothing. Also the YLO is educating everybody to the fact that our people are the ones that make these clothes at the garment center and then have to pay for them, when they are rightfully ours!

Not only that, but the mere fact that billions of dollars are spent to wage a war of aggression against other human beings, and then they say that they don't have enough money to provide clothing for our people (not even providing decent jobs for our people to pay for the damn rags).

The 13th point of the YLO Program and Platform says: "We want a Socialist Society." We understand that the only way all of the things that are necessary for a human being to exist in this technological society can be provided is by taking control of the institutions, the government, the life and death of our people. This can only be done by organizing ourselves into a solid group of people that are armed and will put their lives on the line for the interests of the Poor and Oppressed People of the World. Revolution.

CLOTHING BELONGS TO THE PEOPLE!

David Perez
Minister of Defense
New York State
East Coast Region

....

Breakfast Programs

(From the newspaper *Palante*, 3 July 1970, volume 2, number 6)

One of the Free Breakfast Programs run by the YOUNG LORDS PARTY is located at 930 East 4th Walk in the Lower East Side, the PARTY feeds up to 25 children each and every weekday when school is in session, from 7:30 to 8:30 in the morning. The reason that the YLP has these Free Breakfast Programs is that many of our children go to school hungry every day.

We feel that the morning meal is the most important meal of the day. In order for us to have a thinking mind we must have a full stomach. Free Breakfast Programs will not change the racist brainwashing educational system in this country, but they do deal with the immediate physical needs of our people. We feed the children a full meal that will help them function throughout the school day. The meals include eggs, bacon, sausages, french toast, pancakes, hot and cold cereals, and fruits. The food is obtained from community merchants and donations.

Besides feeding the children, we teach them their true culture and history and show them how to get along with their brothers and sisters. Point 13 of our 13 Point Program states that we want a Socialist Society, with free food, clothing, education, medical care, and housing for all. The Free Breakfast Program is a step in this direction.

NEWARK

The YOUNG LORDS PARTY in Newark has begun a Breakfast Program in which the children of our community will eat and continue to eat as long as we are here. The program was started in honor of Manual Ramos, who was murdered by a Chicago pig on May 4, 1968. We here believe that asking the congressmen, the businessmen, the churches, and the schools has gotten us nowhere, an absolute zero. So, we're not asking anymore. We are taking what is rightfully ours. The age of compromise is over.

Our Breakfast is being served at 75 Park Avenue, where we also have our headquarters. It is from here that we, the people, manage to serve the children that the congressmen promised to, that the businessmen write memos about, that the churches say prayers for, that the schools ignore. The YOUNG LORDS PARTY is not promising, writing memos, praying, or ignoring. We're doing, and we will continue to do—HASTA LA VICTORIA!

One Phantom Jet Fighter costs $5,000,000—How many hungry children could be fed with this money? DESPIERTA BORICUA! Think! Think! For a non-thinking person is a dead person.

Juan Garcia
YOUNG LORDS PARTY
Newark Branch

....

Socialism in Practice

(From the newspaper *Palante*, 17 July 1970, volume 2, number 7)

Free food, clothing, education, health care, community control, and employment for all are a few of the things that make up Socialism. The YOUNG LORDS PARTY wants a Socialist society, a society that is constructed to meet the needs of our people and to make their lives easier instead of more difficult. As servants of the people (revolutionaries), we are devoted and wholeheartedly committed to making it possible for our people to get what is theirs. The YOUNG LORDS PARTY is doing this through practice. We have programs that relate to the needs of our community. One of the programs is our Free Clothing Drive. This program has reached thousands of Puerto Ricans and Blacks in the past.

On Saturday, July 11, the YOUNG LORDS PARTY held its latest clothing drive. Over 1,000 people showed up at Casita Maria, on Simpson St. in the Bronx, where we held the drive.

As the people in the community picked out the things they needed from the many different types of clothing that were there, we rapped with them about the different problems that exist and that will continue to exist unless we unite to fight the system responsible for the murder of our nation and our people. We talked about how Puerto Ricans came, and still come, to this country hoping to find good jobs in order to be able to provide for their families; but once they get here they find out that this amerikkkan dream is a nightmare. We talked about how we kill ourselves working in factories and in garment centers hoping to be able to pay for the things that we kill ourselves making. We talked about the system which makes money off the backs of our people.

Our people have lived under oppression for too long and are sick and tired of it. As long as this decadent system continues to use and oppress Third World people, the people and the YOUNG LORDS will fight against it.

ALL POWER TO OPPRESSED PEOPLE!
CLOTHING BELONGS TO THE PEOPLE!
REVOLUTION IS THE ONLY SOLUTION!

Herman Flores
Field Ministry
YOUNG LORDS PARTY
Bronx Branch

....

People's Child Care Center

(From the newspaper *Palante*, 15 August 1970, volume 2, number 9)

One of the seven demands presented to the administration of Lincoln Hospital by the community of the South Bronx, the YOUNG LORDS PARTY, the Health Revolutionary Unity Movement (HRUM), and the Think Lincoln Committee was that we must have a free day care center for the children of patients, workers, and visitors at Lincoln Hospital.

A day care center is needed for a number of reasons. Patients need a day care center so that they can go to the hospital and get attended to with full attention given to their medical needs and not have to worry about their children. Visitors should be able to go and see sick family or friends and be able to know that their children are in a safe place. Workers should not have to pay $15 to $20 a week for a baby sitter, especially since their weekly wages are no more than $90 or $115. A worker with three children would have to spend more than half a week's pay on a baby sitter.

This demand was presented to the administration of Lincoln Hospital about one month ago, and the people waited for a response. Predictably, nothing happened. So the people of the South Bronx gave the administration a deadline—one week to have the Day Care Center open and functioning. The week ended on the morning of July 31.

At 1 a.m. on July 31, a day care center was opened at Lincoln Hospital. It was not opened or run by the administration of the hospital, but rather by the people of the South Bronx.

On the first day, the center held 50 to 60 children, the sons and daughters of patients, workers, and visitors. The children ranged in age from 6 months to 12 years.

The parents were pleased, and they asked: "Why hadn't anyone thought of this before? What took so long for a center to open? This is beautiful." What some of these parents did not realize was that this was not the result of individual action; this was united power. The power of the people created this day care center.

Since that day we have been enjoying the company of 50 to 60 children every day from 7 in the morning to 8 at night, serving them free lunch and snacks, teaching them Puerto Rican history, African history, karate and art, and answering any questions they have.

What we need now are volunteers from the community to help us staff our day care center, to help us serve our children a little better. We are also asking for more volunteers for the committees which we have formed to push for our other six demands. These demands will lead to changes at Lincoln Hospital, changes that will convert Lincoln Hospital into the People's Hospital.

[Call us at (212) 887-1222 if you would like to help.]

ALL POWER TO THE PEOPLE!
QUE VIVA PUERTO RICO LIBRE!

Raphael Viera
Ministry of Health
YOUNG LORDS PARTY
El Barrio Branch

Message to a Dope Fiend

(From the newspaper *Palante*, 8 May 1970, volume 2, number 2)

Spics going to the cooker
never realizing they've
been cooked
Mind shook, money took
And nothing to show for it
but raw scars, railroad tracks
on swollen arms
And abscesses of the mind

Go ahead spic
Stick it in your trigger finger
You ain't got nothing to lose
but your freedom
And yo' mama—who wails futilely at
the toilet door
wants to tear down the whole plumbing structure
but can't
cause you still inside
shooting up, when you already been shot

You ain't got nothing to lose but your freedom.
Shoot the poison, the smack of your oppressor
Shoot Pepi, on 8th Ave. pulling a mule cart
of cheap dresses
to be sold en la Marqueta.
Shoot mami, sweating like her brown ancestors
long ago, killed by Columbus and the Church,
to make that $60.00 in the tombs called factories
Machines rape your mother every day and spit her out
a whore—

Don't throw dagger stares at men
who cruelly crunch your
sister's buttocks between
slimy fingers
You ain't doing nothing
to change it spic
You ain't got nothing to lose
but your freedom

Shoot up our island
of Borinquen
Populated by writhing snakes

who we nicely call gringos
Green Go
Green Go
Green Berets en el Yunque
Green Marines on Calle del Sol
Green bills passing from trembling hand
to calloused palms,
And you shoot the poison 'cause you don't
want to stare at your own ugly reflection—

But it's there spic, Hanging off the stoops,
dripping over on firescapes, in the eyes
of your hermanito, who wants to be
like you—when he grows up.
Better get hip—Quit lying and jiving
and flying like you own something
Cause you don't own nothing but your chains
And when the revolution comes
Very, very soon—You shoot, and I'll shoot
You shoot, and I'll shoot, You shoot, and I'll shoot—
And unless you shoot straight,
I'm gonna get you
Before you get yourself!

Felipe Luciano
Chairman, N.Y. State
Young Lords Organization

....

Heroin! From Where?

(From the newspaper *Palante*, 4-18 July 1971, volume 3, number 12)

Every few months, the nixon administration announces a new "drug-control" program. They act surprised and shocked at heroin's destructive powers. We, who are forced to live in communities that have been flooded with heroin for years, are not so shocked. In December, 1969, nixon called drug addiction a "national problem." In July, 1970, it became a "national threat." And in May 1971, nixon cried that it had become a "national emergency."

In our communities, we all know that dope has been killing us for years. But for the politicians, it didn't become an "emergency" until heroin spilled out of our ghettos into white communities and into the amerikkkan army.

Nixon is a liar, and he's surrounded by other liars and hypocrites. Since 1969, the white house has known about the increase of drug addiction in the army. They have received many reports about this, but instead of being honest and presenting this problem to the people they are supposed to represent, they covered it up. We should examine some of the facts that have been made available to the politicians and ask ourselves why they are being covered up.

Heroin comes from opium. Opium is grown from poppies, a flower. 80% of the world's opium comes from Southeast Asia, according to the United Nations Commission on Drugs and Narcotics. It does not come from the Middle East as the nixon administration claims.

The main production area for opium is the area of northwestern Burma, northern Thailand, and Laos. These areas are controlled by Nationalist China (Taiwan) and by the u.s. supplied and equipped troops of Laos.

The main growers of the opium poppy are the Meo hill tribespeople. It is the only crop the Meos sell. They sell opium for $50 a kilo. The same kilo will sell for $200 in Saigon and $2000 in San Francisco. But the Meos don't only grow opium. In the late 1950's they were selected by the CIA (amerikkkan central intelligence agency) to be trained against the Pathet Lao guerrillas in Laos. As part of the deal, the CIA is now making arrangements and providing protection for planes flying opium out of the area where the Meos live.

Another factor in the opium trade is the Kuomingtang (Nationalist Chinese) 93rd Division which controls a major part of the opium flowing out of Burma and Thailand.

In 1949, the Kuomingtang were being defeated by the Chinese Communist Party and the majority of them fled to the island of Taiwan. Some of the Kuomingtang also escaped to Burma where they now survive by buying opium from the Mao tribespeople in Laos and then reselling it at higher prices. They are also paid by Nationalist China (Taiwan) and the u.s. to do spying missions into the People's Republic of China.

For some time, opium had been transported in planes owned by Corsican Mafia. But as the civil war in Laos intensified, it became impossible for the Mafia to operate and the Meos had no way to transport their opium.

This transportation gap was filled by the Royal Lao Air Force which began to use helicopters and planes that the u.s. had given them to fight the Pathet Lao—they are using them not only to try to crush the people's movement in Laos but also to fly opium out of the Laotian hills to Saigon.

The route from Laos to Saigon is one of the well-established and often used trails of heroin-opium trade. A big part of the opium and heroin remains in Saigon where it is sold directly to u.s. troops or distributed to u.s. bases throughout the Vietnamese countryside.

This drug traffic operates with the knowledge and participation of the u.s. supported Saigon government. Investigations by senator ernest gruening in 1968 revealed that Marshall Nguyen Cao Ky used to fly missions for the CIA into North Vietnam. He was fired, gruening said, because he was caught smuggling opium from Laos back into Saigon.

The opium trade in Southeast Asia brings in a lot of money—from $250 to $500 million a year. Much of this blood money is used to support the rotten, crumbling governments that the u.s. is backing—South Vietnam, Laos, and Nationalist China.

And nixon talks about "stamping out the traffic in illegal drugs." He makes believe that it is beyond his control to stop heroin from slipping into La Perla, El Barrio, and all our other communities. But he knows where it's coming from. It's coming from his allies and puppets.

We say that if we want to stop the flow of drugs that is killing our people, we have to go to the source, to the root of the problem. Smash the corrupt puppet governments of

South Vietnam, Laos, and Nationalist China (Taiwan). And smash the puppet-master too—the lying united states of amerikkka.

ALL POWER TO THE PEOPLE!
QUE VIVA PUERTO RICO LIBRE!

Richie Perez
Deputy Minister of Information
YOUNG LORDS PARTY
National Headquarters

....

Fight Drugs—to Survive

(From the newspaper *Palante*, 16-29 August 1971, volume 3, number 14)

There are over 4,000 drug addicts in the South Bronx. There is only one city hospital for the people of the South Bronx. Before November 11, 1970, there was no Detox Program for these 4,000 addicts. On this date ex-addict workers and community people took over the 6th floor of the Nurses' Residence at Lincoln Hospital. They demanded a Detoxification Program for the South Bronx. HRUM and the community organized 25 addicts for the take over that first day. 30 addicts were detoxed. They asked lacot, the hospital administrator, for the space and equipment, and he told them they had to leave.

100 ses (special events squad) police busted in and arrested 15 people. Finally the administration agreed, but only 25 addicts were to be detoxed. But the community saw the need to take care of at least 200. The hospital was forced to deal with the demands because they couldn't fight the community and workers. So the ex-addicts, workers, and community people did the work themselves with the help of one doctor. When more doctors volunteered, they negotiated for the program to be funded. The administration threatened to close the program two or three times, but 3,000 addicts mobilized against the threat.

Some people might ask, what makes this program different from other programs?

This is one of the first community-worker controlled Drug Programs. In this program, Political Education Classes are given to answer why we use drugs in the first place? What are the real problems we face? We rap about the big-time pushers (not the poor brother or sister that sells dope in our communities) that bring heroin in from other countries so that they can get richer and kill us poor people. Because the rich are afraid we will rebel against the poverty, and drugs are a way to keep us quiet.

Today the program is in its 20th cycle (a cycle lasts 10 days). For 10 days, addicts come in, get methadone, and see a counselor. Most counselors are ex-addicts, so they know best the problems of addicts. After detoxification, they continue to see a counselor and do volunteer work. The program has taken care of about 2,000 addicts. We are trying to get a warehouse together for addicts to stay in while they detox.

Addicts want to kick. They are beginning to understand that drugs are another way of controlling people. Poor people use drugs to escape all the misery in our lives. But there is no escape and addicts are seeing what's happening and don't want to run away anymore. They are going to stay clean ("drug free") to fight these problems.

Why did 15 people have to go to jail to get this program?

Isn't the government supposed to meet our needs and if not, we should change this government to one that would be in the interest of poor people. But instead, the government is taking this program to court for so-called "unamerican" activities. That proves they want us to stay drugged up. When we try to get clean, they call it "unamerican."

FIGHT DRUGS—TO SURVIVE!
ALL POWER TO THE PEOPLE!

Olguie Robles
Ministry of Education
YOUNG LORDS PARTY

Seize the Jails

(From the newspaper *Palante*, 28 August 1970, volume 2, number 10)

> We rioted because of the stink and the stench and the roaches and ants and fleas. And the food, the slop food they gave us.
> —George, a prisoner in the Tombs (August 13, 1970)

Tombs are a place where people are buried. The Tombs—Manhattan House of Detention for Men—is a place where Puerto Ricans and Blacks are buried—alive—and forgotten.

On August 10, our brothers imprisoned in the Tombs moved against the mistreatment, the beatings, the rotten food, the bugs, and the long trial delays and said "Basta Ya. We are men. We won't be treated like animals!" They seized first the 8th floor and later three other floors to protest conditions in the Tombs. Their list of grievances explained that the Tombs on Centre and White Streets was designed to hold 932 men, but on August 11 was holding 1,992 prisoners. Most of our brothers have not been sentenced, but they are serving time. They have not been tried by a jury of their peers, but because they don't have money to post bail, they're forced to suffer, three in a one-man cell, until the courts get to their case. Forget about our constitutional right to a speedy trial. Our constitutional rights in this country were thrown out long ago.

The brothers reported that:

1. The Legal Aid Society does not provide its clients with a vigorous defense.
2. There is brutal treatment of prisoners, primarily Blacks and Puerto Ricans.
3. Wives, sisters, and mothers who visit are "indecently proposed to" by officers at the prison.
4. There are not enough law books available to prisoners preparing their own legal documents.
5. Food is uneatable and "not fit for human consumption."
6. The prison is infested with "body lice, roaches, rats, and mice."
7. Clothing is not supplied to prisoners detained for long periods of time so that some prisoners are forced to wear the same clothes for months.
8. There is an inadequate medical staff.
9. There is no due process, speedy justice, or adequate legal representation.

These conditions have existed in amerikkka's prisons for years. Amerikkkan jails are overcrowded; but so are our schools, hospitals, and neighborhoods. Third World people are forced to live in substandard and subhuman conditions on many different levels—in the jails, in the schools, in the hospitals, and in the streets. We must support our brothers in the Tombs and in every other jail. They are all political prisoners. Their crime is being Puerto Rican or Black and too poor to post bail.

The brothers are moving. One brother who was released after 7 months (the time it took his family to raise $150 bail) said that he began to sense a new spirit in the jail in the last 2 months. "The other times I was in, prisoners were sort of conditioned to accept brutality. There was a feeling that if you said something or complained, you were a punk. It's different now. People are not giving in." Part of the difference, he said, came from an identification with the Black Panther Party and the YOUNG LORDS PARTY.

The press has tried to cover up the news about the prisons. It is made to seem in the news coverage that the Tombs is a unique case. Actually, prisoners revolted in every jail and prison in the city. In Kew Gardens County Courthouse in Queens, the prisoners gained control and demanded they be tried by an international court of law since they are political prisoners (as are all Third World prisoners in amerikkka). Also, for blacks and Puerto Ricans, jail has become another form of genocide, of extermination against a people.

We should not let the importance of this escape us. It is no accident that the prisoners' demands took place a week after the attempted escape of 3 brothers, led by Jonathan Jackson, from a courthouse in California. There is a direct connection: People are moving towards liberation, and the madmen and madwomen in the jails and prisons, knowing the oppressor first hand, are telling us on the outside to intensify our struggle. The message of revolution gets across all barriers. How else did the brothers at the Tombs hand out a banner proclaiming "Power to the People!"

> LET THE MADMEN AND MADWOMEN OUT!
> LIBERATE ALL PRISONERS!
>
> Ministry of Information
> YOUNG LORDS PARTY

....

Free Martin Sostre!

(From the newspaper *Palante*, 15 January 1971, volume 3, number 1)

Martin Gonzalez Sostre is a political prisoner serving a 41-year sentence in jail! His crime is opening an Afro-Asian bookshop in a Black community in Buffalo and beginning to educate that community about the struggles of poor people in the u.s. and around the world. He saved money to run the store by working at the Bethlehem Steel Plant. Soon it became a place where the people of the community could come to learn their history. From the beginning, the FBI and the local police tried to intimidate him. Periodically, the pigs would smash the front windows destroying displayed posters, and the firemen would ransack the inside of the store destroying the literature.

In the summer of 1967, the Black community exploded in three days of rebellion ending in the arrest of 259 people. During the rebellion Martin kept his store open late into the night, providing refuge for the people from the tear gas being sprayed by the police. Afterwards the cops were determined to do away with Martin; on July 14, several carloads of pigs stormed the store, arrested Martin and Geraldine Robinson, a co-worker and mother of 5 children. Then Martin Gonzalez Sostre was charged with riot, arson, possession of narcotics and assault.

The u.s. constitution guarantees speedy trial, provides against excessive bail and cruel and unusual punishment. Yet Martin spent months in jail before his trial came up because he was unable to pay bail (ransom) which was first placed at $50,000 then lowered to $25,000. Both amounts were too much for a man who barely made $60 to pay. For his defense, he was not able to have a lawyer and the public defender was hooked up with the police. The most prominent law firm in Buffalo dropped his case because it was too hot. Martin was his own lawyer in court.

During pre-trial hearings, he was brought in chains. When he talked longer than what racist judge marshall wanted, he was gagged with towels. As further torture, he was put in solitary confinement in a dark cell especially used for mental cases. The court tried to say he was crazy, but Martin proved that the psychiatrists were all racists and their testimony was invalid. In the end, the all white racist jury met for 60 minutes found him guilty and sentenced him to 30-41 years plus 30 days for "contempt."

Martin Gonzalez Sostre was well experienced with the injustices committed by this government in the name of justice and law because he had already spent 12 years in jail between 1952-64. In 1957, when his case came up for parole, he took it upon himself to question the composition of the parole board which was all white—so he was not paroled. Between 1960-64, he was in and out of solitary confinement at Attica prison because of his belief in the Islamic Religion. It was through his struggle that finally Islam was allowed in the jail. This kind of injustice continued during his second imprisonment.

In 1969, Martin Gonzalez Sostre bought a lawsuit against the state for cruel and unusual punishment, torture in solitary confinement for 373 successive days and other torture like short food rations, dirty bare mattresses and 24 hour day lockup without exercise. As a result of this he was taken out of solitary confinement but still faces the other messed up conditions all brothers and sisters face in the joint.

But why has so much repression come down on Martin Gonzalez Sostre? He is a Black Puerto Rican brother from the streets of EL BARRIO who has struggled for the rights of all poor people. That's why he's considered a threat to this government. That's why in the joint they put him in solitary to prevent him from organizing threat to this government. That's why in the joint, they put him in solitary to prevent him from organizing the brothers. That's why he was framed on phony charges when he was out in the streets. Martin Gonzalez Sostre has shown the police that the revolutionary takes the struggle wherever he's at!

FREE MARTIN GONZALES SOSTRE!
FREE ALL POLITICAL PRISONERS AND PRISONERS OF WAR!
FREE ALL OPPRESSED PEOPLE!

Iris Morales
National Education Captain
YOUNG LORDS PARTY

....

We Are All on Trial

(From the newspaper *Palante*, 25 October–7 November 1971, volume 3, number 18)

In the 1940's members of the Nationalist Party of Puerto Rico refused to register with the amerikkkan draft system (called the "Selective Service"). They were then jailed by the amerikkkans. Today, we have exactly the same situation where people who believe in the liberation of Puerto Rico are refusing to serve in the army of the nation that has enslaved our people. Pablo "Yoruba" Guzmán, Minister of Information of the Young Lords Party, has been indicted by a federal grand jury for refusing to report for a medical examination and refusing to report for induction. The amerikkkan government wants to put Yoruba in jail for 5 years. If they can do this, it will be a double victory for them. They will have jailed one of the leaders of the national liberation movement (as they did in the past with members of the Nationalist Party), and they will have set an example of how they are going to deal with all the other people who dare to refuse to be in their army.

The amerikkkans will succeed in this—unless you, the people who are reading this article, decide that you want to work to stop them. Unless you understand that it is not only Yoruba on trial here, but that all Puerto Ricans are on trial.

At the present time, we have presented our arguments (called "briefs") to the court. If the judge accepts our arguments, we will have a long trial; and we will be able to bring witnesses to give testimony on why Puerto Ricans should not be subject to the amerikkkan draft.

Our position is that in 1917, the amerikkkan government passed the Jones Act, making all Puerto Ricans amerikkkan citizens. But the elected representatives of the Puerto Rican people, the House of Delegates, rejected amerikkkan citizenship. As far back as 1914, they, House of Delegates, sent a "Memorandum to the President and Congress of the United States." This message said: "We firmly and loyally oppose our being declared against our express will or without our express consent citizens of any other than our own beloved country which God granted us as an inalienable gift and incoercible right." We are arguing therefore that we, the Puerto Rican Nation, have been forced to become amerikkkan citizens against our will and because of this we are not subject to the amerikkkan draft.

But the judge may refuse to hear our arguments. All we have to depend on is the power of the people. And that's not just a slogan, because it was only the presence of angry, disciplined Puerto Ricans in court that forced the judges to lower Carlos Feliciano's bail. And only the presence of many Boricuas in federal court will force the judge to consider our argument against the amerikkkan draft.

So the only way this situation will be resolved depends on you. We can be free if we are willing to fight for our freedom. In November, when you get word about this case against the amerikkkan draft, come to court. ¡Unidos Venceremos!

NO BORICUAS IN THE AMERIKKKAN ARMY!
QUE VIVA PUERTO RICO LIBRE!

Palante Collective
YOUNG LORDS PARTY

12

Puerto Rican Revolutionary Workers Organization

In 1972, the Young Lords transformed themselves into the Puerto Rican Revolutionary Workers Organization—an internationalist labor organization that followed closely the writings of Mao, Lenin, Stalin, Marx, and Engels. The transformation into the PRRWO represented a dramatic shift for the group from a community activist organization to a workers' organization. The selections contained in this chapter document the shift from Young Lords to PRRWO and include official explanations from the new organization about how they arrived at such a major organizational shift.

....

Editorial: 1st Party Congress

(From the newspaper *Palante*, 12-26 May 1972, volume 4, number 10)

The time is coming near for the first Congress of the Puerto Rican Revolutionary Party. From June 30 to July 3 members of the Young Lords Party along with delegates of the Puerto Rican Workers Federation, the Committee to Defend the Community, the Puerto Rican Student Union, the Third World Students League, and the Women's Union will meet in New York City.

During these four days we will discuss and plan the work of the new Puerto Rican Revolutionary Party. Before this time, all the people in Puerto Rico and the United States will participate in Peoples Assemblies, on the 18 of June in Aguadilla, Santurce, Philadelphia, Bridgeport, and New York.

In all these meetings the discussions will be the same—Why a Puerto Rican Revolutionary Party? What are the Young Lords doing? What is the purpose of this new party?

In the past the government has called us a gang, a bunch of criminals, hoodlums, extremists, etc. They have called us everything but what we are—a political party, a party of a new type—not a PNP [New Progressive Party] or PPD [Popular Democratic Party], the parties of the rich, of the yankees who dominate the people—not like the other political parties composed of lawyers and professors, of the well off, comfortable rich.

We are a party built by the people, with the same sweat of the working people. We are a party of the workers, the sons and daughters of workers, the unemployed, the poor students, the inmates, the housewives of Puerto Rico and the United States.

We are a party determined to end this system of oppression, of suffering, of the misery under which we have lived since the first division of people into rich and poor, especially since the time the United States invaded Puerto Rico and made us all slaves.

Many people say that things can never change, that there will always be the rich and the poor. But we do not believe this. The poor produce all that there is in the world and everything belongs to us. The dirty lazy rich have robbed us for years and this will change.

Our people have always struggled against oppression. But in the past rich "leaders" have sold us out. We need an organization, not an individual, because one individual never knows everything and individuals die, as Don Pedro Albizu Campos did die.

We need an organization of working people, a revolutionary party, a disciplined party, a party that will guide all the people correctly, because it is of the people. A party learns from all the rich experiences of the poor and working people of the world in our common struggle against the rich. A party that will organize in the schools, in the factories, in the country, and in the community.

All over the world the poor are organizing and struggling against this capitalist system to establish new socialist societies, with the working people in power.

We believe that three peoples organizations are needed to insure our victory—

The Puerto Rican Revolutionary Party

A Mass Movement under the leadership of the workers

A Peoples Liberation Army. This is the form the struggle for the liberation of Puerto Rico will take. This is the form the struggle for a first socialist society will take.

The Peoples Assemblies will be the first step to unite this mass movement. The first Congress will be one step forward for this political party. Standing against the unity of poor and working people; the yankees, Cuban counter revolutionary refugees, and the "puerto rican" puppets have very little time in power.

LONG LIVE FREE AND SOCIALIST PUERTO RICO!!!

WORK PLACES BELONG TO THOSE WHO WORK THEM!!!

Central Committee

YOUNG LORDS PARTY

....

Editorial

(From the newspaper *Palante*, 21 July–4 August 1972, volume 4, number 15)

During June 30, July 1, 2, and 3 Young Lords Party held its first and last Congress.

A year ago we decided to hold a congress so that the whole membership of the Party would sum up all the work and experiences of the 3 years since we began to organize in 1969, in order to make the decisions of how to carry out our work in the future and in order to rename our organization the Puerto Rican Revolutionary Party. The Congress changed from this original plan and this is what this editorial is about, but first we want to thank, first all the mass organizations, the Workers Federation, the Committees to Defend the Community, The Third World Student League, The Puerto Rican Student Union and the Women's Union, for helping us to understand through our common practices, the errors we were making. But more important for staying with the Young Lords Party in the struggle, both during the good and the hard times. All mass organizations participated in the Congress. Second, we are gratified to the revolutionary organizations of the United States and Puerto Rico who also participated. The Black Workers Congress, Revolutionary Union, I Wor Kuen, Kalayaan, J-Town Collective, Rising Up Angry, Los Siete de la Raza, Spirit of Logos,

El Comite, Venceremos, El Gremio Puertorriqueno de Trabajadores (Puerto Rican Work-ers Guild), Kokua Hawaii, and the comrades from the Albanian Affairs Study Group.

Juan Gonzalez, member of the Central Committee, opened the Congress announcing the program and explaining briefly the changes that would come about during the next days. We showed the film "The People Rise Up" (about the history and development of the YLP).

Next day, Gloria Fontanez and Pablo Yoruba Guzman from the Central Commit-tee, opened the Congress with the presentation of the Resolutions, which were to be approved by the people after waging ideological struggle during the workshops and dur-ing the closed meeting of the YLP.

The 4 part resolution was:

1. The World Situation
2. History of the YLP
3. Our tasks
4. Suggestions for a new Central Committee (this last part was not presented to the general body). The Resolutions will be published in a pamphlet along with the speeches by the organizations—I Wor Kuen, Black Workers Congress, Revolutionary Union, and a report on the anti-imperialist meeting, all of which will be out soon. Look for the ad in Palante.

Briefly, during the first part of the Resolution on the world situation, we explained that the people have 2 main enemies: the U.S. with its imperialist system that attacks and exploits and robs the fruit of the labor of poor and working people in general, especially in Asia, Africa, and Latin America.

And the second enemy, the Soviet Union who has betrayed the socialist revolution where workers took power in 1917 under the leadership of the Bolsheviks and the great leader V. Lenin. Today the Soviet Union represents social-imperialism. In Russia, they defeated the Socialist Revolution to build capitalism, these liars are the center of world revisionism and today they compete with the U.S. to divide the world.

The other principal point of this part of the resolution is our analysis of Puerto Rico and the United States. In this part we mainly concentrated on struggles in Puerto Rico against the North American imperialism, and the struggles within the United States.

Later we went into the second part of the Resolution, the history of the ideologi-cal struggle, class struggle within the organization. In this analysis we were able to see that our organization has made many contributions, especially in raising consciousness inside the U.S., about the National Liberation of Puerto Rico. We have also mobilized the people many times to fight against the exploitation of the poor people, especially the Puerto Rican part in New York, Philadelphia, Bridgeport, and Boston.

In the 3 years of our history the Young Lords Party gathered many young people, unemployed, permanently unemployed, students and a small number of workers. With this base, we began to work and the ideas that developed were mainly petty-bourgeois ideas of right opportunism or left opportunism and extremism. These ideas were shown, for example, during a struggle waged by right opportunists, like Felipe Luciano, during the first stage of our development; and they wanted us to ally with the cultural national-ists, people who say they work for the people, Blacks, Puerto Ricans, but who in reality are reactionaries that are only after their own interests, wealth and fans, like Leroy Jones.

These ideas were defeated. Later more right opportunist ideas came up, during a struggle against the study of Marxism-Leninism, Mao Tse Tung thought, the ideology that best represents the interest of the universal working class. At the same time, left extremism was being developed and this was seen in the way we dressed, as if we were an army, our way of talking, of living, so different from the rest of the working people. We also believed that the permanently unemployed (lumpen) were the vanguard of the revolution, when in reality the only class that can lead the revolution is the working class.

These ideas of left wing extremism went on developing to the point that after the split with Chicago YLO, we decided to become a party. This idea hurt us a lot because we were not dealing with reality, with what we were, a progressive anti-imperialist organization, learning how we have to struggle but representing the interests of the lower petty bourgeoisie. Believing we were a party we began to have attitudes that we were the vanguard of this struggle. In December, 1970, we made another error when we decided our nation was divided 1/3 inside the U.S. and 2/3 in Puerto Rico.

This idea begins the period of left opportunism. Puerto Rico is not a divided nation. Puerto Rico is a nation in Puerto Rico, and the Puerto Ricans inside the U.S. are an oppressed national minority part of the North American working class.

But we didn't understand this when we took that decision.

Instead we began to organize in Puerto Rico many times the same way we organized in the United States, still organizing out of the working class. We organized for a year and that year we had the split when both branches in Puerto Rico with the exception of 2 cadres, split on May 21st, 1972. Some of the comrades were waging struggle around some of the mistaken positions we were defending.

Nevertheless the director of the division, Fi Ortiz, took a right opportunist position who, while he criticized the YLP position of left opportunism, stated at the same time that PSP represented the party of the working class, when the party of the working class has not yet been built.

In these 3 years, we have learned a lot, the class struggle within the organization, our commitment to change in any way necessary to defeat the united states government, in the interest of the poor and working people in general; the split that came up, all this made it clear that we were not a party and that our line and practice had to change. For this reason we are *not* the Puerto Rican Revolutionary Party.

In the next Palante, we will explain why we chose the new name and our tasks, how we will continue to struggle, and how we will correct our errors in practice, forwarding our strong principles.

We will also announce the new Central Committee.

Central Committee
Puerto Rican Revolutionary Workers Organization

Resolutions of the Puerto Rican Revolutionary Workers Organization

(From the pamphlet *Resolutions & Speeches, 1st Congress, Puerto Rican Revolutionary Workers Organization,* 1972)

INTRODUCTION

From Friday, June 30 to Monday, July 3, 1972, the Young Lords Party held a congress of all our members. This Congress took place in the South Bronx.

Other organizations which base themselves in Marxism-Leninism-Mao Tse Tung Thought also participated: the Black Workers Congress, I Wor Kuen, and the Revolutionary Union. Mass organizations that supported the ideology of the YLP and have worked very closely with us also took part: the Workers Federation, Committee to Defend the Community, Puerto Rican Student Union, Third World Student League, and Women's Union.

Also taking part were organizations such as: El Gremio de Trabajadores (Workers Guild) of Puerto Rico; Rising Up Angry from Chicago; Los Siete De La Raza, J-Town Collective and Kalayaan, all from San Fransisco; Kokua Hawaii from Hawaii; El Comite, Spirit of Logos/White Lightning, both from New York; Venceremos from California; and the Albanian Affairs Study Group.

The Congress approved a three-part resolution and voted on changing the organization's name. We are no longer the Young Lords Party, but the PUERTO RICAN REVOLUTIONARY WORKERS ORGANIZATION. In addition, the new central committee was elected: Gloria Fontanez, Carmen Cruz, Juan Gonzalez, Willie Matos, David Perez, Pablo "Yoruba" Guzman, Elba Saavedra, Richie Perez, and Lulu Limardo.

We feel that the Congress was an important step forward in the growing proletarian revolution. For this reason, we are reproducing, in this pamphlet, the resolutions and speeches presented at the Congress.

ANALYSIS OF 3-YEAR HISTORY OF Y.L.P.

Comrades here present:

Welcome to the first and last Congress of the Young Lords Party. These following days are very important to us for we understand that in our three year history as an organization, we have gained some valuable experience, have made big contributions in the progressive and revolutionary movement in the U.S. and Puerto Rico, as well as committing some errors which we will share with our comrades and friends here today, in the interest of advancing the proletarian movement through greater and greater unity to go forward towards the defeat of u.s. imperialists, committed to the successful building of socialism and finally world communism.

This history of class struggle in our organization has been intense, always moving forward, and progressing to clearer and clearer proletarian stands.

However, proletarian ideology, Marxism-Leninism-Mao Tse Tung Thought, does not pop from the sky; proletarian ideology develops as a result of struggle against right and left opportunism and in contrast to it.

The following is a summary of the history of the struggle against right and left opportunism in our organization and the proletarian positions which have been combating both.

Young Lords Organization—Founded 1969 in Chicago

The Young Lords Organization arose from a street gang in the streets of Chicago, composed mainly of the unemployed, service workers, small number of proletarians and permanently unemployed, mostly Chicanos and Puerto Ricans.

In 1969, the organization begins to transform from a street gang into a political organization, anti-imperialist and guided by the ideology of the Black Panther Party—a central committee of ministers, and ministries.

The organization began to organize at the community level with the slogan, "Serve and Protect the People." It starts several programs—breakfast, free clothing, and the takeover of the first people's church in Chicago.

The Young Lords start publishing a newspaper, "The YLO," and begin to raise anti-imperialist consciousness and consciousness about the national liberation struggle of Puerto Rico. They distribute the newspaper on a massive scale and particularly in the Puerto Rican community.

In June, 1969, Jose Martinez, Cuban origin, pretty-bourgeois, went to the SDS convention in Chicago. During the convention he meets with Cha Cha Jimenez, chairman of the YLO, and gets permission from Cha Cha to begin a chapter of YLO in New York City. Meanwhile in January, 1969, a group of students, mainly of working class background, had come together to form "La Sociedad de Albizu Campos." Shortly after, the SAC proposes to merge with the Chicago YLO.

Finally, in July of 1969, three groups, the YLO of New York, the SAC, and a group mainly composed of unemployed proletarian youths, Puerto Ricans from El Barrio in NYC, merge with Chicago YLO and form the New York State Chapter.

In the beginning, elements in the New York branch who had right opportunist ideas took the position that in order to have practice with the people, we must first study the 40 volumes of Lenin. On the other hand, others in the Party were saying that to serve and protect the people we must do practice with the people. This struggle resulted in the demotion of Diego Pubon who stood firm and pushed a right opportunist line with revisionist politics. This started a struggle of ideas between the progressive and backward elements in the Party. The social base of the organization was composed of unemployed proletarian youth, students who came from lower petty bourgeoisie (ideologically), permanent unemployed, and a minority of workers employed in service work. The organization continues to develop progressively and for the first time since the fifties a political progressively anti-imperialist organization continues mobilizing the people in New York with manifestations against poor living conditions, especially among the Puerto Rican people (although the organization has never been strictly Puerto Rican, but composed of Blacks, Dominicans, Mexicans, Cubans, Panamericans as well).

The organization continued to struggle against unsanitary conditions which poor people live under; the garbage offensives in New York were part of this struggle. The Young Lords Organization in New York came into contradiction with YLO in Chicago since the early development of the organizations. YLO in New York had previous experience in the anti-imperialist struggle. Some members had previously been in SDS, others involved in the 1969 City College takeover, and there had also been more study of Marxist-Leninist theory. In Chicago, the organization's ideology of the lumpen-proletariat was developed much more, therefore attracting the elements of this class into the organization. Democratic centralism, criticism and self-criticism were implemented in the organization in New York since the early development. In studying the teachings of Mao Tse Tung, we developed a base for proletarian positions and its primitive development.

As the organization consolidated, there arose more ideological and organizational unity with other organizations. In May 1969 in Chicago, there was the Rainbow Coalition composed of the YLO, Black Panther Party, and the Patriots (an organization of unemployed youths, white northamericans—with origin of nine workers from Appalachia and sharecroppers who fell into the category of permanently unemployed).

The organization in leadership, ideologically as well as organizationally, was the Black Panther Party. Of all the organizations in the U.S., the Panthers had the major leading role from the time they began in 1966 until the split in 1971.

The major influence therefore in our development came from the Panther Party. In the Young Lords Org. however the right opportunists were opposed to working with and accepting the ideological guidance given by the Black Panther Party.

The right opportunists, led by Felipe Luciano (deputy chairman of the Young Lords Organization), claimed that the Panther Party "had isolated themselves from the masses of the people by introducing Marxist-Leninist-Mao Tse Tung Thought, and Third World people could not relate to that theory." Another argument was that the Panthers were sectarian "because they attacked the cultural nationalists." The more progressive elements in the organization waged relentless struggle against those positions and raised the necessity of our organizations to study the works of Mao Tse Tung. The organization adopted that position, and all members learned from the Red Book in our daily work, setting therefore a more solid foundation for the rise of proletarian principles.

Around the period of August 1969, some of those opportunist elements leave the organization, some temporarily, others permanently. It is during this period that the organization in New York enters a most progressive period. An office is opened, the 13 Point Program and Platform is drawn up, general meetings of the membership are instituted to give way to a principle level of democratic centralism, a political education curriculum is established, the Serve the People programs go into effect and the organization leads a welfare mothers demonstration.

In October 1969, the organization begins to work with HRUM (Health Revolutionary Unity Movement) founded in October 1969, of health workers who rise from a struggle against proposed layoffs and cutbacks in services in the city hospitals of New York.

HRUM had already adopted the study of Mao Tse Tung Thought as the ideological guide, following the example of the Black Panther Party and the Young Lords Organization.

In December 1969, the Young Lords Organization in New York launches the offensive of the First People's Church takeover. Hundreds of people were mobilized. In the church, we set up health programs, breakfast programs and always raised the question of national liberation for Puerto Rico.

The national minority of Puerto Ricans living in the United States responds once again from the sector of society composed of unemployed proletarian youth and of the people that fall more and more into the lines of the unemployed. As the economic crisis in the United States and Puerto Rico increases the number of permanently unemployed people—

desperately seeking escape and making efforts to struggle against exploitation—rises. The church takeover demonstrates the progressive strength of the Young Lords Organization. From his personal interests, Felipe Luciano sees a growing organization and returns to it. He had left in August. Upon his return the ideology which he represents once again takes hold. Nonetheless, the principles learned in the mass struggle of the church takeover, with HRUM (Health Revolutionary Unity Movement), and during that progressive period form a real base so that proletarian ideas begin to take form in the organization.

In May of 1970, the leadership of the organization in New York has its first retreat, a meeting during which more Marxism-Leninism would be studied and out of which would come the direction of the organization for the next period. During this retreat the relationship with YLO in Chicago is analyzed and it was concluded that in Chicago there was no real development of a direction for what was already a growing organization in the United States, with chapters in Chicago, New York, Newark, and with membership dispersed in other parts of the United States. A criticism was also raised that YLO in Chicago was not producing the newspaper that progressive elements understood to be a key element in organizing the masses. During that retreat it was decided to go to Chicago, in an effort to convince the Chicago leadership to return to New York, so as to train there the cadres, who more and more represented the permanently unemployed.

The organization in Chicago was in a state of disintegration. The division occurred when the Chicago leadership rejected the proposal of the New York leadership. Once the division between New York and Chicago occurred, the leadership of the organization decided to continue using the name Young Lords Party; but at the same time, the left extremist idea of forming a party creates a base for left extremism and also struggles against right opportunism, pushing the organization further and further to the left. One of the ideas that most held back our development was that the lumpen-proletariat was the vanguard of the revolution. At the same time, it was said that the working class was conservative because it had much more to lose than other sectors of society and would therefore join the struggle after the other classes.

These ideas did not permit for the change of the social base of the organization, and so two basic principles around which we would organize were maintained: the national liberation of Puerto Rico and serving the interests of the people.

A preliminary analysis on class in Puerto Rican society which came out of the May 1970 retreat established a firmer base for ideological struggle within the party. Proletarian ideas were expressed more strongly although from a minority base in the party, and only in terms of positions, not of ideology clearly identifiable with the proletarian class.

There was still much resistance to the study of dialectical materialism and Marxism-Leninism, although during that period ideas on socialism were reaching a higher level, and we began the study of the work by Huberman and Sweezy—Introduction to Socialism. The right opportunists in the party were getting into more and more contradictions with the party line, and they made an attempt to ally themselves with groups that were clearly reactionary, such as the cultural nationalist organization of Leroi Jones. The struggle against that attempt was difficult and at the same time, left extremist ideas consolidated themselves in the party.

The right opportunist line had some support from the Newark Branch where Amiri Baraka (Leroi Jones) had one of his strongest bases, but the struggle against such an alliance extended itself not only in the party, but also in the Black Panther Party which opposed the alliance.

It was during the period after the May retreat that we undertook the task of publishing a national newspaper, and Palante comes out. A first publication of 10,000 issues distributed primarily in the New York City area begins the strengthening of a mass movement in the Puerto Rican community. At the same time, we begin to develop ideas on what our relationship to Puerto Rico would be. During that period we began to do a study of and to give support to MPI (Movimiento Partido de Independencia), which was founded in 1959 and of which we knew very little, but that clearly identified itself as an anti-imperialist movement. MPI had a branch in New York called the Vito Marcantonio branch. We are not sure of the exact date it was founded, but MPI had not been able to raise itself as a significantly strong force among the Puerto Rican people in the U.S.

What we knew of MPI in Puerto Rico was that they had raised a very progressive struggle against the draft and against ROTC (Reserve Officers Training Corps) in the University of Puerto Rico. The latter mostly led by the FUPI (Federacion Universitaria Pro-Independencia) founded in 1956, which became in later years the student arm of MPI. We were also mostly aware of the Nationalist Party of Puerto Rico, which had been the main anti-imperialist force in Puerto Rico from the 1930's–1950's, the only organization which to this day has a number of political prisoners. Don Pedro Albizu Campos, President of the Nationalist Party, holds a position of respect among our people and is known as a defender of the Puerto Rican nation.

Other anti-imperialist organizations that we had some knowledge of were CAL (Conando Arnado de Liberacion), a clandestine armed organization, and PIP (the Puerto Rican Independence Party), an electoral, broad mass-based establishment party, founded in 1947.

CAL, like MPI, claimed an "economic crisis had to be created to drive the U.S. imperialist out of Puerto Rico." CAL had declared the Condado, haven of the tourist, a war zone, and had taken credit for several bombings of hotels, american restaurants, and other small businesses.

We knew little about other organizations, such as La Liga Socialista (a PLP branch in Puerto Rico), Projecto Piloto, a group which had split off from MPI in 1965, and the revisionist handful remainder of the CPPR (Communist Party of Puerto Rico). That was our limited understanding of the movement in Puerto Rico. However, of all the organizations, we supported MPI, and most especially FUPI, CAL as they seemed the most progressive, clearly anti-imperialist organizations.

In the Party we began to study Puerto Rican history from the very limited educational materials found in the U.S. We knew that in the future members of the Party would visit Puerto Rico to do a more intense investigation of the situation there.

Meanwhile, left wing extremism was taking root in the Party and it manifested itself in several ways. In the months of June and July 1970, we took on many skirmishes with the police in the streets of El Barrio. We entered a period of more building takeovers.

During this period was the Lincoln Hospital takeover in July 1970. The takeover lasted one day, but we were able to get a lot of support from the people since Lincoln was known throughout the country for the butcher shop that it is.

In August 1970, the Party expanded to Philadelphia. A group of unemployed proletarian youths—some workers, and some permanently unemployed, decided to join the Party. With that merger, the Party expanded to another mostly working class community. However, our extremist line prevented many working class people from responding actively and joining the organization although the different programs gained a lot of support from the people in Philly as a whole.

In August of 1970, Juan Gonzalez and John "Fi" Ortiz leave on an investigative trip to Puerto Rico. In Puerto Rico they met with many of the organizations mentioned before. When they met with PIP, we were able to understand that PIP represented the interests of the higher and middle level petty bourgeoisie, as well as the interests of that sector of the bourgeoisie which is in contradiction with the foreign capitalists and imperialists in general. It became clear that MPI represented the upper middle, middle, and lower petty bourgeoisie. Its class composition and its struggles were geared to those interests. Some of these struggles we refer to were: "beaches for the people," "university for the people," and "mines for the people or no mines." In studying their political thesis we understood that they were unclear about many things. Their analysis of how they would create an economic crisis to drive the Yankees out did not explain the class antagonisms between the imperialist ruling class and the masses of exploited people. Their position on mass struggle didn't have clear distinctions, and their position on armed struggle was unclear except to say that they upheld the right of all people to armed self-defense.

Out of those investigations we realized a need for the Party to exist and organize in Puerto Rico. At the time we made that decision, we had failed to see the first investigation was only a beginning, *not* a complete understanding.

We failed to understand that concrete conditions were different from conditions in the U.S. and that historical development of Puerto Rico was almost completely unknown to us. However, of one thing we were certain, PIP represented the interests of the national bourgeoisie (we are in the process of investigating the size and strength of the national bourgeoisie). We also understood that MPI represented the interests of the exploited masses of the people, and we are convinced today that no one represents the interests of the proletariat.

We proceeded, however, with this partial analysis to make our second gravest error, as we began to plan to take leadership of the revolution and movement in Puerto Rico. Objectively, for the reasons stated before, that was not possible. We did not understand the conditions and our development was still too primitive and influenced by the conditions which had developed in the revolutionary movement in the U.S. The revolutionary movement in the U.S. had gone through tremendous defeat since the Communist Party of the U.S. turned into a totally revisionist party.

In 1970, the Party continued to expand. An organization called Spanish People in Command (SPIC) united with the Party to form a branch in Bridgeport, Connecticut. Mainly an industrial city, it was a city where we would learn a lot more about the interests of the class that we have to respond to. Because of the left wing extremism in the Party, the branch did not grow in size. Nevertheless, the branch has mobilized large numbers of people for mass demonstrations on different occasions. Above all, it has been the place where we have recruited some of the most advanced leading cadre in the Party.

September 1970 was a very important period in our development. This was when we confronted the right wing opportunist positions which were stopping the development of the Party. Because of his growing contradictions with the Party's political line, Felipe Luciano commenced to fail openly as a leader in the Party. He was criticized for his extreme individualism, male chauvinism, and for creating a situation of self-cultivation. Felipe refused to accept this criticism. At this point the membership started waging struggle. On one side, comrades lined themselves up with the right opportunist ideas of Felipe, and on the other side, the comrades who wanted to change the Party, even though it took positions that were extremist. The right opportunist ideas were defeated. With these struggles there is a qualitative change in our work. We enter one of the most progressive periods of our history. The student conference in September 1970 where 1,000 students are mobilized to a conference with the objective of forming Liberate Puerto Rico Now Committees consolidated our ties with the Puerto Rican Student Union. The Party wages struggle with the nationalism of the Union (PRSU) at that time. We learn that we could not isolate ourselves from the student movement and its importance to the revolutionary struggle. We went on to consolidate in the community. We advance our struggle in health programs, unsanitary conditions in our communities, and police harassment, especially in El Barrio. Julio Roldan is killed, and we occupy the People's Church for the second time in October 1970.

We mobilize 10,000 people for the October 30, 1970 demonstrations at the United Nations, demanding liberation of Puerto Rico. In November, 1970, the Philly branch takes a church and gains more support.

In general, the defeat of a highly opportunist line in the Party opens the way for progress and enables us to take positions which enabled us to gain experience in mass mobilization. We were also able to develop centralism to a higher level. We began to develop a more collective leadership, and criticism and self-criticism became a more real part of the Party.

By December 1970, we fell into a crisis of stagnation in the Party. Basically, we lacked a sense of direction; we had not summed up our experience and didn't have an ideology. We therefore went into another retreat. In that retreat we consolidated left extremism— mainly because we really were unable to deepen our understanding of class society and class analysis. In fact, we reaffirmed our belief that the lumpen-proletariat was the leading and most exploited in the U.S. We did however begin to have a primitive understanding of dialectical materialism as shown in our first edition of the ideology of the YLP. In the ideology we further develop the extremist ideas of the Party and the State, the divided nation theory, protracted struggle in Puerto Rico (these are the most significant of that trend). In general, the analysis gave us some ideas to work with although it was not based on scientific analysis. In looking back on our ideology, we realize that it does not represent an ideology based on class analysis, scientific analysis utilizing the universal principles of Marxism-Leninism-Mao Tse Tung Thought. As a result, the national question was not correctly analyzed.

The third fundamental error was in taking that theory to practice we initiated the Break the Chains Offensive (Ofensiva Rompecadensa). In dealing with the reality that there was no party representing the interests of the people, we concluded that we were that party, and we called for a demonstration in Ponce on March 21, 1971, from which we would begin organizing in Puerto Rico. That idea caused a qualitative change in left extremism which developed into left opportunism. This took us further away from Marxism-Leninism-Mao Tse Tung Thought, and further away from reality.

During the same period in February that the Party was consolidating the left opportunist line, the BPP divided. This division was unprincipled. Although it is significant to analyze the development of the Panther Party, its contribution to the movement and its contribution to right opportunism but to left opportunism, it would be too great a task to do so at this time. Nonetheless, it is important to point out that the division in the Panther Party caused great confusion in the revolutionary movement, especially in the Third World sector. Every organization was forced to take a position under extremist conditions. The two factions began to resolve contradictions in an antagonistic way, a way totally different from revolutionary principles. We already had vast differences with Huey Newton's theory of intercommunalism as we did with the ultra-extremist and opportunist position of Eldridge Cleaver regarding armed struggle. We took a principled stand that we could not support either faction. We stated that they would have to correct their errors in practice and in practice show their commitment to serve the interest of the people.

While all this was happening in the U.S., we had begun to organize in Puerto Rico. We had a very successful demonstration in Ponce and mobilized 700 people. The reactionary press played up the extremism and the opportunism of the Party to create further contradictions with the movement, by saying that we were in Puerto Rico to show the other independentistas how to make revolution. The tactic worked; we were further isolated from the movement. A combination of left extremism which we outlined here plus the lack of understanding of the concrete conditions set the base for further errors in Puerto Rico. We began to work as we were accustomed to in the U.S. We had several tasks. One was to spread Palante, which was half in english, plus the fact that most of the information was about the states. We created a contradiction which only affirmed the extremism which manifested itself more clearly each day. Without dealing with the reality of the capacity of our organization, we began programs and struggle in the community. The struggle to open the only hospital in Aguadilla and the struggle against Model Cities in Santurce were the two major ones.

One of our contributions to the struggle of Puerto Rico was to bring on an understanding of the struggle of the U.S. In the first place we had to explain to people why we were a Puerto Rican organization with the name in english. While doing this we would go into the history of the U.S. and raise a lot of consciousness about the terrible exploitation of our people, especially Third World people living in the U.S. In many cases, we broke down the "american dream." In the different programs we showed films of the struggles of other nations, especially that of the people of Viet Nam. This helped to raise the consciousness of the people in Puerto Rico on the international struggle which is usually at a very low level of understanding. This is for two reasons: one, because of the material conditions of its colonial state where strict vigilance is kept on the type of news that the people receive through the media, and second, because of the class composition of the independence movement in Puerto Rico that has failed to raise an international consciousness.

In our struggle with the rest of the movement we have been able to understand this very well, and it was in this area that we could raise consciousness about the importance to the movement[–increasing] learning to the point of being familiar with the struggle in the U.S. and especially the struggle waged by Black people in the U.S. We managed to make some very important contributions in this aspect, although there is still a lack of understanding about this question in Puerto Rico.

To sum up, every object has two different points of view. In our work in Puerto Rico, we made many mistakes, but our positive results can be seen in the raising of consciousness, sometimes at the minimal level, and other times at a greater level, attained in the U.S. about the colonial situation in Puerto Rico, and because of the work we did in Puerto Rico, about the real exploitative conditions that our people suffer in the u.s. We see the necessity to unite the people in the oppressing country to the people of the oppressed country. During the time that we were in Puerto Rico and working in the u.s. we consolidated the left opportunist line in both places. On one side we continued the incorrect idea of the divided nation, and we began to put into practice the theory of the party and the state.

In April, we decided to establish and unite people's organizations. All were to rise in NY at the same time. At this time, the period of transition and restructuring begins. In an idealist way, without planning, we overexpanded again and the organizations fell into chaos.

In July 1971, we entered into another retreat; once again we fail to sum up our experiences in a scientific manner. We didn't have at hand the data necessary as to how many members were active in the organization in order to deal with our reality as an organization. At the same time this retreat sets the base for the proletarian position to develop and creates a big impact on the party. In the first place, we began to recognize that the lumpen-proletariat are not the vanguard of the proletariat. We began to study about the dictatorship of the proletariat, about Marxism-Leninism, and with the minimal understanding we began to plan the task of organization on a class base.

In the struggle against the right opportunist line which had developed as to the position of the popular classes (that the classes had to unite, but not under the leadership of the proletariat, but the same as the other classes in society) and from the base of the left opportunism is developed the phrase "the work places belong to those who work them."

In that retreat of July 1972, we derived a better understanding of the mass line:

1) QUE VIVA PUERTO RICO LIBRE (LONG LIVE A FREE PUERTO RICO)
2) LOS SITIOS DE TRABAJO PERTENECEN A QUIENES LOS TRABAJAN (THE WORKPLACES BELONG TO THOSE WHO WORK THEM)
3) CONTROL COMUNAL DE NUESTRAS INSTITUCIONES Y TIERRAS (COMMUNITY CONTROL OF OUR INSTITUTIONS AND LAND)
4) SOLIDARIDAD CON INDOCHINA (SOLIDARITY WITH INDOCHINA)

In November a member of the central committee went to China. This trip was very significant to our development. In that trip, the Chinese comrades wage struggle with our line and point out incorrect things, especially our position on the divided nation. When the member of the central committee returns, he and the other two members in the absence of two central committee members wage a rectification movement in which they break democratic centralism of the organization. On the arrival of the two other members there were already many conclusions reached and put into practice, without the acknowledgement of the two other members of the central committee. In that situation, the position of right and left opportunism clashed, with the opportunism of the left position managing to take control of the situation and consolidate positions. The national question is not solved in a correct way, and the proletarian positions which had been raised remain outside of the ideological struggle, yet establishing a base for ideological struggle more real and vigorous in the party.

In December 1971, the Workers' Conference took place where more than 100 workers participated. With the Conference is established a stronger material base so that the proletarian position could take more root in the organization. In the conference we have to establish the organizing of the working class, what methods to use, and start to question some fundamental problems of the party. Yet in the conference is consolidated and accepted as a slogan "the workplaces belong to those who work them."

The months which follow this analysis of our development is the period we are in now. The division which has just occurred in the party.

May 21, 1971 was another stage of our development which has much importance. The division in the party, as will any division in any organization, will hurt us and caused subjectivity and an initial lack of analysis. But at the same time, it made us analyze the YLP objectively. In an investigation initiated by the central committee and cadre assigned to Puerto Rico, an analytical process of our development starts. The first thing in question is the idea of the YLP, whose interests do we represent, and third, how would we correct our mistakes and move forward.

In answering the question of whether or not we are a party, the logical answer is no. Not in the United States where the party of the proletariat must reflect the characteristics of that class. In the United States, the proletariat class is multi-national; therefore, the party, the most progressive organism of the proletariat in the U.S., must be a multi-national communist party. In Puerto Rico, we weren't a party. Our class composition and lack of understanding of Puerto Rico were only two objective reasons why we weren't a party. Then what are we? We are generally an anti-imperialist organization that tries to apply itself to understand the necessity for the study of Marxism-Leninism-Mao Tse Tung Thought.

What class interest do we represent? Our history shows that right and left opportunism have been our prominent tendencies, responding to the interests of the lower petty bourgeoisie. We are developing more and more to the proletarianization of the organization. We are committed to change in whatever way necessary. We understand that as long as we are not based in a large scale on the industrial proletariat class and the masses of workers in general, we will commit errors to the right and left. However, we must be dialectical and historical materialists and understand that we are a product of society and that if we correct our errors in the interest of the proletariat, that this is one more step in the right direction.

Our organization is a strong one comrades; it's been a hard struggle. However, we are committed to the development of communist parties in the U.S. and Puerto Rico. We have always said we exist to serve the people. Understanding a little bit more now what that means in itself is the beginning of serving the people with all our might. We cannot even for a moment separate ourselves from the masses.

Comrade Mao Tse Tung has said:

"All our cadres, whatever their ranks, are servants of the people, and whatever we do is to serve the people. How then could we be reluctant to discard any of our bad traits? Our duty is to hold ourselves responsible to the people, and if mistakes occur, they must be corrected—that is what being responsible to the people means."

Therefore comrades, we have to grasp the theoretical base that will guide our thinking. Marxism-Leninism-Mao Tse Tung Thought will help us as communists struggling for the interests of the proletariat and the exploited masses in general!

Bibliography of Materials on the Young Lords

MAJOR MANUSCRIPT COLLECTIONS

Boxed Newspaper. *Palante: Latin Revolutionary News Service.* Tamiment Library and Robert F. Wagner Labor Archives, New York University.

Juan Gonzalez Papers. Centro Archival Collection. Centro de Estudios Puertorriqueños, Hunter College of the City University of New York.

Pacifica Radio Archives, Los Angeles, California.

Young Lords Documents, Vertical File. Centro de Estudios Puertorriqueños, Hunter College of the City University of New York.

Young Lords Party (Publications and Pamphlets), Microfilm Reels. *A La Izquierda: The Puerto Rican Movement.* Centro de Estudios Puertorriqueños, Hunter College of the City University of New York.

PUBLISHED RESOURCES

El Pueblo Se Levanta. New York: Newsreel, 1971. Videocassette.

Elbaum, Max. *Revolution in the Air: Sixties Radicals Turn to Lenin, Mao, and Che.* London: Verso, 2002.

Enck-Wanzer, Darrel. "Trashing the System: Social Movement, Intersectional Rhetoric, and Collective Agency in the Young Lords Organization's Garbage Offensive." *Quarterly Journal of Speech* 92 (2006): 174-201.

———. "The Intersectional Rhetoric of the Young Lords: Social Movement, Ideographs, Demand, and the Radical Democratic Imaginary." Dissertation, Indiana University, 2007.

———. "A Radical Democratic Style? Tradition, Hybridity, and Intersectionality." *Rhetoric & Public Affairs* 11 (2008): 459-65.

Fernández, Johanna. "Between Social Service Reform and Revolutionary Politics: The Young Lords, Late Sixties Radicalism, and Community Organizing in New York City." In *Freedom North: Black Freedom Struggles Outside the South, 1940-1980*, edited by Jeanne F. Theoharis and Komozi Woodward, 255-85. New York: Palgrave Macmillan, 2003.

———. "Radicals in the Late 1960s: A History of the Young Lords Party in New York City, 1969-1974." Dissertation, Columbia University, 2004.

———. "The Young Lords and the Postwar City: Notes on the Geographical and Structural Reconfigurations of Contemporary Urban Life." In *African American Urban History Since World War II*, edited by Kenneth L. Kusmer and Joe W. Trotter, 60-82. Chicago: University of Chicago Press, 2009.

———. "Denise Oliver and the Young Lords Party: Stretching the Political Boundaries of Struggle." In *Want to Start a Revolution? Radical Women in the Black Freedom Struggle*, edited by Dayo F. Gore, Jeanne Theoharis, and Komozi Woodard, 271-93. New York: New York University Press, 2009.

Gandy, Matthew. "Between Borinquen and the *Barrio*: Environmental Justice and New York City's Puerto Rican Community, 1969-1972." *Antipode* 34 (2002): 730-61.

González, Juan. *Harvest of Empire: A History of Latinos in America.* New York: Viking, 2000.

Guzmán, Pablo. "Puerto Rican Barrio Politics in the United States." In *The Puerto Rican Struggle: Essays on Survival in the U.S.*, edited by Clara E. Rodríguez, Virginia E. Sánchez Korrol, and Jose Oscar Alers, 121-28. Maplewood, NJ: Waterfront Press, 1984.

———. "La Vida Pura: A Lord of the Barrio." In *The Puerto Rican Movement: Voices from the Diaspora*, edited by Andrés Torres and José E. Velázquez, 155-72. Philadelphia: Temple University Press, 1998.

———. "My Life as a Revolutionary." *Village Voice*, 21 March 1988.

———. "Ain't No Party Like the One We Got: The Young Lords Party and *Palante*." In *Voices from the Underground: Insider Histories from the Vietnam-Era Underground Press*, edited by Ken Wachsberger, 293-304. Ann Arbor, MI: Azenphony, 1991.

———. "Pablo 'Yoruba' Guzmán on the Young Lords Legacy: A Personal Account." In *Proceedings from the April 8, 1995, IPR Community Forum*, edited by Joseph Luppens. New York: Institute for Puerto Rican Policy (IPR), 1995.

Kc Diwas. "Of Consciousness and Criticism: Identity in the Intersections of the Gay Liberation Front and the Young Lords Party." Masters thesis, Sarah Lawrence College, 2005.

Laó, Agustín. "Resources of Hope: Imagining the Young Lords and the Politics of Memory." *Centro Journal* 7, no. 1 (1995): 34-49.

Laó-Montes, Agustín. "Niuyol: Urban Regime, Latino Social Movements, Ideologies of Latinidad." In *Mambo Montage: The Latinization of New York*, edited by Agustín Laó-Montes and Arlene M. Dávila, 119-58. New York: Columbia University Press, 2001.

Lee, Jennifer. "The Young Lords, a New Generation of Puerto Ricans: An Oral History." *Culturefront* 3, no. 3 (1994): 64-70.

Lopez, Alfredo. *The Puerto Rican Papers: Notes on the Reemergence of a Nation*. Indianapolis: Bobbs-Merrill, 1973.

Luciano, Felipe, and Hiram Maristany. "The Young Lords Party: 1969-1975." *Caribe* 7, no. 4 (1983).

Melendez, Miguel. *We Took the Streets: Fighting for Latino Rights with the Young Lords*. New York: St. Martins, 2003.

Morales, Iris. *¡Palante, Siempre Palante! The Young Lords*. New York: Third World Newsreel, 1996. Videocassette.

———. "¡Palante, Siempre Palante! Interview with Richie Perez." *Centro Journal* 21, no. 2 (2009): 142-57.

Moreno, Marta. "The Young Lords Party, 1969-1975: 'Publisher's Page.'" *Caribe* 7, no. 4 (1983): 2.

Nelson, Jennifer A. "'Abortions under Community Control': Feminism, Nationalism, and the Politics of Reproduction among New York City's Young Lords." *Journal of Women's History* 13 (2001): 157-80.

Ogbar, Jeffrey O. G. "Puerto Rico en mi Corazón: The Young Lords, Black Power, and Puerto Rican Nationalism in the U.S., 1966–1972." *Centro Journal* 18, no. 1 (2006): 148-69.

Pantoja, Antonia. "Puerto Ricans in New York: A Historical and Community Development Perspective." *Centro Journal* 2, no. 5 (1989): 21-31.

Perez, David. *Long Road from Lares: An Oral History*. New York: Community Documentation Workshop at St. Mark's Church-in-the-Bowery, 1974.

Pérez, Richie. "A Young Lord Remembers." Virtual Boricua, May 2000. Http://www.virtualboricua.org/Docs/perez_00.htm (accessed on March 13, 2005).

Rodriguez-Morazzani, Roberto P. "Puerto Rican Political Generations in New York: Pioneros, Young Turks, and Radicals." *Centro Journal* 4, no. 1 (1991/1992): 97-116.

———. "Political Cultures of the Puerto Rican Left in the United States." In *The Puerto Rican Movement: Voices from the Diaspora*, edited by Andrés Torres and José E. Velázquez, 25-47. Philadelphia: Temple University Press, 1998.

Silén, Juan Angel. *We, the Puerto Rican People: A Story of Oppression and Resistance*. New York: Monthly Review Press, 1971.

Torres, Andrés. "Introduction: Political Radicalism in the Diaspora—the Puerto Rican Experience." In *The Puerto Rican Movement: Voices from the Diaspora*, edited by Andrés Torres and José E. Velázquez, 1-22. Philadelphia: Temple University Press, 1998.

Yglesias, Jose. "Right on with the Young Lords." *New York Times*, 7 June 1970, 32+.

Young, Cynthia Ann. "Soul Power: Cultural Radicalism and the Formation of a United States Third World Left." Dissertation, Yale University, 1999.

Young Lords Party and Michael Abramson. *Palante: Young Lords Party*. 1st ed. New York: McGraw-Hill, 1971.

Index

About the Editor

Darrel Enck-Wanzer is Assistant Professor of Communication Studies at the University of North Texas.